book and for helping to keep my dad's words alive. And thank you for your contribution to the book.

Best wishes,

Jeff. Kent

STORIES FROM STOKE

CYRIL KENT

WITAN BOOKS

STORIES FROM STOKE

First published in November 2012 by Witan Books, Cherry Tree House, 8 Nelson Crescent, Cotes Heath, via Stafford, ST21 6ST, England.
Telephone: (01782) 791673.
E-mail: witan@mail.com
Website: www.witancreations.com

Copyright © 2012, Cyril Kent.

WTN 070

ISBN 978 0 9529152 9 4

The right of Cyril Kent to be identified as the author of this work has been asserted by him in accordance with the Copyright, Designs and Patents Act 1988.

A Cataloguing in Publication record for this book is available from the British Library.

Design and cover concept: Jeff Kent.
Cover artwork: Danny Rowe and Steve Billington.
Editor: Jeff Kent.
Editorial advisers: Sue Bell, Gill Evans and Hazel Statham.
Main research: Jeff Kent and Cyril Kent.
Printed and bound by: Hanley Print Services, Units 90 & 79, Shelton Enterprise Centre, Bedford Street, Shelton, Stoke-on-Trent, ST1 4PZ. Tel. (01782) 280028; E-mail: gstock1@btinternet.com.

Front cover photo: Cyril showing off a piece of ware, which he'd thrown at the Wedgwood Visitor Centre, near Barlaston, on a trip there on 31 May 2004.
Back cover photo: Cyril signing copies of his previous book, *A Potteries Past*, at its launch at the New Vic Theatre, in Etruria Road, Basford, Newcastle-under-Lyme, on 27 November 2010.

All rights reserved. No part of this publication may be reproduced, stored in a retrieval system or transmitted in any form or by any means, electronic, mechanical, photocopying, recording or otherwise without the prior permission in writing of the publisher.

Witan Creations
2012 Main Catalogue

WTN 001: *Butcher's Tale/Annie, With The Dancing Eyes* – Jeff Kent & The Witan (animal rights protest single), 1981 - £2.50, including p & p.

WTN 027: *The Mercia Manifesto: A Blueprint For The Future Inspired By The Past* – The Mercia Movement (128-page radical political manifesto), 1997 - £8.25, including p & p.

WTN 030: *Only One World* – Jeff Kent (13-track environmental concept CD), 2000 - £11.15, including p & p.

WTN 032: *A Draft Constitution For Mercia* – The Mercia Movement (20-page draft constitution for an independent Midlands), 2001 - £2.20, including p & p.

WTN 038: *The Constitution Of Mercia* – The Mercian Constitutional Convention (22-page constitution of independent Mercia), 2003 - £2.20, including p & p.

WTN 059: *A Potteries Past* – Cyril Kent (214-page story of the author's life and times to 1962, the antecedent of *Stories From Stoke*), 2010 - £16.50, including p & p.

WTN 060: *What If There Had Been No Port In The Vale?: Startling Port Vale Stories* – Jeff Kent (191-page counterfactual football history), 2011 - £16.50, including p & p.

(All other publications and releases by Witan Creations are now out of print or unavailable from the catalogue.)

For Helen and Jeff

ACKNOWLEDGEMENTS

The author and publisher would like to express their thanks to the following people and organisations for their invaluable assistance, not credited elsewhere, in the production of this book:

Age UK, Alsager Library, Argyll and Bute Council Archives, Ashbourne Library, Dennis Aston, Bill Austin, Roy Bainbridge, Steve Ball, SJB Bands Limited, Shireen Barry, Kathryn Bate, Emma Bayles, Shaun Beardmore, John Beckett, H. Eva Beech, Yvonne Bell, Keith Bennison, Jim Bentley, Beswicks Solicitors, Beth Johnson Housing Group, Lily Birch, John Birchall, Blackpool Central Library, Bodycare (Hanley), John Booth, Boots (Hanley), Bristol Reference Library, Rose Brooke, Dave Brundrett, Burton Library, Josie Cabie, Caernarfon Library, Cairnbaan Hotel, Joan Cameron, Carlisle Library, Care Homes Stoke Ltd, John Clewlow, Communication Workers Union, Ian Cook, Royston Cooke, Susan Cooke, Les Cooper, Tony Coram, Ann Cotton, Crewe Library, Crossroads Care, Crown Prosecution Service, Ken Cubley, Jean Done, Driver and Vehicle Licensing Agency, Bill Duncalf, Kevin Duncalf, Rachel Dunckley, Derek Durose, Eaga WarmSure, Mark Eardley, Pam Edwards, Jim Egginton, Paul Farmer, First Potteries Limited, Rod Fletcher, Flintshire Record Office, Tom Freer, General Register Office, Gentleshaw Wildlife Centre, Julia Gibson, Glenshee Ski Centre, John Goodwin, Tony Goodwin, Ted Green, Alf Halliburton, Lynn Halliburton, Eddie Hampton, Jim Hankey, Harley Street Medical Centre, Carol Hassall, Heatex Group Ltd, Highland Archive Centre, Jeff Hollins, Maureen Hughes, A Hurd Opticians, Judy Hutchings, Images4life Limited, Grahame Jeffries, Jodrell Bank Discovery Centre, Peter Johnson, Ray Johnson, Lorraine Jones, Peter Jones, Ray Jones, Jumbo Self Storage, Keele University, Mark Kennerley, Dorothy Kent, Rosalind Kent, Keswick Library, Anne Kirkwood, Dr Christine Kusiar, Kat Lacey, Nick Lawrence-Downs, Leek Library, Paul Lewis, Lifeline, Little Moreton Hall, Llangollen Tourist Information Centre, Robin Llewellyn, Lochbroom and Coigach Registration Office, Lochgilphead Delivery Office, Dave Lovatt, Sue Lovatt, John Lumsdon, Dennis Lyth, Reg Maddison, Don Maddocks, Joanne Malcolm, Manifold Valley Cycle Hire, Arthur Mellor, Barry Meredith, Mark Meredith, John Middleton, Mill Meece Pumping Station Preservation Trust, Marie Minshall, Jean Mitchell, Moorcroft Medical Centre, Gordon Moore, Howard Moore, Shirley Moore, Jenny Morgan, Mormon Family History Centre (Newcastle-under-Lyme), John Morrey, Mandy Morrey, Newcastle-under-Lyme Library, North Stafford Hotel, North Staffordshire Magistrates Court, Nuffield Health North Staffordshire Hospital, Steve Oakes, Oban Library, Oxfordshire History Centre, Ern Parkes, Eddie Parrish, Penrith Library, Angelo Pezzaioli, Bill Pollock, Gill Poole, Harry Poole, Matthew Poole, Portmeirion Ltd, Mandy Posnett, Prestatyn Library, Lindsey Purcell, David Rayner, Mary Reece, Dr Christine Roffe, Liz Rogers, Bill Rowley, Margaret Rowley, Royal Mail, Royal Oak

(Braithwaite), Evelyn Royle, Joe Rushton, Ruthin Library, Jannette Ryan, St. Andrews Care Services, Sale Library, Janice Sare, Helen Sargent, ScotRail, James Scott, *The Sentinel*, Alex Severn, Severn Trent Water, Phil Sherwin, Shires Veterinary Practice, Shuropody, Anne Sloan, Owen Sloss, Bob Smith, Helen Smith, Lesley Smith, Betty Smithson, Specsavers (Hanley), Stafford Library, Staffordshire County Record Office, Allan Staples, Gary Stockton, Stoke on Trent City Archives, Stoke-on-Trent City Council, Stoke-on-Trent Crown Court, Stoke-on-Trent Register Office, Stoke on Trent Repertory Theatre, Tony Stoker, Stone Library, Reg Street, Ken Talbot, Norman Tatton, Ray Tatton, Karen Taylor, Dr Andrew Thompson, Derek Thompson, Julie Tomasik, Terry Tomasik, Trafford Register Office, Trent Country Club, Margaret Trevor, Ullapool Library, University Hospital of North Staffordshire, Victim Liaison Service, Derrick Wain, Vincent "Danny" Waldron, Maureen Wallett, Bernard Walton, Emily Waqanivere, Phil Warrington, Wedgwood, Lindsey Westerholm-Smith, Irene Whalley, Whitehaven Archive Centre, Joan Wilding, Alice Williamson, Pete Williamson, Vicky Williamson, Williamson Brothers, Sharron Willis, Ian Wilshaw, John Wood, Workington Library, Neil Wright, Susan Wright and Pete Wyatt.

ILLUSTRATION CREDITS

Illustrations were kindly supplied by the following:
John Baddeley – 48; Sue Bell – 70, 78, 81, 82, 84-86; Ken Cubley – 3; Chris Doorbar – 17; Lynn Halliburton – 13; Cyril Kent – front cover, 2, 4-7, 10-12, 14-16, 20-22, 25-29, 31, 32, 34, 35, 38, 40, 42, 43, 47, 49, 50, 53-57, 59-62, 67-69, 71-73; Dorothy Kent – 51; Jeff Kent – 19, 23, 30, 44, 63, 65, 66, 74, 76, 77, 79, 80, 83, 87, 88; Nick Lawrence-Downs – 41, 45; Dave Lovatt – 9; Gill and Harry Poole – 1; *The Sentinel* – back cover, 8, 18, 24, 33, 36, 39, 75; Dave Wallett – 37, 46, 64; Maureen Wallett – 52, 58.

Contents

Preface 1

1 Magnificent Movies! 3

2 Have Wheels, Will Travel 33

3 Rowing With The Routine 67

4 After The Post 100

5 New Horizons 131

6 The Turning Of The Tide 161

7 The Exit Door Opens 190

8 Slipping Away 219

9 Just As Usual 246

10 Then And Now 279

Postscript 280

Preface

It was never my intention to write the preface for this book. Had my father not died on 6 February 2012 and instead remained in sufficiently good health, it was anticipated that the task would ultimately have been his. No doubt he'd have asked me for guidance, which I'd have given, but the final choices of what to put would have been his. However, it's likely that he'd have dictated the text to me, rather than written it, because he'd been finding it difficult for several years to put pen to paper unless he had to. Although I acted as his editor in the production of the first volume of his life and times (*A Potteries Past*) and this sequel, he had the final say on the text and so his story is his own, as he saw it.

At the beginning of 2012, the bulk of the work had been done on this second volume and it was hoped that a big push would have seen it published before Easter. However, after Dad's unexpected death, I was extremely busy for a period arranging his funeral and sorting out the main aspects of his affairs that needed attending to. Also, as readers will probably gather from his books, we had a really close relationship and so his death seemed to symbolize the end of the project. We'd spent years working on it together, discussing endless aspects, carrying out research and producing the text for publication. It was a shared interest and, with Dad's death, all my heart went out of it. Initially, I couldn't face continuing my editing work, alone, with no reference point, and I had to run away from it.

However, as the months passed, the fact that the book was in limbo gnawed away at me and I realized that I needed to complete my work on it, however painful that might be to do. I felt that if I didn't, it would forever haunt me like a spectre prowling the corridors of my mind. In addition, copies of *A Potteries Past* continued to sell and several people asked me what was happening with Dad's new book. Thus his story had taken on a life beyond his physical existence and so it would have been extremely difficult to have abandoned it permanently.

Therefore, in trepidation, I gradually resumed work on the book from 16 July, increasing my efforts as time went by, and overall I found it to be an enjoyable and not a disturbing experience. It brought back many happy family memories and, if anything, kept me closely connected to Dad, at times even seeming like we were together at some point in the past, most especially when I had to check something on one of his cine films. The only time I had a problem was when I was writing the postscript, which I decided was essential, so that the readers would know the details of the end of his life. That was distressing to do and brought back the raw emotion I felt at his death, but I got it done.

From time to time, Dad had continued to tell me recollections of his continuing life for inclusion in this book and he carried on doing so until 17 January this year. As a result, his final memories are still quite contemporary.

In the preface of *A Potteries Past*, Dad expressed his opinion that he had only limited ability to write a book and compared his efforts very unfavourably to those of established writers. However, he completed it, which is more than most would-be book writers achieve, and he has added a second volume with this work.

Fortunately, no criticism of his efforts has been forthcoming and only a tiny handful of errors have since been uncovered in his first book. Of course, with the sheer magnitude of the text, a miracle would have been needed for every single fact to have been absolutely perfect. Having said that, it is the duty of the writer and publisher to inform the readers of subsequent works, like this one, of any earlier inaccuracies at the first opportunity. Therefore, below are comments on and corrections to mistakes that have been discovered in the first volume:

Dad's research showed his maternal grandparents, George and Ann Wallett, to have had nine children. However, last year, Margaret Rowley, the elder daughter of Dad's cousin, Wilf Wallett, got in touch with me and revealed evidence that the full tally was actually eleven!

In 1943, Dad joined 454 Battery of the 3rd Mountain Regiment of the Royal Artillery and said in his first book that when he was posted to the Scottish town of Beauly, the officers slept at the Beauly Arms. It was in fact the Lovat Arms Hotel.

The caption to photograph 67 in *A Potteries Past* states the young girl on the left to be Rosie Green. However, an E-mail I received from her (as Rose Brooke) last year said that the child is actually her sister, Pat. The error was my fault rather than Dad's because I was sure that it was Rosie, whilst Dad was more tenuous about which of the sisters was shown. We'd long lost contact with Rose's family and so no inside help could be found with our identification efforts at the time.

The Greens were victims to a second error in Dad's first volume, but this time he only had himself to blame! A photograph in his possession showed us on a Blackpool beach with their family at Easter in 1960. We knew that the Greens had moved from Cobridge to the seaside resort in the early 1960s. I discovered at Stoke on Trent City Archives that Rose's parents (Jack and Rose) were still on the electoral register in Cobridge at the qualifying date of 10 October 1960, but not a year later. I contacted Blackpool Central Library and was told that the Greens were registered there on that date in 1961, but not in 1960. Therefore, it was near impossible that they could have moved by Easter 1960 and I told Dad so. However, he was convinced that we'd never gone there on a trip with them nor bumped into them in Blackpool and so we must have visited their house. The story as published was therefore placed in 1960, but Rose later said that they'd moved to Blackpool in 1961, so, unusually, Dad's memory was at fault.

In Dad's first book, in 1962, Frank Swinnerton was stated to have been the managing director of F. Swinnerton & Son Limited. However, an E-mail this year from Joan Cameron, the widow of Frank's brother, John, said that the two brothers were in fact at that time joint-managing directors of the company.

Finally, in *A Potteries Past*, Dad said that he'd continued to do the regular Post Office walks that he'd been allocated in 1962 (5, 10, 13 and 17) until he retired, apart from odd occasions. However, four ex-postmen (Jeff Hollins, Ken Cubley, Phil Warrington and John Clewlow) have since independently stated that he also did the Town Road walk (11) for a while at a later stage in his career. Also, John Clewlow, who was Dad's section mate at that time, said that they both did walk 28, which was part of Abbey Hulton, on a regular basis during the same period.

I will be overjoyed if this book proves to be as error free as Dad's previous one and I hope the readers will feel that it was well worth our while in committing this second half of his life to print. I'd like to think that, as the story of a very long working-class life well lived, through rapidly-changing times, there is value in what Dad has had to say and that there are also lessons for us to learn from his words.

Jeff Kent, Cotes Heath, November 2012

1 Magnificent Movies!

The news came through that "Young" Harry Poole was getting married. He was the nephew of my wife, Helen, and his bride to be was Gill Martin, whom he'd met in Oxford, which was where the wedding was going to be held. He'd got to know her when he'd played football for Oxford City during his national service with the RAF in nearby Abingdon. Helen was very excited because she loved weddings and Harry was her favourite. She started planning things right away and one of the first things that came into her mind was that we should get a cine camera. It seemed to me to be rather expensive just for a wedding, but, of course, it was for the wedding of the year! I was detailed to purchase one of these highfaluting gadgets and get it in plenty of time so I could practise with it. These cameras were becoming popular at the time.

I went to have a word with my cousin, Stan Palin, at his photography shop at 3 Vale Street, in Stoke, about buying a model and he fixed me up with a simple affair, a Kodak Brownie, and a Kodak projector in May 1962. I then bought a roll of 8 mm film from Hanley for about a pound and set about reading the camera instructions.

The next morning was a Sunday and Helen, my ten-year-old son Jeff and I got up fairly early to walk from our home at 335 Leek Road, in Shelton, to Hanley Park for a trial run. I looked around for a suitable background and came upon one near the main entrance at the junction of Cleveland Road and The Parkway, where there was a nice array of flowers. First I filmed Jeff walking down the path, sucking an ice lolly that he'd got from an ice cream van outside the park gates, and then I shot him bouncing and kicking a tennis ball. As I did so, I tried to remember the operating and technical aspects of filming motion, as given in the instruction booklet.

Helen and I then went near to the lake and I shot her in front of a tree in blossom. She felt embarrassed in case people didn't understand why she was moving in front of a camera, but, of course, with movie film, motion is essential. She and I then moved on to the detached part of the park, between College Road and Stoke Road, which we called the "Flower Park" because it was so pretty. I then filmed her there looking at a lovely bed of tulips.

Afterwards, I got some shots in our back garden of Janet Bennison, the niece of our next-door neighbour, Nancy Cadman, of number 333. Also on the film I took there was our rabbit, Bobby, in its hutch.

There was a triangular flower bed just inside Hanley Park, by the lodge behind Cleveland Road, and, at the time, it was filled with tulips. Helen practised walking around the flowers, even though her feet were killing her because she had a lot of hard skin that dug into her flesh. I then got some shots of her walking by the tulips and sitting on a park bench.

I just carried on shooting until I'd run off 25 feet of film. Then I had to open the camera, turn the roll of film over and put it back in, to take another 25 feet of footage. The film was split right down the middle and the two lengths were spliced together, making a length of fifty feet. The film was exposed down one side and then the other when shooting.

As soon as I'd run off the whole fifty feet, I sent it off to be processed by Kodak.

Helen and I were pleased with the result. It was amateurish and nothing like the professional movies one sees at the pictures, but it was my first epic! I then bought another roll of film.

Also in May, our next-door neighbour (at number 337), Brian Cotton, and I took down the wooden fence that stood between our back yards and replaced it with a brick wall, which still stands. He knew a bit about building, so we did it ourselves and shared the cost, which was eight pounds.

The location for the next cine film shooting, in June, was again Hanley Park, where I took Jeff playing cricket with some of his friends. Then I moved on to our back garden, with Helen in the starring role, hanging out the washing. Also, I took shots of Brian and Joan Cotton's baby son, Philip, and again Helen and I were pleased with the result.

About June, Helen and I were given the very good news that Jeff had passed his eleven-plus exam, which meant he could go on to study at a grammar school, as we'd hoped he would. At the end of the month, we received a letter from Wilfrid Barwise, the headmaster of Hanley High School (which was off Corneville Road, in Townsend), saying that Jeff had been awarded a place there. With the letter was a copy of the school rules. Also, Helen and I were told that he'd been put in Wilson House and so we'd need to get him a school tie with the right house colour, which was yellow.

The same month, I shot part of another film, at Rhyl and Ffrith (in Prestatyn), on a family trip to the seaside, and completed it by filming Jeff playing with his friends, Glenys Chell and Raymond Tatton, and practising his football skills in the "Dingle", in Hanley Park. By then, I felt I could do with a better cine camera, so I went back to Stan. I got him to change my model for a Kodak Automatic, which was more expensive, but Stan accepted my Brownie as new and so I only paid the difference between the two. I didn't have time to try my new camera before the big wedding, but I was fairly confident I'd be okay with it.

I'd written to Oxford to book boarding house accommodation at 14 St. John Street for the three of us for two nights. The bed and breakfast terms per night were 17s. 6d. for Helen and me and 10s. for Jeff. We travelled by train and were accompanied by Helen's brother, Elijah Middleton; his wife, Ethel, and their children, Lynn and John. Also with us were Helen's Aunt Sally and Uncle Bill. When we detrained, we went to our boarding house, with Aunt Sally and Uncle Bill, and the Middletons went to theirs.

The next day, 7 July, we all went to St. Matthew's Church, which was in Marlborough Road and next to Oxford City's football ground. There, we waited for Young Harry to make his appearance. He came out of 100 Marlborough Road, the house of his best man, John Sheppard, and because it was only a short distance away from the church, they walked there. I had my cine camera ready and shot Harry as he walked to the church. I filmed the proceedings outside the church before and after the wedding and I used nearly two rolls of film doing it.

We then went to the reception at the Elms Hotel, in Church Way, Iffley, in the south of the city, but were late getting there, I think because there was a problem with the transport. The reception had been in full swing for some time and by the time that Helen, Jeff and I arrived, there were only scraps of food left! I took a few more movie shots while we were there, especially of Harry and Gill cutting their three-tier wedding cake.

After the reception, there was a football kickabout, which took place on the lawn of the hotel. Gill's youngest brother, Philip, had done a home-made programme for it, which had Danny Blanchflower, Stan Matthews and Alfredo Di Stéfano advertised as appearing, although they didn't turn up! But Young Harry, "Big" Harry (his father), Port Vale's Peter Ford, and Gill's father and three brothers all played and the game was refereed by Uncle Bill.

Harry and Gill left for a honeymoon in Bournemouth after the reception and Helen, Jeff and I finished the night in the supporters' club at Oxford City's ground. While we were there, Vera (Harry's mother and Helen's elder sister) did the twist to Chubby Checker's song, *Let's Twist Again!*

Helen, Jeff and I stayed another two nights in Oxford at a different boarding house. We walked by the River Thames and watched punts going by and we all went on a pleasure boat. I was going to hire a motorboat for about half an hour, but they had a gear change on them and, not being a driver at the time, I didn't want to risk causing any damage. So Jeff and I had a rowing boat out. Also, we all strolled through the streets of Oxford and into the grounds of one or two of the university colleges. Deer were running loose in a field by Magdalen College and they seemed tame, so we fed them. I shot another roll of film on these post-wedding activities.

On our last night (9 July), we went to the New Theatre, in George Street, to see and listen to a production of *The Student Prince*, a musical starring John Hanson. There was some good singing and Helen and I enjoyed the show, which included interesting costumes and scenes. Jeff was pretty good, sitting through it, but it must have seemed a long time to him.

On 17 July, Helen and I had to go to a meeting at Hanley High School, along with parents of other new boys. We were given information about the school and the subjects that were studied and we had to sign a form, which admitted Jeff to go there. Afterwards, we were taken on an inspection of the buildings, which were impressive.

Jeff brought us his final report from Cauldon County Junior School on 27 July and he'd finished fifth out of forty pupils in his class (1A), in scoring 617½ marks out of 700 in his tests. Harry Whalley was still his teacher and had written that Jeff had produced 'very good work' and wished him success in his new school. Helen and I were really pleased with how Jeff was doing.

I became dissatisfied with my cine camera again because it wasn't as sophisticated as I wanted it, so I went to see Stan once more. Again, he swapped it, this time for a Bolex, which was the top manufacturer at the time. The camera was old-fashioned, but had a good reputation. Its motor was wound up by hand and there was a photoelectric cell, which got its power from daylight. This gave the correct lens aperture, but any adjustment needed to be made manually. Unfortunately, I put the first roll of film in back to front and, when I got it back from processing, it was no good.

In August 1962, Helen, Jeff and I went by train to Southport for a day trip and had a nice time. I particularly remember us going to the model village, the Land of the Little People, which was on the Promenade and had miniature trains going round. I'd not seen anything like it before and it was interesting. We also went to the zoo, which was nearby and had quite a number of animals that you could get very close to because there was only a small dividing rail. I filmed Jeff stroking a baby elephant and there was an ostrich towering above his head. I suppose it was quite dangerous really and I don't think it would be allowed today. We also went to the fair at Pleasureland, but, as usual, we didn't go on any of the rides.

On 18 August, I took my cine camera into the Butler Street Stand, at the Victoria Ground, for the Stoke City versus Leeds United Second Division football match and shot some of the action. The great Welsh international, John Charles played centre-forward for Leeds, who won 1-0.

By then, I was doing all my own interior decorating – painting the woodwork, papering the walls and putting Walpamur Water Paint on the ceilings. Walpamur was an early kind of emulsion, but it required water to be added and the mixture then to be given a good stir. That summer, our ex-neighbour, Harold Bentley, who lived at 141 Ridgway Road, told me about a kind of paint I hadn't heard of before, called emulsion. I tried it on the kitchen ceiling and it came out okay, so I carried on using it after that. It required little or no stirring and brushed on very nicely.

Before long, I was doing all our decorating, including the outside the house, and I did it more or less every year. I seemed to be decorating all the time! I did it mainly in the spring because the inside of the house, especially the lounge, kept getting dirty from the soot flying about from the coal fire. The walls would get blackened up over the winter, but we didn't use the fire so much from the spring onwards, so the walls didn't get so dirty then.

At the beginning of September, Jeff started at Hanley High School, along with a number of other lads from his junior school, who'd also passed their eleven-plus. Jeff had been put in class 1A, which was the top stream, and Helen and I were very pleased about it. On his first morning, one of his friends, Robert Stockton, called on him and I filmed them going off to catch a bus to their new school. I was very proud of Jeff. He had his new school cap on, but later bigger lads snatched it off. I believe the headmaster, Mr Barwise, insisted that the boys wear their caps, so, after that incident, Jeff kept his in his satchel and then put it on when he got to school. He was also wearing short trousers on his first day and they had to last until they'd been worn quite a bit. Then we got him some long ones.

Mr Barwise was a pretty good head, but some of the other masters were a bit kinky. Jeff said that one of them, John Freer, his French teacher, had some lads take off their shoes and socks so that he could hit their feet with a strap! Nevertheless, Jeff settled in pretty well and made no complaints to us about the school, as far as I can remember.

With Jeff being out at school all day, Helen went back to working full time for F. Swinnerton & Son Limited, the caterers. She was 42 on 29 September and she liked to be busy, so going back to full-time work was good for her, really. I left her to make her own decision to do that, which was okay with me, and the extra money helped out. She became the manageress of both the firm's catering business and its production of Kia-Ora, a kind of orange squash drink.

On 13 October, Young Harry, who was a regular in the Port Vale team, played at centre-forward at home against Brighton & Hove Albion. I took Jeff along and, of course, my cine camera. I only filmed a small amount of the game and I concentrated on Harry when he was attacking, but I missed him scoring Vale's only goal in a 2-1 defeat! The team played in black and amber striped shirts and amber shorts then. My footage was later used in the 1998 *Up The Vale!* history video.

One day not long after, Helen called me to our front windows. When I looked out, I could see Nate Copeland (who lived at 358 Leek Road) and another fellow shepherding a swan along the road! I think they were trying to get it to the nearby Caldon Canal or the lake at Hanley Park. I don't know how the bird got onto the road, but it was lucky because there was very little traffic about and so it was unhurt. I dashed for my cine camera and took some of the incident.

In late October, the Cuban Missile Crisis took place. The Yanks had spotted Soviet nuclear missiles in Cuba, which was only ninety miles south of the U.S.A. The American president, John Kennedy, decided to send warships to stop any more arms going to Cuba from the U.S.S.R. and said they'd sink any ships that tried to get through. He also demanded that the missiles be removed. In the evening on the 24th, I heard on the news that a Soviet convoy was heading for Cuba and the Americans were going to stop it. That would mean war starting and war would mean the use of the nuclear bomb or something even nastier. I went to bed that night really worried because I couldn't imagine either the Soviets or the Americans backing down. In fact, I didn't expect to wake up again because I thought the British population would be wiped out, with us being allies of the Yanks. Fortunately, good sense prevailed because the Soviets turned their ships away from the confrontation and their premier, Nikita Khrushchev, agreed to remove the missiles.

I filmed two flowerpots and a scrubbing brush moving about in our back garden as if they were alive. Then I did the same kind of thing with some packets and containers of cleaning materials. I did it by taking a series of single frames and moving the items between each frame or two.

Later, on a rainy day, I filmed the view from the front of our house, which included the Remploy factory, the General Post Office depot and, in the distance, the old Berry Hill Collieries' spoil tip. Although the tip was no longer used, there was smoke coming out from the right side of it and the dismal weather made the scene look a bit grim.

I used my cine camera quite a lot, even though it was rather expensive, because it was a novelty and more money was being brought in as Helen had gone back to working full time. That meant I could afford to use it without thinking too much about the cost.

Helen used to have splitting headaches and would ask me to press her head, I suppose to try to relieve the pain. Doing so must have made a difference unless the effect was psychological. Eventually, they stopped happening, but that was years later.

On 14 December, I was 47 and, although I was getting older, I was pretty happy. My job was nice and steady and I had a settled home life with Helen and Jeff, so things in general were okay.

We spent our Christmas at home as usual and Jeff again had all his presents laid out in the lounge, so he'd be in the warmth instead of being in his cold bedroom, where there was no fire. I filmed him opening many of them and a number were books because he was very interested in reading. We had a small artificial tree in the room, which we'd decorated, and streamers on the walls.

The winter of 1962-1963 turned out to be the coldest since 1739-1740. One

Saturday in January 1963, Jeff went out on a hike with a party from the school, led by Graham Eardley, one of the teachers. It was a bitterly cold period, with plenty of snow about. Helen and I thought it was crazy for children to go out in those conditions, but hoped things would be okay because we thought that surely the teacher would know what he was doing. When tea time came and Jeff hadn't got back, we became worried because it was dark and snow was falling. We didn't know what to do for the best. We kept looking through the window for some sign that would give us hope. We didn't even know which way to look because we didn't know where the lads had gone.

Eventually, about eight or nine o'clock, Jeff turned up, frozen to the bone. The string on the hood of his anorak was pulled tight, so we couldn't see much of his face. It seemed that they'd been walking on the moorlands between Leek and Buxton and left it so late that they had to wait for the last bus home. By some miracle, the bus was running in the atrocious conditions, otherwise it could have been midnight or even after before the lads had got home. Helen and I stripped all Jeff's wet clothes off and then got a hot bath ready for him, in which he had a good soak. He was none the worse for his experience, thank goodness! Helen and I thought of complaining at the school, but wondered if they'd take it out on Jeff, so we kept silent.

Jeff wasn't doing as well as expected at his new school and came 27th out of 34 pupils in his class in the January exams, although he finished second in history, with a mark of 81%. He was one of the youngest boys in the class and was four months below the average age, which must have made it difficult for him to keep up with the older ones. Unlike at junior school, where he'd mainly been taught English and mathematics, he was studying a lot of different subjects: art, biology, chemistry, divinity, English language, English literature, French, geography, history, maths (which included algebra and geometry, as well as arithmetic), music and physics. His report said, 'His attitude seems to be rather silly on occasions and he needs to concentrate.' Helen and I were very disappointed with him.

In February, I visited Swinnerton's factory in Wood Terrace, Shelton, because Helen had asked me to make a movie of the Kia-Ora production process, which, along with the catering business, had been moved there from Raymond Street. I took my floodlights, which I'd bought for filming indoors, and fixed them on top of my camera. They were awkward to fit, wobbled about and got red hot, but I made a nice little documentary. After processing, I took the film to the factory to show the staff the result, but nobody got too excited at seeing themselves moving around and performing. I suppose they were just doing their duty by watching!

Helen had been worried about a lump in her left breast for some while, so she went to see Dr Kerr at 4 Jasper Street, in Hanley, which was where our surgery had moved to, from 108 Lichfield Street. He fixed up for her to see a specialist, Mr William Sewell, for a fee at his consulting room at Windsor House, 5a King Street, in Newcastle. He told her that he thought the lump was just a cyst, but Helen was concerned it might have been something more serious. So, at her request, he got her into the City General Hospital for an operation as a private patient, with her own room because she thought going into the main ward might upset her.

She had notice to report to Ward 4 on 19 March, so I went to see the acting chief inspector of the Stoke-on-Trent Post Office (where I worked), Bill Shore, to ask him for some time off. He told me it wasn't that easy because the Post Office would have to pay someone to do my job for me, maybe on overtime at double time. He said that I'd have to foot any bill paid above ordinary time. I told him I'd have to take the chance because I'd require time to take my wife to hospital, look after the household chores and see to my son. He said Jeff was big enough to look after himself, but I disagreed. Anyway, my time off was arranged on the above condition.

I took Helen to the City General and she had her operation, which was carried out by Mr Sewell. It was a success and the lump was after all only a cyst. On the 21st, she told me she could come home, so I got a taxi and home we went. She was feeling pretty good and it seemed she'd soon be alright again. She thought I could go to work, but I was doubtful about it. I then got a message to report to Bill Shore, who told me they'd been able to fix my duty without me losing any money, but they wouldn't be able to do it any longer. I thanked him and said I'd start back the next day.

Jeff had taken the upset of routine in his stride and had been little trouble. Helen hadn't told many people what was going on, including most of those at her factory, who thought she was having a few days' holiday. After a couple of days or so, she went back to work, but took things very easy at first.

On 27 March, Stoke-on-Trent Hospital Management Committee sent Helen a demand for seven pounds for the cost of her two-day stay in the private room and, on 30 April, Mr Sewell sent her a bill for fourteen guineas for his 'professional services', which meant for his know-how and doing the operation privately. Of course, we paid both bills straightaway.

Helen's brother, Elijah, bought a car, a Volkswagen Beetle 1300, and came to our house to show it off to us. He had a few driving lessons and then drove about unaccompanied by a qualified driver for quite a while, taking his family with him, until he passed his test! He was taking a risk because that was illegal.

Vera and Harry bought a newsagent's business at 136 Greasley Road, in Abbey Hulton, just round the corner from where they lived, at 9 Holdcroft Road. It was with Young Harry in mind because being a footballer was only a temporary job and they doted on him. To help pay for the shop, Big Harry had his pension contributions back, even though he was giving up a decent works' pension. Even then, they didn't have sufficient money to pay for the shop and had to borrow some. They came to Helen and borrowed sixty pounds. They were really broke and we found out later that they went short of food. Helen would have helped them out more if she'd known.

Vera and Harry put the business in Young Harry's name and let him and Gill run it as their own, but Vera and Harry both retired from their jobs to help them behind the counter. The business proved a little gold mine and it wasn't long before the money started rolling in.

The Beatles were becoming really popular at that time with their very catchy tunes. People loved their new type of music and girls were screaming when they played, which was good publicity that pushed things even more in their favour. All the excitement was called Beatlemania and it was over the top! I didn't particularly like the group at first and thought they might have been a flash in the pan, but they kept producing songs and sold millions of records. After I'd listened to the group a few times, I decided their songs were pretty good and more or less liked all of them. I particularly remember *Yellow Submarine* and *All You Need Is Love*.

The Beatles had got long hair and looked a bit odd. It didn't seem quite the thing, but teenagers started copying them, including Jeff eventually. I suppose things changed through the group so that youngsters seemed to be getting more of their own way. Some of the things they did were crazy, but I wasn't bothered about it a lot. The Rolling Stones were also very good, but Mick Jagger, the lead singer, stood out like a sore thumb because he was pretty ugly, so people remembered him.

Other similar groups became very popular as well so that there was all this new music coming in, which took over. It did away with most of the old ballad style of music that I liked, but some good old-fashioned-type songs still came up occasionally.

In June, Helen, Jeff and I had a trip to Llandudno on a steam train from Stoke Station. We sat in a compartment, but Jeff was so keen to see the scenery on the journey that he put his head out of a corridor window, even though it was dangerous to do so. I wasn't much better myself because I took shots out of a window of scenes along the way, which included the approach to Harecastle Tunnel, Beeston Crag and Castle, Chester Racecourse, the Dee Estuary, the Clwydian Hills, Colwyn Bay and Conway Castle. When we got to Llandudno, I also got some nice footage, from partway up the Great Orme headland, of the Little Orme, Llandudno Bay and the town itself.

On 15 June, I took Jeff to the Tunstall Park Annual Carnival, which had a demonstration of police dogs in action, supposedly apprehending a crook. There was a women's football match, between Foden's Ladies and Handy Angles [sic] of Brierley Hill, and I was surprised how well they played. I'd imagined that, if anything went wrong, they'd be scratching each other's eyes out or would be crying, but there wasn't a bit of it. There were also a motorbike stuntman, who rode through a flaming frame; a miniature steam train and a children's procession, and I took a fair amount of film of the various events.

Jeff still wasn't doing particularly well at school, but went up one place, to 26th, in the June exams. His report said his marks 'must be improved next term', but that, 'Generally he seems to be working with more enthusiasm.'

On 13 July, Helen, Jeff and I went on a trip, organized by the Railway Mission, to Colwyn Bay, on the North Wales coast. The mission was on the opposite side of Leek Road from our house, where Stoke on Trent Repertory Theatre is now located. Helen attended the mission's services fairly regularly, while Jeff went to the Sunday school and they'd both been going there for a long time. While we were in Colwyn Bay, we went to Eirias Park, which had a model yacht pond, a miniature golf course and a boating lake, but what I remember most clearly was a talking parrot on a perch. It was in a mini-zoo, which also included a black bear, separated from the public only by a wire-mesh fence, and I filmed Jeff just a few feet away from it!

Our neighbour, Julia Noone, of number 319, got married to Peter Gibson, a bus driver from Penkhull, at the Church of Our Lady of the Angels and St. Peter in Chains, in Hartshill Road, on 27 July. I went along to Julia's house on the morning of the wedding to take some movie film of her getting ready for the big occasion. I think it was a little unusual taking pictures of that part of a wedding, but we were pretty friendly with her family. I shot her getting into the wedding car, with some of the neighbours standing around, and also took some footage of the scenes at the church after the ceremony.

The same month, I took Jeff to Dudley Zoo. It cost me two shillings to get in and I paid one shilling for Jeff. We had a nice day there and I got some good movie shots of the animals. We saw two performing chimpanzees having a drink, while they sat on chairs at a table, and riding a tricycle and a scooter. There were seals, which were enjoying sliding down a long water chute into a pool, and we were there to see the tigers and lions being fed with great chunks of meat. Amongst the other animals we saw were polar bears, brown bears, giraffes and flamingos, and Jeff also enjoyed the train ride there and back.

We also had a trip to Alton Towers by train, which was a thrill. Unlike now, there wasn't a lot to do when we got there, but it was very scenic and we went walking in the grounds. There was a fairground, but the rides weren't anything like the real hair-raising ones that they have now! Also, there was a display of old steam tractors and I filmed Jeff turning the steering wheels of two of them and opening up the boiler of another. I also took shots of the boating lake and exotic fountains that they had.

At the beginning of August, Helen, Jeff and I went on the railway to Barmouth, on the west coast of Wales, for a day trip. The journey through Wales was spectacular and I filmed the River Dee at Llangollen from the train, which was a diesel. More and more diesel-powered engines were coming into use and they were replacing steam trains, which eventually became obsolete. For most of the route after Llangollen, the railway was only a single track. Down the line at Dolgellau Station, there was a beautiful display of flowers, but the highlight of the journey was crossing the half-a-mile-long Barmouth Bridge over the Mawddach Estuary. The scenery around Barmouth was nice, but there wasn't much to do there except to go on the beach. After we'd done that, we got a ferry from the harbour to Penrhyn Point on the other side of the estuary and then had a ride on the two-mile-long, steam-powered Fairbourne (miniature) Railway.

We also had a look at Hanley Wakes, which was on some spare ground off Harding Road, where there'd once been a marl hole. The fair was Pat Collins', just as it had been when I was a boy. There were side stalls and fairground rides, but not big ones (except for the big wheel) and we didn't go on them because Helen and I didn't fancy them. But Jeff and I liked the Dodgems because we could operate them ourselves and go where we wanted. Mainly, we tried to avoid the other Dodgems because if you bumped people you didn't know, they might not have liked it. There were also slot machines, of course, and the largest rat in the world was advertised as an attraction, but we didn't go to see it!

On 12 August, a new sorting and distribution post office was opened on the corner of Leek Road and Station Road, at a cost of nearly £300,000. It had been built on the site of a reservoir, which the Post Office had bought and drained. The lake had originally been created by the railway as a water supply for the boilers of the steam engines. It seemed silly for the Post Office to build there then because the ground wasn't stable and, a year or two after the office's completion, some of the walls began to crack. These were repaired a number of times until eventually they had to be covered by false walls. Nevertheless, the new office was better because there was a lot more room. The Station Road and Regent Road offices were closed, as was our Lytton Street depot, where our vans had been kept and repaired, and this operation was also brought to the new site.

The mail was then run from the new office to the railway station on trains of trailers, pulled by tugs, but the practice was dangerous because it involved crossing busy Station Road. The bags of parcels were conveyed by vans to the far end of the station, where there were sidings. Trains backed in and the mail was thrown into different trucks, depending on their destination.

The letters and parcels were all sorted on the ground floor of the new office and there was a chute for the sorted parcels to go down to the van bay below, ready to be picked up. In the basement, we had a canteen, but, like most of the postmen, I took sandwiches for my meals and made myself a cup of tea from their urn.

We each had a full-length locker allocated to us and that was a big improvement on the small wooden boxes that some of us had been lucky enough to have had previously. But even the new lockers didn't give a lot of room. The top part was used for storing a teapot, cup, tea, milk, sugar and odds and ends. The lower part housed our winter jacket, summer jacket, overcoat, raincoat, leggings, overalls, wellingtons and shoes. We also had to fit our lamp in somewhere.

Like Helen, Jeff and I, Elijah still supported Vale and started to go to the ground in his car. He usually gave Vera and Harry a lift home after the matches, but if they didn't attend, Helen used to push the three of us into his car instead. She thought that, as Elijah's sister, she was privileged to do so. When just Jeff and I went to the matches, Helen told us to get into Elijah's car to be run home, which we did two or three times. However, I got the impression that my brother-in-law resented our cheek, so I didn't bother again. He didn't ask why and never gave us a run out into the country or to the seaside, so my impression must have been correct.

In September, Jeff started his second year at high school, but, because of his low position in his first-year exams, he'd been dropped into the W (West) stream, which wasn't the top division. The school must have thought that would suit him or other pupils better, but the average age of the boys in 2W was another month higher, which put him at a bigger disadvantage. However, Helen and I wondered what was happening with him dropping down.

I decided once more to get a new cine camera because I wanted a more up-to-date automatic one and part exchanged my Bolex for a Kopil, a Japanese make. I didn't really like doing that because the Japs had been the archenemy in the war, but they made first-class goods, often superior to British ones.

I first tried out my new camera on the North Staffordshire Homes and Food Festival, which was held in Hanley Park from 14 to 28 September. Swinnerton's were the caterers for this event and Helen was helping them out at it. It was mainly held in a great marquee and there were lots of different products on sale from a variety of stands. Outside the marquee was an old ornate, horse-drawn Gypsy caravan.

Around that time, Helen and I became members of Shelton Club and Institute (a working men's club), in Richmond Terrace, and paid an annual subscription. These clubs were all the rage, partly because families could take their children with them. Otherwise, they'd have had to have stayed in because children weren't allowed in pubs. So it gave us a Saturday night out and we took Jeff with us. It was the first time we'd been out at night regularly since he'd been born. There was a concert room, which was quite large, and the tables and chairs were laid out in rows, with corridors in between so that people could move about. The entertainment was provided mainly by groups, playing the current pop songs, so we could sing along with the tunes we could remember, some of which were pretty good.

The first night we went, Helen had been nervous and shy because we didn't know anybody. We sat by an older couple from 8 Edge Street, in Burslem, Lucy and Charlie Dean, who made us welcome, and we quickly became friends. They were of low intelligence, but were very pleasant and Charlie was quite a character. Sometimes, he danced up and down the passageway and even got on stage and sang in a high-pitched voice, with everybody urging him on! Lucy wasn't too happy with his antics and called him 'a damned fool'!

Later, we also became friends with Les and Joan Brown, who were a bit younger than Helen and me. They lived at 43 Boon Avenue, in Penkhull, and Les was a builder, while Joan had a wartime hairstyle, but didn't always tell the truth!

Jack Hodgkiss worked with Helen in the office at Swinnerton's. He was made a director and put in charge of the orange squash factory, but was a nice fellow, who was anxious to please, so people tended to put on him. He was easygoing and wasn't much for telling the production girls what to do. In reality, Helen did the managing and Jack was more like a labourer!

Helen became friendly with him and one day he took us in his Triumph Herald to Fradswell, a hamlet between Uttoxeter and Stone. Helen had wanted to go there for a while because she'd spent some happy times there during her school holidays on her Uncle Alf's smallholding. She used to set off on her own from Northwood and get a train from Stoke Station to Leigh. Even though the train compartments were separate at that time and she had to walk through narrow country lanes for three miles or so, she was never molested. It certainly wouldn't be safe for a girl to do that nowadays. Uncle Alf had since moved to Mirfield, in Yorkshire, and when we got to Fradswell, we found there was no longer a smallholding, but the cottage was more or less the same as it had been before.

Another time, Jack and his wife, Flo, took Helen and me for a run towards Buxton. Flo was a bit of a snob, but we seemed to get on alright. When we drew near to Ramshaw Rocks, Jack pointed to a rock formation and told us to look for the shape of a man's face, with an eye in it. We did so and, as we drove past, the eye seemed to wink. This was known as the 'winking man'. It's still there today.

While I was working at the new Post Office one day, a fellow postman told me that we could be under surveillance. I asked him what he meant and he pointed to some black glass windows at the top of the building, which ran the length of the office. He told me that the glass could only be looked through from the other side and at the back was a corridor where someone could watch what we were doing, without us being any the wiser. That was the observation corridor and it was mainly used when someone was suspected of stealing from the mail. Occasionally, I'd hear about one of our postmen being caught and it was always a shock to learn of a colleague getting into trouble. The Post Office was hard on thieves and they were nearly always imprisoned.

That Christmas, Helen and I bought Jeff a Dansette Conquest automatic record player. He'd wanted to be able to play records for some time, so we were happy to get him a machine to do so on, although we were concerned that he'd have it going bang, bang. There was a lot of noise generated by the kind of pop music that he liked, though it was quite good. He was so keen on the music of the time that he'd already bought a number of singles, even though he'd had nothing to play them on! After he'd opened his presents on Christmas morning, I filmed him putting the first record on, which was *Yesterday's Gone* by Chad Stuart and Jeremy Clyde.

The latest action film, *Lawrence of Arabia*, about the First World War hero known by that name, was on at the Odeon, in Trinity Street, Hanley, for a season from 29 December and I took Jeff to see it. Lieutenant Colonel T. E. Lawrence had led Arabs in a revolt against the Turks and I remember him riding across the desert on a camel in the film. The story started off with him getting killed in a motorbike crash and it went back to his war exploits from there, which was an unusual way of doing things. There were quite a few big stars in the film, like Peter O'Toole, Alec Guinness, Omar Sharif and Anthony Quinn.

Jeff did a little better in his exams in January 1964 than he'd done before and came nineteenth out of 32 pupils. He was by then studying two additional subjects, metalwork and Spanish, making fourteen in all!

Helen and I occasionally bought a record to play if we really fancied it. I think the first one I got was an LP of the soundtrack of *The Alamo*, the 1960 film, starring John Wayne, which Jeff and I had seen at the pictures and liked. The LP was alright and my favourite song on it was *Ballad of the Alamo*, sung by Marty Robbins. When I listened to it, I was visualizing the Mexicans milling about and volunteers, like Davy Crockett, riding in. I also bought Robbins's single, *Devil Woman*, which had got to number five in the pop charts in 1962. I liked the story it told, which was about the singer's true love, Mary, having him back after he'd escaped from the clutches of the "Devil Woman", who'd tempted him by her charms.

Helen loved The Bachelors, an Irish trio, and I too thought that they sang very nice songs. They weren't very exciting, but they were good harmony singers. We bought five of their records, starting with *Charmaine*, which had made number six the previous year. On 22 February 1964, they topped the charts with *Diane* and we got that as well. In the same year, they also made the hit parade with *Ramona*, *I Wouldn't Trade You for the World* and *No Arms Can Ever Hold You*, all of which we bought, so we were pretty keen on them at that time.

In March, Helen and I noticed water dripping down the dividing wall between our kitchen and that of Hannah Bradbury (Nancy Cadman's mother), so we had to get a plumber out. It seemed that the hot water lead pipe was leaking under the floorboards of our back bedroom. The pipe had a right-angled shape and, as it warmed up and cooled down and so expanded and contracted, the pipe sprung a leak at the corner. The plumber, Ivan Pointon, of 18 Jasper Street, in Hanley, had to get the floorboards up to get at the leak, but put them back without securing them, so they still tend to creak when trodden on! The cost of the job was £3 7s. 10d.

At that time, I used to fill in a Littlewoods Pools Limited football coupon each week and send it off to them through the post. The pools involved betting on the results of forthcoming football matches, but I only ever gambled the smallest amount of money possible. One week, I did well with my predictions and won about ten shillings, so I sent off my claim. I didn't hear anything, so I wrote to the company. A few days later, a fellow from the firm knocked on the door and said my postal order had been cashed in Burslem. He wanted to look at my signature, so I got out my old National Registration Identity Card (which I still had handy) and showed it to him. He then revealed the cashed postal order and the signature on it was nearly identical to mine. However, he seemed to be satisfied with what I'd shown him and so I got the prize money.

On 18 April, Stoke played at home to Manchester United in the First Division and I went to the match to have a look at United because they were a big club with big stars. They were an attraction to a lot of people and there were long queues outside the turnstiles at the ground. Although United were in second place and had George Best, Bobby Charlton and Nobby Stiles playing for them that day, Stoke won 3-1. I stood in the Butler Street Stand and took some action shots of the match with my cine camera.

A new television channel, BBC Two, started up on 20 April, but it was years before we could get it on our set. Stoke was one of the last cities in the country to have proper coverage of it and the station wasn't even advertised in the *Evening Sentinel* till October 1965. Of course, Helen and I tried it out when it became available. It gave us more choice, but I don't think the programmes were much better than those we were watching on the other two channels. We tended to have the set mainly on ITV because our favourite show, *Coronation Street*, was on there. Of course, there weren't any remote controls then and we didn't want to keep getting up to change the programmes over. When the new channel came in, we carried on more or less the same.

In May 1964, Helen, Jeff and I paid a visit to Southport. We went on the train as usual because we didn't bother with coaches. I didn't particularly like them because they were more enclosed, whereas on a train you could get up and walk around. While we were at Southport, I filmed a speedboat tearing across the lake and we had a ride on the miniature railway in one of the open carriages pulled by a small steam locomotive. Of course, we went to the zoo because Jeff was very keen on animals and I filmed two monkeys grooming each other, which was interesting. Also, we went for a walk along Lord Street, in the town centre, which was supposed to be one of the most famous and attractive streets in Britain. I think Helen wanted to be filmed strolling along the pavement there, so I duly obliged with my camera.

On 25 May, I read in the *Sentinel* that the old Majestic Ballroom, in Pall Mall, Hanley, had been gutted by a fire and the dance floor had been destroyed. Four months before, the dance hall had been renamed the Rave Cave and had been putting on well-known pop groups. I was sad about the fire because the ballroom was a place that I'd gone to a lot before and during the war and, of course, I had memories of meeting Helen and dancing with her there many times.

Jeff seemed to be getting the hang of his studies at school because he rose ten places to ninth in his class in the June exams and his report said he'd made 'a very creditable effort'. He finished second in divinity and geography and third in science. It was a relief that he was improving.

Our friends, Jack and Flo, offered to take us in their car to Anglesey for a two-day holiday on 4 and 5 July. The car had a fairly big boot, but we were cramped in the rear seats. Jeff sat between Helen and me and was alright until we were near Conway when he felt sick. So I asked Jack to stop, which he did, and we had a cup of tea that he brewed on a Calor Gas stove while Jeff got his "sea legs" again. When we started off once more, I sat in the middle seat. It wasn't very comfortable because I couldn't get my legs in a good position owing to the raised floor in the centre of the car, where the propeller shaft ran through, but Jeff was alright because he could look through the window.

It was the first time the Kent family had been to Anglesey and it was so off the beaten track that it seemed like a foreign country! It was interesting to see the two different bridges across the Menai Strait: Thomas Telford's suspension bridge carrying the road and Robert Stephenson's tubular bridge containing the railway. We got some good B & B accommodation in Benllech, on Anglesey's east coast, and had a look at nearby Red Wharf Bay, where there were a number of yachts moored. This was where we saw our first frogman, who was wearing a rubber suit and used a snorkel as he went under the water.

The following morning, Jack drove us to Bull Bay, on the north coast of the island, but there it rained and we had to put our coats on. Later, the weather improved, so we had a picnic, overlooking the sea, which was enjoyable. We then moved round to the west coast, where we had a look at the village of Rhosneigr. After that, we started the journey home, but stopped off at Betws-y-Coed and visited the nearby impressive Swallow Falls, where the River Llugwy plunges down past quite a number of jagged rocks. Of course, I made a film of the trip and used up two reels in doing so.

The Lord Mayor's chauffeur, Ralph Cotton, used to visit his son, Brian, our next-door neighbour, in the Rolls-Royce and park it outside his house! One day, in August, while the car was there, I took a movie shot of Helen trying to get in the passenger seat, but the door was locked! The idea of it was to be swanky and it was a bit of fun. Also, I liked to shoot anything that was different and of interest. The *Sentinel* later said that Ralph was the chauffeur for forty Stoke-on-Trent Lord Mayors and clocked up over a million miles driving them around!

Brian and Joan used to attend motorcycle scrambles in their bike and sidecar and one day asked Jeff to go along with them. Helen was nervous about him going on a motorbike, but he travelled in the sidecar, where he kept Brian and Joan's son, Philip, company. A couple of months earlier, Helen had sat on the bike to be filmed, but Brian hadn't been able to get her to take a ride!

Helen and I decided to have a fluorescent ring light in the kitchen because it was brighter than a normal bulb, used less electricity and lasted longer, although it was dearer to buy. I didn't know how to fix one up, but Brian knew and he got me one from F.W.B. Products Ltd., the mechanical supply company, where he worked. At that time, the firm was based at 292a Waterloo Road, in Cobridge, and they later moved to Whieldon Road, in Fenton. Brian and I got the light fixed up between us in October, but he did the main work and I helped him.

Roy Orbison had a song out at that time, which I was keen on, called *Oh, Pretty Woman*. The thing I particularly liked about it was the beat, which was more up-tempo than the kinds of songs I normally listened to. Orbison had an unusual voice and Helen wasn't as keen on him as I was, but I bought the record anyway. It got to the top of the charts on 10 October.

Another very popular song at that time was *The Wedding*, which was sung by Julie Rogers and reached number three the same month. It was very sentimental and easy to sing along with. Helen and I both liked it, so we bought that as well.

On 5 November, we had a newfangled washing machine, from the M.E.B. (Midlands Electricity Board), with an electrically-operated agitator and wringer. The water was heated by electricity and there was an electric pump to empty it out. The delivery man asked if he could have our old one for an exhibition being held at their offices at 234 Victoria Road, in Fenton. We agreed to let him have it and later went to see it on display! Our new machine just kept working, so we continued to use it for over 25 years!

One day, Helen was by the pantry door and shouted to me to come quickly. I saw she was holding the door shut and she said something about a mouse. I looked and noticed she'd closed the door against the jamb and in between, partway up the door, a mouse was wriggling. It seemed to be trying to climb up. I took over from Helen and gave the door some extra pressure and so killed the little varmint!

There was a song out at that time that I particularly liked, called *Ringo*. It was by Lorne Greene, who played Ben Cartwright in the television cowboy series, *Bonanza*. The record was a story about a lawman and an outlaw and Greene spoke the words, instead of singing them, which made it all seem more dramatic. The song got to number 22 in the charts.

That Christmas, Helen, Jeff and I went to Vera and Harry's for our tea. Young Harry, Gill, Elijah, Ethel, Lynn, John, Uncle Bill and Aunt Sally were also there and it was a bit cramped with so many people in the small lounge. However, it made a change from being in our house and I filmed Vera cutting up a turkey for us all.

Jeff was continuing his improvement at school and moved up to fifth in the class (3W) out of 34 pupils in his January 1965 exams. He finished top in history, with a mark of 82%, and second in divinity. His report said that his progress was 'very creditable'. Helen and I were very pleased with him.

About that time, Jeff stopped going to the club with us. He'd made some friends there and behaved himself, but he wasn't supposed to go outside because the doorman was pretty strict and stopped the kids running about. I think Jeff got fed up with the restrictions after a while. He decided he'd stop at home on Saturday nights instead and watch our black and white television. We fixed him up with lemonade, crisps and nuts and he seemed to be happy enough with that. We told him not to open the door to anyone.

On 27 February, the students of the University of Keele held their annual rag, Keele Karnival. Helen and I went along to Stoke Road to watch them pass by the "Flower Park", on forty floats in a mile-long procession, and to give them a few coppers. Of course, I had my movie camera with me and took some film of them. They were showing off all kinds of crazy things and a student was playing a piano on one of the floats, whilst on another a student was dressed as a surgeon and pretending to saw into a patient! I took more shots of the procession going through Church Street and then on Hartshill "Bank".

One of the postmen I worked with was Derrick Wain. His uncle and aunt, Horace and Gladys Wain, lived in my old house in Windermere Street (number 27). Derrick didn't know I'd lived there, but they showed him a piece of paper they'd found with the name "Cyril Kent" scribbled on. I must have hidden it when I was a lad and they'd come across it by chance. I suppose they'd then told Derrick that they'd found this item from one of the previous owners or tenants. Derrick must have said, 'We've got a postman named that! I'll ask him if he knows anything about it.' So he came out with the story and asked me if I'd lived there at one time. It was quite remarkable!

Billy Smart's Circus was in town in April and set up on the Wakes ground off Harding Road. I went along on the 4th to watch the marquee being put up and to see and film the elephants arriving in a parade. The 'Elephant Trek', as it was called, started at Stoke Station and went up Stoke Road, Snow Hill and Broad Street and then along Bethesda Street and Regent Road to the site of the circus. There was a line of adult elephants walking along the street, each being ridden by a woman, with a number of baby elephants following. All around them were people milling about and it was a wonder that nobody got trodden on by the elephants!

One early morning, when I was going to work, a couple of swans, coming from the direction of Stoke, flew about ten feet over my head and continued along Leek Road towards Milton. As they flew out of sight, they seemed to be even lower down. There was no traffic about and I wondered what happened to them.

Stan Matthews was given a testimonial game by Stoke on 28 April and a lot of international footballers played in it. Amongst the stars of the all-British Sir Stanley's XI were Stan himself, Johnny Haynes and Jimmy Greaves, whilst the International XI included the famous Soviet goalkeeper, Lev Yashin, and the Real Madrid forwards, Ferenc Puskás and Alfredo Di Stéfano. A crowd of 34,450 turned out to see the International XI win 6-4. Unfortunately, I was working when the match took place, but Helen went with Jeff and took my cine camera with her. Unfortunately, the shots she took were poor because she didn't know how to use it properly. As it turned out, the best of the action was on the television, so I was able to film off this and, at the end of the match, Stan was carried off shoulder high by the other players.

Jeff had become interested in wrestling and began to watch it quite regularly on Saturday afternoons on the television, especially when Vale weren't at home. It had become a regular feature of ITV's new *World of Sport* programme, which had been screened since 2 January. Jeff was convinced that the action was all genuine and wouldn't believe that it was fixed. One of his favourite wrestlers was Jackie Pallo and, at Jeff's request, I filmed part of a bout Pallo had with another tough guy of the ring, Mick McManus.

There was a lot of activity in our garden in the late spring. We had two tortoises, which wandered around our lawn looking for vegetation, like dandelion leaves, that they liked. Jeff was keen on them and they were pretty trouble-free pets. Also, our rabbit, Bobby, was still going strong and living in the same two-compartment hutch that I'd built three years before. As well as our own animals, there was a nest in one of our hedges, in which baby birds had hatched and I filmed them, with their mouths wide open, waiting for their parents to feed them.

On 25 May, there was a world heavyweight boxing championship match between Muhammad Ali and Sonny Liston, which Ali won in the first round. It appeared to be fixed because the great Liston just seemed to cave in. I took a movie film of this from the TV, which turned out quite well.

MAGNIFICENT MOVIES!

Helen and I were so pleased with our kitchen fluorescent light that, in June, we had one installed in the lounge, by the M.E.B. The light cost £8 9s. 5d. and the labour was £2 18s. 9d. Unfortunately, the workers told us that all the wiring in our house needed replacing. Helen's brother, Elijah, knew an electrician, Frank Wiseman, of 4 Swaffham Way, in Bentilee, who worked for the M.E.B., so we fixed up for him to come and do the job after his work hours. The job took a number of days and I helped him with it, as he suggested, to keep the cost down. He showed me the old wiring and I was shocked by its condition because the rubber covering was as stiff as hard plastic! It had also cracked and split in a number of places, exposing the wire, from which sparks would flash and so be a fire hazard. He said the new cable, which was covered with pliable plastic, would keep for thirty years and last me out. The total cost was £29 10s., which was very reasonable because it included plugs and a new fuse box.

Jeff dropped a place, to sixth, in his June exams, but still topped the class in history and improved his mark to 85%. Also, he finished third in geography, with 80%, and maths. However, he hadn't done very well in biology, chemistry, physics and music and his report said, 'A special effort is needed to bring the standard of his work in the scientific subjects in line with his very sound performances elsewhere.' Not surprisingly, Helen and I had mixed feelings about how he'd done.

I decided to change my cine camera again and part exchanged my Kopil for another Japanese model, a Minolta Minoltina 8. This was made of plastic and was lighter and more compact than my previous camera. Also, it had more gadgets and a cassette was used to put the film in. Previously, I'd had to thread a new film into the camera each time the old one had finished. With this model, I loaded the film into a cassette and then more or less shoved that into the camera. Because it had two cassettes, I could load the second one with film ready to replace the first when it had been run off, so it was more convenient. It was a very good camera and I still have it, but it was made obsolete by video.

On 29 July, I was trying to deliver a letter through the letter box of a house in Etruria Vale Road when a dog on the other side bit my middle and ring fingers on my right hand. My flesh was ripped and blood was flowing, so I knocked on the door to complain and a little old lady answered. I told her what had happened, which flustered her. Then she went into the house, brought out a bandage, wrapped it around my fingers and told me it had been used before! I was annoyed about that, but didn't want to upset her any more, so I didn't say anything further to her. When I got outside the gate, I pulled the bandage off, hoping my fingers wouldn't turn septic! Blood was running on my letters, but I carried on with my delivery because I only had half an hour to do.

When I got back to the Post Office, I reported the incident. The chief inspector sent for me and said I'd have to go to the hospital. I didn't want to and told him so a couple of times, but he insisted and provided me with a lift in one of the vans to get there. So I went to the North Staffordshire Royal Infirmary, in Prince's Road, Hartshill, and had an anti-tetanus injection in my arm and some stitches in my middle finger. A stiffener was fastened to it to keep it straight and I thought that would make it difficult to do my deliveries, but the doctor said I'd be alright. I disagreed with him because I thought I'd knock my finger, perhaps hundreds of times, going in and out of garden gates. He gave way and gave me a sick note and so I stopped at home.

The next day, my finger started to swell up and the day after I could see there was pus in the wound, so I went back to the hospital. I was told it had become septic, so they cleaned it and wrapped it up in a bandage. After a day or two, it improved, so I went back to work, sorting and facing the mail. I asked Joe Boulton, one of the bosses, if anything could be done about the dog that had bitten me. I was told that, because my fingers had gone through to the other side of the letter box, technically I was trespassing and so the dog had been entitled to its bite! It took a couple of weeks for my finger to get right and I had to be careful with it while it did so.

That still wasn't the end of it because I had to go back to the hospital on 7 September for a follow-up jab and then again on 17 August the next year for a 'reinforcing' injection. I was also supposed to go every five years after that, but I didn't bother. In total, while I was working for the Post Office, I got bitten five or six times, so there were further visits to the hospital, but a couple of times I took a risk and didn't go.

About that time, pedal cycle speedway racing was all the rage and there were a number of clubs around the area, mainly involving lads. Shelton Tigers raced not far from us on spare bits of land before the council constructed a special track for them off Compton Street, in Shelton. In August, I went along to see a match, which I filmed, but I wasn't too impressed with the sport because it seemed amateurish. The riders were young lads, there didn't seem to be any proper officials and there wasn't much of a crowd there watching. The *Sentinel* gave them publicity by reporting the results, but the craze didn't last very long.

We had our holidays in August. Helen and I had seen an impressive advert in the *Sentinel* for a detached bungalow, Caer Gors, to let in Rhosgadfan, about five miles from Caernarvon, in northwest Wales. It described the property as overlooking the Menai Straits, with an uninterrupted view of the whole of Anglesey. The bungalow was fully furnished, with three double bedrooms and a lounge with a television. It was equipped with crockery and cutlery and had central heating and a large garage with plenty of tools in it. The cost to rent it was eighteen guineas a week. There was a train service from Stoke to Caernarvon and a regular bus from there to the village. It sounded alright and we'd become a bit more ambitious by then, so we sent a deposit of four pounds and received a booking for a week, with instructions on how to get there.

Helen mentioned it to Jack Hodgkiss and he and Flo offered to run us there. In return, we said they could stay with us for the night or the full week. Jack had to get back to work on the Monday, so they decided to stay just the Saturday night. We had a good journey to Caernarvon and then asked the way. It was south along the A 4085 (which is now the A 487) and then left and up a hill for a couple of miles. We found the owners of the bungalow a short way along the village, where they were living, and they gave us the keys. It was just as described and was lovely. All the doors were glass panelled, but one was patched up because it looked as though someone had fallen against it. They appeared to be rather dangerous for children and it seemed silly having a glass toilet door, especially when there was more than one family staying!

The Hodgkisses had been in the area before and took us to a private village called Portmeirion, by the Afon Dwyryd estuary, where we had to pay an entrance fee. It was a marvellous place because its design seemed futuristic and we were told that the Prince of Wales had stayed there with Mrs Simpson. It was a very discreet and classy type of place and one could imagine royalty and millionaires being inside the villas.

The following day, Jack and Flo set off back home and, from then on, when we went out, we caught a bus in the village, except on the Thursday when there were none running. That day, we had to walk down the lane to the main road to catch one from there. It would have been nice to have had a car because Rhosgadfan was a good centre to travel to places from.

We'd taken some food with us and were able to top up from a store in the village, so we could make our own meals. We preferred to do that rather than eat in cafés and restaurants. It was part of the holiday and a bit like roughing it. We didn't want to spend more money and some of the eating places in those days didn't look clean.

We tended to go to Caernarvon because the bus from the village went there and, of course, we went into the castle. Jeff and I went up onto the walls and looked down at Helen sitting on a bench.

On the holiday, we also toured around the countryside and one day we had a trip on a coach to Portmadoc, Criccieth and Abersoch. As part of the day out, we had a ride on a steam train on the narrow gauge Festiniog Railway. At that time, it ran from Portmadoc to Tan-y-Bwlch, but later the line was extended to Blaenau Ffestiniog. As we went down the track towards Portmadoc, I took shots of the lovely scenery and stations we passed through. I remember putting my head out of a window to film the train when it went around a bend. The main danger from doing that was from flying red-hot cinders from the locomotive, Merddin Emrys, and, in any case, I wasn't setting a very good example to Jeff!

Portmadoc was a scenic but busy place and from there the coach took us to Criccieth via Tremadoc, where we passed the birthplace of "Lawrence of Arabia". I filmed the ruined castle as we came into Criccieth and we spent a bit of time on the East Shore beach while we were there. We then carried on to Abersoch, where we again went on the beach and I shot Jeff and Helen clambering up some rocks behind it. The weather wasn't very warm and Helen wore a coat for most of the day, while Jeff had his anorak on.

One day, when we were at the bungalow at Rhosgadfan, Jeff was messing about with the plentiful supply of tools that were lying around. He picked up a hammer and tapped a Carborundum stone with it, but, because the stone was brittle, it broke! We insisted on him replacing it out of his pocket money, which was only right. We took the broken stone home with us and I still use it for sharpening knives!

As we were in the area, Jeff wanted to go up Snowdon, which was 3,560 feet high and the tallest mountain in Wales. I was interested in doing it too, so, one day, we all got a bus to Llanberis, which was where the climb started from. There was a rack-and-pinion railway to the summit, but it was expensive, so we decided to walk up. I had my movie camera with me and intended to make a recording of the climb. We walked along a street and then came to a track. I expected the mountain to be right in front of us, but instead the ground rose steadily. We came to the railway line and followed it partway, but it was a bit boggy around there. After a while, we reached the Halfway House refreshment place.

We plodded on, getting higher, till the ground sloped rather steeply downwards from the path. Helen was getting nervous and didn't wish to go any further. She told Jeff and me that she'd wait there for us and so the two of us carried on until we got to the summit. There was a restaurant at the top! The highest point was a great pile of rocks and several children were standing on it. I pushed Jeff up, so he could say he'd been at the very top, and took a movie shot of him there. After a while, we made our way back to Helen and then down to Llanberis. Unfortunately, when I had my film processed, I found out that all I'd taken from the Halfway House was no good, which was very disappointing.

We had a good time on the holiday and the weather was kind to us overall. At the end of our stay, I think we went home by train from Caernarvon.

There was a downpour on 8 September that lasted for hours. The next day's *Sentinel* said that it had led to the River Trent rising six feet above its usual level at Hanley Sewage Works, which was across the road from us, so that swans were seen swimming across its humus tanks! I didn't see them doing that myself, but it was scary that the water was above the tanks, although I can't remember anything being said about whether the flooding was a health hazard. In any case, I was confident that the water wouldn't reach up to our house, no matter how much it rained.

Helen, Jeff and I had long got used to the occasional smell that came from the works, but eventually the council decided to transfer its functions to their Strongford Water Pollution Control Works, south of Trentham. It took quite a while to get a link sewer built, but the Hanley Works finally closed down in the mid-1970s.

West Midlands Gas Board had decided that we needed a new pipe connecting the main to our meter and did the job on 30 September. They put the pipe under our front garden and, from there, removed the concrete flags of our front path to take it to our back gate. They were able to put the soil and flags back more or less how they'd been before, but, to get the pipe from the gate to our meter, they had to break up the concrete on a small section of the path at the side of our house, so they could dig down. They didn't make too much mess, but we were left with a temporary filling in the concrete path.

Maureen Machin, the Swinnerton's directors' secretary, was getting married at St. Mary's Church, in Marychurch Road, Bucknall, on 2 October. Her bridegroom was Jim Longmore, who came from Tunstall and worked for Simpsons (Potters) Ltd, in Waterloo Road, Cobridge. Helen was excited about the wedding and persuaded me to go along to it with her and take some shots of the occasion with my cine camera, which I did. Unfortunately, Maureen was later divorced, but she did remarry. Her second husband was Stan Hughes, who came from Northwood and was a dairyman, and they went to live in Canada in 1973.

Helen and I were keen on and bought a sentimental song called *Tears*, which was sung by Ken Dodd and got to the top of the charts on 2 October. He was a well-known comedian and was alright, but I didn't think he was all he was cracked up to be. He wasn't a top-class singer, but he sold plenty of records and Helen and I bought another one that he made, *The River*, which was also a big hit the same year and got to number three.

On 9 October, the Railway Mission burned to the ground. Helen was still a member of the congregation, but Jeff had stopped attending nearly eighteen months earlier and we hadn't been able to get him to go again. The mission was built of wood, so it made quite a large blaze and it didn't take long to be gutted. I took a film of the debris after the fire had finished. I can't remember if Helen was very upset by it, but she must have been.

The Post Office football team (Postal Sports Club) were still playing on Thursday afternoons in the Half-Holiday League and were doing really well. I still went to watch them play when I had the time. Amongst the best players were Bert Ash, who was the captain and tall and slim; Ted Green, who was a good centre-half and trained by jogging along Leek Road, and Dave Lovatt, who was a skilful little player. Also, they'd got a new centre-forward, Jeff Walker, who just stood on the spot and seemed to be anchored to the ground, but if the ball came his way, he'd let go and nearly always scored! He couldn't be knocked off the ball and, with him in the team, they were almost unbeatable. One of the old players, Bill Bishop, had become the team's secretary and manager and they got better and better, whether it was partly down to him or not.

On 8 November, Parliament put the death penalty for murder on hold and it was abolished in 1969. That was a good thing because many had been the man who'd been hanged when he was innocent. The death penalty was barbaric and you could never be absolutely sure that somebody was guilty of murder. It was too late if new evidence came up after someone had been hanged.

A lot of people, perhaps including me, were racist and looking down on coloured people at that time, thinking they were inferior to us white people. I kind of agreed with Enoch Powell that the numbers of immigrants into Britain should be controlled and wondered what would happen if a very large number of foreigners came in. On 8 December, the first Act of Parliament on race relations came into being and said that it was against the law to discriminate in public areas against people of a different race. After a while, I got used to seeing foreigners and accepted them and there's not a lot of trouble between different races today, really. I talk to people of different races and treat them more or less normally now.

Helen, Jeff and I went to Vera and Harry's for our tea again that Christmas and the same family members were there as had been the previous year. I took my cine camera to take some shots and they showed people getting in each other's way when the food was dished up because of the lack of space, but nobody seemed to be bothered about it.

My basic rate of pay at that time was about £14 a week, but, over the Christmas period, I was able to boost my earnings quite a bit by working overtime. On 23 December, I was paid £34 0s. 1d., but £4 18s. of that went to the government in income tax. On the 31st, I received £25 2s. 3d., of which £2 17s. was paid in tax, and even on 7 January 1966, my pay was £20 2s. 3d., less £1 14s. income tax, presumably as a result of the extra work I did in helping to clear the remaining mail of the festive season.

Jeff dropped down to thirteenth out of 33 pupils in his January exams, but he remained top of the class (4W) in history, with an 80% mark. His report said that he'd got only 11% in chemistry, but that he'd still finished in 23rd position in the subject, which was strange! Also, the report's general remarks suggested that he was improving: 'Most subjects show that he is working well and he seems to be making a more serious effort.'

An advertisement was put up on the notice board at the Post Office asking for volunteers with three or more years' service to apply for available postman higher grade positions. These were indoor jobs and involved sorting the mail, mostly on afternoon and night shifts. P.H.G. was the grade from which inspectors were recruited. I put my name down, but I don't know why. Some time later, the duty assistant inspector, Walter Holmes, came to me and said I had to report to Birmingham the next week to train as a P.H.G. That meant living there for perhaps a couple of weeks and I thought of Helen and Jeff staying on their own at night. I knew Helen would be terrified and I didn't fancy staying indoors to work, so I told Walter I'd changed my mind. He said, 'Okay,' and there was no trouble.

On 20 March, it was on the television that the World Cup had been stolen from Central Hall in Westminster, where it had been on display. The 1966 competition was being held in England in July and so the theft was very embarrassing. The Football Association offered a £3,000 reward for the cup's discovery and, a week later, it was found by a dog, Pickles, in a hedge in Beulah Hill, in Norwood, London. Even though it was all trivial really, it was one of those stories that made the world go round!

One day in April, Harry and Gill came to see us with their Rottweiler dog, named Hans. Harry had read about the breed in a magazine, which had said they were good family dogs and would protect their owners. Hans was a very big dog and put his front paws up on our 3½-foot-high concrete back wall with ease. He wandered around our lawn and then went to the hutch and had a smell of Bobby, but the rabbit seemed to have frozen in terror and kept perfectly still.

The Postal team won the Half-Holiday League by a mile, having been victorious in every league match until the very last one of the season when they lost 2-1 to the joint-runners-up, Fire Services. They completed a marvellous season by winning the Haig and Haig Trophy (the league's cup competition), beating Stafford Police 1-0 after a replay, and Jeff Walker scored 72 goals in total!

Helen and I celebrated our silver wedding anniversary on 21 June and we held two parties at home to mark the occasion. We had Helen's family round for the first one on Saturday 18th and our friends from the club the following night. Of course, I made films of the occasions.

With us for the family party were the regulars on these kinds of occasions: Uncle Bill, Aunt Sally, Big Harry, Vera, Young Harry, Gill, Elijah, Ethel, Lynn and John. Also present were Helen's Aunt Rachel; the latter's daughter, Edith (Helen's cousin); her son-in-law, Jack Elson, and her granddaughter, Susan. However we all fitted into our small lounge I'll never know! I filmed the guests arriving and then took a rainbow, which appeared over Remploy just afterwards. Helen and I had two of our wedding photos up and Young Harry shot us cutting our celebration cake.

The second party was more relaxed because we only had Charlie, Lucy, Les and Joan round. I filmed Les demolishing chicken legs from our buffet and finally I shot our wedding gifts and cards, but with a difference. I took them both frame by frame and moved them between each shot so that it looked as though the gifts were wandering about and as if the cards put themselves up on a table!

The same month, Jack and Flo took Helen and me for a run to Shrewsbury, where we had a walk around a beautiful park called The Quarry, which ran alongside the River Severn. In the middle of the park was a lovely sunken garden called The Dingle, which was looked after by the park's superintendant, Percy

Thrower, the famous television gardener. We had a good look at the garden and then had a nice walk along a path by the tranquil river.

Jeff moved up three places in class, to tenth, in his June exams at school and was top again in history, with a mark of 83%. His report said that, 'He has worked well and should continue to make this determined effort.'

Our wooden fence and gate by the pavement were rotting, so Helen and I decided to have them replaced by a brick wall and an iron gate and, at the same time, have the privet hedge behind the fence removed. The job was done in July by Joe Davies, a property repairer, who lived at 384 Leek Road, at a cost of £33 5s. The removal of the hedge saved quite a bit of time because it had to be cut every so often.

Some of our red roof tiles were flaking and coming off in slices and bits because they hadn't been very well fired when they'd been manufactured. So we got Joe to replace them. He put about a hundred new tiles in and also cemented over where the Gas Board had laid the new pipe down the side of our house. He charged £20 2s. 10d. for the two jobs combined.

The main thing I remember about England beating West Germany 4-2 on 30 July to win the World Cup was watching Nobby Stiles chopping somebody down! I can't remember Geoff Hurst scoring his three goals on the day, although I've seen highlights of the match since.

After England had won the competition, the Post Office issued a stamp with the words 'England Winners' overprinted on their fourpenny World Cup 1966 originals. Clive Dunn, a postman who was a second-hand stamp dealer, was advising collectors to buy them because he was forecasting that they'd increase in value in a short time. So I bought a sheet with 120 on, but there was a stampede to get hold of the new issue. Because large numbers were sold, the stamps didn't gain any great value and so Clive was wrong. I've still got them, but they won't be worth much.

Helen fancied a new fire grate and surround, so we had a look around Caterham's, the fireplace manufacturers, in Waterloo Road, Burslem. She ordered one to her specifications, but when it arrived, the surround was not what she'd asked for. It had creamy-grey tiles, with some mottled effects and a wooden shelf along the top of it. However, she decided to accept what had been delivered. It cost us £45 and Joe Davies fixed it in on 8 September for £8 1s. 3d. The basket that held the coal in the grate was supposed to be an all-night burner, but we never tested it because Helen and I liked to let the fire out before we went to bed, for safety's sake. The surround is still there in the lounge.

The same month, Elijah removed the picture rail from our lounge because such things were going out of fashion. He then plastered over the area where it had been and put up a cornice all the way round, in the angle of the walls and the ceiling. It was a fairly straightforward job for him because he was a plasterer by trade. I then had to wallpaper the whole of the room.

Helen received a letter, dated 16 September, from the solicitors, Challinors & Dickson, of 32 Cheapside, in Hanley, saying she'd been left a sum of money in the will of Ivy Barker, who'd died on 29 December the previous year. Ivy had owned a second-hand shop in Bryan Street, Hanley, and was a cousin of Helen's mother, Leah. Because Leah was dead, her share of the money was divided between her surviving children (Helen, Vera and Elijah) and her granddaughter,

Helen Asher. As a result, of the £39 2s. 6d. estate, Helen got the princely sum of £1 12s. 7d.!

The Postal team had packed in playing on Thursdays and joined the Potteries and District Sunday League, where there were better sides and they didn't do as well. I stopped watching them because Helen was at home on Sundays and it wouldn't have been fair to her if I'd been out at a football match every week.

Les and Joan Brown told us about a decorator named William Cooke, of 17 Epping Road, in Trent Vale, who'd done some work for them cheaply. We decided to try him and asked how much he'd charge to paper the walls of the landing and the stairs and paint the ceiling. He said he'd do the job and take the old wallpaper off for five pounds if we supplied the materials. I think he was working at a low rate of pay to get his business going. We gave him the go-ahead in November and he did a pretty decent job in a couple of days. So we asked him the price to paper the lounge and paint the ceiling. He told us it would be four pounds, so again we accepted. Once more, he did okay, so we then asked him for the cost of doing the kitchen, to include painting the picture rail, the skirting board and a door. He quoted £4 10s., so again we agreed to that and once more he did a decent job. At those prices, it wasn't worth me doing the job myself!

Some time later, we were discussing with Les and Joan the possibility of Mr Cooke coming to do some more decorating for us. Les told us that he'd asked Mr Cooke to do a job for them, but that he was by then asking too much money. We didn't bother to get in touch with Mr Cooke and in the future I did my own jobs.

About that time, the Post Office was advertising on their notice board for van drivers. Although I wasn't really interested in becoming a driver at work, I put my name forward because I thought I'd try to get my driving licence and then buy a car. The chief inspector tried to dissuade me, I suppose because I was getting on a bit, so it would lessen their return on their cost of training me. However, I insisted on going ahead, but, because I couldn't drive, I was given some tuition by their official instructor, an Irishman, who lived in Stafford. I didn't impress him, so I didn't get any further instruction because they could get someone who could learn and pass the test more quickly!

On Christmas evening, we all went to the family party at Vera and Harry's house in Holdcroft Road, as had been the custom for several years. I enjoyed it on the whole and it saved us from bothering about getting our tea ready! At night time, we'd go to Abbey Hulton Suburban Club, in Greasley Road, which was okay, but Vera and Harry were regulars there and Helen and I didn't know any of their crowd. This year, there was an addition to the family because on 4 December Young Harry and Gill had had a daughter, who was named Amanda, and I took a shot or two of the newcomer being bottle fed by her mother.

My wages, including overtime, for the week ending 30 December were £26 10s. 3d. and I paid £3 4s. income tax. The following week, my wages were £19 5s., with income tax of £1 9s. My basic rate at that time was about £14 5s.

In January 1967, Jeff took his O level mock exams and got pass grades in six of the seven subjects he was studying, including a Grade 1 (the highest possible) in history. Because percentage marks were no longer being given, the pupils weren't put in a finishing order in class as they'd been before. His report said: 'Some very pleasing results, promising well for the future. An all-out effort should now be made to remedy the few weaknesses.' Helen and I were hopeful he was on the way to success.

Early in the year, our rabbit, Bobby, became poorly, so I took it to the PDSA clinic, at 40 Epworth Street, in Stoke, which was cheaper than going to a normal vet's. The rabbit had an examination, but no problem was found, so I brought it home. Bobby had a run around the hutch, but then suddenly collapsed and died. I looked at the rabbit and touched it, but there was no life in it. So I phoned the vet to ask what it was all about and he said, 'Which rabbit?' He pooh-poohed it and said, 'Perhaps it had a heart attack.' I can't remember what Jeff's reaction was, but I reckon he must have been upset and recently he told me that he was.

Helen and I really liked a sentimental song called *Release Me*, which was very popular at that time. It was sung by Engelbert Humperdinck, whose conventional appearance fitted in with the style of the song. He was a good singer and his name caught the public imagination. The record got to the top of the charts on 4 March and Helen and I bought it, although it wore a bit thin after I'd heard it for a while.

Around that time, Jeff seemed to think that he was superior to Helen and me and that we were slaves to attend to his needs. One day, I came in from work and wanted to get by the fire to warm up, but Jeff was sitting in front of it with a newspaper spread out across his legs so that I couldn't get near it. I asked him to let me in, but he told me he couldn't as there wasn't enough room because of the newspaper! When I said that wasn't fair, he told me he was clever, which he thought gave him more right to be in front of the fire! Anyway, he folded one side of the paper back, which gave me a bit of room. Then, in 1995, when he was asking me to tell him stories about his early life, I happened to mention the tale. He didn't remember it and was shocked. He gave me a hug and was very apologetic.

Stoke signed the England goalkeeper, Gordon Banks, from Leicester City for a then club record fee of £50,000 on 17 April, which seemed an ambitious thing for them to have done. I wasn't really excited, but getting such a big name in encouraged me to go to the matches. He did well, but I think his ability was exaggerated and signing him meant that Stoke's promising young goalkeeper, John Farmer, got pushed into the reserves, which was a pity.

In May, it was announced by the Post Office that a new grey postman's uniform would gradually be brought in to replace our traditional navy blue one. Grey didn't seem the right colour because it wasn't traditionally associated with postmen. It was at least two years before I had mine and I eventually got used to the colour. Also, the uniform was made from artificial material, whereas my original one was wool, but I can't remember it feeling any different.

In 1966, a new issue of National Savings Certificates had been introduced at a fixed five-year compound interest rate of 4.57%, which was quite a bit ahead of inflation. The certificates at that time were available at various prices from a pound to £200. Helen and I decided to buy some because they seemed a good investment. We also bought one for four pounds for Jeff on 6 May 1967 and got more for him from time to time over the next five years.

On 10 May, I read in the *Sentinel* that more than £7 million was going to be spent on building a ring road in Hanley and a new link road to Derby, as well as making an improved Etruria Road from Cobridge Road to Etruria Station. I didn't take any notice of the ideas because I couldn't imagine alterations coming on that scale. But all those changes took place and the new roads seem normal now.

Jeff took his O levels in June and did quite a bit of swotting for them. Because it was thought he'd do well, he stayed on at school until his summer holidays, preparing for A levels that he was hoping to study in the sixth form from the autumn.

In our office was a postman called "Chitty" Shenton, who was a bachelor and lived with his mother. He was known by that name because he was always saying, 'I've signed a chitty,' for overtime. He gave the impression that he was a country yokel and he was quite a character. He did a lot of drinking and was always in debt. He was therefore constantly borrowing from somebody, but always paid his debts when he got his wages each Friday. Every Monday, though, he was borrowing again! Some of the postmen he tapped seemed to love this arrangement and fell for Chitty's patter time and again.

He approached me, with a pen and a piece of paper in his hands and a big smile on his face, and said, 'Have I got you on my list?'

I just said, 'No!'

He wasn't offended because he had a thick skin, but he never tried it on me again.

In July, Jack and Flo took Helen, Jeff and me in their car to Llangollen, which was a very nice place. At the side of the River Dee was a small girl, paddling and running about without any clothes on, and she looked cute. Further along were professional photographers, taking pictures of a model in a bikini, posing with a dagger. It reminded me of the famous scene in the film, *Dr. No*, where Ursula Andress came out of the sea with the sunlight shimmering on her hair!

We later went further on, to the impressive Horseshoe Pass and parked for a while partway up to have an ice cream from a nearby store and shoot some film of the impressive scenery. While we were there, a sheep came along, begging for food. We didn't have any, but the cheeky devil kept nudging us!

Helen had Jeff working for her at the orange squash factory at Swinnerton's in his summer holiday from school. He was paid a wage and got a bit of work experience. Helen told me that Jeff had said he wouldn't take any orders from her, but that he would do from Jack, so she simply told Jack what to tell Jeff to do! Anyway, I think it worked out alright.

I've still got Jeff's weekly pay slip from 10 August. It shows that his gross wage was £3 15s. 3d., that he'd been stopped 9s. for national insurance and that he'd brought home £3 6s. 3d. That wasn't much, even in those days.

In August, Jeff got the news that he'd passed six of the seven O levels that he'd taken: English language, English literature, French, geography, history (in which he'd got a Grade 1) and maths. He'd failed chemistry, but that wasn't too surprising because he hadn't been doing very well in it. It would have been nice if he'd passed in all the subjects, but he hadn't let Helen and me down and his success meant that he was able, as expected, to carry on at school in September, studying at A level.

On 29 August, Young Harry and Terry Miles, a fellow long-standing Port Vale player, were given a benefit match at Vale Park. They played in a Vale side that won 5-4 against an International XI, which included Stan Matthews, Neil Franklin, Ronnie Allen and Nat Lofthouse. Of course, Helen, Jeff and I went along and I recorded a bit of the occasion on my cine camera. 4,789 supporters turned out to watch, which brought in some extra money for Harry and Terry, but they had to share it.

On 9 September, Engelbert Humperdinck got to number one with a sad song called *The Last Waltz* and Helen and I liked it so much that we bought the record. It told a story about falling in love during the last dance of the night and then having a romance, but eventually the girl saying goodbye.

Jeff settled back in at school in September in his new form, Lower Sixth Arts Beta, which seemed a bit of a mouthful, but Helen and I thought taking A levels would help him in the world. Even if he hadn't passed them, it would have meant he'd had a try, but, as it turned out, he did well enough. Also, being in the sixth form pushed him up a bit on the social ladder. I suppose it was important to Helen and me as well because the type of people you associate with rubs off on you, so Jeff's success made us look good in front of our friends and neighbours.

The hippies were around at that time. They were just another craze and I remember the guitarist Jimi Hendrix being connected with them. It was on television and in the papers that youngsters were taking drugs. I was despairing and wondering what would happen to the world. I kept hoping that Jeff wouldn't get involved because he wasn't always attending to his lessons.

One day, when I was on the Hope Street walk at work, I was about to deliver a letter to 32 Mulgrave Street, in Cobridge, when I noticed that the surname on the envelope was Skerratt. I wondered if it could be for someone from the family who'd lived there when I was a lad, so I decided to knock on the door and find out. A lady answered, but I didn't recognize her. However, I asked if there was a connection and she said she was Evelyn, the youngest sister of my old pal, Lenny, and the letter was for her mother, Edith. We had a short talk about the old times and she told me that she'd married one of the lads I'd known, Monty Royle, who'd lived at 5 Windermere Street, eleven doors away from me!

On 12 November, I attended the Remembrance Day commemoration at the cenotaph in Albion Square, Hanley, as I did most years, and Jeff may have gone with me, which he did a time or two. By that time, it was always on the nearest Sunday to the 11th, the date that the First World War armistice had been signed in 1918. I remember the commemoration being like a church service and there was a two-minute silence followed by the laying of wreaths to remember the dead of both wars. I kept going because I was an old soldier, perhaps out of duty, but I don't think Helen ever went with me.

The country had been having money problems and, to try to sort them out, the pound was devalued by 14% on 18 November. Prices were going up anyway, so I was worried that things would get much dearer, but I can't remember them doing so and I just carried on as normal.

It was in the *Sentinel* on 19 December that the French president, Charles de Gaulle, had blocked Britain's application to join the "Common Market", which was what the European Community was usually called. I was happy about that because I hadn't wanted us to become a part of it. I thought it would lead to a load of foreigners telling us what to do. Unfortunately, we eventually went in, in 1973, and it seems to have worked out as I'd feared.

On 29 December, I was paid £75 6s. 5d. in wages, which included overtime and arrears from a pay rise backdated to 1 July. It was a nice Christmas present, although I had to pay £19 11s. of it in income tax!

Jeff did pretty well in his January 1968 exams and got B grades in history and British government, but only a D in economics. Because grades down to E were passes, he was on target to get three A levels and so Helen and I thought he was doing okay overall.

I'd started to have a bit of difficulty hearing, so I went to the doctor's on 28 January. It was the first time I'd needed to go since 1949! It was discovered that my ears were blocked with wax and I had them syringed, which was a queer affair. Warm water was squirted into my ears and the wax came out with it into a bowl that the doctor held to the sides of my head. Afterwards, everything seemed to sound pretty loud and I could hear things I hadn't noticed before!

Around that time, I started having driving lessons, at about a pound each, with the British School of Motoring, which was the only place I knew that offered them. I called into their office in Piccadilly, Hanley, to sign up. They asked me what kind of car I'd like to learn in and, because I had no knowledge of which would be best, I said any would do. They said I could use a Ford Cortina and that was okay with me.

When I reported for my first lesson, I got in the passenger seat of the car and the instructor drove me to Avenue Road, in Shelton, where he turned off the engine and started talking to me. He asked if I had any driving experience and, like a fool, I told him I had a bit. I think he therefore thought it wouldn't take me long to learn. He asked if I'd brought my Highway Code book with me and I said I hadn't because I didn't think it was necessary at that stage of learning. He gave me a stern lecture on my lack of concern! He kept on talking till my hour was up and so the first lesson was a complete waste of time because I'd learned exactly nothing!

On the next lesson, I did occupy the driver's seat and I started to learn the art of driving. I was supposed to have an hour's tuition each time, but I almost always had to wait about ten minutes for the instructor to appear and then the lesson would always finish five or ten minutes early! I had quite a number of sessions with the same instructor, but I found the car cumbersome and was only improving slowly. He seemed to be getting impatient and told me I'd do better in a Morris Mini-Minor. I took him at his word and, as soon as we got back to Piccadilly, I asked to be transferred to a Mini, which also meant another instructor. I got on pretty well with the new fellow and found the new car easier to handle, although I was still a slow learner.

I told Les Brown that I was having driving lessons and he volunteered to take me out in his car for a bit of practice. I accepted his offer and he took me to the Fenton area a time or two. I was grateful, but nobody else ever offered their services. I was pleased about that really because it meant I could eventually say I'd passed the test without their help.

At that time, Jeff had a girlfriend, Janice Leigh, who lived at 15 Freehold Terrace, in Middleport. Her parents invited Helen and me to visit them, but I wondered why that was because he'd only been seeing her for a few weeks. Anyway, we went up there and I remember that their settee was right by the fire in their small front room and it was sweltering! They made quite a fuss over us, which was too much for me, and her mother gave us some plates from Burgess & Leigh's Middleport Pottery, in Port Street, Middleport, where she worked. It was very unusual and I wondered if they were trying to marry their daughter off. As it turned out, Jeff only went out with Janice until April, so her parents' interest in Helen and me was all for nothing, really.

In March, Helen asked me to film a presentation and farewell celebration for Frank Swinnerton, who, until three years before, had been a joint-managing director of the firm she worked for. He was emigrating to Malta, with his family, because he was fed up with the rate of tax in Britain and was planning to sail to his new home in his thirteen-ton ketch, *Harp Song of Spinola*, on the first suitable tide after the 12th! I went to the factory, where the event was held and shot a number of scenes, which were very jolly and included the handing out of a glass of sherry to each of the factory staff.

There was a distribution of prizes to lads of Hanley High School at the Victoria Hall, in Hanley, on Thursday 21 March 1968. Jeff had won the Elizabeth Campbell Prize for history as a result of his performance in the subject at O level the previous summer. Of course, Helen and I were proud of him. We attended the event in our best clothes and were on our best behaviour! Jeff was presented with a prize on the stage and I was apprehensive about what would happen, but it turned out alright. He was given a book token, which he exchanged, with some money, for a book on dinosaurs!

The following month, he went with his class and teachers on a trip to London. While they were there, they visited the House of Commons. I suppose Helen and I must have paid towards it, but we were pleased because it was all part of Jeff's growing up. However, we did wonder if he'd be okay away from us.

On 14 May, Vale announced their list of retained players, but Young Harry wasn't amongst them and was given a free transfer, having played 498 competitive first-team matches, made one substitute appearance and scored 79 goals. Harry and Gill thought he could have carried on playing for them and criticized the manager, Stan Matthews, for letting him go. It was a comedown and I was surprised that no other league club came in for him. Jeff was also surprised and very disappointed that he'd finished with Vale. Helen and I hadn't been turning up as regularly in recent years to watch him play, but Jeff had been going to quite a few Vale away games for a couple of seasons and getting free tickets to go in from Harry most of the time. So, after that, Jeff had to pay to watch Vale!

Eric "Ecker" Copeland was one of the postmen I worked with in the Leek Road office. One day around that time, he was on railway duty and was driving the tugs that pulled trucks of mail from the sorting office to the station. He was on platform one, with one or two other postmen, and decided to clear his nose over the edge of it, so that he wouldn't make a mess on the station. He hadn't noticed that behind him there was a moving train, which hit him on his head and knocked him over, but, fortunately, he wasn't seriously injured.

My driving instructor eventually told me that he was putting me in for a test, which was fixed for 19 June. I had an hour's tuition before the test, for which I had to report to the Ministry of Transport office, at 4 Mollart Street, in Hanley. I was tested by the chief examiner, but it went okay. The first thing he asked me to do was to read the numberplate of a car coming up Windsor Street, on the opposite side of Lichfield Street, but I struggled to do so because it was outside my reading distance. Fortunately, the car turned down Lichfield Street and moved out of sight. So he then turned round, looked down Mollart Street and said, 'Read that one, there.' It was a parked car and I read that one alright.

Then we got in the car and he said, 'Off you go.' There was traffic coming and I wondered how long I could hold it on the clutch, but a fellow flashed his lights and I was able to edge out. We went into Bethesda Street and down to Etruria, where we turned into one of the streets between the park and the Caldon Canal. Halfway along, he told me to do a three-point turn and I did it pretty decently. On the way back, he asked me to turn right from Broad Street into Bethesda Street, but I was behind a bus, which was obscuring my vision, and traffic was coming down the other way. However, I managed to hold the car on clutch control and drove back to Mollart Street okay.

When I stopped the car, he said, 'I'm pleased to tell you you've passed.' I was delighted and my tutor, who was waiting, was pleased too, especially when I gave him a five-pound note! While I was talking to him afterwards, he tried to sell me his old car, but I refused it! I had some time left on my tuition lesson, but my instructor said: 'Don't drive any more. You're bound to make a mistake.' I suppose he just wanted to get back to his office and get his feet up!

I wished him goodbye and made my way to Swinnerton's to tell Helen. She could hardly believe the news till she saw the pass certificate. I then walked down to the Motor Taxation Department office, in Woodhouse Street, Stoke, where I bought a full driving licence (number 41643) for fifteen shillings.

Jeff didn't do quite so well in his June exams and dropped down a grade in economics and history, but still passed in all his three subjects. However, his end-of-term report was pretty positive and said: 'He has now shown his ability to maintain a good standard of work. With continued effort he should do very well.'

2 Have Wheels, Will Travel

A few days after I'd passed my driving test in June 1968, Helen and I decided to get a car. I started looking around, but I didn't know what I was searching for, how much to pay, if we should pay cash or take out hire-purchase or whether we should have a new one or a second-hand model. Helen suggested that we have a Volkswagen because Elijah hadn't had much trouble with his. So I went along to W. H. Jervis & Sons, the VW dealer in Botteslow Street, Hanley, where I had a look at what was on offer and brought away some literature. After studying it, we decided to buy a brand-new 1192 cc Beetle, the cheapest car in the range at £714 6s. 9d. (including £25 road tax), although that was a lot of money in those days. Its colour was chinchilla, which was grey with a touch of brown. I then went back to Jervis', ordered and signed for it and put down a deposit of £44 6s. 9d. But I decided to buy it on 1 July, so as to get the full value of the road tax from the beginning of the month.

I paid £27 10s. for fully comprehensive insurance, but then had to wait to pick the car up. When the time came for collection, I walked to the garage, where I met Helen, who'd been driven there from work by Jack Hodgkiss. The car was parked outside the showroom, ready to be driven off, and the firm said they'd given me two free gallons of petrol. 'What a big deal,' I thought! Also, there were 39 miles already recorded on the speedometer, even though I'd bought it as a new car, but I think it had been driven over from another agent's. Nevertheless, I paid the balance in cash and took possession of my new car.

I arranged to meet Helen by the electricity works in Ridgway Road, to where she was being driven by Jack. I don't think she trusted my driving! They set off up Botteslow Street and I followed. It was very strange being alone in a car, but I started it and got it going okay. We turned left into Derby Street and then came to Lichfield Street, which had to be crossed and I managed it. We got to the meeting place, where we had a look around our new car and it seemed rather basic. I then purchased four gallons of petrol, at a cost of £1 2s. 4d., and we had a little run, calling at Vera and Harry's to show off our new possession.

The car engine was at the back and it was air cooled, which made it rather noisy, but that didn't really bother me. Under the bonnet at the front was a kind of a boot, which had a fair amount of room and could house a large suitcase. Also, there was space between the back seat and the engine compartment for a second suitcase, which could be dropped in the gap!

I discovered that the car didn't possess a petrol gauge, so there was no way I knew how much fuel was in the tank! If it was used up, the car would stop, of course, but, at that point, there'd still be an emergency gallon of petrol left, which could be brought into action by kicking over a lever with your foot. That was a poor show, so I wrote out a table, giving how many miles I should do to each gallon, but the problem was that that varied according to whether I was just dodging around the town or on a big run. So, once or twice, while I was travelling along, the engine faded out and I had to look towards the floor to find the lever to switch on the reserve petrol!

I had to think of a better way of indicating how much fuel was left in the tank. I decided to try a dipstick, but it had to be flexible, so I used an old clock spring, which I unwound and marked off. After I judged the tank to be about empty, I put two gallons in and scratched a mark on the dipstick with a file, then added another two gallons and made a further mark and so on. The method was pretty successful and I didn't run out of petrol again.

At first, we had to leave the car on the street, but then we found a garage to rent from 5 July, in Haywood Street, Shelton, at ten shillings a week. Unfortunately, it was about three-quarters of a mile from home, but it was the best we could do.

Whenever we needed any shoe repairs, we used to go used to the cobbler's shop at 142 Lichfield Street. The cobbler recommended that we visit Knypersley Reservoir, so Helen, Jeff and I had a run out there and it was quite nice. We wandered round the reservoir and came across the Warder's Tower, which looked like a miniature castle and had been inhabited by a gamekeeper. Of course, I filmed it, as I did the Head of Trent cascading down the dam wall of the reservoir and another waterfall, as the river left the Mill Pond, slightly further downstream.

However, we soon ran out of places to drive to! Although it may seem strange, that was because we hadn't moved outside the city much, except on holidays, mainly to the seaside, so we didn't know where to go. Then, one day, I was working on parcel duty with a fellow postman, Bill Hammond, and the subject of my new car came up. I asked him if he knew of anywhere decent to drive to and he gave me a route to the Manifold Valley, in the Peak District, which became one of our favourite places.

We went there for the first time through Werrington and Ipstones to Warslow and turned right just afterwards into a lane. As we were going down it, there was a storm and the heavens opened, so I pulled up and we sheltered the car under some trees! When the storm was over, we carried on and, at Swainsley, went through a converted railway tunnel to Wettonmill. We parked up and walked about half a mile down the lovely valley before we turned back. We then wandered across a bridge over the river to a farm at Wettonmill, where the National Trust now has a café. We watched a herd of cows come in for milking and Helen stroked a calf that had been carried in by the farmer and didn't seem to be able to get up onto its feet. We took a different route back home, through Butterton, but I had a job to get up the narrow, bending road from the valley. It was a thrill to have been to such a beautiful place and we visited it many times over the years.

I started to notice one or two drivers waving or signalling to me, which was puzzling, but a friend from the club, Reg, who also had a Volkswagen, told me it was because I was driving that make of car. He said it was a kind of salute that VW drivers gave each other and he put his hand up to show me. After that, I began to look out for Beetles and waved back when their drivers saluted me. Then I started saluting straightaway when I noticed another Beetle, by opening my hand and putting it near the windscreen. It was a thrill at first and continued for a fair number of years, but, eventually, drivers stopped bothering and it faded away.

In July, we also had a run to Chester Zoo, where we had a good day out. We saw a number of animals feeding: hippopotamuses on vegetables, rhinoceroses and bison on cut grass, lions on great slabs of raw meat and seals on fish thrown to them by a keeper. The zoo also had elephants, giraffes, tigers, leopards, zebras, chimpanzees, orang-utans, flamingos, penguins and different types of bears, as well as many other types of creatures. I shot one scene with my cine camera where a little boy gave a monkey something to eat through the wire of its enclosure and another in which a woman stroked a sika deer on its nose!

We didn't go away on holiday that summer owing to the great expense of buying the car. Instead, we had trips out and Jeff came with Helen and me on a number of runs. He did the navigating, which allowed him to sit in the front passenger seat, but it really wasn't fair on Helen.

Not long after we'd had the car, Helen and I had a trip to Bearstone Farm, on the B 5026, near Woore, to pick our own fruit. We liked it so much that we went every summer after that for thirty years or more, mainly to get potatoes and strawberries. We took Aunt Sally and Uncle Bill a time or two, but Uncle Bill would light up his pipe in the car straightaway, which I didn't like him doing because it was horrible and poisonous. Aunt Sally loved the idea that we could pick and eat as we went round. It was an accepted thing because, if you ate anything, the farmer couldn't tell. We'd go in, pick up a basket from a pile and wander round the strawberry fields, eating and gathering at the same time. I didn't eat too much because I liked to wash the strawberries first. It was a novelty picking our own fruit and sometimes we'd pick raspberries instead. It was nice to have a run out in the countryside and we'd also buy potatoes, beetroot and carrots from their counter. The farmer mentioned to us that he could hardly get any paid fruit pickers, so he was glad people went round and helped themselves.

Young Harry and Terry Miles, his old Vale colleague, joined Sandbach Ramblers, who were stepping up from the Mid-Cheshire League to the Cheshire County League. Harry was a regular in the team, but they still finished third from the bottom of the table! He was very busy with his shop and so he packed football in after one season with them to concentrate on his business.

At the beginning of September, Jeff returned to school for his final year. He moved into a new class, Upper Sixth Arts Beta, for his second year in the sixth form. It was a very important year for him and Helen and I hoped that he'd concentrate on his studies and do well.

At the time, the Vietnam War was taking place. The Americans were trying to stop the communist North Vietnam from taking over South Vietnam, but they made a mess of it. The war had been going on since the 1950s and, by 1968, the Americans had over half a million men in Vietnam. But it was all to no purpose because they eventually lost the war and were humiliated. Fortunately, Britain didn't get caught up in it, but Jeff might have been called up if we had done. I dread to think what could have happened then. We get involved in too many wars alongside the Americans and they keep costing too many lives and too much money.

One day around that time, when I was delivering post in and off Greasley Road, a brown mongrel came up to me, so I had a word or two with it. It started following me and carried on doing so regularly for a while. That was useful because it tended to attract the attention of the other dogs I encountered, so it took the pressure off me. It tended to drift off eventually, but one day it jumped on the bus with me, which I caught in Leek Road to get back to the office. The conductor assumed it was a stray and shouted 'Get off!' at it. The dog slunk off and I felt ashamed that I'd disowned it, but I couldn't really have taken it with me.

I don't think I ever saw the dog again.

Jeff was very good friends with Paul Lewis, who lived at 399 Victoria Road, in Hanley. We'd first met Paul and his parents on a train on the way back from a holiday in Prestatyn one year when Jeff was a boy. Paul's father, Dan, was a bricklayer for British Rail and I was shocked to read in the *Sentinel* on 28 October that he'd been hit by a Euston to Liverpool express train and died from his injuries in Staffordshire General Infirmary the day before. It showed how dangerous his job was and it made me feel glad that I was working in a pretty safe job on the Post Office.

The council decided to improve the way Stoke-on-Trent looked through a land reclamation plan. There was a lot of derelict land about and big slag heaps had been left from mines that had closed. There was a huge area of wasteland off Town Road, where Hanley Deep Pit had been, and the council wanted to clean it up and make it into something attractive. On 19 November, they made an agreement with the National Coal Board, the owners of the land, to reclaim it and turn it into a public open space called Hanley Forest Park. The wasteland was a real eyesore and I couldn't imagine what it would be like when the job was completed. Obviously, I thought it was a good thing and the area, which was actually named Central Forest Park, now looks much better than it did, with a lake and trees, and is a pretty popular place to visit.

In November 1968, *Lily the Pink*, by The Scaffold, became a popular sing-along song. It had a swing to it and got to the top of the charts on my 53rd birthday, on 14 December. I bought the sheet music of it and it turned out to be the last one that I ever purchased. I tried it on the piano, but it was too difficult for me to play.

Because Young Harry wasn't playing for Vale any more, Helen and I had stopped going to their matches and she hadn't been to Stoke for quite some while either. On Saturday afternoons, she wanted to go out in our car, but I was watching Stoke every other week or so. It didn't seem fair on her, so I more or less stopped going to their matches, although I carried on supporting them from my armchair!

That Christmas, the family party was held at Harry and Gill's semi-detached house, 146 Greasley Road, which they'd bought a year or so before. It was in a very handy place because it was just a few doors up the road from their shop. All the usual members of the family were at the party and we were all able to fit around Harry and Gill's dining table to eat our tea, which was much better than the cramped room we'd always been in before at Vera's.

In his January 1969 mock A level exams, Jeff got his grades back up to where they'd been the previous year and so things were looking promising. His report said, 'If his present efforts continue he should achieve commendable results in the summer.' Because he was in the second year of his A level studies, he was leaving school that summer and so he needed to decide what to do.

On 30 January, we postmen were called out on a one-day stoppage by the Union of Post Office Workers, of which I was a member. The action was in support of a pay claim by the overseas telegraphists. I can't remember the strike, but I'd have been involved in it because I automatically followed the union's decisions whether I agreed with them or not. That was because I thought we should all stick together and the officials didn't call strikes for nothing. I wasn't worried about losing my job by supporting the union because the bosses couldn't sack large numbers of postmen who went on strike. By 1 February, the backlog of mail in the city was still 50,000 items and it was estimated that it would take a few more days before things were back to normal.

In February, a fund was set up to try to raise the money to buy a Supermarine Spitfire fighter plane so that it could be put on display in Stoke-on-Trent. The reasons were that it had been invented by a local man, Reginald Mitchell, and it had played a very important part in the vital Battle of Britain victory in 1940. A Mk XVI model, built in 1945, was given to the city in 1969 and put in a glass house in Bethesda Street. I went to see the plane and thought it had a nice, streamlined design. It was appropriate for the city to have a Spitfire because its designer was local and it was a good reminder of what had gone on in the war.

Sometimes, when we were working on the facing table at the Post Office, we'd come across loose coins and banknotes. Everybody at first would tend to ignore the money, wondering if it was a trap and they were being tempted to steal it, but, eventually, someone would pick it up and take it to an inspector. On odd occasions, somebody working alone would put the money in his own pocket, thinking he couldn't be seen. Sometimes, the money was placed on the table deliberately as bait, to tempt a postman to pocket it. The Investigation Branch would be looking from behind the one-way glass in the watch gallery and occasionally a culprit who was seen would be arrested. I suspected that the gallery was also used by the bosses to check on our work practices, perhaps with a view to making cuts or increasing our workloads.

One day, I was walking across the sorting office and these three fellows were coming towards me. One of them was a fairly new postman and I smiled at him, but his face was ashen. The other two were Post Office security detectives. After a while, I realized that he was under arrest and that they'd marched him off.

Jeff resolved to train as a history teacher and applied to study at Bishop Lonsdale College of Education in Western Road, in Mickleover, Derby. I drove him there for an interview on 26 March and, on 3 April, he was sent a letter by the college accepting him onto the course as a residential student for the following September. But I was apprehensive about it, wondering whether he'd fit in there.

While I was delivering letters in Etruria Vale Road one day, I thought I'd look up my Aunt Florrie Bryant, who still lived in the same house (number 336) as she'd done when I was a lad, although her husband, my Uncle Fred, had died during the war. When she answered the door, I tried to explain who I was. She was in her mid-nineties by then and it took a while before she accepted who I was. Finally, she invited me in and we had a bit of a talk.

One of Frank Sinatra's best songs was *My Way*, which was popular at that time and got to number five in the charts. I suppose he was pretty good for his time and he was almost talking, rather than singing, the words of the song. It was about a man looking back on his life and saying that he'd lived it his way and had few regrets about it. I bought a copy of the record, but Helen wasn't as keen on it as I was.

Swinnerton's had a big wedding reception job to do for William Tatton & Co. Ltd., of Upper Hulme and Buxton Road, Leek, who were silk dyers. It was being held under canvas in a field at Birchall, in Leek. Helen's job was to supply all the tableware out of Swinnerton's own supply, which wasn't as easy as it appears because they hardly ever had any in stock. They always had a number of receptions on the go and so, to prepare the required amount of items, she had to wait for them to come in from other receptions. There were also tablecloths and napkins to be washed after their return, so it was a big headache, especially as the directors didn't take into consideration the stocks of equipment they had when they took catering orders. But they muddled through in British fashion!

Helen asked me to take my movie camera and record a few scenes, which I did, at a preview on 21 June. It was a marvellous setup, especially considering it was under a tent. It was laid out as though it was in Buckingham Palace! There was a four-tier wedding cake and I shot Helen organizing the table that it was on. The presents were displayed in what appeared to be a large garage nearby and were in the charge of a plain-clothes policeman. I asked for and received his permission to shoot the scene and found the place packed out with gifts!

By then, members of the pop groups, like The Beatles, were growing their hair really long and so influencing their male teenage followers to do the same. Like lots of other youths, Jeff was growing his hair longer and by that time it covered his ears, so that they couldn't be seen any more. It wasn't all that long really, but older people were used to men's hair being short, so we didn't like the new style. Helen was going on at him all the time to get it cut and I left him a note one day, saying, 'Get your hair cut or else no television.' It was too late to threaten him with something like that, though, because he was out a lot of the time and had a life increasingly separate from Helen and me, so my note didn't bother him and he didn't get his hair cut.

He left school in July, having taken his A level exams. His school report said: 'His work has always reflected his interest and industry. He deserves to succeed.' I was pleased that he seemed to be doing well, but I wondered how things would turn out.

We decided to have a tour of Scotland for our summer holidays. That was mainly because of my experiences there in the army during the Second World War and I suppose Helen and Jeff were interested in where I'd been. We'd not been on a long car run before and had only been on the motorway as far as Stafford, so it was to be quite an experience for us. For the trip, we bought a Calor Gas stove, a kettle, a teapot, a collapsible table and chairs and a large water container. Also, Eva Jeffries, our neighbour at number 311, gave us an AA road map book to keep, to help us with the routes, and Jeff has still got it!

We started off on Sunday 13 July and drove through Stoke and along Campbell Road, to join the motorway link road at Hanford, as the A 500 had not then been built through the city. We joined the M 6 at Hanchurch and made steady progress north. After a while, I found myself occasionally passing another motorist, which surprised me a little. About 50 mph was about the fastest I went because Helen got worried at anything quicker, so I'd expected everybody would have come whizzing past me. Helen had given way to Jeff and let him sit in the front passenger seat because he'd have been very awkward otherwise. This had been a problem before and he seemed to think he was the most important person in the family! He sat there like he was the monarch of all he surveyed and had the AA book on his lap because he fancied himself as something of an expert on navigation. I must confess, however, that he was pretty good at it and I was glad he'd come along for the ride.

We had a break at one of the motorway service stations, but, after we'd resumed our journey, a funny noise started and continued for mile after mile. We couldn't understand it and Helen was most upset because she thought something was happening to the car. She wanted me to stop or get off the motorway, but we were miles from an exit, so we had to keep on going. Eventually, the noise stopped and we noticed that the surface of the road was a different colour and texture. We then deduced that the noise had been caused by the concrete surface we'd been on.

The motorway finished just beyond Carnforth, in Lancashire, and we went onto the A 6, which was an ordinary road. Traffic jams soon built up and we were ages crawling along. It was very frustrating, but Helen was very patient, sitting in the back without complaining. Further on, we went up a fairly steep hill near Shap. I'd been told by one of the postmen at Stoke that it was a terrible climb, that his car had had a hard time getting up it and that at the top he'd had to stop to let the engine cool off! But our Beetle went up it with the greatest of ease.

Eventually, we came to a sign, by a bridge over the River Sark, which stated that we were going into Scotland. That really thrilled us because it seemed as if we were entering a foreign country. On the other side of the bridge, we came into Gretna, which was another thrill. There was a fellow in Highland dress, parading up and down, playing the bagpipes in front of the Old Toll Bar. The building was advertised as the "First House" in Scotland and a sign on it said that over 10,000 marriages had been performed there since 1830. It had been the first place where English couples between sixteen and twenty could get married without the agreement of their parents because the law on marriages was different in Scotland. So the Old Toll Bar was used by runaways, as were many other premises in Gretna and nearby Gretna Green. Sometimes, the couple's parents would be chasing after them, trying to prevent their marriage!

We parked the car behind the building and paused to brew some tea and have a bite to eat from our supplies. On the holiday (and others afterwards), we generally ate our own food in lay-bys in the open air, so we bought food in as we went along and had picnics, using our own plates and cutlery. It was only on occasions that we'd pay for something in a pub or café.

After a short while, we continued northwards on the A 74, which I was surprised to find soon became a very good dual carriageway. I didn't expect decent roads in Scotland! Unfortunately, Jeff had been a bit awkward with Helen and she got fed up of the situation. To make him get in a better frame of mind, she said she wanted to go home, so we went back a few miles, until she judged things were going to be alright, and then we turned around. I just went along with it, but was worried that she did want to go all the way back and was relieved when she decided to carry on with the holiday.

Further on, we went through the streets of some towns and then came to Bannockburn. Jeff was interested in this place because of the battle that had occurred. We started looking around for somewhere to stay the night and saw a farm just off the main road, which had a sign out advertising B & B. We drove up the track towards the building and stopped and had a look. Helen had an eye for getting good digs that we liked and, after studying the place, she decided it wasn't up to standard. We drove on and came to another sign. So we had a look at that place and it seemed okay. We had a check around and everything seemed alright, including the price, so we accepted it. It was seven or eight o'clock by that time and it had been a long day, so we were glad we'd got somewhere to stay.

The man of the house was a bee keeper and asked us what we wanted for breakfast. He said, 'We've got this, that and the other and oatcakes.'

'Ooh, ah!' we said.

The breakfast was very nice, but no Staffordshire oatcakes appeared. What a disappointment it was. We'd been dreaming all through the night of bacon, egg and oatcakes! There were some small, hard biscuits, though, and we later discovered that they were Scottish oatcakes! They weren't a patch on our own local soft, floppy oatcakes.

We then had a look at a monument to Robert the Bruce, which was close by. He was the king of the Scots, who beat the English at the Battle of Bannockburn in 1314 and made sure that Scotland stayed independent. On the statue, he was holding an axe in his right hand and both he and his horse, on which he was mounted, were wearing armour.

In a field nearby were some lovely horses. We stroked them and tried to feed them with handfuls of grass, but Helen was timid and offered only one small piece of vegetation at arm's length!

A short distance away was Stirling Castle. We decided to have a look around it and it cost us a shilling each to get in, as I had to pay full price for Jeff. It was worth it because the castle was very impressive. It had been maintained in good condition and I was surprised to see that inside there were well-kept lawns and gardens. I remember looking down from the walls and across the open countryside, and I filmed the spectacular views.

We carried on to Callander and then turned left to a beautiful area called the Trossachs. There we stopped in a lay-by and got our chairs out. As we sat there, Helen felt a bite on one of her legs, but didn't think much about it. Later, though, it swelled up and remained like that for weeks. We thought the insect responsible must have been a horsefly because there were some buzzing about.

While we were in the lay-by, a bus load of old folks pulled up and we heard a piper playing for them. After the bus had gone, Helen went to the piper and asked if she could pose by him so that I could take them with my cine camera. He agreed and I took some film, but he stood quite still because he didn't understand that it was a movie. Such cameras were still unusual to many ordinary people.

We moved on to Balloch, on the southern edge of Loch Lomond, and then up the western side of the loch until we came to the village of Luss. We saw a B & B sign out, at Arnburn House, so we called and made enquiries. Everything seemed alright except that the toilet was outside, but there was a consolation – the car could be kept overnight in a garage. The landlady was very nice and Helen said that she was just like my mother. After we'd fixed up our stay and deposited some of our luggage, we drove back to Balloch, which was like a little seaside town, with a steamboat tied up at the quayside. We spent a couple of hours wandering around and then made our way back to the B & B.

In the morning, we headed north on the A 82 to Tarbet, where we turned off to Inverary. We then got on the A 819 and headed for Oban. A few miles from there, at Taynuilt, we spotted a nice bungalow, with a B & B sign up, so we pulled up and Helen and I went to have a look at it. It seemed satisfactory and, after a few niceties and unloading some of our luggage, we headed to Oban to have a look around.

It was an interesting town and port and it was fascinating to see fish being unloaded and boats going out to the islands. There was a folly, McCaig's Tower, on the hill behind the harbour. It was circular and had archways in the walls, but no roof. Jeff wanted to have a look at it and I went with him, leaving Helen on a bench in the town, watching the locals and tourists go by. The folly was interesting and we had a great view looking out over the sea. Later, we all went around the town, looking at the shops. Afterwards, we made our way back to our B & B and had a walk to the nearby village, where we had a drink in the tavern. Although Jeff was almost eighteen, and would therefore very soon be permitted to buy alcohol himself, I don't think I got him beer because I didn't want to encourage him to get into bad habits.

In the morning, we headed towards Oban, but turned right at Connel onto the A 828, which took us to Ballachulish, where there was a car ferry. There were two boats operating and we decided to queue to get on one to save us driving twenty miles around Loch Leven. The ferries made two or three journeys across the narrows before our turn came. The current flowing out to sea was strong and our boat had to have its engine going nearly full blast to hold it steady by the slipway so that the cars could roll aboard. I think Helen was visualizing me driving the Beetle overboard and so I got on with some trepidation! The ferry powered its way upstream so that the current would bring us level with the opposite slipway and again the engine worked strongly to hold us steady for disembarkation.

We were then on the A 82 and drove through Fort William and on to Spean Bridge, just past where there was a monument to the commandos who'd trained in that area during the Second World War. We stopped to have a look at it and it was pretty tall and impressive, towering over us.

Further on, we came to Fort Augustus, which was at the southern end of Loch Ness. There we had a look for a B & B and found a council house that seemed alright. Unfortunately, after we'd booked in, we discovered that the place was swarming with houseflies, but we couldn't for shame have left because it would have been most embarrassing. When our breakfast was served in the morning, the flies were all over our food, but we made the best of the situation and hoped that we hadn't eaten any of the insects! I'd never seen so many flies in one place and I was glad to get out of the area.

We carried on on the A 82, which turned and twisted along the northwest side of Loch Ness. After a while, Jeff suddenly said: 'Look, Dad! There's the Loch Ness Monster!' I couldn't look because the road was snaking in and out, but I wasn't impressed because I took his remark as some kind of a joke. A mile or two further on, round a long bend, we came upon a group of people by the road side and a few cars parked nearby. We decided to have a look at what was going on and walked over to the group. We followed their gaze and way out into the loch there was a monster, about fifteen feet high! It had a long, snake-like neck and head and behind were three humps sticking out of the water. So Jeff had been right – it *was* the Loch Ness Monster, or so we thought as we looked in disbelief! Then we saw a motorboat near to the creature and heard the sound of its engine. The boat moved forward and "Nessie" followed it. Sadly, the monster was a fraud because the boat was towing it along! I got my movie camera and shot a length of film off, showing the monster in the loch, with the ruins of Urquhart Castle in the background. We made enquiries and were told by someone in the crowd that filming was taking place for an episode of the popular television series, *Dr. Finlay's Casebook*.

After a while, we got back in the car and proceeded to Inverness. I can't remember stopping there, but we went on to Beauly and Muir of Ord, where I'd been stationed in the war and I wanted to have a look at them again. I parked the car in Beauly and had a look around the back of the Lovat Arms Hotel for the building where our mules had been stabled. It had become a garage, but I still poked my head inside to reminisce. There was a fellow standing inside and I tried to explain in a few words what I was doing, but he looked blank. I didn't linger because sacrilege seemed to have been committed.

We moved on up the road to Muir of Ord and had a look around. I couldn't see any Nissen huts and could only guess where they and the stables had been, so I was disappointed.

That was the furthest north we got. We headed back to Inverness, but there was a terrific rainstorm on the way, so we pulled in to the side of the road until it had eased off! From Inverness, we went onto the A 96 to Nairn and then turned onto the A 939 to Grantown-on-Spey and Tomintoul. We came to Ballater, where I'd also been stationed during the war. I picked out the railway station buildings as we passed. That was where I'd allowed a prisoner to have a drink at the bar with his mate! I should have liked to have had a good look around, but I don't think Helen and Jeff were as interested as me, so we carried on. Things did look different and I wondered whether Monaltrie House and its grounds, where we'd been billeted outside the village, had been handed back to its former owner or perhaps even knocked down to make way for a council estate. As it turned out, it was still there and today is used for luxury self-catering accommodation.

I drove towards Braemar and then we came upon a cottage, which was doing B & B, so we booked in for the night. An old man lived there and he sat in a big chair, with a cup and saucer on its arm. It seemed as if he wanted a drink of tea because he rattled his cup and saucer and his daughter (I presumed) came in and filled his cup. The incident amused us and, for many years afterwards, Helen rattled her cup and saucer when she thought back to the event! The lady at the B & B remembered the soldiers and mules marching past their cottage when Helen mentioned it.

We visited the grounds of Balmoral Castle, which was nearby and was owned by the queen. The grounds were open to the public when royalty weren't in residence, but there were very few people about when we visited. I was rather disappointed with the castle and grounds because I'd expected to see something more glamorous than they were. As we left, as a bit of fun, I filmed Helen pretending to wave goodbye to the queen, so we could swank about it when we got back! On the other side of the River Dee was Crathie Church, where the queen worshipped when she was around those parts. Helen went inside to have a look at it and was impressed. We had Jeff take our photo on the entrance steps.

We then continued along the A 93 to Braemar and onwards and upwards till we came to the Glenshee ski chairlift, which was in operation, despite it being the middle of the summer! As we stopped to look at it, two or three sheep came along and one of them started butting the car! I had to shout at it to drive it away. Despite the interruption, I managed to shoot a bit of film of the lift in action.

Shortly afterwards, as the road began to drop downhill, there was a nasty steep section called the Devil's Elbow, which I'd heard about. Eva Jeffries had come down it some years previously, with her husband, Vin, and had screamed with terror as they negotiated the double hairpin bends, which reached a gradient of one in three! I pulled the car to a halt, just previous to the descent, to have a look. It was rather steep, but we had to go on or take a very long detour, so I edged slowly down and I think we were all glad when we got to the bottom.

A bit further on, we got to the Spittal of Glenshee, another place where I'd been stationed in the army. We couldn't see my old camp site because it was way up a private estate side road, which was a shame.

We carried on to Blairgowrie, where I'd been on a short pass during the war. We stopped a short while, but it didn't bring back any memories of the town, so we continued to Dundee. We then drove over the Tay Bridge and had to pay a toll to go on it. Helen was a bit nervous, I suppose because of the drop. Eventually, we came to St Andrews and had a look around. We saw the ruined cathedral and the famous golf course.

After a short stay, we got on the A 959 to Anstruther and then turned right onto the coast road, where we found a B & B in a village after a few miles. The house was stone built and had some beautiful furniture inside. After depositing our suitcases, we drove further along to Elie, a little seaside place, where we parked and went to look at the beach and the sea. We sat for a while, enjoying the view, and then Helen and I went into a nearby public house to have some refreshment. I just had a shandy and took a glass of lemonade and some crisps to Jeff outside.

The next morning, we set off towards Edinburgh and came to the Forth Road Bridge. I wound down my window, paid my dues to a fellow in a little cubbyhole and drove onto the bridge. I looked up and saw very thick cables slung between the supporting towers. I mentioned to Helen that the cables were holding the bridge up, but she went to pieces and said if she'd known that she wouldn't have crossed over!

We drove into Edinburgh and came to Princes Street. Jeff wanted to have a look at the castle, so we thought we'd go in. I parked pretty easily in a side street nearby, but, just then, a motorist pulled in and, in doing so, bumped another car. He got out, had a look at the damage, smiled and walked off! We didn't know what to do, so we also walked away, to the castle. At the entrance were two guardsmen, who saluted a passing officer. We went in, at a cost of two shillings each, and found a lot of interesting items on display. One was a crown in a thick glass container and Helen asked me which crown it was. Without thinking, I turned to the soldier guard and guide, who was standing nearby, and asked him the same question.

He looked at me and asked, 'What country are you in?'

Again without thinking, I said, 'England.'

His face coloured up and I thought he was about to have a fit. Then he exploded and bellowed, 'It's the Scottish crown, man!'

I sidled away before he struck me and I got lost in the crowd. Helen, Jeff and I then went outside, round the top of the castle, and there was a good view. There were a number of old cannons, the largest of which was Mons Meg, one of the most ancient in the world. It was over thirteen feet long and had been built to fire 330-pound cannonballs!

I wanted to have a look at Redford Cavalry Barracks, in Colinton, another place where I'd been stationed in the war. They were only about three miles away, to the southwest, and I found them okay. I stopped the car, walked across the road and gazed through the railings onto the parade ground and the barracks beyond. I had a reminiscence and then thought that, while we were in the area, we could go to Juniper Green, where I'd visited the Crawford family, with whom I'd become friendly. I drove to the village, but couldn't recognize where they'd lived. There was a shop nearby, where I explained my predicament. I was told that Mr and Mrs Crawford were dead and that the children had dispersed. Ian was still living in Edinburgh, but I hadn't known him because he'd been in the air force, so I didn't think it was right to look him up. I was sad not to meet the family again, but it was time to be on our way.

We got on the A 7 and drove to Selkirk, where we looked for a B & B. We were told by the landlady of a likely-looking place that she was full up, but that her mother had a vacancy and that she would ring her to tell her to look out for us. We followed the instructions and came to a row of cottages. One of them had an old couple standing by the doorway, but it looked dowdy and therefore we thought it couldn't be the correct place. We carried on to one which seemed smarter, but no-one came out to greet us, so we reluctantly reversed the car and found that the old couple were the people we were looking for. They showed us around their cottage and it was clean, but old-fashioned. We decided to stay and were very comfortable.

The following day, we'd been intending to take the B 7009, but the old chap persuaded us to go on the A 708 instead. I couldn't understand what he was saying at first because of his accent, but he eventually got through to me that there was a waterfall along this road, called the Grey Mare's Tail. We took his advice and eventually came to it. It was aptly named, being grey, twisty, narrow and long. It was in a lonely valley, with hills on each side. We climbed upwards to have a closer look, but Helen only went partway.

We then carried on driving until we came to the lovely little town of Moffat. Jeff had been looking at his map and wanted to go to a place a few miles to the north, called the Devil's Beef Tub. So off we went and came to it in the hills. There was a hollow deep in a valley off the road and it was quite impressive. It had been used, hundreds of years before, by raiders along the border area with England to hide stolen cattle. The thieves temporarily kept them there until it was safe to drive them off.

Afterwards, we went back to Moffat and, for a change, had a meal at one of the restaurants, which we enjoyed very much. There was a carnival going on in the town square, which we watched with interest, and I filmed the Moffat Pipe Band and a float with the gala queen on.

We then moved on and made our way to the A 74, which took us to Carlisle. From there, we went on a B road into North Cumberland, where we found a farm that did B & B.

The next day, we visited a number of places in the Lake District, which we enjoyed very much. After we'd had our tea, Helen wanted to know how long it would take us to get home and I told her it would be two hours or a bit more. It seemed to me that she'd had enough of the holiday and she then suggested that we get back to our own house. I agreed, so we packed our utensils and set off.

We got back without a stop and it was nice to see the old homestead again!

It had been a very interesting holiday and it was something new. The only trouble had been the travelling because of the long distances and it hadn't been all that comfortable in the car. Memories had come flooding back and I'd relived the past glories and tragedies, especially the deaths of my parents, which had come back to my mind a bit.

Jeff received the news that he'd passed all the three subjects he'd taken at A level, but his grades were disappointing (D in history and E in British government and economics). However, that didn't seem to matter because they were good enough for him to go on to do his teacher training at Bishop Lonsdale College. He'd also passed another O level, in general studies, which was nice to know, but it didn't make any difference to his plans.

I managed to get a council garage to rent off Trentmill Road, in Eastwood, which was a bit nearer home than Haywood Street. It cost eleven shillings a week and I moved the car there on 20 August.

Helen and I were invited to attend Pam Kent's wedding with Alan Edwards on 23 August. They'd been students at Oxford University at the same time, which was where they'd met. Bernard (Pam's father and my cousin) told me that Alan's parents were farmers in Weston, near to Crewe, with his father being in effect the squire of Weston. Bernard also told us that he was hiring Swinnerton's to do the catering for the reception, so Helen became responsible for supplying the tableware.

Except for Bernard's immediate family, I was the only relative on the Kent side to be invited! Pam's Uncle Sam and Aunt Annie hadn't been invited because they'd been at odds with Bernard for years. Also, the parents of Bernard's wife, Dorothy, hadn't been asked because she was at loggerheads with them.

The weather was nice on the day and Helen and I picked up Pam's grandmother, Aunt Florrie, and arrived in good time. I was making a film of the event and took shots of the wedding party before they entered the Church of All Saints, in Cemetery Road, Weston, and as they came out after the ceremony. We then went to the church hall, which was almost opposite, where we were served with a nicely-cooked meal. Afterwards, we were invited to the Edwards' house at Red Lion Farm, on Main Road, but Helen and I were the last to leave the church hall and there was no-one in sight to ask where the farm was. I drove along the road and into the open countryside, but I couldn't find it, so I asked at the first farm we came to. I was sure we'd get the help we required, especially considering that I understood "Farmer" Edwards was the local squire and a wedding in the village would have been a rare event known about by everybody. But I was disappointed because the fellow at the farm had never heard of Squire Edwards nor the wedding! It turned out that Alan's father was a tenant of the Duchy of Lancaster and wasn't actually the local squire at all, so Bernard's description of him had proved to have been rather flamboyant! Anyway, I turned back and found the farm pretty quickly, fairly close to the church hall!

I developed a rash on my left arm and went to the doctor's about it on 25 August. I was told I'd got shingles, but I don't know if I was given anything for it, although my medical records show it was improving by my next visit on 3 September.

In September, Jeff started his college studies in Derby. Helen and I were paying his main expenses, but we also gave him something to get by on while he was there. He'd been awarded a grant of £48 by the council for his first year at the college, but it was nowhere near enough to cover all the costs, so Helen and I had to make up the difference. Because we were both working, we were told to contribute £115, but Stoke-on-Trent Education Department said they'd pay Jeff's college fees.

Jeff had expected to have all the money from his grant, including our contribution. He wasn't very pleased that we wouldn't let him have any of it and couldn't understand the reason for our decision. Also, he'd worked out in his mind that he was having our car to run himself there, where he'd then knock about in it, even though he hadn't had any lessons or passed a test! His idea was that one of the other lads who could drive would sit in. However, Helen and I got down to brass tacks and drove him there, with the stuff he needed, and then drove back after we'd dropped him off.

He was billeted in a semi-detached house with three other fellows, who were quite a bit older than him, and I understand they put on him. He wanted to come home at the weekends, as much as anything because he was keenly following Vale, who were doing very well in the Fourth Division. The first time or two, I collected him. He then said he'd hitchhike, but that wasn't successful and he finished up getting a bus, so we returned to picking him up.

On 1 October, the Post Office ceased to be a government department and became a public corporation. The government had thought of this brilliant idea to cut down on civil servants because it would look good and give the impression that money was being saved. So postmen were no longer civil servants and we were given a 6% pay rise to compensate for stoppages from our wages for superannuation, which we hadn't had to pay before. The real pay, though, worked out about the same.

After a few weeks at college, Jeff said he'd had enough of it, so we brought him home. I thought it was something to do with him being bullied by his house mates, but he later told me that it was mainly because he didn't like the course. Also, he said he didn't want to miss out on Vale's promotion challenge, so he found that he was having to keep travelling back and forwards to see them, and, as well, he had a girlfriend in Hartshill (Joy Mellor), whom he was keen on.

Before Jeff left, the fellows in his house tried to throw him into a bath of cold water fully clothed and told him it was a leaving ceremony. I understand that he wrestled with them, so that they only managed to push him partway in before they gave up. I suppose they thought it was funny, but I'd call them bullies!

Helen and I told Jeff that he'd better get a job and he agreed, so I went with him to Stoke Town Hall. I think that was because we thought we'd see if he could get a nice, safe job there and it would be convenient, being just down the road. He got an interview right away and was immediately fixed up with an office job, in the City Treasurer's Department. However, his interviewer advised him not to take his father with him when he went for another job! He seemed to settle into his work, but it appeared to me that he didn't have a lot to do. His student days weren't over, however, because he was sent to the College of Building and Commerce, in Stoke Road, part time in the evening to learn accountancy and study for the Local Government Training Board's Clerical Examination.

On 12 November, Harry and Gill had a baby son, whom they named Matthew.

Helen was delighted that they'd had a lad because she really liked baby boys, although I've no idea why.

Vale were top of the division and had gone eighteen league games unbeaten from the start of the season, one short of the Football League record. On 22 November, Jeff went all the way to Scunthorpe to see if they could equal it, but it was not to be because they lost 2-1. He was very disappointed.

Our sorting office in Stoke had started to bring in machines to sort letters automatically and it was announced in the *Sentinel* on 1 December that we were the first place in the Midlands to be doing so. The machines came in gradually and postcodes were eventually introduced for all addresses in Britain to try to save money by cutting out manual sorting. For a long time, people were reluctant to use the codes, especially if they had to find them out, and many customers didn't want to put extra writing on their envelopes. Even now, plenty of mail is sent without the codes on and I've never put mine at the top of my letters! At first it was like a protest I had against the Post Office replacing postmen with machines and I've never bothered with it since.

A great barrel, about six feet wide, was used in automatic sorting. Postmen who'd collected mail would tip it in the barrel, which had slots inside and turned around. The thinner items would drop through the slots and the thicker ones, including the packets, would stay in the barrel, be removed every so often and have to be sorted by hand. The letters that had come through the slots would be sorted into first and second class and put into a cancelling machine to cancel the stamps with a black mark. It didn't matter which way up the letters had been put in because the cancelling machine would turn them to the way they were required. Then the letters would be conveyed to a postman who'd look out for those with missing postcodes, which he'd print on through a coding machine. The letters would then be automatically sorted, so that all those for whichever walk I was doing would end up on my sorting table, ready to be put into order for delivery. The system saved on labour, but it wasn't perfect and letters with difficult addresses or bad handwriting still had to be sorted by hand.

My pay on 12 December 1969 was £18 16s., which was fairly typical of what I got at that time, and £1 4s. tax was taken out of it. The next week, there was overtime on the Christmas mail and my earnings went up to £24 9s. 4d., but I had to pay £4 3s. of it in tax. The overtime, of course, carried on over the Christmas period and the following week my gross pay was £28 8s. 5d. Then, on 2 January 1970, I was paid £27 5s. 3d.

On 10 January, the prime minister, Harold Wilson, spoke about 'booming Britain' and said the workers 'have a right to be proud of their achievement'. I suppose there were more things in the shops, but that didn't matter much to me because I didn't want a lot. I was more or less happy with what I'd got, but I still had to go to work no matter how the country was doing.

A week later, it was in the *Sentinel* that there were still 4,500 houses in the city unfit for people to live in and that the council was hoping to clear all the slums by 1974. Sixteen years earlier, it had been said that they were hoping to clear them by 1963! So I'd learned to take with a pinch of salt what the council said and most of the changes that happened seemed to be very slow.

On 4 February, a white paper, the Redcliffe-Maud Report, was published and two of the changes it proposed to local government were that Staffordshire should cease to exist and Stoke-on-Trent should become the centre of a new county made up of North Staffordshire and South Cheshire. I couldn't understand why the government wanted to alter the country's local areas. I don't think most people were bothered about changing things and I don't suppose the alterations would have made it better for us. As it turned out, though, the Labour government lost the next election on 18 June and their plans never came about.

The government was calling for there to be more coloured policemen on the beat, but that didn't seem reasonable to me at the time. It didn't seem right for a coloured policeman to be telling white people what to do in England. I wondered what would happen if one of them started pushing me around. I thought the British were a superior race, but, of course, that was nonsense.

One of Jeff's lecturers at the College of Building and Commerce asked him whatever he was doing on the course when he had such good credentials. When Jeff came home afterwards, he asked Helen and me if he could go in for a degree at the North Staffordshire Polytechnic (now Staffordshire University), which was just being set up. We agreed, so he filled in an application form to study on a University of London BSc course in Economics, which was being run at the polytechnic for external students. He was sent a letter on 20 March, offering him a place as long as he could get a Grade B in British government. He then wrote to Hanley High School to ask if he could retake the exam there and Mr Barwise agreed to it. Jeff found out that the title of the subject had been changed to British constitution and he paid a fee of £14 5s. to enter for the exam.

In March, Helen and I had a new ceiling put in our lounge by Elijah because cracks were appearing in our old one. We cleared everything out of the room and then he dug the ceiling plaster and laths out, which all fell on the floor. What a mess it was! Next, he nailed large plasterboards over the exposed ceiling beams and then covered them with a thin layer of plaster, which made a nice smooth ceiling, as it still is today. We put all the rubbish in bags and Helen got permission from Swinnerton's to use one of their vans and a driver to take them to the refuse tip. We gave Elijah five pounds for his work and tipped the Swinnerton's driver.

Vale were still gunning for promotion and Jeff travelled all the way to Hartlepool on 28 March to watch them win 2-0. He then cheered them on at Notts County on 8 April, where Vale won again, that time 2-1. He was spending a lot of time and a fair amount of money going round the country to watch them, but then again they weren't in a promotion race every year!

Helen and I went to Matthew Poole's christening at St. John's Church, in Greasley Road, on 19 April. I took some film of the guests coming out after the event, especially of Helen carrying Matthew. She had been chosen as the godmother, which she thought was just the right thing to have happened and so she was very pleased.

Vale were promoted on 22 April and celebrated by playing a friendly at Stoke nine days later. To nearly everyone's amazement, Vale won 3-2 and it didn't seem that Stoke had thrown the game because it was quite rough and a number of players were injured. Of course, Jeff was cock-a-hoop, not least because we lived in an area of Stoke supporters, who often kidded him about Vale and how poor they were!

That spring, I was busy with DIY at home. I made a fitted wardrobe in the front bedroom, stained it and fixed a rail inside it, to hang clothes on. I put sliding doors on the shelves of the small storeroom off the kitchen, which we used to house books and called the library, and also I redecorated the inside of nearly the whole of the house!

Helen and I were invited to the marriage of one of the Swinnerton's office girls, Mandy Moore, to David Harvey, a draughtsman from Birches Head. The wedding was at St. Mark's Church, in Shelton, on 30 May. Of course, Helen wanted me to film the occasion, which I did, as usual taking the guests and bride as they arrived and the events afterwards outside the church.

Jeff took an exam in the Outlines of Central and Local Government on 26 May and also had to sit one in the Use of English, both of which he passed, to get his local government Clerical Examination certificate. In June, he took his A level exam and was later informed that he'd got a Grade A, which was the highest possible and better than he needed to get into the polytechnic. Helen and I were very pleased with him.

About then, our neighbours at number 333 decided to get rid of their white and pink stones, which were around the edges of their front garden, and to have cement edgings instead. Helen and I had stones of the same colour in our front garden, but ours were smaller, so we had some of their larger ones, for free, which made our borders look better. We should have had some of the bigger stones in the first place because they'd all been bought jointly by my father and William Evans, our then next-door neighbour, in 1933, but the latter had helped himself to the biggest and best blocks when they'd been delivered. Helen had always felt annoyed that Dad had been cheated and said she wouldn't have allowed it to have happened had she been living with us then. So, when we finally got the bigger stones, justice had been done!

The Kinks were a very popular group at that time and were to appear on *Top of the Pops*, a Thursday night TV show on BBC 1, on 9 July. They were performing their new song, *Lola*, which had just got into the pop charts. Jeff asked me to take a movie of the event and said he'd pay me half the cost of the film. I did as he asked and set up my camera in front of the TV and recorded some of the programme. I looked at the result and it seemed odd seeing a group playing, but hearing no sound! I didn't ask Jeff for any payment. The song was a big hit for the group, though, and reached number two.

Helen and I booked our holidays for July and decided to tour the Lake District. That was because we'd enjoyed our brief visit the previous year and it wasn't as far as Scotland. Jeff agreed to come with us again. We drove up the M 6 and, shortly afterwards, came to Windermere, the largest lake in England. It was a thrill to see it.

We went on to Keswick and then headed south down the B 5289, alongside Derwent Water. From there, we turned up a track and came to the quaint stone Ashness Bridge, which was in a lovely spot. A stream ran under the bridge and beyond was a beautiful view of Derwent Water and Skiddaw, which was one of the highest mountains in the Lake District. The scene was on a lot of novelties that were sold in the Lake District and I filmed Helen on the bridge.

Jeff wanted to see the famous Hadrian's Wall, built by the Romans in the second century, so another day we headed eastwards from Carlisle to try to find it. We came across a section of it northeast of Brampton, at Banks East Turret, a fortification on the wall. Of course, only the remains of the wall and the fort were left, as a load of old stones, which weren't very high. It was a marvellous feat for the Romans to have built the wall, but we had to use our imagination to picture what it might have been like at that time.

While we were in the area, we called at Carlisle. Helen said she'd stay with the car while Jeff and I explored the castle, which we did. There were a lot of military exhibits, such as weapons, medals and uniforms, and I was particularly interested in an open book, which listed punishments of men of the Border Regiment, whose headquarters had been at the castle. One soldier had been awarded 800 lashes for some crime. I wondered how a man could survive taking such a beating, but I was later told that the punishment would have been given in small amounts, say twenty lashes at a time. Apparently, the scars would have been allowed to heal and then the next twenty lashes would have been inflicted and so on!

After we'd spent about a couple of hours in the castle, I felt we weren't being fair to Helen, who was still waiting for us, so we made our way back. Then we all had a picnic in the car park and afterwards had a look around the town.

From Carlisle, we headed west and came to Bowness-on-Solway, which was on the north coast of Cumberland. We booked into a house by the side of the firth for B & B and, through our bedroom window, we could see a herd of cows grazing by the side of the water and the Scottish town of Annan in the distance. Hadrian's Wall had started near to Bowness, but there was nothing left of it there. Also, there were two bells in St. Michael's Church, in the village, which had been captured from Middlebie, in Scotland, in the seventeenth century.

From there, we went along the coast to Silloth, which had developed as a seaside resort for the workers of Carlisle in the nineteenth century. We had a walk along the promenade, but it was a pretty quiet place.

We then went back to Keswick and walked up to some high ground just south of the town. From there, I was able to film the marvellous view across Derwent Water and beyond to Bassenthwaite Lake. It was a very clear day and the footage came out a treat.

After that, we travelled to Haweswater Reservoir and drove to the far end, where the road stopped. Jeff wanted to climb up into the hills and I went with him partway. He wanted to go further up, so I agreed, but told him not to be too long away. He must have been at least an hour and I was getting a bit concerned because I didn't know where to look for him. Eventually, he turned up as large as life and I protested at the length of time he'd been, but he didn't understand.

We also drove along Ullswater and then up the Kirkstone Pass, which was a narrow, twisty and pretty steep road. Towards the top, we pulled into a lay-by to give the engine a rest. There we met another family, who told us that they'd previously been towing a caravan up the same pass in fog and had pulled into the lay-by because they didn't know how far away the top was. They'd left the caravan there and called back for it when the fog had gone! The family had a daughter with them and she and Jeff wandered up a hill at the side of the road, but they soon returned because he wasn't impressed with her.

From there, we went down to Ambleside and had a look at the north end of Windermere. There were boat trips out on the lake and there were plenty of people about.

The next stop was Coniston Water, which was where Donald Campbell had made some water speed record-breaking attempts in his Bluebird speedboat. His last effort, on 4 January 1967, had ended in disaster when his boat had flipped over at more than 300 miles an hour and killed him. Nothing of him was found afterwards, which was mysterious, but his body was finally recovered in 2001.

We then booked in for B & B at Yew Tree Farm, just outside Coniston. The accommodation was in an old farmhouse, which dated back to the early sixteenth century. It was a gloomy place where you could imagine ghosts doing their haunting. Jeff was put in a room downstairs, but the house gave Helen the creeps and she insisted on having him in our room. The room was peculiar too because the floor sagged in the middle, which made the furniture at the sides tilt inwards! At the top of the stairs was a huge chest, which must have been six feet in length by thirty inches high and about the same in depth. It could have held half a dozen bodies! At the side of the farmhouse was a long, narrow building of two floors and our landlady told us that it had been a spinning gallery, where people had worked in the old days on spinning machines.

When we returned from Coniston later on, our place for the night looked rather sinister, with dark hills immediately behind and black storm clouds covering their peaks. Fortunately, the night passed without incident, but I think we were all glad when morning came!

Jeff wanted to look at an old fort, which was situated somewhere in the hills. He guided me in the car to a track in a field, which was rather rough and got worse as we continued till it became like an old packhorse trail. There was nowhere to turn around and Helen was getting agitated because she imagined us getting stuck. Eventually, we came to a hamlet, where the track went straight on, but on our left was a decent road, which we took, and it led us back to the main road near Coniston. So Jeff didn't see his fort after all!

Our next destination was the village of Grasmere, where we had a look at Dove Cottage. It was a quaint place and had been the home of the poet, William Wordsworth, from 1799 to 1808. While we were there, we had a wander down to the mere itself, which was quiet beautiful, and Wordsworth had described the place as 'the loveliest spot that man hath ever found'.

We finished our holiday with a visit to the Lake District National Park Centre, at Brockhole, which was about two miles south of Ambleside. The centre had only opened earlier in the year and it had marvellous terraced gardens, which stretched down to the shore of Windermere. We had a walk around and Jeff filmed Helen and me sitting on a bench there, enjoying the surroundings.

Vale's first season back in the Third Division began with a long trip to Swansea on 15 August and Jeff went with a coach full of supporters to cheer them on. The journey was worthwhile because the team won 2-0, but Jeff said there'd been a major disturbance after the game when the Vale fans were bombarded with pebbles, which the home supporters had thrown at them. I'd heard about football hooliganism on the television and read about it in the papers and I wondered if Jeff was safe when such dangerous things were going on.

In September, Jeff finished working for the City Treasurer's Department and enrolled for his studies at the polytechnic, in College Road, on the 21st. He went nicely dressed on his first day of lectures, but when he got home, he pulled off his tie and told us he wasn't wearing it again because the rest of his class and the lecturer were dressed casually! I wasn't really bothered about that and Helen and I were pleased he was studying.

On 7 October, Stoke-on-Trent Education Department sent Jeff notice of the money they'd decided he should have as a student for the academic year. They awarded him a grant of £204.11 and asked Helen and me to make a contribution of £120. As he was living at home, we were keeping him, so that more than covered our contribution. We also paid for some of his other expenses. He put his grant cheque in the bank, to use as he went along, but he was unhappy with the arrangement and thought we ought to pay him the £120 parental contribution as well.

Helen and I were keen on a sentimental song called *Snowbird*, by Anne Murray, which was in the charts at that time and which we bought. It was about a woman with a broken heart who wanted to fly away with the snowbird. It was sung very nicely, but only got to number 23.

At that time, the council was trying to set up an airport for Stoke-on-Trent at Seighford, near Stafford, where there was a disused airfield. The council was looking for an alternative to Meir Aerodrome, which was pretty undeveloped and due to be closed. The aerodrome had never been very important and I thought it was beyond Stoke to have a proper airport, although at that time I didn't understand the implications of the growing numbers of foreign holidays. Wellington bombers had flown from Seighford during the war and it had a 2,000-yard runway and a modern control tower, but the scheme was turned down by the Department of the Environment in 1972 after a public inquiry. So the city carried on as normal, without an airport.

Helen had developed hard skin under the ball of each foot, which made it painful for her to walk. So she got a chiropodist, Albert Williams, of 19 Neville Street, in Oak Hill, to call round and he cut the skin off. Unfortunately, it kept coming back again, so he'd visit us every now and again to redo the job. Her feet would be sore to stand on afterwards and the situation wasn't very satisfactory, but it was better for her than doing nothing.

One of the council's land reclamation schemes was to remove the two million tons of waste from Berry Hill tip. Spoil had first been tipped there in 1930 and had finally stopped being dumped in 1952, by which time the pile of waste had become 200 feet high! We could see from our house huge machines digging up the spoil and putting it on lorries to be taken away. The waste-moving machines had to move at high speed because of the risk of their tyres catching fire through the intense heat of the tip, which was reported to be up to 600 degrees Fahrenheit! I wondered where all the material was going to and eventually heard that some of it was being used to fill the old Loop Line tunnel, under Myott's Pottery, because it was no longer in use. When I was delivering mail around Waterloo Road, in Cobridge, I saw lorries coming with the slag to put in the tunnel. Most of the tip, though, was used to help to fill in the great disused marl hole of Berry Hill Brick Works, about a hundred yards to the east of it. Amazingly, the marl hole was over double the area of the tip! The job took about four months to complete and the whole levelled area then provided land for Fenton Industrial Estate to be built. Although I suppose the tip at Berry Hill was an eyesore, I was a bit sad about it being removed because it was an interesting part of the view from the front of our house.

On 7 December, the Electrical Trades Union got their members on a work to rule in support of a five pounds a week pay rise. The result was power cuts and on the 9th nearly a third of the country's electricity supply was off. There were periods when it was on and others when it was off. So at times we had to rely on candles for our lights at home and there was nothing we could do except to wait for the power to come back on. Because we had a coal fire and a gas cooker, the power cuts didn't stop us keeping warm and having hot food. Of course, we couldn't watch the television when the electricity went off, but, apart from that, the cuts didn't inconvenience us too much and everything went back to normal after a week.

My hearing had become quite poor again, so I went to the doctor's on 30 December. It was found that I'd got a build up of wax once more and I was given a solution to put in my ears for a week to soften it up. Then I went back on 8 January 1971 and had my ears syringed, which again did the trick.

On 20 January, I went on strike for better pay, along with almost all the country's other postmen. Our basic wage was less than twenty pounds a week and our union wanted a minimum three pounds a week rise, but the bosses would only give us 8%. Tom Jackson, our union general secretary, said that if we accepted the offer, we'd be worse off than the year before because of inflation. We were then told, not asked, by the union to strike. I think if there'd been a ballot, there wouldn't have been a stoppage. There'd never been a proper national postmen's strike before. Matters were made worse because we were in a vital industry and the government didn't want anything to affect the national way of life. We were threatened with the sack, but, of course, there were too many of us for that to happen. Then there was an outcry because it was said that the old age pensioners couldn't draw their pensions and so they wouldn't be able to buy any food and pay their bills.

The only postmen who got any union pay were those in bad circumstances, who received 'hardship' payments. Some others got money from social security for their wives and children, but not for themselves. I didn't get anything because Helen was working. Some of the fellows said that we were bound to win our claim because the public couldn't do without their mail, but the people managed. The union had got on the bandwagon because other unions had got good settlements when they'd gone on strike or threatened to. However, the government clamped down on us and refused our claims, so we were forced to go back to work after nearly seven weeks on strike. We were compelled to accept 9%, which was only slightly more than we'd been offered in the first place. One of the postmen, Arthur Williams, said to me, 'We've lost £150 in wages,' and I agreed with him.

While the strike was on, the Post Office covered up the pillar boxes to stop people using them because the mail was piling up and a lot of business was lost because some firms found alternative ways of dealing with their correspondence. One of these, Littlewoods Pools, used to send football coupons by post to nearly every house in the land every fortnight. Most people used to fill their coupon in and send it off, along with a postal order. But, when the strike was on, Littlewoods got hundreds of agents to hand out the forms (in factories, shops and so on), take them in completed, with the cash, and pass them on to a central agent, who then delivered them to the firm. When we went back to work at the Post Office, most people stopped using the post for the delivery of their coupons because they'd realized they were better off by continuing to use the agents. That was because they didn't have to buy postal orders and stamps.

When we went back to work, everywhere was stacked out with letters, packets and parcels. We tried to clear the backlog, but it was slow in reducing, so the management had to ask the union for assistance! We then got overtime for working on it and everything was soon back to normal, except for the relationships with the postmen who'd been into work while the strike had been on. Only one or two of them had been guilty of that, I think because their wives had put the screw on. They were sent to Coventry to some extent for a short while. I'd have hated to have been in the position of nobody speaking to me.

During the strike, decimalization had come into being (on 15 February) and, of course, it had affected the postage rates, so a new set of stamps had to be printed. Before the changeover, a first-class stamp had been 5d., which was the equivalent of just over 2p. But the Post Office rounded the amount up to 3p, so actually the stamp went up by over 2d.! After a short period of time had elapsed, all the old stamps became invalid excepting the one pound ones. That didn't affect us much, except that we had to knock on people's doors, asking for a surcharge when we found letters with old stamps on. Obviously, the recipients weren't very pleased, but there wasn't a lot of trouble. I found it quite difficult getting used to the new decimal coinage and, by 31 August, we had to use all the old coins that didn't exactly convert to the new system. The first time I purchased petrol after the change, it was being sold at 34p a gallon.

Sometimes, Jeff would be out when we got in and he used to leave Helen little notes requesting beef 'samos' (sandwiches) to be made and left ready for him when he came in at night. By then, he was coming in pretty late, often after one o'clock in the morning. Then he started frying chips when he got in in the early hours and I noticed scratches on the draining surface of our stainless steel sink, where he'd been cutting up the potatoes!

The old Loop Line railway had closed to passengers in 1964 because there'd been hardly any customers and trains by then. The track between Cobridge and Goldenhill had been taken up by 1968 and the council decided to turn the route into a 'greenway', where people could walk and cycle. It was reported in the *Sentinel* on 19 April 1971 that the council had been given the money by the government to get the job done and eventually you could walk or cycle all the way along the route from Cobridge to Kidsgrove. It was a good idea to make use of it and give people more open space.

The council also had the idea of having a dual carriageway built through Stoke-on-Trent to connect the city to the M 6 to the southwest and northwest. At first, it was called the "D" Road because of the shape of its route and its cost was said to be £8¼ million. The exact route was announced on 19 May and 230 properties were listed to be compulsorily purchased and demolished. I supposed the road was needed because there was more and more traffic and the ordinary roads which led to the motorway were getting jammed up, but it was very hard lines for those people whose houses were in the way because they were shifted off. The building of the new road, which became the A 500, started in 1974 and was finished in 1977. It did help to take the weight of traffic off ordinary roads in the city and I think there'd be chaos without it now because of the number of vehicles that there are today.

It seemed as if there was a fashion for building roads in 1971 because less than a month after the "D" Road announcement, it was in the *Sentinel* that at least 561 houses in the city would be demolished to make way for an £11 million 'mini-motorway' from Sideway to Catchem's Corner, in Meir, as part of the proposed link road to Derby. I wondered where all the road building was going to end and if our house was safe from future plans because it seemed that roads could be put just anywhere. As it turned out, it took decades before the 'mini-motorway' was built and it opened as part of the new A 50 in stages between 1996 and 1998.

Jeff had become very influenced by the informal environment at the polytechnic and, along with many of his fellow students there, wasn't having his hair cut any more, so that it grew longer and longer in the hippie style that it is now. After a while, I realized that he didn't see his long hair as a flash in the pan and I gradually got used to it being like that. Eventually, I didn't think about it any more, but Helen never gave up trying to get him to have it short again. Even decades later, she still went on about it, but Jeff just took no notice of what she said.

We didn't go away on holiday in the summer of 1971, owing to my loss of wages, so we just pottered about. One day, we all went to Dove Dale, which was a lovely place in the Peak District. While we were there, Jeff climbed to the top of Thorpe Cloud, which overlooked the stepping stones across the river and the entrance to Dove Dale. Also, we saw some lads walk into the river and carry on for about a hundred yards for the devilment! I quickly got my cine camera into action and filmed them doing it. I also shot Helen crossing the river on the stepping stones, but another woman decided to cross the opposite way at the same time, so they met in the middle. There wasn't much room for them to pass one another and it was a bit precarious for a few moments. I don't know what we'd have done if Helen had lost her balance and fallen in the river. We then wandered further up the dale, where cows were lying on the path and we had to go round them, but it was a nice, leisurely walk anyway.

Another day, we all had a trip to Lathkill Dale, near to Bakewell, in Derbyshire, which also was a beautiful river valley. We had a relaxing stroll alongside the river there as well and Jeff took some very nice film of Helen and me beside it.

On 29 July, Aunt Sally died in Bucknall Hospital, in Eaves Lane, of thrombosis and pneumonia. She was cremated at Carmountside Crematorium on 2 August and Helen had her name put in their Book of Remembrance, which is opened every year on the date of the person's death, to display his or her name in copperplate writing. Helen told Uncle Bill that she'd provide him with a Sunday lunch-time dinner each week and did so right up to the time he went into an old folks' home in 1985. Helen used to cook our dinners and I'd take Uncle Bill a portion in the car to his home at 29 Rose Street, in Northwood. It was a bind and he wasn't very clean, but it was a job to be done.

There'd been trouble in Northern Ireland for a long while between the Protestants and Catholics, but by this time it was getting much worse. On 9 August, the Northern Ireland government brought in a law that allowed people suspected of being terrorists to be detained without a trial for as long as was wanted. Within three days, 342 people had been rounded up. None of them were Protestants, so there was uproar and things got much worse, with endless violence and murders. Then it became dangerous in England because there were Irish

Republican Army bombings here. I became worried that the IRA might attack postboxes, as I remembered them doing in 1939. I wondered if they'd put any bombs in the pillar boxes that I collected mail from towards the end of my walks. They never did, but I couldn't imagine the troubles ever finishing.

Jeff had passed his first year exams at the polytechnic and decided to specialize in international relations as the main subject of his degree. I didn't know what that really meant and the title didn't make sense to me. Helen and I didn't know if it would be of any use to him, but we just left him to it, hoping things would turn out okay.

It was reported in the *Sentinel* on 24 September that a motorway was going to be built around Hanley at a cost of £7½ million. It was going to run from Leek Road to Waterloo Road on the west side of the town centre and have a number of flyovers. On the other side of the town, a dual carriageway was planned to run from Waterloo Road to Lichfield Street and the whole thing was being called the Hanley Ringway. I couldn't visualize such a thing and thought it was too much, especially because about 350 houses would have to be demolished. I couldn't see how it would make an improvement. However, the plans were wishful thinking because the motorway never came about, although there's most of a ring road round Hanley now.

On 9 October, Vale played Bolton Wanderers at home and drew 1-1, but the *Sentinel* said the police had had a job keeping the rival supporters apart. Jeff didn't tell us there'd been any problem, so I just hoped he was keeping well away from trouble like that when it happened.

Helen thought we should visit her Uncle Joe and Aunt Florrie because we hadn't seen them for a long time. They still lived at 39 Sussex Road, in Coventry, but we hadn't driven there before and lost our way after having got tangled up with some roadworks. We stopped to ask a man where Sussex Road was and he knew exactly, so we got there without any further trouble and had an hour or two with Uncle Joe and Aunt Florrie. They then pointed us in the right direction towards home and we returned okay.

On 6 November, Aston Villa were in town and Vale drew 4-4 with them. Jeff said it was a very exciting game, but he knew nothing about damage caused in Burslem by the visiting supporters, which was reported in the *Sentinel*. I wondered what the world was coming to when people could behave like that just because of a football match.

In November, the Local Government Reform Bill was being discussed in Parliament. The idea was to get rid of the old county boroughs like Stoke-on-Trent and put their areas under the control of the counties. So it was proposed that Staffordshire County Council should take over the main powers in the Potteries. Not surprisingly, the leaders of the city council were up in arms about it, but there wasn't anything they could do. I didn't agree with it either because we should have been sorting out our own situations, not being put in with other places miles away and run from Stafford. The bill was passed by Parliament in 1972 and the county council took over on 1 April 1974. After they'd done so, I can't say I noticed things were any different and in 1998 Stoke-on-Trent got its main powers back, so it was all a waste of time.

Earlier in the year, I'd given Jeff a few driving lessons in our car and Helen and I had then paid for him to have more with the British School of Motoring. He'd passed his test at his first attempt, but I think he then became increasingly frustrated with not having a car as time went by.

On 10 December, after Helen and I had gone to bed, Jeff woke me up and asked if he could borrow the car because he wanted to run a girl he knew from the polytechnic (Gill Hirst) to 7 Silverton Close, in Bradwell, where she lived. They could have been halfway there if they'd walked it from Hanley, where he'd met her, but I suppose he wanted to impress her. I was annoyed at being awakened, as was Helen, and I refused permission. I thought of the annoyance that would have been caused to people when they heard an engine starting up and further noise when the car returned.

One of the problems I'd had when I'd been decorating was that the paint tended to drip and so it would get all over the place if I wasn't careful. But in December, I thought I'd try some nondrip gloss paint, which I'd heard about, so I got some Dulux Super 3 and painted the lounge and kitchen woodwork with it. I found it to be an improvement, but it wasn't perfect because the paint could still drip, so I still had to be careful that it didn't happen.

On 5 January 1972, Jeff bought a 1964 Mini from Rex Downing, one of his colleagues in the City Treasurer's Department, where he'd been working during the Christmas holiday. He was cheated because the chap asked him for £170, which was too much because the car didn't look roadworthy at all. So he was taken advantage of, though it was partly his own fault because he was so eager to get a car that he didn't stop to think about what he was buying or to get advice. He rushed to cash some of his National Savings Certificates and hand the money over to the fellow, who must have been laughing!

On 29 January, Helen and I went to Lynn Middleton's wedding at the Church of St. Michael and All Angels, in St. Michael's Road, Great Chell. As usual at such events, I filmed scenes before and after the ceremony. Lynn married Alfie Halliburton, who was a computer analyst at ICL (International Computers Limited), in West Avenue, Butt Lane. Alfie's father's side of the family came from Jamaica, which was ironic because Lynn's father, Elijah, didn't like coloured people! He'd picked up the white attitudes to the natives when he'd been in South Africa in the war and he'd brought that home with him. Then his daughter got involved with this person of mixed race! Elijah didn't talk to me about that, but I suppose his view softened as a result.

Around that time, Helen and I started to take Mandy and Matthew Poole out for runs in our car on Saturday afternoons. We mainly went around the Peak District, especially to a brook near Earl Sterndale, in Derbyshire, which Matthew loved and called 'Splish Splash'! I think he called it that because he paddled in it and he recognized it from that name whenever we mentioned it.

Stoke won the Football League Cup on 4 March by beating Chelsea 2-1 at Wembley Stadium in front of a crowd of 100,000, to lift a major trophy for the first time in their history. Helen and I went to Stoke the day after to welcome the players back. I took my movie camera to record them as they came past us in their tour bus. Along with thousands of other people, we waited for them in Wharf Street, which was later obliterated to make way for the A 500. After a while, news got around that our victorious team would be late, but we still hung on. Darkness fell, but eventually a police car appeared and the team rolled by. I attempted to shoot some film, but it wasn't successful and, when it was developed, all we could see were flashing lights! The following night, the *Sentinel* reported that at least 250,000 people had lined the 8½-mile victory parade route from Barlaston to Kingsway, in Stoke, making it the biggest ever turnout in North Staffordshire.

One day, Helen and I thought we'd give Mandy and Matthew a treat. It seemed as if they'd never had a train ride and Matthew had never been on a bus! They'd always moved about by car, which seemed strange to us because at their ages we'd never been in one. I drove Helen and the children to Alsager Station, where they got on a train to Stoke and I waved them off. I then drove to Stoke to pick them up, as arranged, and parked opposite the station entrance, but they weren't there. So I asked the ticket collector if the train had come in and he told me it had and that it had gone out again. I asked if he'd seen a woman and two children come through the barrier and he said 'No.' I then asked if there'd been an accident further up the line and he again said 'No.' I didn't know what to think because the instructions I'd given Helen were simple.

I waited for perhaps half an hour, thinking they'd turn up, but they didn't. So I rang Harry and Gill, but they hadn't seen them either. Harry and Gill weren't in the least concerned and told me Helen and the kids would be alright, but I was worried about the mystery. I waited a while longer and then drove home, where I found them all! Helen said that, as soon as the train had pulled out, Matthew had got terribly upset, probably because he'd never been in one before, and she hadn't been able to pacify him. She'd been forced to take him off the train at Kidsgrove, the next station, where they'd got on a bus. Although Matthew had continued to cry a lot, they'd got to Hanley and then walked down to Leek Road. I was very relieved, having lost somebody else's kids!

Two or three weeks later, Harry and his family went to Switzerland on holiday and they set off on the train from Stoke. We went along to wave them off and wondered how Matthew would react. We came away speculating as to whether they'd all have to get off at the next station, but we later learned that Matthew had been no trouble!

Harry and Gill were fortunate in having Harry's parents to look after their shop when they went on holiday. Some newsagents were reluctant to go away because it was hard to get someone who could be trusted to run their business and look after the cash.

Helen and I were still going to Shelton Club for a drink on Saturday nights and walked there because it wasn't very far. Our friends, Les and Joan, insisted on running us home in their car, even though we protested against it because we dreaded it as Les usually had pretty fair to drink. One night, he was driving us along Avenue Road, but didn't stop at the junction with College Road and drove straight across, even though he didn't have right of way. Luckily, there was no traffic coming. Another time, we came across a police car attending to an incident. Les quickly drove his car down a side street because he didn't wish to be breathalysed. Eventually, we managed to persuade him that we didn't mind walking home.

One night, someone used a bolt cutter on the locks of the Trentmill Road garages, including mine, and broke in. Helen and I didn't know anything about it until one of the victims informed us and told us that our garage doors had been left open. Fortunately, our car was undamaged and nothing had been stolen from it, although things had been taken from other garages.

One Sunday morning, a policeman knocked on our front door and wanted to know whose Mini was parked outside. We had to tell him that it was our son's and he asked why a road licence wasn't being displayed. I said I didn't know, but that there was one. As we were talking by the car, Jeff's face appeared at the front bedroom window and the policeman beckoned him to come out, which he did in quick time! The policeman asked him where his disc was, so Jeff opened the car door and found it on the floor of the vehicle. It must have fallen off the windscreen. He then gave Jeff a lecture about not displaying the disc and the poor and dirty state of the car. It was the Mini's appearance that had caused the policeman to look around in the first place and the incident was humiliating for us because the neighbours would have been looking at the scene. Helen and I gave Jeff a good talking to when he got back in the house, but he was defiant and cocky, even though he was a bit sheepish!

In July, Helen and I went to Scotland and the Lake District for our holidays, but Jeff stopped at home. First, we headed for Portpatrick, in Galloway, which I'd been told was wonderful and the nearest place on the British mainland to Ireland. (Actually, the Mull of Kintyre is closer.) We had a nice, steady journey to the border and turned left at Gretna onto the A 75. We passed through Dumfries, Castle Douglas and Newton Stewart and found nice accommodation some miles from Portpatrick. We went on to the village the following day and spent a pleasant morning there. It was lovely watching the waves dashing over the rocks and the boats in the sea. We saw something swimming out of the water and, for a second, I thought it was a seal, but it was a dog!

After a while, we moved on and took the A 712 to New Galloway and then the A 702 to Thornhill, which was a one-horse town. We found accommodation in the main street, but we didn't like it much.

The next morning, we motored towards and then past Glasgow and crossed the Clyde on the Erskine Bridge, which had only been open for a year. We continued to Loch Lomond and found a suitable B & B at Balloch – Fiveways, on Drymen Road. Then we sat and watched a paddle steamer, the Maid of the Loch, take passengers for a trip on the loch. I liked Balloch. It was like an English seaside town in its atmosphere.

The next day, we moved on towards Oban and, some miles before we got there, booked in at the same place in Taynuilt that we'd done on our last visit to Scotland. We then drove into Oban and wandered down to the docks, where we watched a ship, flying a Royal Mail flag, unloading mail and fish. Nearby, a gull was pecking at a fish and dragging it along the dock side. Maybe it had stolen its prize from a crate! For a change, we had a meal in one of the restaurants. Later, we sat on the rather poor beach and watched a large ferry going past, towards the docks. I suppose it had been on a trip to one of the islands.

We then drove east, on the A 85 and A 82, to Crianlarich, which was in a very mountainous area. We stopped just before we got there and I filmed a train, high on the hillside, travelling south from Fort William. In the background was Ben More, which was 3,852 feet high, and it still had a large patch of snow near its summit, even though it was the summer.

We carried on going south and decided to head to the Lake District. There, we stayed a couple of nights at The Marshalls, a B & B in a detached house at Ruthwaite, south of Ireby, which became a Grade II listed building in 1986. The couple who owned it, Joyce and Cyril Hood, made us most welcome. Cyril was an ex-policeman and they kept goats. At night, we went for a drink in Ireby, where there was on old steamroller dumped on a spare piece of land. There was also a small, old Aspatria Industrial Co-operative Society store, which we heard was going to be converted into a bungalow. That intrigued us and we said we'd come back to see the result, which we did in 1977.

Jeff was informed by the Education Department of his money award for his final year of studying at the polytechnic. The total amount had risen, to £364.80, but his grant from them, of £201.80, was slightly less than that in his first year. That was because the contribution from Helen and me had gone up, to £163, perhaps because we were earning more by then.

On 28 July, Jeff celebrated his 21st birthday. I didn't particularly regard it as being an event out of the ordinary, but Helen and I sent him a greetings telegram, wishing him 'happiness and success for the future'. We bought him an Accurist gold automatic watch, which wound up from the movement of the hand when being worn, so it didn't need any batteries. We also paid for the hire of an upstairs room at The Observatory, in Bucknall Old Road, Hanley, so that he could have a party with his friends in the student pub that he went to regularly.

In August, Helen and I had a trip to Bamford, in Derbyshire, where there was a lovely rose garden, which was open to the public. I think we paid to go in and Helen enjoyed it very much. We also had a look at the nearby Ladybower Reservoir, which was beautiful with its big stretch of water and woods.

The same month, we took Mandy and Matthew to Chester, where we had a stroll along the side of the River Dee. Afterwards, we went to the zoo and had a good look around. Most of the species that had been there on our previous visit were still to be seen. The kids were amazed at the sight of an orang-utan and there was a lovely show of begonias. Also, we watched the elephants, one of which extended its trunk towards Matthew, who was alarmed and ran off!

Jeff couldn't believe his ears when he heard that Vale had lost 7-0 at Rotherham on 26 August! He was even more amazed when they won their next five league games and were top of the table in the middle of September. He was certainly finding it interesting following the team at that time!

Helen persuaded me to get my cine camera out again to shoot scenes at another wedding of a Swinnerton's office girl. This time it was Carol Dale, the directors' secretary, who married Clive Hassall, a caster from Etruria, at St. Mary's Church, in Bucknall, on 16 September. I dutifully did my usual sequences!

Helen and I bought a song by Faron Young, which we were keen on at that time, called *It's Four in the Morning*. It was about an on-off love affair and reached number three in the charts. It was sentimental and a lot of our generation seemed to go for songs like that.

One day, after I'd been delivering the post in Abbey Hulton, I was waiting in Leek Road for a bus back to the sorting office. A Rolls-Royce pulled up by the bus stop and a voice said, 'Get in then!' I looked up and realized it was the Lord Mayor, Bill Austin! So I got in and I thought the chauffeur would drop me off outside the Post Office, but he drove right to the loading bay. I was expecting there to be postmen working there and that they'd come crowding round, asking me what had happened and then spread the news, but there wasn't a soul about! I had to go to find some of them and tell them, but they didn't seem to think much of the story.

I was shocked to hear that Stoke's goalkeeper, Gordon Banks, had been seriously injured in a car accident in Whitmore Road, Trentham, on 22 October. His car windscreen had shattered and he was taken to the Infirmary for an emergency operation to remove splintered glass from his head and right eye. He was in hospital for three weeks and his eye was permanently damaged, so that he never played professional football in England again. It was a great shame.

The trouble in Northern Ireland was at its height this year and it was in the news a lot. On 10 November, there was a wave of letter bombs in London, which was worrying in case it spread here, to Stoke-on-Trent. I was handling a lot of letters every day and wondered if I might get injured or killed or whether my job could be at risk if the bombing increased and the Post Office closed because of postmen being too afraid to go to work. As it turned out, I needn't have worried because such bombs were never used in Stoke.

One day, when Helen and I visited Harry and Gill, I was persuaded to take out Hans, their Rottweiler dog, for a walk to the top of Greasley Road because they were busy in their shop. In fact, the dog took *me* for a walk! Because he was so big and strong, he pulled me all over the place and I was tempted to let go of his lead. But I thought, if I did, he might run across a road and get injured and I'd get in trouble. So I kept hold, but I was thankful when I got the disobedient dog back to his owners.

Another time, when we were leaving from visiting Harry and Gill, I put one of my hands out to stroke Hans's head, but he made a grab for my hand. My skin wasn't broken, but my bones became bruised and my hand hurt for days afterwards, though the Pooles weren't very concerned.

On 20 December, it was the silver wedding anniversary of Helen's cousin, Edith, and her husband, Jack Elson. Helen, Jeff and I were invited to their celebration at their home, at 96 Eastbourne Road, in Northwood. It was a good party with plenty of drink to be had! Jack had been a projectionist at one or two local picture palaces, including The Abbey Cinema in Leek Road, Abbey Hulton, and later became a driver for Securicor.

At the end of December, Harold Bentley asked Helen and me if we'd like to rent the garage at his house (141 Ridgway Road). He was asking for two pounds a calendar month, whereas I was paying eleven shillings a week for my council garage. Harold's house was a lot nearer and he'd also be able to keep an eye on things, so I accepted his offer and moved my car in on 1 January 1973, the same day that Britain joined the Common Market.

Jeff had started going out with a girl from Stanfield, Pat Clarke, who lived at 12 Norris Road. On 18 January, they had a mix-up and she came to our house to see where he was. He wasn't in and Helen answered the door, but she got into an argument with the girl, which didn't go down very well with us.

I didn't come into contact with Pat very much, but she didn't seem to be the kind of girl that I'd have liked around and Helen had the same opinion as me. I didn't like her behaviour and I thought she might lead Jeff astray.

On 28 January, I went to a charity football match at the Red Cow ground in Werrington and filmed some of it. Gordon Banks was playing on the right wing for a representative eleven. Although he was still recovering from his road accident, he made a big effort by turning out to play for charity. Young Harry was also involved in the game.

Aunt Florrie Bryant had stopped being able to look after herself in 1970 and had become a resident of Leek Moorlands Hospital, in Ashbourne Road, Leek. Because of her advanced age, the *Sentinel* and the *Leek Post & Times* printed a photo and a report on her a few times. I went to see her on odd occasions, but she didn't know who I was. I explained and she said, 'Oh, yes, Cyril,' and seemed to grasp it, but then a short while after, she again asked who I was. Jeff was with me at least once and he found it quite amusing!

About that time, Helen and I had a letter from Tony Thorndike, one of Jeff's lecturers at the polytechnic and his degree course organizer. It said he was concerned about Jeff, who was running the students' union entertainments and wasn't attending to his studies as much as he had done. We had a word with Jeff about it, although I don't think it made much difference.

Vale were in the hunt for promotion to the Second Division and Jeff was amongst their 2,000 supporters who went to cheer the team on to a 3-2 win at Shrewsbury Town on 27 March. One of Jeff's old friends, Alan Challinor, had walked all the way there to raise money for the club's Buy A Player Fund!

On 1 April, the government brought in a new tax, VAT, on things that were being sold. We were told it was part of going into the Common Market, but I thought it was another way of getting money out of people. It was the same old talk and we had to pay out regardless of what we thought. People have always had to pay too much.

Vale were still in with a chance of going up when they played at home to Bolton Wanderers, who were already the champions of the Third Division, on Easter Monday. Vale were winning 2-0 thirteen minutes from the end of the match in front of a crowd of 14,168, but ended up drawing 2-2, which finished their hopes of promotion. Jeff wasn't very pleased and said there'd been a lot of trouble at the game. The *Sentinel* reported that 'rival fans caused havoc' and threw 'half-bricks at each other and the police'. Also, the newspaper said that the different groups of supporters on the Bycars End, which was where Jeff stood, had had to be separated by police dogs. Helen and I were worried that Jeff would end up in trouble, but Vale built a steel fence at the Bycars End and from then on supporters were stopped from moving around the ground. Things seemed to quieten down after that.

The numbers of fish in the oceans were reducing because there'd been too much fishing. Iceland relied on fish and decided to extend its sole rights to fish from twelve to fifty miles from its shore. That meant that foreign trawlers were supposed to keep out, but our boats carried on fishing there. So the Icelanders sent in patrol boats to harass our ships. On 19 May, it was in the news that we'd sent three frigates to protect our trawlers and a struggle followed, which became known as the Second Cod War. It's hard to say who was right and who was wrong, but I remember the little country rebelling against us and it was dodgy sending the frigates in because it made us look like bullies. I wondered if it was going to lead to a full-scale war and the Yanks wouldn't have liked that. I wanted it to be smoothed out peacefully and in November an agreement was reached, which gave us limited fishing rights in the Icelandic zone. There was another "war" with Iceland over a similar problem from 1975 to 1976 and that ended up with them having sole fishing rights for 200 miles out. So it seemed as if they'd beaten us, which was remarkable, really!

Fortunately, when Jeff's exams started approaching, he buckled down and got on with his work, revising for them. He had to take eight exams overall, which was a lot, but then he was studying for a degree.

On 7 June, he left home. I don't think he'd been very happy living with Helen and me for a while, but he hadn't realized how lucky he'd been. He didn't know what he wanted to do and we didn't know where he'd gone. His friend, Paul Lewis, told us he'd moved to 37 Sheppard Street, in Stoke, to rent the house with a friend from the polytechnic, Stewart Merricks. After a few days, I called round and asked Jeff to come back home. The house was a bit rough and he seemed to be unhappy, but he said, 'Leave me alone, Dad.' After a while, he said he'd come back, so I left relieved because I didn't like seeing him unhappy.

Jeff had a tiny kitten in his bedroom, which was the only bit of comfort he'd got, and I don't think he was fitting in too well with the other fellow. Jeff wanted to bring the kitten home with him, but Helen and I couldn't have done with having a cat about the house, so he came back without it. He settled in again after that.

On 30 June, the 1st Battalion of the Staffordshire Regiment Band played for about half an hour in front of several hundred people in Hanley Park. I filmed the band beating the retreat, which involved playing their instruments and marching and interweaving at the same time, but it wasn't outstanding like I'd expected.

Helen and I had seen something in the press about Wester Ross in Scotland and it looked attractive, so we thought we'd go there in July for our summer holidays. We mentioned it to Jack and Flo, who decided to go with us. That couldn't have happened previously because Helen and Jack couldn't both have had the same time off with them being co-bosses at Swinnerton's. However, Jack had retired in June. He'd told the other directors he wouldn't work a day after his 65th birthday and he'd kept on repeating the statement. Helen told me that really he would have loved to have stayed on, even if it had been only part time. The directors would no doubt have asked him to carry on, but he'd talked himself out of a job!

We took both cars on holiday because they gave us more room to pack our things. We went in convoy, with Jack and Flo in the lead, because Flo liked being the navigator and ruled the roost, but I took over when she got fed up! We had a straightforward run and stopped at a parking place a few miles from Callander. The River Teith was running by and tumbled over rocks. It was a lovely sight to behold while we had a brew and something to eat.

We then drove into Callander, where we found a very good B & B called Rock Villa. That was one of the best places we ever stayed and was a cottage next door to Arden House, where much of *Dr. Finlay's Casebook* had been filmed. We had a look around the town, which was nice, and had a drink at one of the pubs.

In the morning, we went north on the A 84 and came to Killin, where we stayed for the night. We wandered around the village and found it was a beautiful little place, with a number of shops. We stood on the bridge and watched and heard the river thundering over the rocks in the spectacular Dochart Falls.

The next day, we drove northeastwards on the A 827, which ran along Loch Tay, and towering above us was Ben Lawers, 3,984 feet high. At the end of the loch, we came to Kenmore, where we watched some water skiing. We then carried on till we reached the A 9, where we turned left and drove to Pitlochry. There, we watched a fellow land a big fish, which I assumed was a salmon because of its size. We then went into an unobtrusive building, which had a glass viewing window of part of the fish ladder that every salmon had to pass through to get up the River Tummel, past Pitlochry Dam. Through the window, I saw one or two of them going up, which was very interesting. There was also a fish counter, to monitor the salmon for scientific purposes.

A few miles up the road, we came to Blair Castle, which was a beautiful place, all gleaming white. We saw an old cannon outside and there was a peacock glaring at us. There were some horses in a field and Flo attempted to feed them. She fancied herself in handling horses.

Further up the road, we turned onto the A 889 and then the A 86, which brought us to Spean Bridge. There, we turned right onto the A 82, which took us to the Commando Memorial and then Invergarry. We turned left at that point and soon came to Loch Garry, where we pulled up to stretch our legs and admire the glorious view.

We were then on the A 87 and looking for somewhere to stay because we'd been on the move for quite a long while and time was getting on. Helen liked to book into a B & B in the afternoon, when it was easy to get fixed up, but Flo preferred to leave it till later, when there'd be less chance of finding somewhere. She'd even said that she wouldn't mind sleeping in the back of the car. I didn't fancy that because it wouldn't have been very comfortable for me in the front seats of our car! This particular day, we were struggling to see anywhere to stay and we were almost about to give up hope when we finally came upon a B & B a few miles from Kyle of Lochalsh. It was very welcome, even though the owner was pretty strict. Afterwards, Helen referred to her as 'the sergeant major'!

After breakfast, we made our way to Kyle of Lochalsh and all agreed we'd visit the Isle of Skye. We got on the next ferry and were soon across the half-a-mile strait. We drove on a few miles and then stopped, got our chairs out and sat down. We hadn't been there long before Helen was bitten, we thought by a horsefly, on her left leg. There were plenty of them about and she wanted to get away from them, so we packed our things away and went back to the ferry. Her leg was swelling up, so we took her to the local doctor in Kyle of Lochalsh. He looked at the swelling and asked if she'd been in contact with anyone suffering from chickenpox. She said she hadn't, as far as she knew, but he gave her an injection in her bottom and put a bandage on her leg. She asked if there was anything she could do to prevent any further bites and he told her to try different kinds of fly repellant and to keep away from places where horseflies were, which was easier said than done in Scotland!

Helen said she'd be alright, so we decided to carry on with our tour, but, as the days went by, the area around her bite got harder. She suffered pain all through the rest of the holiday and her leg still wasn't right when we got home.

From Kyle of Lochalsh, we took a minor road north and, after a few miles, came to Plockton, which was on the coast in a bay, where yachts were sailing around. It was a beautiful spot, but the little post office was a broken-down place. There were palm trees growing and I was amazed that they survived so far north. I'd read in a magazine that Wester Ross had a mild climate, but I hadn't expected to see the palms! We parked right by the sea and had a meal with a view!

After a while, we moved on to Gairloch, which was further north and a small fishing port. We found a decent B & B, which had a toilet seat that felt warm to the touch because it was made of foam or that type of thing. We went out to the quayside to watch fish being unloaded and Helen picked two of them up, each about a foot long, and held them high, just like you see fishermen do on pictures!

Near to was Inverewe Gardens, which was well worth a visit. Subtropical plants were being grown in the mild climate and the locals we met said they hardly ever had any snow! It was remarkable. I particularly remember a tree in the gardens, with its bark partly stripped off in layers, showing different colours in the wood underneath.

Further along the road, we stopped in a lay-by, with a good view of Gruinard Bay. It was a beautiful spot and I took a panorama shot of it with my cine camera.

We then carried on, on the A 832, to Braemore Junction. Shortly before we got there, we parked for a while at a wonderful viewpoint down to Loch Broom in the distance. While we were there, we kidded Flo to bend down and touch her toes, just to see her reaction. As she was proving that she could still do it, I took a movie shot of the incident and, because her dress was fairly short, I captured her knickers on the film!

At the junction, we turned north onto the A 835 and continued until we came to Ullapool, where we found some suitable lodgings. We then went to look at the town and especially the boats at the quayside. Ullapool was a lovely place, jutting out into Loch Broom and I took a film looking down at it from the road above.

In the morning, we headed north on the A 835 and, after about three miles, came across Ardmair, a beautiful place, where we stayed for quite a while. There was a lovely curved beach and in the background was a flat-topped mountain, Ben More Coigach. Helen fed some sheep that were wandering along the road and Jack went to the water's edge and started to skim flat stones on its surface, so that they bounced off several times. I thought I'd have a go, but he beat me. He then took his shoes off and had a paddle and I did the same. When I tried to put my shoes on afterwards, my feet wouldn't go into them. I was puzzled and thought my feet must have swollen up in the sea. It was an awful moment and I didn't know what to do, but then I discovered I'd put Jack's shoes on by mistake!

We then started moving south and stopped for a while by a river to pick and eat wild strawberries. Further on, we pulled in by Corrieshalloch Gorge, where there were a couple of bagpipers playing. Jack, Flo and I went onto a bridge, which was limited to six people at a time, and gazed down at the Falls of Measach, a long waterfall in the 200-foot-deep narrow gorge. It was pretty dramatic, but I don't think Helen joined us on the small bridge because she'd have been terrified being suspended in the air like that.

We had some difficulty in finding a B & B for the night and landed back at Spean Bridge, where we were offered a big bedroom, with two double beds, in a bungalow. There didn't seem to be anywhere else available in the district, so, after some discussion, we accepted it. At night, Jack and I waited in the lounge for our wives to get into their respective beds. After a decent interval, we entered the bedroom, requested the women not to look and then quickly donned our pyjamas. In the morning, Jack and I had our wash and shave, dressed and then got out of the way while the good ladies sorted themselves out.

We then set off and made for the Lake District. We arrived at the village of

Braithwaite, near to Keswick, and decided to try the Royal Oak Motel for our accommodation. It wasn't very comfortable and the food was dished out in packs, so we weren't impressed with it.

In the morning, we made our way to Buttermere, over Honister Pass. It was scary because it was very steep and pretty narrow. When we got to Buttermere, we went for a walk, but when we returned, a youth was lying on the bonnet of my car. I said: 'Hey! Get off!' He didn't say anything, but just got off and wandered away. We then sat about and Flo and Jack dangled their feet in the river by the side of the road, while she sang a little tune. Then we packed up and made our way home to Stoke, though Flo insisted that where she and Jack lived at 64 Uplands Croft, in Washerwall, was in the countryside and not a suburb of the Potteries.

Jeff was told that he'd passed his final examinations and achieved a second-class honours degree. On 1 August, he was awarded his certificate by the University of London and so became a Bachelor of Science (Economics). Helen and I were very proud of him.

The swelling on Helen's leg still hadn't gone down, so she went to our doctor's and was given more treatment with antibiotics. The affected area was red and moist, which was supposed to be a sign that it was healing, but months went by before the swelling finally disappeared!

3 Rowing With The Routine

In September 1973, Jeff started to do a Keele University teaching certificate at Crewe College of Education, which was on the outskirts of the town in Crewe Road. Helen and I were happy that he'd decided to go into teaching and things were turning out well. I imagined he'd be alright at it because I thought it would suit his abilities, as long as he was able to cope with the kids.

At first, he rented a room in a house, 159 Ruskin Road, Crewe, to save him driving over to the college every day, but after a while he returned home. I think that was mainly because he had to keep driving back to Stanfield to see Pat. So he was back to square one, but then he palled up with another student, Niall Rogers, who lived in Trent Vale, and they took it in turns to use their cars to go to the college.

It was in the *Sentinel* on 8 October that the government was planning an extra day's public holiday for 1 January, from 1974. That was very good news because we on the Post Office still worked on New Year's Day, even though it was becoming a holiday for more and more people. A lot of people celebrated the arrival of the new year and some of those who were supposed to go to work later the same day weren't in any condition to do so. Therefore, by making the day a public holiday, it made the government look good when they were only jumping on the bandwagon because more and more people were taking time off anyway. I was never bothered about New Year myself, but I was happy to have a rest from going to work when the holiday came about as planned.

Around that time, an Italian lad started working at the Post Office. He was very pleasant, but confided in me that he always carried a knife for self-protection. He didn't show it to me and I don't know if it was because he'd been picked on, but I'd got the impression from newspapers and books that that was normal practice for Italians. I didn't report it and I don't know if he'd have been warned if I had.

On 9 November, Helen and I went to Jeff's polytechnic passing out in the ballroom at Trentham Gardens, but he and some others wouldn't wear a gown for the ceremony. I wasn't too bothered about that because gowns were swanky and seemed ridiculous things to put on. He was also invited to attend one of the university's presentation ceremonies at the Royal Albert Hall, in London, but he decided not to go because he wouldn't have known anybody there.

One of the postmen, Les Pearson, became nicknamed "Paper Roses" after the way he sang the popular song of the time in his broad Bolton accent. During the Second World War, he'd been captured by the Japanese and it's well known that they starved their prisoners. In the compound where Les was, the Japs kept pigs and they were fattened with leftovers and vegetable peelings. As soon as the Japs had left the pigsty, the prisoners got in among the animals and pushed them on one side to eat the choicer bits of the pigswill!

On 1 December, petrol was restricted to only two gallons a time at filling stations in the city, which was a shock. A shortage of fuel had come about because we'd backed the Yanks in supporting Israel in the Yom Kippur War in October against the Arabs. In retaliation, the Arab oil producers decreased their oil supplies to us by 15%. The AA appealed to motorists to reduce their use of petrol and the government issued coupons, although they didn't actually bring rationing in. I didn't use my car regularly and always walked to work, so the shortages didn't affect me. On the 8th, the maximum speed limit was reduced to 50 mph, but that didn't bother me either because I thought it was plenty fast enough anyway.

At the same time that all this was going on, the Arabs increased the price of oil dramatically because they'd got fed up of getting very little for it. They were the main suppliers and by then our economy depended on oil, so we had no choice except to pay up. The price of petrol rocketed and the average cost of a gallon of four star increased from 38.7p in 1973 to 73.2p in 1975! I didn't feel the rise too much myself because most of my motoring was for pleasure at the weekends and it was only when Helen and I went on our summer holidays that I did many miles.

The situation in the country was made worse by the National Union of Mineworkers (NUM) banning overtime and weekend working to back up a pay claim, so that stocks of coal began to run low. To try to make sure that they didn't run out altogether, the government decided that, from 1 January 1974, electricity would be supplied for non-essential workers on only three days each week. Fortunately, getting the mail through was considered to be vital and so the cuts didn't affect my work at the Post Office.

When the three-day week had started, television broadcasts stopped at 10.30 p.m. to save on electricity. People weren't very happy about that, but it didn't bother me much because I was often in bed by then during the week as I still had to get up very early for work a lot of the time.

As part of his college course, Jeff had to go on teaching practice and in January 1974 was sent for two months to St. Joseph's College, a Catholic boys' grammar school in London Road, Trent Vale. That was because he'd put down that he wanted to teach in a college and so he was given quite a lot of sixth form classes. I'd thought it was a real class place, but Jeff told me that some of the younger pupils were troublesome, even after the headmaster had caned them, but Jeff passed his teaching practice okay.

In February, the NUM decided to go on strike in support of their pay claim and the Conservative prime minister, Ted Heath, called a general election for the 28th. I don't think he could have done otherwise. The big unions were pretty cocky because they were strong and they seemed to be dictating things to the country. The Tories used the slogan 'Who governs Britain?' in their election campaign, but Heath didn't seem to be very strong. I voted for the Labour Party because I thought they supported working-class people.

The result of the election was that Labour had four more MPs than the Conservatives, but the party was in a minority overall. Its leader, Harold Wilson, still became the prime minister, but he didn't seem any stronger than Ted Heath. Wilson offered the NUM pay increases of up to 35%, which, of course, they accepted and the country went back to a full working week. It seemed like a fiddle because as soon as Labour got in power, the strike ended. It was as if it had been arranged because most trade unionists were Labour supporters and I suppose they wanted to make a laughing stock of the Conservatives.

It was on the television and in the newspapers that a Japanese soldier, Lieutenant Hiroo Onada, had been roaming about on Lubang Island, in the Philippines, still fighting the Second World War on his own and nobody had been able to get him to surrender. Eventually, his commanding officer from the war,

Major Taniguchi, had to be brought over to order him to give in, which he did on 9 March 1974, over 28 years after the war had ended! He was a hero and I admired him for sticking it out for all that time, but I was intrigued because I couldn't see the reason for him carrying on when he could have been sleeping in a nice soft bed. Surely it had entered his head that the war was over, but perhaps he was trying to win it on his own! It brought memories back to me about my time in the army and how I could have been killed if things had turned out differently, especially if I'd had to face fanatics like Onada in Burma.

Jeff was still seeing his girlfriend, Pat, and they were out together most of the time, but they seemed to be having quite a lot of arguments. One day, he told me she'd slapped him across the face when he was driving and I was worried about how it would all turn out.

Aunt Florrie Bryant was going to be 100 on 13 April and Helen thought she should have a visit from the Stoke-on-Trent Lord Mayor, Arthur Cotton. Helen wanted the glamour of asking, but wasn't very good at writing letters, so I sent a request in her name. By the time I posted the letter, it was already too late and the reply from the Lord Mayor's Parlour, on 25 March, told Helen that he wouldn't be able to pay a visit because he'd be in Germany on Aunt Florrie's birthday, but he did send her a congratulatory telegram. She finally died in 1976, aged 102.

In April, I put emulsion on the ceilings and walls of our bedrooms and later did the same in our lounge and kitchen. That was something I did almost every year because of the continuing problem with soot from our coal fire. That was in spite of the fact that we still normally had our chimney swept every year.

On 13 April, Helen and I attended the wedding of her niece, Helen Asher, at the Church of St. James the Great, in Clayton Road, Clayton. She married Derek Stubbings, a bearings salesman, and an old Rolls-Royce was used to take her to the church and to drive them both off afterwards. Helen wore a broad-brimmed white hat, which was very smart. The reception was held at the Dick Turpin Hotel, in Gallowstree Lane, Westlands, and, of course, I took some cine shots of the whole occasion.

Helen and Derek later got divorced and Helen remarried on 19 September 1992 at Newcastle Register Office, at 20 Sidmouth Avenue. Her second husband was Charles Sargent, a Michelin casings warehouse manager, who was from Basford.

The following month, Helen and I drove to Coventry to see Uncle Joe and Aunt Florrie, which we did from time to time. We used to go on spec because they didn't have a phone and neither did we, but they always seemed to be in when we got there.

It was Lucy Dean's seventieth birthday on 18 May and celebrations were held at Scotia Club, which was in Scotia Road, Burslem, near to her home. Helen and I went on the bus, to boost the numbers. Unless we were going on a trip, we didn't use our car because our garage was away from our house and, in any case, unlike many people, I never drove when I was going to have a drink. I thought it was important to have a clear head when I was driving and since 1967 there'd been a legal limit to the amount of alcohol that could be drunk when doing so.

There was an announcement from the stage, by the club chairman, about Lucy's notable occasion and everybody then sang 'Happy birthday'. That kind of thing was quite normal in working men's clubs. When the night had finished, Helen and I got a taxi home.

Flo and Jack had suggested that the four of us should book a holiday in a caravan in Devon and Helen and I had agreed. We set off on the M 6, on 19 May, with Jack leading the way, as usual. He was an excellent driver, but he hadn't got much idea about navigation, so he relied on Flo to do that job. We got on the M5, which soon reduced to two lanes and that seemed strange. The motorway ended just before Bristol and the extension over the Avonmouth Bridge was about to be opened, so we were shuffled around on some ordinary roads. Flo had wanted to take us over the 245-feet-high Clifton Suspension Bridge, but we missed it and finished further up the River Avon. Flo pointed out the bridge to us and, when she saw it, Helen was glad we'd missed it. Looking up at it, it did seem a terrifying height above the river!

Flo then led us to Cheddar Gorge, in the Mendip Hills, which was quite impressive. We drove into it on the B 3135, which ran along the bottom of it. The gorge was almost 450 feet deep at its maximum and the limestone cliffs on the southern side of it were nearly vertical. Of course, we made a stop there and got our chairs out so that we could sit and admire the scenery.

After a while, we carried on towards our destination and came to the village of Dunster, near to Minehead, in Somerset. It seemed an interesting place, so we stopped to have a look around, even though it was raining. It had a beautiful main street, with a covered market place in the middle, and on the hill behind was a castle.

Finally, we arrived at Mortehoe Caravan and Camping Park, at Twitchen House, in Mortehoe. We reported to the site office and were directed to our caravan. Helen and I had never had a holiday in such accommodation and we were apprehensive about it. The caravan was very nice, large and supposed to sleep six, but we felt rather cramped. It was alright for a single family, but I didn't think there was enough privacy for separate families. Anyway, it was an experience.

We unloaded our cars, settled in and then drove to nearby Woolacombe, where there was a huge stretch of sand. It was there that I saw what appeared to be an early attempt at hang-gliding. In the distance, someone ran down a hillside, holding onto a large kite, but it was unsuccessful because he didn't get airborne.

We then returned to the caravan, where we had to decide who'd have the double bed and who'd have the two single beds. The site had a social club, with an alcohol licence, and I asked Jack if he cared to go there with me for a drink, but he declined, so I went on my own.

In the morning, the ladies prepared the breakfast and afterwards Jack and I went to the village bakery to get some fresh bread. We all then had a drive to look at the scenery. We came to Lee, which was a lovely little village just around the coast, with some thatched cottages. There was also a sand and pebble beach, with large rocks, where Jack indulged in his stone-skimming game.

After that, we went back to the caravan, where Flo made us some soup. We then visited Lynmouth, where the flood disaster had occurred in 1952. We had a look at the marker, which gave the height of the water as it had thundered down the Lyn gorge that August night. However, looking at the small river running by, it was impossible to imagine the force of the water moving huge boulders and sweeping cars away.

We then drove up to Lynton, which was perched on a cliff high above Lynmouth, and from there we went west for about half a mile to the spectacular Valley of Rocks. It ran above the coast and was very rugged, so we decided to have a walk down it.

We travelled on to nearby Watersmeet, where the East Lyn River was joined by Hoar Oak Water. It was a beautiful spot, with a lot of little waterfalls, so we stopped for a wander round and walked over the two bridges over the rivers.

After that, we took the A 39 and then the A 399, which brought us to Combe Martin, a seaside village, which had a very long main street. We went down to the beach and I filmed some boats in the bay. We then called in at Ilfracombe, which was further along the road and was busy.

After we'd got back to the caravan, there was a knock on the door, which I answered. Standing there was the owner, who said he had some bad news for Mrs Kent. It seemed that Young Harry had sent a message to the effect that Elijah had died. I thanked the fellow and passed on the information to Helen, who'd already got the gist of the story. We were shocked and, after some discussion, Helen said she wished to go home. I told her that there was nothing we could do to help, but she was insistent on making the journey back. Because of the lateness of the hour, we decided to travel the following day.

In the morning, we packed our belongings, said goodbye to our friends and set off for Stoke. It wasn't exactly a happy journey and we drove straight to Vera's house, 208 Greasley Road (where she and Harry had moved to about five years before). She told us that Elijah had been at work in Chester on the 20th when he'd suddenly had a heart attack and died. He'd been having treatment from his doctor, who, apparently, had made light of the pains Elijah was having in his chest and told him that he had indigestion. Elijah's funeral service was on 24 May at Central Methodist Church, in Madison Street, Tunstall, and afterwards he was buried in Carmountside Cemetery.

Helen started complaining to me about a security light being left on all the time on the side of the building directly across the road from us. It was owned by Post Office Telecommunications and seemed to be pointing at us, rather than down towards the ground. It was shining through our lounge windows into Helen's eyes when she was watching the television and reading, but it didn't affect me as much because my chair was at a different angle from it. I didn't want to bother doing anything about it, but Helen wanted me to do something. So I wrote to the area office, at 35 Stafford Street, in Hanley, and their Executive Engineer, Mr C. Bell, replied on 21 June. He said he'd told his staff to mask the part of the light facing us and they'd blocked out the centre part of it, but a thin strip all the way round was left shining, so it wasn't much better.

Helen and I were invited to the twenty-first birthday party of Edith and Jack Elson's daughter, Susan, at their home on 15 June. Included amongst the guests was a well-to-do man, Edward McCombe, whom Edith cleaned for. She told us he had some beautiful furniture in his home, at 187 Greasley Road, but he didn't have a wife or any near relatives. Helen used to tell Edith that she'd be left his whole estate, but Edith ridiculed her statement. Helen was eventually proved right because Mr McCombe died in 1977 and Edith got most of his assets.

Edith's brother, Ken Johns, was at Susan's party and he was still quite a ladies' man, chatting them up and putting on the style. The party was very successful, there being plenty of drinks, but Jack seemed intent on pushing drink onto Helen, I think on purpose to get her drunk. He kept saying, 'Do you want another drink, Helen?'

It seemed as if Edith was joining in as well, so I don't know if they were conspiring. Then I said, 'I think you've had enough,' but Helen insisted on having another one.

I wanted to get her home and fortunately Jeff dropped in and volunteered to run us back in his Mini, which was still on the road! When she got home, Helen wanted another drink, but I said: 'No! You'd better get off to bed!' She did do and was alright.

Another night, when we were watching the television, Helen had a bottle of whisky on the hearth. She must have kept drinking because she later started talking in a slurred way, so I said: 'You're drinking too much there. You've had enough!' I took the bottle away and she must have been drunk because I had a job getting her upstairs to bed. Then, in the middle of the night, she got up to go to the toilet, but couldn't make it and just stooped down and urinated on the carpet by her side of the bed! I couldn't get any sense out of her, but the next day she couldn't remember what had happened. There wasn't another incident, but I had to keep an eye on things after that.

Helen and I decided to have a tour of South Wales with the Hodgkisses in July because our earlier holiday had been cut short. We drove to Leominster, in Herefordshire, where Jack did a U-turn and went the wrong way up a one-way street and I followed because I didn't want to lose him! The traffic was very heavy and everybody was looking at us. Then a police car came towards us and I thought we'd be copped, but the driver looked away, pretending he hadn't seen us! We kept on driving and eventually sorted ourselves out.

We motored on to Saundersfoot, in Pembrokeshire, which had a lovely sandy beach, and there we found a B & B, named Leecroft, to stay at. We then had a look at Tenby, which was a classy seaside resort. We took a boat trip from there to Caldey Island, where there was a monastery run by a group of Trappist monks, but we didn't see any of them.

On returning, we went to Lydstep and paid a fee to go onto a private beach, which was very nice. We then moved on along the coast and had a look at the thousands of marvellous lilies, in the lakes on the Stackpole Estate, which were in flower. We carried on to nearby St Govan's, where we went down a lot of steps from a cliff to a tiny chapel built on some rocks by the sea. A mile or so inland was the small village of Bosherton and we decided to stop there for a while. All of a sudden, hundreds of horseflies swarmed around us and we dived back in our cars to escape them! We'd heard about Elegug Stacks, which were a few miles away, so we drove there and walked along the cliffs to see them. They were two huge isolated limestone pillars in the sea, which had become detached from the cliffs behind them.

We then drove north to Pembroke Dock, where we got a ferry across Milford Haven, which was a wide waterway. We moved on to St David's, in the far west of Wales, where we got a B & B. While we were there, we had a tour around the cathedral and the ruined Bishop's Palace.

The next day, we worked our way up the magnificent Pembrokeshire coast and had wonderful views of the cliffs as we went along. We moved on to New Quay and, although it was raining when we arrived there, we got out to have a look at the harbour and Dolau Beach.

We then continued up the coast, through Aberystwyth, to Aberdovey. That was a very nice seaside town and we found a B & B there for the night on 12 July. We had a walk to the harbour and then sat on a bench on the sea front admiring the lovely scenery, but we wore our coats because it was chilly. Unfortunately, Helen had to go to see a doctor while we were there because she was being troubled by a bite on her right arm, which may have come from a horsefly at Bosherton. She usually had a fairly serious reaction to insect bites, but it seemed to be a hazard of going on holiday.

The next day, we drove to Fairbourne, on the opposite side of the Mawddach estuary from Barmouth. The miniature railway was still running and I filmed it and the lovely view across to Barmouth. Flo wanted to get another B & B, in Barmouth, but Helen felt she wanted to go home. I'd have liked to have stayed longer, but Helen always wanted to get back home as soon as she'd gone anywhere! So we started off towards Stoke, but spent some time at Bala Lake, sitting on our deck chairs, watching boats and people go by. We had a picnic while we were there, although we had to wrap up because there was a strong wind blowing, which made the water on the lake choppy. When we'd finished the picnic, we packed the things away and made the final run home, where we arrived in the evening.

As Helen and I looked up at our house, we noticed that there seemed to be a party going on. Jeff had stayed at home and, when we looked through a window into the lounge, we found that there really was a party in the house! We were shocked that he'd held it behind our backs. The furniture had been moved, music was blaring and several youngsters were sitting around with drinks. There was even a couple upstairs sitting on our bed! It was a good job we came back when we did and I shuddered to think what might have happened if we'd not turned up at that time.

Helen and I told Jeff's guests to clear out, but one of them, Dick Hall, who was a strange character, wanted to know what the setup was. We told him to clear out! I was visualizing having to call the police, but there was no trouble – they all left. Some of them only went as far as the lawns on the other side of the road, where they sat drinking for a while. Later in the night, a couple knocked at the door and wished to know if this was the house where the party was being held. Helen got rid of them by saying that there'd been a party, but that it had finished.

Jeff thought he was entitled to do as he did. He couldn't understand that it was our house and that he was a privileged guest, who paid hardly anything towards his keep. He was upset at what we'd said and done and things were a bit awkward at first, but they settled down.

The bite on Helen's arm still hadn't healed up and had turned into a big blister surrounded by smaller ones. So she went to our doctor's on 15 July and was given Fucidin, an antibiotic ointment, which did the job.

Around that time, Jeff told us the news that he'd passed his teaching course and was being awarded a Certificate in Education, with a commendation in the Theory of Education. That meant that he was qualified to work as a teacher and so he started applying for jobs. He first went to Burton-upon-Trent to be interviewed for one at the boys' grammar school and got it, but turned it down in favour of another he was offered, as a teacher of history and geography, at Maryhill Comprehensive School, in Gloucester Road, Kidsgrove.

Because Jeff's job was fairly local, it meant that he could carry on living at home and drive to school and back every day, which he did. He started early in September and Helen and I were glad that he'd got something settled and had money coming in, but I wondered how he'd do in dealing with the kids.

One weekend morning, when Helen and I got out of bed, we found a note that Jeff had written when he'd come in the previous night. The message was to the effect that there'd been a stray dog outside our back door and it had been making a noise. Jeff had given it some chocolate cake to eat and had fetched an old carpet from the hut for it to sleep on. Helen and I had heard a dog whining in the night, but had thought that it was a neighbour's animal.

When we opened our back door in the morning, the dog was still there. I caught hold of it and looked for information on its collar. This said that it lived in Avenue Road, so, as soon as I was able, I walked the dog to the given address. An old lady answered the door and I explained what had happened. She was pleased that her dog had been returned and asked for my address so that she could send me a Christmas card, although I never did get one.

There was a girl, who lived in one of the terraced houses across the road from us, who had a cat. She didn't allow the animal to run wild, but took it out on a lead for its exercise pretty often! They came along the lawns in front of Remploy and it didn't seem to struggle, even though there was traffic going past, although it pulled a bit on occasions.

One of Helen's eyes had become very bloodshot and she was really worried about it. So she went to the doctor's on 5 December and was told that it might have been caused by coughing, was probably harmless and would very likely clear up within a couple of weeks, which it did.

Jeff got engaged to Pat on 31 December and I wondered what he was letting himself in for because their romance was still stormy. They went to Macclesfield on New Year's Eve and he bought her an engagement ring while they were there, but they didn't have any kind of event to celebrate the occasion.

On 3 January 1975, the Post Office announced that it was putting up the cost of first-class stamps from 4½p to 7p and second-class from 3½p to 5½p. The Post Office was in the red and needed to get some more money in, but the rises weren't really quite as high as they seemed because inflation in the last year had been 19.1%. Also, because the Post Office had a monopoly on delivering mail, I suppose the bosses thought they could get away with those increases and I can't remember the new prices making much difference to the number of letters I handled.

Jeff wasn't very happy teaching and decided he wanted to go back to studying, so he got in touch with Tony Thorndike at the polytechnic to see if he could do a master's degree in international relations. One of Jeff's old lecturers, Trevor Taylor, was put onto the job of tutoring him, but Jeff couldn't get a grant to study full time. He knew what he wanted to look into, but it wasn't straightforward for him to do that, so he had to discuss it with his tutor. The idea of getting a better qualification seemed very good to me, but I didn't know if Jeff would have the time to do it with working full time.

Around that time, I occasionally used to go to The Terrace Inn, along the road at number 185, to get a drink in for Helen and me. She had a bottled drink and I used to take an empty bottle to get some bitter put in for me. One night, I was going there in the dark when I saw a gang of youths coming along Leek Road towards me, shouting and acting silly. I was wary, wondering what was going to happen because there was nobody else about. One of the youths threw a bottle in the road and it smashed. Of course, I could hear passing traffic crunching on the glass, which didn't do the tyres much good. I started to be afraid, wondering if the youths were going to do something to me, but they just passed by, thank goodness! After that, though, I was more wary about going out at night.

It was headline news that the body of a young woman had been found at the bottom of a sixty-foot drainage shaft in Bathpool Park, near Kidsgrove, on 7 March. I was surprised that ordinary people could get into something like that. The woman turned out to be Lesley Whittle, who'd been kidnapped from her home in Highley, Shropshire, by Donald Neilson, known as the "Black Panther". It was a fearsome nickname and was used by the press to make him sound even more evil. He'd demanded a £50,000 ransom for her release and became the country's most wanted man. Helen and I were shocked when we heard about it all. It was a strange affair and it had happened on our doorstep, but I don't think it made me any more careful when I was going out at night than I had been before. Having said that, there seemed to be more violence about by then and older people became more frightened to go out in the dark. Neilson was later captured and in 1976 was given life imprisonment for Whittle's murder and three earlier ones.

Helen and I attended the wedding of Eileen Noone and John Moran on 31 March. Eileen lived a few doors away from us at number 319 and was Julia's sister. The ceremony was at The Church of Our Lady and St. Benedict, in Abbey Lane, Abbey Hulton, and I filmed people arriving and the celebrations after the ceremony despite the fact it was raining.

On 12 April, Jeff was able to apply to the Council for National Academic Awards to study for a Master of Philosophy degree in international politics. The idea was that he'd work on it for an average of twelve hours a week over three years.

Helen asked me to take some movie footage of the wedding of her nephew, John Middleton, which she and I went to at Stanfield Methodist Chapel, in High Lane, on 19 April. John's bride was Pauline Jones, who came from Tunstall and was working for Hanley Economic Building Society. I was short on film, so I took a shot of the church notice board and then waited until the bride and groom came out of the church after the ceremony. My camera then started to roll, but, unfortunately, I ran out of film after a few seconds!

Flo and Jack persuaded Helen and me to go with them on holiday to the Cotswolds in May. We hadn't been there before, but had heard it was beautiful. We set off in convoy from our house and got to St. Peter's Church, in Glebe Street, Stoke. We should have turned right into Lonsdale Street, but Jack went left and then made an illegal U-turn round a traffic island before going into Lonsdale Street after all! I didn't wish to make this unlawful manoeuvre, so I carried on, then turned right into Bowstead Street, right again into Woodhouse Street and finally left into Lonsdale Street. Unfortunately, by then Jack was nowhere to be seen. I thought that he was looking for us, so we waited a while, but he didn't turn up. So I drove home to see if he was there, but he wasn't and Helen was getting agitated. I then drove to Campbell Road and we waited there for quite a while till Jack and Flo eventually appeared from the Hanford direction, looking for us. It seemed that they'd nearly got to Stone before they'd missed us!

Anyway, we finally got going and our first stop was at Stratford-upon-Avon. There we saw William Shakespeare's birthplace, which was a half-timbered house in Henley Street, and we had a walk in Bancroft Gardens, by the River Avon, where there were swans swimming about and a barge going past. In the background was the Royal Shakespeare Theatre, built in the playwright's honour.

After a while, we moved on and came to Chipping Campden, where we found B & B over a shop in the main street. It was a quaint village, which had a market hall of a great age right in the middle of the street.

In the morning, we went on to Broadway, which was a lovely place, with a very wide main street, which we wandered up. I was already impressed with the Cotswolds and we then came to the beautiful hamlet of Snowshill nearby, which we also explored.

We carried on to Bourton-on-the-Water, which was a lovely village, with the River Windrush running by the main street and little stone bridges over it. Flo had got a couple of addresses for B & B, so we tried one of them, which was several stories high and in a square. The property was old and so were the owners. Our bedrooms were on the top floor, but they were okay and had an electric kettle, tea, sugar and milk for our own use. That was the first time we'd ever come across that facility. We were pleased with the novelty and made use of it!

In the morning, we toured around the area and came to Lower Slaughter, which was another beautiful place, with the River Eye running through it. There was an old water wheel and at the back of it was a post office, where we got an ice cream.

After that, we carried on to Bibury, near Cirencester, where there was a trout farm, which we had a look at. It was another very pretty village, although it wasn't at its best when we were there because it was raining. There were beautiful beds of flowers by the River Coln, which ran through the village, and a lovely group of fourteenth century cottages – Arlington Row.

We then turned back and drove to Stow-on-the-Wold, where there were some old wooden stocks, in which people in the past would have had their legs fastened as a punishment. Helen decided to try them out, for a bit of fun, and I took a movie shot of her.

Finally, we went to Churchill, near Chipping Norton, where we had a picnic. Afterwards, we all had a go on some swings that we found!

In May, Helen and I had a new three-piece suite made for us by John Banner, of 40 Crediton Avenue, in Bradeley, for £216, including VAT. Because our lounge was small, we only had a two-seater settee. Gliders were fitted underneath, but it was fairly hard to move the suite around. To give an idea of the real value of the suite, the price of petrol at the time was 66½ pence a gallon.

On 5 June, there was a referendum on whether to stay in the Common Market or not. We'd been taken in by Ted Heath whether or not we'd wanted to be, but the Labour government had promised us a vote to decide if we wished to stay in. Because I hadn't wanted us to join in the first place, I voted to leave, but more than two in every three people favoured remaining in, so that was that.

The weather was strange in June because there was snow on the 2nd and it was almost unheard of at that time of year. Then, three days later, a heat wave started and it lasted for nine days. That was the beginning of the hottest summer since 1947 and it showed how quickly the weather can change.

Helen and I decided to go to Lastingham, in Yorkshire, in July because we'd seen a big write-up glamorizing it in our *Sunday Express* one week. On the way, we went through York, which was a nice old city, but its one-way streets were confusing. We found Lastingham to be a beautiful village and we drove straight to the Blacksmith's Arms, which had been described in the newspaper, to see about booking in for B & B. I went in, but discovered the place was packed and I was told rather abruptly by the barmaid that the rooms were full too. So I came out and told Helen about it. We then looked elsewhere and came across a nice place run by the local policeman's wife, which we took.

We toured all around the area and visited some beautiful places. Firstly, we had a look around Hutton-le-Hole, which was nearby. It was a pretty, small village and the Hutton Beck ran down the middle of it.

We then went west along the A 170 to Helmsley and we had a wander around the town. I took a cine shot of Helen by Borough Beck, with a quaint stone bridge and the All Saints Church tower in the background. There were also the remains of Helmsley Castle, where there was a peacock on display.

From there, we turned south onto the B 1257 and came to Hovingham, which was a large village built around the seventeenth century stately home, Hovingham Hall. The hall had an unusual entrance, through an archway, and I captured it on film.

While we were in the area, we had a look at Pickering, which was a nice country town, with an outdoor market on when we visited. It was also where the North Yorkshire Moors Railway started.

Helen and I also had a run to Scarborough, which was a seaside resort about half an hour's drive from Pickering. It had beaches, cliffs, a harbour and a ruined castle and it didn't seem to have changed a great deal since we'd last been there in 1948.

After a few days, we decided to move on and headed more or less to the west. We drove over the Hambleton Hills and later came to within a few miles of Catterick. We spoke to a fellow, who told us we should have a look at Wensleydale, so we drove in that direction.

That was all part of our holidays, going mainly on spec, with no plans. That was the beauty of it. We just saw what cropped up. We'd decide where to head for at the start and see how things worked out from there. We wouldn't book up anywhere in advance, but there was always somewhere to stay. That gave us freedom and we could go anywhere we fancied whenever we wanted to.

We came to Leyburn, from where there was a pretty impressive view of the River Ure and the dale down below. We carried on up the valley and arrived at the little town of Hawes, where we got B & B in a stone house, which was typical in the area. We then drove on to the nearby hills, but a thunderstorm developed, so we returned to the B & B. After about an hour, it abated, so we had a stroll in the town to find a pub. Having a drink at night was a part of our holidays and we did it regularly. We came to a river running under the main road, the Gayle Beck, and heard a roar. When we looked over the bridge, we saw the water going as fast as an express train. The surface water from the storm had poured into the river and made it into a torrent. We quickly moved away because the force and weight of the water threatened to sweep the bridge away!

In the morning, we were on the move again and headed roughly south. We came to Gisburn, where it was market day, and we wandered around having a look at what was going on. We saw a fellow with a gadget punching holes, about half an inch in diameter, into sheep's ears and he was going through a whole flock, doing just that! He'd catch hold of a sheep, slip one of its ears in the gadget, press two handed and then release the animal, which would run off minus a piece of ear! It must have been painful because their punched ears twitched like mad.

About a week after we got home, we set off again, to Anglesey, in convoy with Flo and Jack. Our first stop was at Beaumaris, which was a nice seaside place, where we sat on a bench and watched boats sailing about on the Menai Strait. Form there, we went a few miles northeast and paid a twenty pence toll to drive to Black Point. There, we sat on a large rock on the shingle beach, looking out to the lighthouse in the sea and Jack found some flattish stones to skim in the water.

We later went to Porth Eilian, on the north coast, where there was a small beach. There, by chance, we came across Edith and Jack Elson walking towards us! They were also on holiday there and it seemed a miracle that we'd just bumped into them.

Helen, the Hodgkisses and I then moved on to Amlwch, which was nearby and the most northerly town in Wales. We had a look at the harbour and saw a trawler coming towards us through the narrow passage.

We continued to Holyhead, which was a fair-sized town on Holy Island, just off the west coast of Anglesey. There was a road bridge to it, so we had no problem going there in our car. We had a look at the harbour, where there were quite a lot of boats, before moving on to nearby South Stack. To get to the lighthouse there, you had to go down over 400 steps, so we thought it would be dangerous to do that and admired it from above instead. Nearby, we saw someone climbing up an almost sheer cliff face and it was very daring.

On 15 August, Jeff set off for France with Pat in his Ford Escort van, which he'd bought the year before. They were planning to sleep in the back of it, as they'd done a number of times on holidays in Scotland. Jeff had never been overseas before and they didn't really know where they were going to go, so Helen and I were worried whether he'd be alright. In those days, before mobile phones had been developed, it was much more difficult to keep in touch with people who'd gone on holiday. As it turned out, they were okay and got back on the 25th as planned, having also been to Belgium, Luxembourg, West Germany and Switzerland!

Jeff had got fed up with teaching at Maryhill school and had given in his notice, which ran out at the end of August after his summer holiday. On 1 September, he became unemployed and signed on the dole, so he seemed to be going backwards. For the next four months or so, he spent most of the daytime at home writing a book on rock music, which he hoped to get published, but I didn't think he'd get anywhere with it. Also, he didn't seem to be making much headway in getting his master's degree studies set up and in October he had a letter from CNAA, saying they wouldn't accept his study plan, so he didn't appear to be progressing.

At the Post Office, I was told a story about Sid Rutter, a P.H.G., who'd been in the army in India during the Second World War. There, he'd been drafted into a special force, the Chindits, under General Wingate. They operated behind the Japanese lines in Burma, but, unfortunately, Sid became ill and required treatment in a hospital. As there was no way they could have got him there, it was decided that he'd have to fend for himself. So they left him under a tree, with a revolver and one round of ammunition! That was so that he could shoot himself if need be, to prevent the Japanese getting their hands on him and torturing him! I don't know why they left him with only one bullet. Perhaps they hadn't any more to give him.

I don't know how long he was on his own, but a miracle happened. Merrill's Marauders, a Yankee mob, similar to the Chindits, just happened to be returning to India, after being in action against the Japs, and came across him on their way back! So they took him back with them and transported him to hospital.

Jeff was usually out till late with Pat, but on 6 November he came back early. He told Helen and me that they'd had a row and she'd got out of his van and run off across a field off Haywood Road. He'd left her to it and come home and that was it, more or less. I was relieved that he stopped seeing her because things hadn't seemed to be working out very well to me.

At that time, there were still grocers, butchers, newsagents and a post office within a few hundred yards of our house. We continued to use the local shops to get most of the supplies we needed and they were a good thing.

We got our general groceries from W. & L. Jackson's shop, at 398 Leek Road, which was just our side of the Lichfield Street roundabout. Laura Jackson was pretty friendly, but her husband, Walter, was superior and an awkward customer. We'd always just called at their shop when we'd wanted to buy something, but, by this time, local stores were under a lot of competition from supermarkets. Because they'd been losing custom, Mr Jackson had started delivering groceries from a weekly order and that's what they wanted to do, to make sure they got the custom. Helen and I didn't want the deliveries because we liked going in for our groceries when we needed them, but Mr Jackson kept pushing their home service.

The *Sentinel* was delivered to us every day by the newsagent at 431 Victoria Road, who for quite a while had been F. J. Cartwright, and I'd nip into the shop every week to pay the bill. The main post office we used was the Eastwood one, at 465 Leek Road, just the other side of Lichfield Street from us, and we got our fresh meat from W. H. Marks & Sons Ltd, a bit further along at number 537, with whom Helen became pretty friendly.

On 14 December, I was sixty and that was the official retiring age for postmen, but the Post Office wrote to me and informed me that I could carry on working if I wished. I replied, accepting their offer. At one time, the Post Office pensions hadn't been paid out until the postmen had retired, but now I was able to get my full pension and work at the same time. I was awarded a pension of around eight pounds a week, based on my service of eighteen years and four months.

On my sixtieth birthday, Helen and I joined perhaps fifty people in welcoming Kelvin Bowers back to Stoke after he'd run 10,275 miles to Sydney, in Australia, to raise funds for the North Staffordshire Ladsandads Club. Although it had been hoped that the figure would reach £50,000, unfortunately the total fell well short of that. Kelvin ran into Stoke from Hanford and Helen and I stood in Kingsway to greet him. As he rounded the corner, she ran to meet him and gave him a hug, to my surprise and slight embarrassment! The *Sentinel* photographer recorded the incident and there was also a write up in the newspaper of the occasion. We bought a couple of the photos, with Helen on, and I still have them.

A part-time geography lecturing job at Leek College of Further Education was advertised in the *Sentinel* and Jeff put in for it. He went for an interview and was given the job, but it was only 3¾ hours a week. But it was something to keep him occupied and brought him some money in. I hoped it would build up and perhaps become a full-time job. He started on 7 January 1976 and seemed to enjoy it and fit well into the college.

By that time, Charlie and Lucy weren't coming to Shelton Club as often because Lucy's health was deteriorating. However, they decided to have a party there in the afternoon on Saturday 10 January, which was their 45th wedding anniversary. Helen and I were invited and it was a pretty decent get-together. When the club opened for the usual Saturday night's business, we were still there and carried on with our celebrating! But we'd had very little to drink in the afternoon, so the total amount of alcohol we consumed was about the same as usual.

On 24 January, there was a report in the *Sentinel* that a 38-foot-long ketch, Ton-y-Botel, belonging to John Swinnerton had been impounded by the Israelis! He was the managing director of the firm that Helen worked for and was called Mr John by the factory staff. Customs agents had seized the vessel after shots had been fired and an Egyptian man, brandishing a pistol, had been killed. An Englishman (Michael Rohan) and an American (John Mills) were arrested on board when half a ton of hashish, worth over a million pounds, was found on the boat. The customs fellows stripped the boat right down, looking for more drugs, till it was an empty shell! They even ripped the carpets out, some of which reached Swinnerton's factory in Shelton. Helen was given some of it, which we used for matting in our car and it's now on the floor of my current vehicle! It seemed that Swinnerton had hired his boat out to some people, who'd used it for drug running. He had some explaining to do before he was cleared of suspicion, but Rohan and Mills were gaoled in Israel.

Inflation had become a big problem, reaching 24.2% in 1975. There seemed no end to it. Business people kept putting prices up as far as they could get away with and wages had to follow, otherwise the workers would have become poorer. On 11 February 1976, the government's Secretary of State for Prices and Consumer Protection, Shirley Williams, announced the introduction of a new price restraints scheme for businesses, to try to keep increases in the cost of goods to no more than 5% in the next six months. It worked in the main and inflation fell, so the unions no longer had to put in for wage claims as high as before. That made it better because I became clearer as to what my money was worth.

On 3 March, it was in the *Sentinel* that there were at least 200 homeless people wandering the streets of the city. I thought it was shocking that human beings should have to be outside in the cold, with nowhere to sleep. The council should have fixed something up for them and bought empty properties through compulsory orders if they hadn't got any spare council houses for them. If the corporation had been so minded, they could have got around any obstacles, like red tape. But homeless people remained and sadly it's still the same today.

Jeff had applied to Staffordshire County Council to see if he could get a grant towards the cost of his part-time degree studies, which he was still trying to get accepted by CNAA. Unfortunately, he got a letter from the council in April, saying that they couldn't give him anything, so he'd have to pay the fees himself, which was disappointing.

Around that time, Jeff started to fiddle about on my piano, trying to make tunes, and got on Helen's nerves and a bit on mine. I don't think he wanted to learn to play properly. He wanted to put out a tune right away. He was struggling trying to do it, but eventually knocked out some tunes and they were as good as most of those that were around then.

A time or two, Jeff mentioned bands he was getting together, but I didn't really understand what he was doing. Over the years, he recorded quite a few of his songs and sold them on cassettes and CDs, but I can't remember him saying when he was taping his music. I was always in the dark about what he was doing with it.

On 5 June, the sixth stage of the Milk Race (an international amateur cycling competition) ended in Meir. The whole race was 1,100 miles through England and Wales, and it was divided into twelve sections. I went to Victoria Road, Fenton, to watch and film the start of the seventh stage at eleven o'clock on 6 June. A large crowd of people lined both sides of the road, but when the cyclists got going, they soon headed up Lichfield Street and out of sight.

Jeff made a second application to CNAA on 17 June, with a new plan, to try to get them to give his studies the go-ahead. He'd had to do quite a lot of work to change things to their satisfaction and I think he was getting fed up with it dragging on.

In July, Helen and I went on holiday with Flo and Jack to Scotland. We drove up the M 6 as usual, in convoy, and stopped at Lesmahagow, just off the A 74, for a bite to eat near an old railway viaduct. There was no-one about, so we got out our tables and deck chairs and the ladies prepared our food while Jack and I brewed the tea.

Afterwards, we carried on and came to Bridge of Allan, a nice town just past Stirling, where we lingered a while. There, we watched a wedding at the parish church and I took some shots of it with my cine camera, to remember the place by. We then came across Chalmers Church, which had a tall spire, and I filmed that as well. There was a lovely view from the bridge over the river and there was an old water wheel going round at Inverallan Mill.

We then carried on to Callander, where we stayed at Rock Villa again. In the morning, we drove a short way to Kilmahog, where we visited a woollen mill, which still had its original water wheel working. There was a sign in front of it which said, 'All money thrown into the water is donated to the war blinded.' For me to take some film of the whole thing in action, Helen and Flo pretended to throw coins in the water and make a wish.

A few miles up the road, we came to Strathyre Forest, where there were log cabins to let. We went up to one and the people renting it let us have a look inside. We were very pleased with what we saw and we thought we might book one for the following year, although they were rather expensive.

We then turned round and returned to Callander. At the back of the town was a walk we took to Bracklinn Falls, which were nice. Nearby was a wishing well, which had been constructed right in the middle of a field. It was a rather strange location because there was no habitation around, but there was a request on a board to have a wish. Perhaps someone hoped people would throw coins in the water!

From there, we drove west to the Trossachs. While we were there, we visited Loch Katrine, which provided the main water supply for Glasgow. We then turned south and came upon a B & B about three miles from Balloch. It was a farmhouse and, when we knocked on the door, a man asked us in. We soon came to the opinion that it was a great place. In fact, it seemed too posh for ordinary people, but the price the farmer was asking was okay, so we accepted the accommodation. From our bedroom there was a great view. We could see Loch Lomond and, in the distance, Ben Lomond. The farmer told us that it was a beef farm and later we met his wife, who was fairly pleasant, but was a snob. We got the impression that her husband would have been told off for letting four scruffs use her farmhouse! In the morning, we went into a large dining room, where there was a beautiful large table, which was set out with silver cutlery. The breakfast was good, but not overgenerous.

Afterwards, we had a look around Balloch and then drove to Balmaha, on the east side of Loch Lomond. That was a lovely place, where quite a number of sailing boats were anchored. We spent quite some time there and talked to a little girl, with heart trouble, whom we met.

It was then time to look for B & B, so we thought we'd try the posh farm again. The lady farmer didn't want us and made some excuse, but gave us the address of another farm nearby. That turned out to be rough and ready, and, when we got inside, Helen went to open a door, but the door knob came off in her hand, which caused a bit of a laugh.

Helen and I had read in the *Sunday Express* about the Mull of Kintyre, so we suggested to Flo and Jack that we go there the next day and they agreed. So we set off north on the A 82, up the western side of Loch Lomond. When we reached the A 83, we turned onto it, travelling more or less west to Inverary, where we got a B & B. Then we just kept on going, but we didn't seem to be getting anywhere near to our destination, so we stopped for a consultation. I suggested we leave the Mull of Kintyre for this time and go instead to Crinan, which was nearby. Helen and I had a calendar at home with a coloured picture of Crinan on and it looked beautiful, so we decided to go there.

We found the little village of Crinan to be as beautiful as on our picture and we had a walk around it. There was a small armada of sailing boats moored up in the harbour. The village was at the western end of the Crinan Canal, which was nine miles long and had been built to save boats from making the big journey around the Kintyre peninsula. The canal linked the Sound of Jura in the west with Loch Fyne in the east.

Afterwards, we returned to Inverary for B & B and in the morning we set off for the Lake District. Eventually, we got to Pooley Bridge, which was on the River Eamont and just off the M 6. There we got B & B at a farmhouse. The farmer's wife told us that some Pakistanis had stayed with her and she'd found them cooking on the bedroom floor. After that, she'd always been full up whenever any Pakistanis had called!

The next day, we had a picnic on the shore of Ullswater, even though we had to wear our coats because there was a cold wind. It was so blowy that a swan was bobbing up and down in the water near to us, so I took a bit of film of it.

We then visited Aira Force, a seventy-foot-high waterfall, which we walked to from the A 5091. While we were there, Jack sneaked up on a sheep and touched it. The sheep casually looked around, perhaps expecting another sheep to be there, but it took off like a rocket when it saw Jack there instead! Luckily, I got my cine camera going in time and captured the amusing incident.

One Day, Helen and I took Charlie and Lucy for a run to Butterton, in the Peak District. We drove through the ford there and stopped on the other side to wait for another vehicle to pass through the water, so that we could see the effect, but it was a bit disappointing. We then moved on to the hamlet of Ford, a bit further south, where we picked and ate some blackberries from a bush at the side of the road. Charlie and Lucy enjoyed their experience, especially because I don't think they'd ever been to such places.

As Lucy became more poorly, they stopped coming to the club and I don't think we saw them after that. Lucy died in 1981 and Charlie in 1986 and I'm pretty sure that Helen and I went to their funerals.

Jeff carried on teaching geography at Leek College in the new term, which started in September. He must have been doing alright because he was given history to do as well, so it seemed as if he was making progress.

In October, he was finally able to register as a research student at the polytechnic to study for his master's degree, but by then he'd got pretty involved with his work at Leek College, which was taking up a fair amount of his time. So his studying for his degree fizzled out and I was disappointed with that.

I was walking to work one dark, cold morning and had to be there by 5.30. As usual, there was a heavy flow of traffic along Leek Road towards the Michelin tyre factory in Campbell Road, Stoke, as the early shift made a last-minute rush to work. There were cars parked on both sides of Leek Road outside H. & J. Foster, the newsagent's, at number 193, as men dashed in for newspapers and cigarettes. The shop must have taken more money at this early hour than in all the rest of the day, but outside things were going haywire, with people rushing about, so something was bound to happen at some point.

When I reached The Terrace Inn, I heard a clatter and screech of metal against a hard surface. I looked around and it seemed as if there'd been a road accident. There was chaos and confusion as I stood there, trying to make out what had happened. A man came wandering vaguely towards me, with his trousers slashed right from his waist to the bottom of one of his legs. I could see his thigh had a very deep gash, about eight inches long, which had gone down right to the bone. What struck me straight away was that he wasn't bleeding! I gently caught hold of him, got him to sit down on the pavement and tried to talk to him. After a while, he noticed his gashed leg and said in a disturbed tone, 'Bloody hell!'

A policeman came to have a look, although I don't know how he managed to appear so quickly. He told me to keep the injured man where he was, but the fellow had other ideas and wanted to see where his mates were. I told him not to get up, but he insisted and wandered away. The policeman came back and wanted to know why I'd let the man get up. I said I hadn't been able to stop him, but the policeman gave me a filthy look and walked away! There didn't seem much else I could do, so I carried on to work.

When I was out delivering letters around that time, I had a number of brushes with our enemy, the dog. One day, I was delivering in Abbey Hulton and was in the gateway of 103 Blakelow Road when a dog came through a hedge and almost had me. The dog's owner, Eric Goodwin, who lived there, said to me, 'Talk to him.' I tried doing that, but it was to no avail, so he said, 'Stroke him.' Like a fool, I put my hand on top of Eric's on the dog's head and it was growling. I then attempted to talk to Eric about it, but he tried to pass it off as if everything was alright and it was me being awkward!

A few weeks later, another postman, Derek "Lofty" Durose, was bitten by the same dog and the Post Office prosecuted Eric, who was fined a few pounds. That was a surprise because they rarely took anybody to court as it was too much trouble for them. The fine didn't make any difference because we were still menaced by the animal for a while until Eric got rid of it.

In February 1977, Helen and I had trouble with our hot water pipe, which began leaking under the floorboards of the back bedroom and water started coming through the kitchen ceiling. We got out a master plumber, Joseph Brown, of 180 Cromer Road, in Hanley, to attend to it and he was very professional in his work. He found the leak on a bend in the lead pipe and said a crack had opened up through its expansion and contraction over a long time. He melted some lead with a blowtorch and smoothed it over the joint to seal it. He then produced a typewritten invoice, with a breakdown of the job, which was an unusual thing for a plumber to do at the time. The cost was £20 10s.

Around that time, one of the Post Office inspectors was showing a new inspector the ropes and explaining what happened when a postman emptied the coin containers in telephone boxes. They went to a phone box just outside the office, in Station Road, but found the coin holder missing and loose coins in its place! By chance, they'd come across a fraud in operation. It appeared that the postman concerned took out the coin box and didn't replace it with an empty one, as he should have done, but came back later to pick up the loose change that had accumulated and put it in his pocket. He then put the empty box in its socket. He was charged and I think he went to gaol.

Jeff was still supporting Vale, but they weren't doing very well and let in ten goals in two games within six days! They went down 6-2 at Wrexham on 24 March and were then beaten 4-0 at Chesterfield on the 30th. Of course, how well or badly they did didn't make any difference as to whether Jeff went to watch them or not, but they did pick up and weren't relegated that season.

In April, I decorated the whole of our stairs and landing, which was a big job to me because I hadn't tackled anything like it before. To get to the ceiling above the stairs, I leaned a ladder against a stair wall, put a stepladder on the landing and rested a couple of planks of wood between them. When I stood on the planks and looked down to the bottom of the stairs, it felt as if I was a mile up. I was very careful when I stripped the old paper off the walls and then put emulsion on the ceiling. The next job was to cut a length of paper, nearly seventeen feet long, which reached right down from the ceiling to the bottom stair, and then I pasted it. I struggled to stick this very long piece of paper onto the wall, but I managed it. Then I moved on to the next piece of wallpaper. It took me a long time to do the whole job, but I was very pleased with myself when I finished and the wallpaper is

still there now!
    In May, Helen and I went on holiday once more with Jack and Flo and we revisited the Cotswolds. Helen and I couldn't get away until the Sunday, but our friends started off the day before, so we made arrangements to meet them in Bourton-on-the-Water. While I was getting our Beetle ready, round about lunch time on the Saturday, I noticed I had a slow puncture, so I tried a number of garages, but all of them told me that their repair staff had gone home for the weekend. I didn't want to put on my spare tyre because it had never been used before and I didn't fancy the idea of going on a long trip with no spare, but there was no alternative because we didn't want to leave setting out till the Monday.
    We got there okay and met Jack and Flo as arranged at Bourton. They told us they'd fixed us all up at the old B & B that we'd stayed at the previous time we'd been there, which was good news. At night, we had a drink in a pub, to savour the local atmosphere, but most of the people there were holiday-makers.
    In the morning, I got my puncture mended at a nearby garage and then we revisited lovely Lower Slaughter on the way to Guiting Power. There, the landlord of one of the local pubs was looking through an open bedroom window and, after a bit of conversation, informed us that he was from Stoke-on-Trent! We then walked down a slope and came to a long ford, which seemed rather deep. We waited for a while until a vehicle went through it and I was gratified with the wave it created! Also, a couple of grouse were wandering around and they weren't afraid of us.
    When we got back to Bourton, we called in an eating place and each had a waffle or two, which were lovely, but very sickly. The next morning, we returned there for a coffee, after having parked our cars in the main street. I'd noticed that there was no parking after noon, which only gave us thirty minutes. About 12.10, I told Helen I was going to see if our car was okay, but she said it would be alright. I was doubtful about that and went to have a look anyway. It was a good job I did because there was a lady traffic warden standing by my car and she had a pen and a book in her hands! I shouted to her and then waved, and she looked up and lowered her book. I hurried over to her, apologized and quickly moved my offending vehicle to another place. The warden moved onto the next car to write a ticket out, while Jack, who'd followed me out, also speedily removed his vehicle too!
    We travelled further around the area and revisited Broadway and Snowshill. The weather was very nice and we all enjoyed ourselves.
    One day, when I was delivering letters in Bryant Road, Bucknall, I was approaching number 65, the home of Kathleen Finer, one of Helen's workers at Swinnerton's. Coming towards me was Kathleen's dog, dragging behind it a chain, which was attached to its collar. The dog had been fastened by this chain to the back of the house because it was dangerous to callers, but now it had broken loose. As the dog got nearer, it was just trotting along and didn't appear to be aggressive or posing a threat. It passed me and then I felt a pain in one of my ankles. I realized the dog had bitten me – the foxy thing had waited till it was behind me and then made a grab for my ankle! I stopped, pulled down my sock and saw my flesh was bleeding. I was very vexed and felt like putting my boot in the dog, but it had drifted on.
    Kathleen's next-door neighbour, at number 63, was Dolly Owen (who also

worked for Helen) and she was standing gossiping to another woman. So I went up to them and showed them my ankle because I wanted them to witness it, but they didn't want to know about it. That may have been because Dolly didn't want to get into the bad books of her neighbour and workmate or Helen's either.

On getting back to work, I reported the matter to an inspector, who looked at the wound and asked if I'd had an anti-tetanus inoculation. I got out my card from my wallet, to prove that I had, but I was out of luck because I'd gone past the time when I should have had a booster jab. So the inspector ordered me to go to the Infirmary for a new inoculation! I wasn't very pleased because it meant I'd be waiting for the treatment instead of having my lunch and an afternoon snooze.

When I told Helen I'd reported the incident, she didn't like it in case things became difficult with the two Bryant Road staff. I pointed out to her that if I became infected with tetanus, it could be serious and, if I hadn't reported it, I wouldn't be entitled to compensation. Unfortunately, I was then told by an inspector that the Post Office couldn't prosecute the dog's owner because it was entitled to its first bite!

The queen's jubilee celebrations took place on 7 June, which was a public holiday. People in thousands of streets put out decorations and had their own street parties, and traffic was banned in a lot of streets because of the festivities. There were 460 jubilee parties in Stoke-on-Trent alone. Helen and I decided to visit some of the roads and I took my cine camera to record some of the occasions. First we went to Westacre, which was at the side of Finney Gardens Hotel, in Bucknall. The people there had spent quite a bit of money and time decorating their houses and gardens and had made a good show of it, but two little lads walking in puddles nearby seemed unimpressed!

We then moved on to Bold Street, in Northwood, where there was a mass of bunting across the road. There were also window displays and outside wall decorations.

Next, we went to Birches Head Road, where we saw people holding traffic up while they strung a huge Union Jack across the street. It was tied to the upper part of a drainpipe on one side of the road and high up in a tree on the other.

Off Birches Head Road ran Gleneagles Crescent, where the residents had been busy with their own individual efforts. There seemed to be bunting everywhere down the street.

We then came nearer home, to Talbot Street, in Eastwood, where we stayed for quite a while, watching the activities and looking at the displays. These were plentiful and varied, with some having dolls dressed up and photos of the queen. We saw people bringing tables, tablecloths and chairs from their homes into the street and then food and drinks. Soon, adults and children were feasting away. Then music came from an old record player and people started dancing to it. People were walking around in fancy dress and games were organized for the kids and old folks. Also, there was a maypole dance, though this was chaotic, maybe through lack of practice, and I understand the celebrations went on till quite late at night. Unfortunately, all the houses in the street have now been demolished.

Young Harry was telling me how he bought cigarette coupons for cash, from his shop customers, and then used the coupons to obtain gifts. This worked out very well for him and he got a wide range of goods for a very reasonable outlay. Most tobacco companies operated this scheme, whereby a coupon would be inserted in each packet of cigarettes, to encourage people to buy their brand. They had catalogues, from which people could buy items when they'd collected enough coupons. It was big business and Green Shield Trading Stamp Co. Ltd. had a shop at Unit 10, in East Precinct, Hanley, where people could exchange their stamps for goods. A lot of shops and petrol stations gave these stamps out to encourage people to come to them.

Harry agreed to let me partake in the scheme, so I looked in his Player's No. 6 catalogue and picked out a gold-plated, automatic Japanese Seiko watch that I liked the look of. I then handed Harry the thirteen pounds required and he told me that he'd get the company representative to get the watch. When I received it, I was very pleased and it was a good-looker, which wound up by the movement of the arm it was on. It gave me very good, trouble-free service until 2009 when it began to run slow.

Helen and I received an invitation to the wedding of Jack and Flo's daughter, Susan, to Royston Cooke at Werrington Methodist Church, in Ash Bank Road, on 2 July. Susan was a teacher at Bentilee Middle School and Royston was a lecturer at Cauldon College of Further Education, in Stoke Road. I decided to make a film of the event. We'd already received the invitation letter, but I started off by making an arrangement with our postman, Alan Deakin, for me to shoot him walking up the steps and pretending to deliver it to us. Then I filmed Helen picking the letter up from behind the door, taking it into our front room, reading it and looking delighted!

The wedding reception was being held at the Southbank Hotel, in Southbank Street, Leek, and Jack and Flo invited Helen and me to go with them to have a drink there so they could size the place up. When we got there, I noticed a mouse on the floor and told the others, who saw it too. I didn't think a mouse would dare to run round when there were people about and I was concerned that mice would get at the food before the guests did at the reception.

On the wedding day, as Helen was getting into our Beetle, the hem on her new dress came undone, so she had to go back into the house to repair it. That made us late in getting to the church and the service was halfway through when we got there. I took one or two shots inside the church, but the bride and groom weren't on them. Then, when the ceremony was over, the couple were on the wrong side of each other as they walked down the aisle, so the official photographer made them go back and change over!

I also took some footage of the couple and guests outside the church and then we all drove to the Southbank Hotel for the reception. Before Susan went inside, she lifted her skirt to show a garter on one of her legs. That was for a joke and it seemed to be a fashion at the time. Later, I went into the car park to watch some of the guests tying tin cans, a toilet roll made into streamers and a cardboard box, saying 'JUST MARRIED', to the newlyweds' sports car. When Royston came out, he took the joke in good humour. As he drove off with Susan, the tin cans dragged behind the car, making a noise on the road! But, when they turned the corner into Compton, they stopped and removed the offending articles.

Young Harry branched out into another type of business and became a moneylender. It started when a fellow named John Turley (who lived at 204 Greasley Road, two doors down from Vera and Big Harry) called into Harry's shop as a customer and told him that he worked as collector for a moneylending firm. The two of them got their heads together and decided to set up a moneylending business of their own, visiting John's clients. So John left his employment and used his knowledge and connections, while Harry supplied the capital. All went well until John's former employers found out that some of their clients had gone over to the new setup. Then, one day, Harry received a letter claiming compensation for this poaching and, I believe, paid an out-of-court settlement.

Whilst delivering letters one day in Oak Street, Northwood, I saw the letter "V" painted in red on the front wall of a house. I'm sure it appeared on or around V-E Day in 1945 when people indulged in all kinds of celebrations and those in the house, in their excitement, painted a victory sign. Perhaps they later regretted it, but found it very difficult to remove, or maybe they were proud of it.

In July, Helen and I went on holiday again and drove up the M 6 in our Beetle to Cumbria. We got off the motorway at Penrith and headed east on the A 66 to Temple Sowerby, where we found B & B at Skygarth Farm, just outside the village.

Our first trip was to Brougham Castle, which was a ruin just southeast of Penrith and in a picturesque setting by the River Eamont. On the opposite side of the river was Frenchfield, the home of Penrith Swimming Club. There was a sign listing the prices for swimming in the club's part of the river and spectators could watch for just five pence. Helen and I spent some time spectating and saw plenty of youngsters diving into the river and swimming about. It was an unusual idea for a swimming club's pool to be a river!

We then moved on to Haweswater Reservoir, which was a bit out of the way, so we were practically on our own. The Mardale Valley, where it was located, was quite bleak, but looked beautiful in the bright sunshine that we had.

Another day, we watched an outdoor religious gathering in a field in Maulds Meaburn, which was a small village about thirteen miles southeast of Penrith. We listened to the hymns which were sung and enjoyed them.

The next day, we travelled on the A 66 to Keswick and wandered around the busy town and its shops. The weather was glorious and we were happy to amble about.

We then drove on to Ruthwaite and booked in at The Marshalls, where we'd stayed in 1972. This time, Helen plucked up the courage to stroke one of Cyril's goats! While we were in the village, we had a look at the old Co-op store, which had been transformed into an attractive bungalow, with a pretty front garden.

After a while, we revisited Ashness Bridge and found the spot to be as beautiful as we remembered it from our previous trip there in 1970. The day was fine once more and I wandered bare-chested around Ashness Ghyll, which flowed under the bridge. The scenery was so lovely that I shot some film of the same view of Derwent Water and Skiddaw that I'd taken the last time we'd been there.

Another day, we had a drive to Ennerdale Water, which was on the western side of the Cumbrian Mountains. It was a lovely and quiet area well off the main tourist route. While we were there, Helen took the opportunity to try to skim stones across the water like Jack, but she wasn't very successful.

From there, we drove a few miles south to Calder Bridge. A mile or so off the main road were the ruins of Calder Abbey, but a herd of horses, with foals, in a field more caught our attention.

Back home, Helen told me that the Prince of Wales was visiting the city on 15 July, so it meant me getting my cine camera out and checking that it was ready to record the historic scene. His cavalcade was coming along Leek Road from Stoke, on the way to Northwood Stadium, the sports centre on Keelings Road, and, at the appointed time, I was ready near the end of Cauldon Road. A crowd of people were waiting and included pupils from Cauldon Road School. I spotted two motorbikes coming along, which were being ridden slowly by policemen. Just behind them was a green Rolls-Royce, with the registration 20 TU, and it had an open top to give a better view of its royal occupant. His Highness was smiling and waved graciously as the kids cheered and people waved their Union Jack flags. I captured Helen on the film, standing well in the road and only a foot or two from the passing car! Later, we waited with another crowd in Victoria Road for the prince's return journey, on the way to visit Queen Elizabeth II Court, a sheltered accommodation block, in Temple Street, Fenton. As his car went past, I recorded Helen, in the road again, waving goodbye to him.

On 6 August, Helen and I attended the wedding of Paul Kent, the son of my cousin, Bernard. Paul's bride was Anne Jones, who came from Fenton and worked as a personal assistant. The wedding was at Shelton Church, and, of course, I took some shots on my cine camera. Afterwards, there was a reception in the Prince's Hall, in Wedgwood Street, Burslem, which was in the same complex as the Queen's Theatre, where Anne's father was the stage manager.

Young Harry and John Turley bought a static caravan, which was sited at Ffrith. Harry hardly used it and told Helen and me that we could take advantage of it if we wished, but we never did. However, we did visit Harry's family there once, in August, when Vera and Big Harry were with them. We all had a walk along the promenade and then I filmed Matthew coming down a helter-skelter. I also took shots of Young Harry and Matthew, and Big Harry and Mandy in two boats on the little lake.

On 13 August, Helen and I stood by Shelton Church to watch the start of a big parade in the Lord Mayor's Gala, which was the city's main official celebration of the queen's jubilee. It began in College Road and had a lot of beautifully-decorated floats, including one from the Post Office. There was an army band, an air-force band, a Scottish pipe band, the Boys' Brigade, youth organizations, a very old fire engine and the Lord Mayor's Gala horse-drawn carriage. There was also an old-time double-decker bus, with an open top and stairway, as well as what was claimed to be the biggest Union Jack in the world, which was being carried along.

The procession went round Hanley and ended up in Hanley Park, where there was a carnival, which I filmed. The actress, Diana Dors, was there, with her husband, Alan Lake, who was an actor. She was showing herself off, with her big bust, blonde hair and so-called pretty face, but I thought she looked a bit rough! Also there was Peter Adamson from *Coronation Street*, who played Len Fairclough. The decorated floats trundled along the main pathway, past the pavilion, a plane flew overhead and did a roll, a netball game was played, police dogs performed tricks (including jumping through flaming frames) and there were plenty of other events as well, watched by large numbers of people.

When my cine film of our visit to Ffrith came back from processing, I took it to Young Harry's and showed them the footage. I'd taken Matthew coming down the helter-skelter, but, as he got to the bottom, I reversed the motion on my projector, which then had him sliding upwards to the top. He thought it was wonderful, so I repeated the action over and over again for him!

About that time, Helen and I had a walk to the garage of Bristol Street Motors (Imports Ltd), in Victoria Road, which stocked VW Beetles and where an exhibition and wine evening was being held. The place was packed, with quite a number of folk attending just to have a free drinking session. In fact, to our disgust, we saw a woman staggering around drunk! There was a competition in spotting the number of special qualities in the new type Beetle, which were identified by small stickers on the cars. I looked at them and it seemed too easy to win. Then we came across my cousin, Sam Kent, and his wife, Hilda. She told me that she'd counted all the stickers and there were x number, so I got an entry form and put down a slightly higher figure than she'd done. Later, a fellow spoke through a mike and announced that Cyril Kent had won the first prize! It was a pewter tankard and I was asked to step up to receive it. I was a bit embarrassed because I'd not won many things before, but I still went up to get it.

In October, Helen and I bought a Prestige pressure cooker, at a cost of £13.95, because we'd heard how good they were. We tried it a number of times, but didn't get much satisfaction from it because it was too fiddly. We had to put the ingredients in according to how long they'd take to cook, so we had to keep adding them in as we went along. So we went back to the normal way of cooking. We tried it out from time to time, but we still got no joy from it, though I've still got it!

The same month, we bought a spin dryer from Comet, at 52 Town Road, in Hanley, for £43.90, because we thought it would be an improvement on our automatic mangle, into which we had to feed our washed clothes by hand. The spin dryer was a lot better because it was less effort and got more moisture out of our clothes.

The Stoke-on-Trent section of the A 500 finally opened to traffic on 2 November. As planned, it was a dual carriageway and was named Queensway, but most of the local people continued to call it the "D" Road. It had cost £25 million to build, which was over three times as much as we'd been told, when the plans had been announced six years earlier, that it would be! Even allowing for high inflation in the meantime, the building of the road seemed to represent poor value for money.

I didn't use the road a lot myself because most of my journeys weren't in the direction it went, although I did travel on it to get to the motorway when we went on holiday and it was alright. Later, when Jeff moved to Alsager and then Cotes Heath, Helen and I used the road more regularly when we made trips out to see him and Helen took to calling it 'the motorway', I suppose because it seemed very grand compared with the other roads in and about Stoke-on-Trent.

P.M.T. (Potteries Motor Traction Limited) had long been the main bus company in Stoke-on-Trent and a lot of people, particularly those without cars, relied on buses to get about. That autumn, the bus workers went on a 26-day strike, which ended on 18 November. It made it very difficult for people who were some distance away from shops to get their food in, but the strike didn't affect Helen and me much because we had more or less everything we needed in the local shops.

During the Christmas pressure period, I was working on parcel duties at St. Luke's Church Hall, in Mulberry Street, Hanley, which had been hired by the Post Office. One day, Helen walked in and told me she'd left her keys at home and that she wanted to borrow mine. But, when I felt in my pocket, I found out that I'd also left my keys there! Jeff was out somewhere and we didn't know when he'd turn up, so we discussed what to do and I thought I should break a window. Tony Nixon, a P.H.G. from 25 Avenue Road, overheard us and asked if any of the windows were open. I told him that we usually left our small front bedroom window open and he offered to climb up our ladder and get in right away. I didn't really like the idea in case he got hurt, especially in the Post Office's time, but he seemed very keen to do us the favour, so I gave him the okay.

We all got in a Post Office van and Tony drove us to our house. I got our ladder fixed up against the bedroom windows and Tony was up it and through the window in no time at all. He then came down the stairs and opened our front door before we'd got our breath back! We left Helen there and Tony drove us back to work. Later, I gave him a packet of twenty cigarettes as a little gift for his kindness.

On 5 January 1978, there was a story on the front page of the *Sentinel* about the effects of punk rock, a new type of music, on youngsters who liked it. It said that they were behaving badly, which wasn't right of them. I didn't know much about the music, except that it was loud, tuneless and aggressive. Jeff told me that the punk groups used to spit on their audiences, so no wonder teenagers at that time were going off the rails!

The local steelworks, Shelton Bar, had long been under the threat of closing down and in 1971 the men there had set up an action committee to try to stop it happening. But, in January 1978, the workers there who were members of the National Union of Blastfurnacemen and the Iron and Steel Trades Confederation asked for redundancy packages. The steelworks couldn't really carry on without them, so that undermined the campaign to save the main part of the operation and it closed on 23 June, with the loss of 2,100 jobs. So the bosses got their way, even though the workers had put up a good fight. The only part of the works that stayed open was the steel rolling mill, which carried on operating until 2000 when it too was closed down. It was a shame because the steelworks had been a part of the city for such a long time.

On 18 February, the North Staffordshire Polytechnic students had a rag procession, which I shot going up College Road with my movie camera. It was the finale of a week of events they'd organized to raise money for charity, which had included spring-cleaning Josiah Wedgwood's statue in Winton Square, Stoke, and holding a chariot race in Hanley!

I also filmed a visit by Prince Philip to officially open the new YMCA centre, Edinburgh House, in Harding Road, on 10 March. Helen was there to help greet him and was close to the action when he arrived. The opening was part of a five-hour tour he had of North Staffordshire, which also included visits to the Sixth Form College, off Victoria Road, Fenton, and the Michelin factory.

The same month, Helen and I bought one of the newfangled duvets for £49.95. We'd heard that they were used extensively on the Continent and that they were supposed to be warm in winter and cool in summer when used on their own. We found that it was insufficient in winter and too warm in summer! But, being filled with duck down, it was lighter than our old-fashioned eiderdown, which, despite its name, was filled with heavy cotton.

Vale were having another bad season and Jeff was having to put up with it, but it looked as though they might again avoid relegation. On 25 March, they still had ten games to play, but didn't win any of them and they lost all the last four so that they went down to the Fourth Division at the end of April. Of course, Jeff wasn't very pleased with the turn of events, but he was used to Vale not doing particularly well, so it didn't really affect him.

In April, Helen and I drove to St. Oswald's Church, in Church Street, Ashbourne, to see the wonderful annual display of daffodils in the churchyard. Helen made a lovely picture as I filmed her walking amongst a mass of them.

One Sunday, I drove to Uncle Bill's, as usual, to deliver his dinner, but I locked myself out of my car while the engine was still running! I had to walk all the way home to get the spare key and when I got back, the engine was still going, so at least the car hadn't run out of petrol!

May Day was celebrated in Hanley Park with a parade, which included a military band, girl troupes, decorated floats and horses and carts. On the old "Horse Ring", there were pony rides, a small amusement fair and side shows. One of our neighbours, Graham Reece, of number 285, was there with his Shetland pony and small cart, and I made a cine film of the various events. Graham was a small chap with long hair and a beard and he kept horses on land, opposite his house, which is now part of Staffordshire University. Every so often, I collected their manure for our garden and especially our roses, which Helen adored. The idea of using horse manure came from the old days and we carried it on.

Helen and I went with Flo and Jack on a trip to Eyam, a lovely village in the Peak District, where the plague had killed most of its inhabitants in 1665-1666. There were signs up on some of the houses with the names of the people there who'd died from it. We had a look at the stocks, which had been used for punishments in days gone by and were still preserved. Then we came across a revolving roasting jack, which was a strange device used to cook sheep in an old annual custom in the village!

In July, Helen and I once again went on a touring holiday to the Lake District and we were in the company of Flo and Jack. On the way, we called at Grange-over-Sands, on the north of Morecambe Bay, and had a stroll along the promenade, but there wasn't much of a beach. Our next call was at nearby Cartmel, where people were sitting outside the Royal Oak pub in the fine weather. There were also a lovely old church, with wonderful woodwork, and a racecourse nearby.

We then drove up to Ouse Bridge, at the northern end of the Lake District, where the River Derwent flowed out of Bassenthwaite Lake. We had a stroll along the side of the lake, on which there were sailing boats.

From there, we went to Borrowdale, which was south of Keswick. In the valley, close to the B 5289, was the Bowder Stone, a huge rock, thirty feet high and fifty feet across, with wooden steps to the top of it. Jack climbed up them and onto the stone and Helen followed him up, which I was very surprised about. She took every step carefully, even though there were handrails on both sides, and she did the same on the way down. I then climbed up myself and took some shots of the view from the top.

We booked in to stay at Gillercombe, a B & B at Stonethwaite Road End, in Borrowdale, owned by a lady named Rachel Dunckley. One day, we drove from there to Ashness Bridge, where we heard that a young fellow had been drowned in Watendlath Tarn further up the track. We decided to have a look at the scene of the tragedy and walked there.

Another day we spent at Buttermere, around the lake side area, which was very scenic. Jack took the opportunity to practise his stone-skimming skills on the water. That night, we got B & B accommodation at Syke Farm, which was just outside the village of Buttermere in the middle of marvellous scenery, being surrounded by mountains and lakes.

We then went further afield, to Appleby-in-Westmorland, which was on the River Eden, southeast of Penrith. There we inspected the almshouses and St. Lawrence's Church, which had a beautifully-carved pew inside.

After that, we drove southeast on the A 66 and then southwest on the A 685, until we came to the village of Ravenstonedale, which was just off the main road. We had a walk around it and found it to be nice and quiet.

From there, we went back into the Lake District and got four days' B & B for thirty pounds per couple at The Marshalls, where Helen and I had stayed the previous July. Despite being a retired policeman, Cyril, the landlord, didn't have much faith in the local police force! That was because he'd had something stolen and they'd done nothing about it. So he'd done his own detective work, found the culprit and put the facts to the local force, who prosecuted the thief as a result.

After we left there, we called at Hawkshead, which was south of Ambleside and close to Esthwaite Water, one of the smaller lakes in the area. We had a wander around the beautiful and most popular village before going home.

Although Vale were playing in a lower division, they didn't start the new season particularly well. On 25 August, Jeff went to Crewe to support them, as he usually did when the local Derby was played there. This time, he was in for a treat because Vale won 5-1, with their new centre-forward, Bernie Wright, scoring a hat trick. Unfortunately, the result was a flash in the pan, but Jeff carried on following Vale through thick and thin as usual.

In September, Helen and I bought a new Hoover vacuum cleaner, which cost £51.90. It was light and easy to use and was also easy to empty. It had a bag, with a big opening. There was a clip on the top of the bag, which we took off to empty all the rubbish in the bin. It was then ready for use again.

Around that time, Harry and Gill sold their house in Greasley Road and bought a nice detached one, Oakwood, in Cheddleton Road, Leek. Harry had been a member of Leek Golf Club for years, but now the course was almost right across from his new home.

Not long after, Harry and Gill also sold their newsagent's shop and Harry then concentrated his efforts on his moneylending business and a short-lived rabbit breeding and selling scheme he got involved in.

Jeff had been recording some of his songs with other musicians and was sending copies on cassettes to record companies around this time. He was hoping that one of them would take him on and he seemed daring to me, trying to branch out from the normal way of living. There wasn't much chance of it coming off and Jeff selling a million copies because a lot of youngsters were trying the same thing, so I wasn't surprised when nobody signed him up.

In November, there were rumours that the bakers were going to go on strike. On the 4th, the *Sentinel* reported that many of the local shops had sold out of bread because people were panicking and buying up what they could. The news seemed to create more panic because the next working day, the 6th, there were great queues outside the shops. The members of the Bakers' Union went on strike for more pay the following day and all the local supplies were sold out by 9 a.m. Shopkeepers started to ration the amount of bread that any person could buy and the local bakeries were able to carry on enough production, so that people didn't go hungry. I was confident we'd be alright and I'm pretty sure we never went short in our house. Helen was in charge of the shopping and she'd have seen to that! The strike ended on 11 December when the union members accepted a 14.4% pay rise and things then went back to normal.

There was an advert in the *Sentinel* by Stoke-on-Trent Council, offering a grant to householders who insulated their roof spaces. I did ours and what a dirty job it was! I had to clear the dust, grime and fallen roof tile cement out of the loft, which was obviously a confined space. I put a cloth around my mouth, so that my lungs didn't get clogged up with dust, and, for a light, I fixed up our bedside lamp in an extension cable. I had to be sure that I didn't tread off the beams or I'd have gone through the fragile ceiling! The only place that I could stand up straight was in the centre of the roof space, but I managed to lay rolls of fibreglass in between the wooden beams until the space was covered. This took me two or three days to do, fitting it in around work. It cost me £38.25 and I then sent the receipts to the council to apply for the grant. In December, I got £25.24 from them towards the cost.

During the Christmas pressure period at the Post Office, I was sorting letters next to a Polish lad, who was new and seemed nice. I left him to go for a meal break, but when I returned he wasn't there, so I assumed he'd gone for his break or to the toilet. I worked away for a while and then an inspector came over to me and told me that the Investigation Branch had taken him away, having seen him steal something out of a letter. The inspector also said that I'd been under observation at the same time. Perhaps they hadn't known which of us was doing the stealing, but I felt terrible at the thought of someone watching my every move. It made me feel guilty, even though I hadn't done anything wrong.

At the beginning of 1979, I had to replace the fluorescent ring light in the lounge. The experience of having fitted the original one in the kitchen with Brian Cotton helped me to do the job because I'd seen what it was all about. It only had a sixty-watt tube, but it was as bright as a normal hundred-watt light bulb. It lasted for years, but it was quite expensive to replace. Eventually, the light became obsolete, so I had to go back to a normal bulb.

One day around that time, I was looking through one of the kitchen windows and saw a mouse go into our rockery. I went out to trap it by filling the gap up between the rocks with small stones, but I saw it dig itself out another way and it escaped! So I then set traps in our gardens, but I don't think I ever caught a mouse, although I left the traps there in case they were needed another time!

I could hardly remember my Uncle Mo Wallett's son, Dave, as a lad, but, one day, while I was out working in Penkhull as a postman, he recognized me. I take it that it was because I was a similar-looking fellow to his father (so the family thought) and Dave knew I worked on the post. He was an ambulance technician and was driving an ambulance at the time. He stopped outside the Marquis of Granby pub, in St. Thomas Place, and said hello. He kept in touch after that and called at our house every so often for a chat.

It was in the news on 22 March that our ambassador to the Netherlands, Sir Richard Sykes, had been shot dead in The Hague by the IRA and, eight days later, the Conservative MP, Airey Neave, was killed by the Irish National Liberation Army when his car was blown up on the House of Commons car park. It was worrying that two top people had been murdered in such a short space of time and I wondered if it would get worse. I thought for a moment that terrorists might start shooting postmen, but, of course, I quickly realized that killing big names makes more impact than shooting ordinary people. So I then couldn't imagine terrorists wasting bullets on mere postmen.

That spring, Helen and I had a nice show of daffodils in our gardens, as we had done for many years. I took them with my cine camera at Easter and also shot a blooming forsythia bush, which we'd planted in our rockery at the back. Our gardens were ablaze with yellow.

Later, I filmed the cherry blossom in Hanley Park, which covered the ground and where it was white, it looked like snow. I then went into the "Flower Park", which, at that time, had a large conservatory with plants in and I filmed a collection of different-coloured foxgloves that were in bloom there.

Margaret Thatcher became the prime minister on 4 May after the Conservatives had won the general election, but it seemed strange that a woman had taken up the job. It didn't seem quite the thing, but it was right that the job was open to both sexes and it had to happen some time. I wasn't very happy about the Tories getting in because they represented the middle and upper classes, who were, of course, on the other side from working-class people, including me.

On 21 May, it was in the *Sentinel* that climbers were being banned from The Roaches, the popular rocky ridge north of Leek, by the landowners, Alan Edgecox and Frank Sykes, who said that damage and nuisance were being caused. The landowners then started to try to charge people to go there, which led to uproar. The ordinary people had been pushed out of the countryside a long time before, but I think interesting and beautiful places like The Roaches should belong to the people. Banning climbers was a poor decision and I think it was an excuse to get them off the land by saying they'd caused damage. Fortunately, the Peak District National Park Authority bought the land the following year and left it open for visitors to wander about.

The first direct elections to the European Parliament took place on 7 June. I didn't vote because I still didn't want to be in the Common Market, so I boycotted the elections, as I've done ever since. Most other British people have ignored them over the years as well and less than a third of the voters turned out in 1979, which showed what they thought about the organization!

When John Wayne died on 11 June, it was the end of an era. He'd dominated the cowboy acting scene in his day and I'd seen him many times in films. He'd fitted into them very well, but was limited as an actor and always did the same old thing, although I suppose that's what people imagined cowboys had been like.

Jeff had come across a detached house which was being offered for rent to any of its employees by Staffordshire County Council. It was St. Bartholomew's

Primary School House, in Buxton Road, Longnor, which was a small, picturesque town about eight miles northeast of Leek. Jeff was taken with the house and acquired it, even though Helen and I thought it was a fair way from his work at Leek College and would be a hazardous journey in the winter time when snow and ice were on the ground up on the Peak District hills.

In July, Helen and I went with Flo and Jack for another tour around the Lake District. That was the fourth year in a row that Helen and I had been there, but we still found new things to do. We booked in at Rachel's B & B in Borrowdale, which was a good place to stay. There were some nice walks from there and we enjoyed our visit.

The first day there, we had a stroll around nearby Seatoller, which was an attractive hamlet at the eastern end of Honister Pass. In the evening, we walked to Rosthwaite, the first village north along the road. We went into the bar of a hotel there, where we had a round of drinks and a natter with some of the other customers. We then took a stroll back to Rachel's, where we sat for a while, having a word with the other guests.

The next day, we drove to Buttermere, via Keswick, to avoid Honister Pass. We got to the lake and walked alongside it, partly on a privately-owned concessionary path. By Hassness, we walked through a rock tunnel and then came to a stile. Flo had her work cut out to get over it, but then we sat down and fed some gulls, which were flying nearby and swooped down to get the food.

Again, we had a walk to Rosthwaite in the evening and a drink at the same hotel. Although Helen and I had a drink most nights when we could on holiday, I don't think Flo approved and Jack didn't particularly like drinking, but they joined in to make us happy.

Another day, we visited Loweswater, northwest of Buttermere and Crummock Water, where we spent a leisurely hour or two. It was out of the way and rather quiet.

One morning at Gillercombe, we looked through our bedroom window and saw Rachel feeding a baby lamb out of a baby's milk bottle. The lamb was a pet from nearby Chapel Farm, which was run by Rachel's parents.

We had another visit to Buttermere while we were on holiday and this time Jack dropped off to sleep! Also, we watched a fellow and two children throwing water from a brook over one another until they were soaked.

Some time after we returned home, a postman about my age told me that he was retiring under the job release scheme, which had been brought out by the government. He said the idea was that, if an older man gave up his job to a younger one, the government would pay the fellow retiring about forty pounds a week. As my wages were around sixty pounds a week, I had a good think about what I'd been told.

It was a shock when I heard on 27 August that Earl Mountbatten of Burma had been killed by an IRA bomb in his boat in Donegal Bay, off the west coast of Ireland. He'd been the Supreme Allied Commander in Southeast Asia in the Second World War, but I don't think he did all that much. He was a snob and seemed to think he was superior to the lower-down people, like me, but it was a poor show by the IRA, killing him. I couldn't see what they'd gain from it because there's always somebody ready to jump into the places of the top people, so it wouldn't have mattered how many of them they'd killed.

Unfortunately for Jeff, Vale were becoming a very poor Fourth Division team and started the 1979-1980 season with six defeats in a row. By the beginning of September, they were bottom of the league and even Jeff found that hard to take. They bucked up a bit in September, although they were beaten 7-1 at Huddersfield Town on the 22nd, a week after having won 5-0 at home to Northampton Town!

Helen and I went over a time or two to clean Jeff's new house and do some odd jobs. One day, when we got there, we found that the boiler was leaking and water was running over the floor. We turned the stopcock off, emptied the tanks and cleaned up. Jeff then reported the problem to the council, who got it sorted out.

Margaret Thatcher said, at the Conservative Party conference, in Blackpool, on 12 October, that millions of British workers were in fear of the power of trade unions and that she was going to do something about it. I thought what she was claiming was an exaggeration, but there was some truth in her comment in that the big unions were getting too powerful. It wouldn't have done for them to have humiliated or smashed the government because it would have ended up with very high inflation as the unions would have asked for the earth in their pay claims. But I think Thatcher was after trouble because she'd really be the top dog if she beat down the unions.

Then, on 2 November, it was in the *Sentinel* that the government had got plans to 'reform the trade union closed shop'. In firms where there was a closed shop, you could only get a job if you were willing to join the agreed union. It was a good thing for the unions because it made them powerful and meant the bosses couldn't go too far, so everything was more or less comfortable. Perhaps it was right that workers shouldn't be forced to join a union, but the closed shop made jobs more secure and, I think, led to a better service because the workers weren't worrying about getting the sack. Also, it didn't seem fair that workers not in unions would get the pay rises that the unions had negotiated. So I wasn't very happy with the government's plan, but I'd retired by the time they'd made the closed shop illegal.

It was announced on 12 November that there was a 'multi-million pound scheme' to increase the shopping area in Hanley by 22% by building a new centre 'with open-plan shops at gallery level'. I didn't really understand what that meant, but the finished centre was to include a department store, shops, a restaurant and a multistorey car park, which made it all sound very grand. The development eventually cost £45 million and opened in 1988 as The Potteries Shopping Centre, which covered most of the area between Stafford Street, Quadrant Road, Town Road and Market Square. A number of old shops and the general market were knocked down to make way for it, but I'd say the centre is better and more attractive than what it replaced and a modern market was built underneath it.

Jeff didn't sleep at his house many times, I suppose because he was going home to a cold, dark place and having to make the fire every day, do the jobs around the house and get his own food. He didn't use the coal fire much, but mainly switched on a little electric fire that Helen and I had given him. He stayed with us most of the time and, with the winter coming on, gave the house up on 30 November.

On 14 December 1979, I was going to be 64 and I gave a lot of thought to the idea of retiring early. I had to finish working a year later anyway when I was 65 and would be able to draw my old age pension. I wasn't looking forward to delivering letters in the coming winter. I didn't mind the cold, but I didn't fancy walking on icy pavements any more. The last winter had been bitter, the third coldest since the war, and I didn't want to risk having to go through something like that again. Also, if I took early retirement, the difference between the government hand-out and my wages wouldn't be too big when the stoppages were taken off. Helen didn't like the idea of me retiring early for some reason, but I put my application in for release anyway. After a while, I got a letter informing me that I'd be finishing work early in December.

I was sent word that I'd be presented with a leaving certificate. I was visualizing that the managers would stop everybody working and tell them to gather round, but I didn't want a fuss, so I told the chief inspector that I didn't want a presentation in front of other people.

On 1 December, Helen and I went to the wedding of Nancy Cadman's nephew, Keith Bennison, and Kath Armstrong. Kath was from Talke Pits and was a secretary at ICL, in Butt Lane, where Keith was an electronics engineer. The wedding was in the little St. Martin's Church, in Crown Bank, Talke, and, of course, I took some cine film of it. We then went to The George Hotel, in Swan Square, Burslem, for the reception, which was enjoyable. Partway through, I went outside for a breather and was followed by Nancy's husband, Fred. While we were standing there, a youth started hitting a girl a few yards away. We were shocked, but then a coloured lad ran across the road to the girl's rescue. He hit the attacker a time or two, the girl ran off and then they all dispersed!

The following week, I was on afternoons in the parcel office, ending my shift at about 9.30 p.m. On the Friday night (the 7th), I was due to finish work for good and, by 9 p.m., my colleagues and I had completed our duties. We were just hanging about, waiting for the off-duty time of 9.30 to come round. One of the team said he thought I should nip over to the British Rail Staff Association Club, at 4 Winton Square, for a drink to mark the occasion. I thought there was no reason why not, so I walked round and ordered myself a pint of lager. There were a couple of off-duty postmen there, so I treated them to a pint each. One of them, Arthur Taylor, had already had a few and his eyes were glazed. He looked at me and I thought he was going to tell me a few home truths, but he said: 'They't a bloody good postman!' I didn't know what to say, so I just gave him a little smile.

After a while, I finished my pint and strolled back to the office. I took off my overalls and signed off for the very last time. I had one or two handshakes from other postmen and I felt a little sad because working for the Post Office had been alright. It was part of my life gone, but it was no use – that was the end of my Post Office career. I went to the main gate in Leek Road and waited there for one of my colleagues, Bill Pierpoint, to turn up because we'd made an arrangement to have a last drink. I waited for half an hour, but he never showed up, so I just went home, feeling hurt. I was vexed about it because it was he who'd made the suggestion about the meeting! Some weeks later, I bumped into him in Hanley and asked what had happened. He told me he'd been poorly. I then asked him why he hadn't phoned the office and let me know, but he didn't have an answer. I didn't say any more – I just felt let down.

I was sent a letter on 10 December, telling me to go to see the head postmaster, Mr Lowe, to be given my leaving certificate. A day or two later, I went to his office in Tontine Street, Hanley, as arranged. He wasn't there and Ron Angell, the assistant postmaster, greeted me instead. He pulled out a bottle of whisky and poured us a glass each, which we drank. He seemed a nice fellow and said a few complimentary words. I wasn't bothered about having the certificate, but he gave it to me and that was that. The certificate was in a frame and said how much the Post Office had appreciated my services over the years.

4 After The Post

I thought I'd have missed my job, but I settled down to retirement alright. The winter of 1979-1980 turned out not too cold after all and so I could have managed another twelve months, but, when I looked through the window when it was raining, I'd think that I needn't go out if I didn't feel like it. Also, it was nice not having to get up in the mornings at an unearthly hour and the streets were well aired when I decided to go out.

The major disadvantage of not being on the post any more was that my main supply of stamps for my album collection dried up because I was no longer able to ask the people I'd delivered to for ones off their letters. So from then on, I had to rely on finding something interesting amongst the stamps that I got in my post and Jeff got in his. It was ironic that just when I'd got more time to give to my hobby, less time was needed to carry it out!

On 19 January 1980, Helen and I went to the wedding of Barry Meredith and Jackie O'Brien at the Ridgway Memorial Methodist Church, in Bedford Road, Shelton. There was a scattering of snow on the ground and I captured some of the wedding on film, although it was fairly quiet.

Barry and Jackie were friends we knew from Shelton Club and had both been married before. Barry was an electrician with the Post Office and the father of Mark Meredith, who became the elected mayor of Stoke-on-Trent from 2005 to 2009. Jackie came from Liverpool and was quite pleasant. Mark was a nice-looking lad then and was quiet, but really fancied himself at dancing. He was good at it and he and Jackie (who became his stepmother) used to whiz round one another.

Jeff managed to get some part-time work at Stoke-on-Trent Technical College, in Moorland Road, Burslem, lecturing in liberal, general and communication studies, and started on 21 January. It was in addition to the teaching he was doing at Leek and was okay with me because it meant he'd got more money coming in.

By that time, he had a girlfriend, Jill Evans, who lived in Alsager, at 48 Station Road. She was an English lecturer at Cauldon College and was pleasant, but she was still married, so I thought it was strange that Jeff was going out with her. She and her husband weren't getting on very well and I thought that it might become a problem for Jeff. Jill had a son, Jason, to whom Helen took a shine and he came to lunch a time or two when Jeff was taking him to watch Vale.

Not long after I'd retired, Jeff and Jill must have been discussing the time I'd have on my hands and what I might do to fill it. I think she said to him, 'Why don't you get your dad to do his family tree?' He mentioned the idea to me and I showed some interest, so he bought me a short book, *Discovering Your Family Tree*, by David Iredale. Despite that, I didn't go straight into researching my family tree, perhaps because I wanted to have a rest from working, but I got interested in the idea.

In April, Helen and I went again to Ashbourne to see the marvellous carpet of daffodils in St. Oswald's churchyard. They were everywhere. Once more, I filmed Helen in the midst of their glorious sea of yellow. Also, there was a notice up in the churchyard, saying that the church spire was having to be restored at a cost of

£30,000 and it was going to take six months for the work to be done.

One day, when Helen was at work, she found one of her eyes was bloodshot, so she was driven in one of the firm's vans to hospital to have it checked. The nurse, who was taking Helen's blood pressure, said, 'My God, your pressure is high!' Helen was then asked if she smoked. I think they advised her to give up the habit, but she wasn't given any treatment.

She'd sometimes been getting through fifty cigarettes a day because there was so much frustration at work, with problems always needing to be sorted out. She hadn't actually smoked those many because often, after she'd lit up, something would happen and she'd put the fag down and forget about it. It was a terrible waste of money. I didn't think she had the willpower to stop smoking altogether, but the thought of illness frightened her so much that she never smoked again.

One Sunday, we decided to visit Uncle Joe and Aunt Florrie in Coventry. On the way, by the side of the A 446, near to Coleshill, we saw an old fellow living in a broken-down caravan. We stopped near to him, to have a closer look, and he saw us and walked over. He asked if we had any cigarettes, but we hadn't, so I gave him twenty pence instead. I was expecting to hear about how he'd come to be in his present condition, but he didn't tell us anything.

Unfortunately, when we got to Coventry, Uncle Joe and Aunt Florrie were about to be taken out for a run by somebody. The lady taking them said she'd pick up Florrie's sister and call back for them so that we could have a chat, but Florrie said she wanted to go there and then! So Helen and I turned round and went home! I think that was the last time we went to see them.

A full-time lecturing post came up at Stoke-on-Trent Technical College, where Jeff was still working, and he put in for it. I was surprised because he didn't seem to want to do a proper job. He went for an interview on 29 May and got the position. Helen and I were very pleased because we wanted him to have a regular, stable, well-paid job, with a pension attached to it.

In June, Helen and I had a drive to The Roaches and there was a good view of Tittesworth Reservoir from there. We had a wander around and I took one or two shots of some of the climbers on the rocks. We also saw Doug Moller, the Lord of The Roaches, in his "estate" and had a word with him. He looked a bit rough, but in keeping with his surroundings! He had his eye patch on and looked like a pirate! He lived with his wife, Anne, in a tumbledown old gamekeeper's residence called Rockhall Cottage, which was built on to a cave and had no mains water or electricity.

Helen and I didn't go on holiday that summer. I think it was because we thought we'd better see how our money went, with me having retired, and, in any case, I was very busy with jobs around our home. I decorated most of the inside of the house and in June I started building a new fence at the back of our garden, beyond the hedge.

Our old back fence was rotting, so I had to take it out and then dig holes to put the main posts of the new fence in. Helen had got some timber from Swinnerton's and I used that for the job. I cemented the new posts in and then built a horizontal wooden frame, which I screwed onto the main posts. I knocked timber slats onto the frame and finished off by creosoting the whole thing. It took me a week or two to do and it was July when I finished the job. I must have done it pretty well because the fence is still there now.

In July, there were three earth tremors in the city in twelve days. I can't remember if I felt any of them, but they'd been going on from time to time for years and were often blamed on the coal mining in the area. I wondered if the shaking might weaken the structure of the house and thought any damage could be very expensive to repair. There have been many more tremors since and one on 9 November the same year measured nearly $3\frac{1}{2}$ on the Richter scale, but none have caused damage to the house as far as I know.

In or around August 1980, there was a display by two pairs of parachutists over Hanley Park. They jumped out of a plane and all landed a few yards away at most from the small target, which was marked on the ground. I filmed them descending, which wasn't very easy because they kept drifting in and out of the viewfinder until they got near the ground. They seemed to be able to control their chutes more than had been possible around the Second World War, although another parachutist going down over the park on a previous occasion had landed across the far side of Leek Road dangerously near some spiked railings!

Helen usually supplied the flowers for the office of her boss, John Swinnerton, and also arranged them there. She made a very good job of it. One day that summer, she got some gladioli, arranged them in one of our tall Wedgwood vases and put them on a table in his office, where I filmed them. They looked wonderful and I understand that Mr John really appreciated the effort Helen made. She saved him a lot of money too because many of the blooms were free from our garden or the countryside, where we picked them.

Jeff's full-time employment at the technical college began on 1 September, although he didn't have to start work till a week later. He appeared to get on okay and I think it suited him being a lecturer. He seemed to be made for it because he'd got the style (being pleasant), the speech (having a cultured tone) and the looks (with his long hair and the beard he'd grown).

In September, Helen and I had one or two day trips. First we drove with Jack and Flo to Dove Dale, where we walked to the stepping stones. We saw a Labrador dog swimming in the river as we strolled along the side. We then drove on to Milldale, crossed the old packhorse bridge (Viator's Bridge) over the Dove on foot and walked down the river to Dove Holes. These were two caves in the rock and the larger was about sixty feet wide and thirty feet high! We then returned the same way and it was a lovely experience.

From there, we went to Ilam, which was at the southern end of the Manifold Valley. We parked in the village and walked up a path to Ilam Hall, which had been converted into a youth hostel. We sat on a bench in the hall's gardens and admired the lovely view to the nearby Church of the Holy Cross and Thorpe Cloud in the distance.

Another day, Helen and I drove to Oldfurnace, which was a little place on a minor road between Cheadle and Alton. From there, we walked down Dimmings Dale, which was a beautiful valley, with lovely woods. We passed a number of pools and eventually came down an unusual old building, where the dale met the Churnet Valley, which later became the Ramblers Retreat café.

We also went to Lathkill Dale, where we came across a hen with a solitary chick, which only had one leg. It was heartbreaking to see it struggling along, but Helen picked it up and stroked it with one of her fingers. We then came across a cottage for sale and Helen wandered down the path to it, to have a look, wishing it was hers. I wondered whether she'd have liked it if she'd lived in the countryside or whether she'd have missed the town.

We drove on a short distance to Monsal Head, which was up the River Wye from Bakewell. We had a look at the marvellous view down to Monsal Dale from the Monsal Head Hotel and I captured it on my cine camera.

Perhaps because I'd retired, I got to thinking about having a new will done. My old one, that I'd made when I was in the army, had my friend, Jack Green, as the executor, but he'd long been dead and I wondered how that would affect things. So I got in touch with Beswick & Co., the solicitors, who had an office at 50 Broad Street. On their advice, I made a new will, on 13 October, still leaving everything to Helen, but also appointing her as the executor, so she could just get on with it if I died first. It was witnessed by the solicitor, J. V. Meakin, and a clerk of the firm, M. Forrester.

Helen had never made a will and Beswick's advised her that it would be a good idea. So she did, on the same day, leaving everything she had to me.

Ronald Reagan was elected as the president of the U.S.A. on 4 November. When I heard the news, I thought it was odd, a cowboy actor being the top man in the world. I hadn't been aware of him as an actor and I couldn't remember any of the films he'd been in. I don't think he turned out to be the greatest of presidents, but he did the job up to a point. He was mates with Margaret Thatcher, so that was an advantage because it helped to keep us in with the Americans. I don't like America a lot, but you have to look after your own needs and they give us a certain amount of protection. They might help out if somebody attacks us.

All the original gutters on our house were made of wood and I'd creosoted them from time to time to help preserve them. By then, though, the one above our kitchen windows was rotting and part of Fred Cadman's end had dropped down. So we decided to replace it with a plastic gutter and did the job between us in November. The total cost of the materials was thirteen pounds and we split it between us. Eventually, of course, I had to have all the remaining wooden gutters replaced.

On 4 December, Jeff put down a deposit on an old semi-detached house, 65 Audley Road, in Alsager, in conjunction with his girlfriend, Jill. I didn't like the house much because it wanted things doing to it, especially a damp-proof course putting in, and they left it empty for months, which worried Helen and me. Then Jill backed out and left Jeff with the house on his hands.

Mal Kemp, one of the bosses at Swinnerton's, got married in South Africa. I don't think he did much at the firm and Helen told me that he was out golfing a lot of the time, but the other bosses seemed to think he was wonderful. Helen asked me to take her to the blessing of the marriage, which was at St. George's Church, in Queen Street, Newcastle, on 4 December. She also wanted me to take some footage of the event on cine film, which I did. Mal's wife, Dianne, was blonde and good looking and wore a flimsy dress, with no sleeves, even though it was winter. She was a picture! All the women from Swinnerton's were there to watch and John Swinnerton put his Rolls-Royce at the disposal of the couple for the occasion. He also gave them a party at his home, Lake House, in Whitmore, which Helen and I went to.

That winter, we had a robin coming for food, but, on 15 January 1981, there was a heavy snowfall and when we threw something out through the kitchen window, it sank in the snow. Helen went outside and scooped a hollow out, so that our robin could see the food, but there were so many sparrows and bigger birds about that he could hardly get to it.

On 10 February, I was granted life membership of Shelton Club. That was because I was a long-time member and had become 65. It meant that I didn't have to pay any subscriptions again and I was very pleased about it. When Helen and I were at the club the following Saturday night, I was called onto the stage and presented with a life membership card. I don't particularly care for any fuss and so I'd have preferred not to have been called up.

Around that time, I started having migraines and the first time I was worried, wondering what was happening. I could see patterns like sergeants' stripes in a "V" shape going across my eyes, but eventually they drifted out of sight. Also, while it was happening, my sight wasn't so good. I never had a headache with the migraines, but I had them every couple of months for years.

On 4 April, hundreds of bikers drove past our house on their way to Stoke Town Hall on their egg run, with Easter gifts for homeless children. The procession had been advertised in the *Sentinel*, so I went to the Leek Road-Lichfield Street roundabout with my cine camera to get a good view of them coming down the road from Hanley. We heard a roar and then a load of motorbikes appeared, with a police escort. Some of the riders were very smart considering they were riding bikes! With all the fumes they created and the petrol they used, I wondered why they didn't just give the children the money, but I suppose it wouldn't have looked so good! They came past for years, but later they altered their route.

Helen and I went to Flo and Jack's golden wedding anniversary reception at Brooms Hotel, in Stafford Road, Stone, on 5 April. It was a nice affair and we finished the night off at 505 Ash Bank Road, in Werrington, the house of their daughter, Susan, and her husband, Royston.

Helen's pal, Mandy Harvey had become the Swinnerton's directors' secretary and had been divorced from her husband, David. She'd become engaged to her new boyfriend, Bob Morrey, an engineer from Chell, and they went on a canal boat holiday around the beginning of May. Helen wanted to see them off, so we drove to Norbury Junction, southwest of Eccleshall, where they were picking up their narrow boat. It was quite interesting to see how they went about starting off, because it was a different kind of world on the waterways, and we soaked up the atmosphere. Helen waved a little Union Jack flag as they moved off and disappeared into the distance! She was being dramatic and I think she'd copied the idea from films and other programmes on the television.

I often wondered whether we'd have enjoyed such a holiday. Helen didn't think so because she thought there might be mice running around the boat and security problems when leaving it for any length of time. Another thing that didn't seem too good was the dirty water all around the boat. Years before, we'd thought of hiring a boat on the Norfolk Broads, but the same doubts had crept in, especially after I'd read in a newspaper that it was dangerous to swim in the Broads. The report had seemed exaggerated, but it put us off the holiday.

Prince Charles was in Stoke-on-Trent on 3 June to open the new £5 million City Museum and Art Gallery, in Bethesda Street, and departed from the football pitches area in Hanley Park in his helicopter. I believe he took the controls. I was recording the event on my cine camera when a police officer decided I was too near and told me a time or two to get back, but I took no notice because I didn't think I was doing any harm. I did move back after I'd got my shots. I suppose his concern was understandable because the police must have been jumpy with the IRA still being active.

Helen had had enough of work and decided to retire at the end of June, at the age of sixty. When he heard she was leaving, John Swinnerton had her in his office and brought out a collection of gold watches and bracelets, which he'd got on approval from Henry Pidduck & Sons Ltd, the jewellers, at 1 Market Square. He asked her to take her pick for her retirement. She was overawed by them and so she hesitated. Mr John then told her to take them all home and select one there, but Helen said, 'What happens if my house is burgled and they're all stolen?'

He said, 'They're insured,' but Helen declined to have them in our home and so she chose a watch (valued at £430) and bracelet there and then.

Swinnerton's decided to have a retirement party for her on 24 June at the Cock Inn, in Stableford, which was owned by the firm. I went with her and all the bosses were there, including representatives from Schweppes Limited, of Aylesbury, in Buckinghamshire, who were the owners of the Kia-Ora squash that Swinnerton's made. Helen was very pleased with it all and we had an enjoyable time.

On her last day at work, 26 June, Helen was given a good sendoff by the firm. Her retirement gifts were given to her by Mr John at a presentation at the factory, in Wood Terrace, as the staff looked on, and again there were representatives from Schweppes. She also received presents from various other groups and people, and I, of course, filmed the event. The staff then waved goodbye to her as she got into Mr John's Rolls-Royce (JS 66) and rode into the sunset!

As it turned out, Helen didn't fully retire because Mr John still had her going in part time after that. He knew she was a hard worker and the company had saved a lot of money by having her around, not least because she'd set an example to the workforce by mucking in with the work herself, as well as managing the show. Her monthly wage had been £425, but from then on, Swinnerton's paid her a pension of £145 a month and she carried on getting flowers for Mr John's office and arranging them. It was a waste of money, really, paying her to do that, but she also helped here and there and even worked on the factory floor when it was needed. But Helen told me that the new boss, Tony Hawley, who'd taken over from her, didn't understand how to run the factory and stood around with his hands in his pockets!

I'd been hoping that Helen and I would tour the coast of Britain, for perhaps around six months, after she'd retired. The idea had come into my mind when I was coming up to retirement and Helen had seemed quite pleased about it. She'd gone telling people, and especially Jeff, what we'd be doing, but as time had gone on, she'd become less enthusiastic about the plan. Eventually, she said, 'I don't want to go,' so that finished that! I think she thought it would be too much trouble, but I was very disappointed.

Jeff had had to have the plaster at the bottom of his house walls hacked off so that he could have a chemical damp-proof course put in. After he'd had the walls replastered, all the downstairs rooms needed redecorating. It was obviously a big job, so I offered to help him, particularly with the wallpapering, of which he had no experience. We started on 4 July, stripping the wallpaper off, and carried on working most days till the 22nd, by when we'd repapered most of the walls and put emulsion on the others. Also, some of the skirting boards were going rotten, so I made some new ones, from planks of wood, and fitted them.

Jeff finally moved into his house at the end of July. I had mixed feelings about it. My lad had gone and I wondered if he'd be okay. To help him out, Helen and I bought him quite a few things for it, including a black and white television, the licence for it, a second-hand gas cooker, a continental quilt, an electric kettle and a saucepan. We also gave him our old vacuum cleaner. As it turned out, he seemed to cope alright.

When he left, Helen didn't want to lose touch with him, so she offered to carry on doing his lunch-time dinners at the weekends. They could easily be done and would keep us all together around the table. I was happy with the idea and, of course, Jeff was very pleased. He came most weekends, mainly on a Saturday and sometimes both days, and it just carried on from there. It's still happening now, except that Jeff cooks a pizza for the lunch.

29 July was the wedding day of Prince Charles and Lady Diana Spencer and it was a public holiday. Helen was so excited that she'd done a window display for Swinnerton's wine shop in Snow Hill (at the front of the orange squash factory), which I photographed a week before the wedding! I bought a reel of film for my cine camera to record the event off the TV and was able to shoot parts of the journeys of the couple to St Paul's Cathedral, in London, where they married; the ceremony and their return together to Buckingham Palace. The wedding was watched on television by 750 million people across the world! It was something different to look at and discuss, but the quality of my film wasn't as good as usual and the movement was different, with it having been recorded from the TV.

In August, Helen and I once more visited the Lake District, but this time without Jack and Flo. We returned to Gillercombe for B & B and, while we were there, joined a free guided tour from Seatoller, which was very interesting. We walked up Borrowdale on a path which passed by Thorneythwaite Farm and were shown huge rocks that had been deposited on the valley floor by a glacier. We also saw a very thick stone wall, which the guide informed us was actually two parallel walls, with the space between them filled in with loose stones from the adjoining fields. That meant that the fields could then be cultivated with less damage to the ploughs and implements. Eventually, we came to Seathwaite Farm, where refreshments were for sale and there was a fellow shearing a sheep. He was pretty adept in holding the animal and getting the job done quickly. The farm was in the hamlet of Seathwaite, which was the wettest inhabited place in England!

Another day, we stopped in a wooded car park between Keswick and Borrowdale, where we decided to have something to eat and drink. So we got out our deck chairs and Helen rustled up a picnic lunch. While we were consuming it, we noticed a red squirrel running around. We threw it some bread and it came over and ate it. We continued to throw titbits to the red beauty and it kept coming up very close to us to take them. After a while, it disappeared up a tree trunk. It was quite a thrill and a privilege to have seen a red squirrel in the wild for the first time, at such close quarters, and I captured it with my cine camera.

Jeff had got a lot of books by then, but had nowhere to store them, so he piled them up on the floor of his house. I offered to make some shelves for him, to fit in the recesses either side of the chimney breast in his front room. I went over on 17 September and made two wooden supports for each shelf to ledge on and drilled a hole in them. I measured the walls up very carefully, knocked holes into them at the right points and slipped a Rawlplug into each hole. Then I screwed a screw through the supports into each of the Rawlplugs and so fixed the supports to the walls.

I measured the length and width of the two recesses so the shelves would fit snugly, but the walls weren't true. That made things difficult, but I did my best. I also had to get the height between each shelf right so that Jeff could fit the books in as he wanted. I got some planks of wood, sawed them down roughly to size and carefully planed them until they fitted the best that I could manage. I finished the job on the 19th and Jeff seemed very satisfied with what I'd done. When he put his books on them, it all looked rather neat.

On 20 September, there was a parade of RAF personnel and other groups through Hanley, commemorating the Battle of Britain. They came down Parliament Row and assembled around the cenotaph in Albion Square, where they laid wreaths. I shot some of the proceedings with my movie camera.

When Jeff had had the damp-proof course put into his house, the cladding on the bottom of the gable end had had to be hacked off to expose the bricks for the solution to be put in. That had left the wall looking very untidy, so I asked Big Harry if he could cement it over, which I suppose was a bit of a cheek. He'd long retired from doing building work, but had had the experience of doing such jobs. I offered to pay him, but he wouldn't hear of it. I drove him to the house on 7 October and he mixed the sand and cement that Jeff had got in and used his trowel to render the wall. He did a good job and it matched in quite well.

When Jeff had bought his house, there'd been a small wooden shelf attached to the wall of his kitchen which adjoined his neighbour's property. Jeff had decided he didn't want the shelf, so I'd sawed it off for him and put filler or plaster over the wooden support that was still fixed in the wall. Some while later, about this time, he heard a bang and the support block came hurtling out of the wall onto his kitchen floor! The fellow next door, Chris Platt, at number 63, had decided to remove it, without telling Jeff, and knocked it through. There was then some discussion about it and I filled up Jeff's end of the hole that had been left.

A lot of work had been going on to rebuild Etruria Road, from Cobridge Road to the A 500, as a dual carriageway and the new road opened on 6 November. The part of it down from the Trent and Mersey Canal had been built up above the level of the old road, so that it became easier to get up Basford Bank, which had been steep and winding before. It all looked very different from how it had done when I'd been a boy and it was difficult to imagine me having gone down the old road to work at Wedgwood and Sons Limited in the 1930s. I suppose the new road has helped to get the traffic to and from the A 500 more quickly, but there didn't seem to be a problem before.

It became really cold in the middle of December and, on my 66th birthday, on the 14th, when Jeff went to look for his van on the car park opposite his house, he couldn't find it because it was completely buried under a snowdrift! The same day, it was reported that about sixty roads were blocked in the Leek, Ashbourne, Buxton and Macclesfield areas and that AA men had had to dig their own vehicles out of the snow! Soon after then, Jeff's van stopped starting altogether because of the subzero temperatures, so that he had to come for his lunch on a train on the 19th. He carried on struggling to get his van to start, but after the weather turned mild in the middle of January 1982, he had no problem with it!

Mandy Harvey and Bob Morrey got married at Stoke-on-Trent Register Office, in Hanley Town Hall, on 23 December. It was very cold and there was snow on the ground. Of course, I took some cine film of the occasion. We then adjourned to the reception at The Red Lion, in Moorland Road, Burslem, which was run by Mandy's brother, Malcolm Moore, and we had a buffet meal there.

Jeff had been doing a lot of recording at Keele University with a band he'd got together, named The Witan. He decided to have a record made of two of his songs that they'd done and have it put out as a single. The A-side was called *Butcher's Tale* and was a protest song against the killing of animals, which he felt strongly about. The other side was a love song called *Annie, With The Dancing Eyes*. He had 1,000 copies done and ended up with another 33 for free. He started selling them on 25 January 1982 and got quite a bit of publicity. Unfortunately, he wasn't able to get the record played much on the radio, so not many people heard it, but he managed to get rid of most of the copies through sales and promotion.

By then, our neighbours at number 337 were Harry and Alice Williamson. They'd moved in about ten years earlier. Harry was a Second World War Burma veteran and had later lost an eye through an accident. Alice was tall and slim, but kept herself to herself. Their younger daughter, Vicky, came along one day, riding one of Graham Reece's horses and stopped outside to be admired. Helen went out and had a word or two with her. Harry told me that he'd been thinking of buying a pony for Vicky and that he'd asked the council if he could buy or rent the field at the back of our houses, but nothing came of it.

The mudguards were rusting on our car, which seemed to be because of a design weakness, and it had done about 63,000 miles, so Helen and I decided to buy a new one, which we did on 16 February. Because we already knew something about Volkswagens, we decided to have a Polo and bought a brand-new 1043 cc red hatchback, with twelve months' road tax, for £3,895.

Helen and I had seen an advert for this new type of VW, with its water-cooled engine, as against the air-cooled system we had in our Beetle, which was noisier. So we went to have a look at one at T. G. Holdcroft (Motors) Ltd, in Leek Road, who'd replaced Jervis' as the main VW dealers. We liked what we saw, so we got one from them. Helen chose the colour from a brochure they had and they ordered the car in. It already had 187 miles on the clock, but I was given eight gallons of petrol free. It was more modern and quieter than the Beetle and had more luggage room, as well as a petrol gauge, although I now had to top up my radiator with water from time to time.

We mentioned to Young Harry that we were selling our Beetle and he said he'd have it for Gill. He bought it from us on 17 February for our asking price of £450, which he was happy with, but, when he paid, Helen gave him £50 back because he was her favourite nephew!

A few years later, after Harry had sold the Beetle on, I saw it in Victoria Road and it still looked in good condition, although the mudguards were continuing to rust. I had a talk with the owner, who was in the car, and he said he was going to keep it because it would be worth a fortune in the future. Then, in 2011, I found out from the Driver and Vehicle Licensing Agency (DVLA) that the car's final tax disc had expired on 30 June 2003, so the Beetle had carried on for a good many years and it had been registered in the historic vehicle tax class.

On 5 March, having done 217 miles in our new car, I topped it up with petrol for the first time. I put in four gallons, which cost £5.64, and it was a lot cheaper than it is now!

The same month, I found our stopcock was dripping and contacted Joseph Brown, the plumber. He came to have a look, but said he couldn't get the main stopcock under the pavement to turn off, so he'd make arrangements with Severn Trent Water Authority to replace it. He didn't come back, so I went to his house in Cromer Road after a day or two to find out what had happened. He told me he hadn't been able to contact Severn Trent and I got the impression that he didn't want my bit of a job. The repair had to be done, so I went to see them myself, in Westport Road, Burslem. They were very helpful and sent a man out to look at the problem the next day. A couple of days later, the job was done free and the main stopcock then worked perfectly. I got another plumber to repair my inside stopcock. I thought he was going to fit a new one, but, instead, he put in a washer and gave the screw a very hard tightening. For a ten-minute job, the cost was eight pounds!

A few weeks after Helen and I had bought our new car, Harold Bentley informed us that he and his wife, Annie, were selling their house and going into an old folks' home. They thought Helen really fancied their house, which was very well cared for and maintained. She did think it was nice, but liked ours even more, so we refused their offer to sell to us. Not long afterwards, we were told that we'd better look for another garage because they'd be gone in a few weeks. We were concerned for a while, but Helen felt certain that they wouldn't move. Harold reminded me about the situation two or three times and eventually he convinced us that he meant business, so we started looking around for another garage.

With a full-time job and a house to look after on his own, Jeff had got a lot on, but also he wanted to develop his garden. So I went over on 4 April and gave him a hand to dig out his small front lawn and convert it into a flowerbed. We carried on working the following day and that was the start of Helen and me helping him with his garden, which continued until he eventually sold the house.

Helen was still cooking a Sunday dinner for Uncle Bill, which I continued to take him in my car. He gave me a key to get in, to save him the effort of opening the door, and he started to neglect himself. His house began to smell foul and once, when I went upstairs, I found his bed soaking with urine! Helen couldn't bear to see him in the state he was in, so she had me representing her, though she did come along with me on special occasions to see him and have a drink with him in the Cross Keys pub, across the street.

Uncle stopped cooking and relied instead on the Cross Keys for his food. He gave a door key to the publican, John Smith, who, at opening time, would help Uncle into his overcoat and take him over. There, Uncle would have a few drinks and something to eat. He liked whisky and peppermint and a small bottle or two of Gold Label, a strong beer. He was in the pub every night and was a very good customer.

Although he'd become very scruffy and dirty, John didn't mind because, in a way, Uncle was an attraction. On occasions, he'd burst into song, with a rendering of the old hymn, *The Old Rugged Cross*, and he'd settle arguments about the rules of football. He was an expert on the rules, having been a qualified referee and a Football League linesman. He could also remember lots of incidents that had occurred and he used to tell stories about them.

Uncle would stay in the pub till about nine o'clock and then he'd indicate to John that he was ready for home. The publican would take Uncle across to his house and, in later years, even saw him climb the stairs to go to bed. John would then let himself out.

On 16 May, Helen and I went on holiday with Flo and Jack again, but this time it was for a tour of Scotland. We went through Callander to Oban and there were still patches of snow on the mountains. We then visited the Isle of Seil, which was a short journey to the southeast. It was quite interesting.

We drove over the little Clachan Bridge to get onto the island and then pulled in to have a look at it. On its stonework was growing a rare plant, the fairy foxglove, the purple flowers of which were in bloom at the time. The bridge joined the island to the mainland and was known as 'the bridge over the Atlantic'! Whales had been recorded as being stranded in the narrow waters beneath it, but all we saw was a couple of sheep standing head to head and pushing one another!

We drove on a few miles and came to the village of Easdale, where there was a large store, called Highland Arts Exhibition, which sold tourist items. At that time, it was advertised regularly in the *Sunday Express*, with a picture of its owner, C. John Taylor. He told us he'd written the music that was playing in the background, which was a haunting melody called *Islands of Beauty*. We didn't buy anything, but we did have a picnic on the grass by the store's car park!

We then returned to Oban and saw boxes of fish being unloaded. From there, we drove all the way down to Campbeltown, which was 89 miles to the south, because we thought we'd have a look at the lighthouse at the Mull of Kintyre. We'd read about it in the *Sunday Express* and the writer had described a terrifying steep road down to it. In Campbeltown, we booked into an imposing house close to the harbour, with a grand staircase, for B & B.

The next morning, we drove to the Mull of Kintyre, which was about another fifteen miles further on. Our car was in the lead, but when we came to the road leading down to the lighthouse, we stopped. It seemed almost as steep as the side of a house and Helen refused to go down. Just then, an ancient car came past us and went slowly down the hill. I said, 'If that old thing can get down alright, we should be okay!' Helen still wouldn't go, so none of us ever saw the lighthouse.

On the way back north from Campbeltown, we drove along the east coast on the B 842, a slower road, but with better scenery (especially across to the Isle of Arran) than the route we'd come on. We reached Claonaig, where we followed the road northwest to join the main highway. This then swung over to the east coast and followed the western shore of Loch Fyne up to Lochgilphead. Just north of there, we took the B 841 and revisited Crinan. From there, we walked partway along the canal and watched Crinan Bridge (a swivel bridge) being hand operated by a waterways official to allow a yacht to pass by. We then drove a short distance back, to Cairnbaan, where we stayed the night in a motel.

In the morning, we moved northeast to Inverary, where Jack pointed to a watchtower on Dun na Cuaiche, a nearby hill, and told us that it was a toilet for old age pensioners. He was joking, of course! While we were in the town, we had a look at Inverary Castle from the outside and then sat on a bench overlooking Loch Fyne.

From there, it was 309 miles to Stoke and a long way to drive in one go. I don't remember going anywhere else on that holiday and I didn't take any more cine shots, so we might well have undertaken the long trek in a day.

Argentina had pinched some of our land by taking over the Falkland Islands on 2 April, but British troops recaptured them on 14 June when the Argentines finally surrendered. The prime minister, Margaret Thatcher, made a good job of standing up to the enemy. If there'd been a man in charge, I don't think he'd have taken the risk of fighting, but Thatcher had guts. The Falklands were thousands of miles away, so there was a problem with backup and things had to be put together quickly. I was worried about how it would turn out and whether it might lead to a general war or the Yanks telling us to get out. But the Forces did very well with the limited equipment they'd got and then things seemed to go back more or less to normal.

On 20 June, Helen and I went to see the Around The Towns Marathon, which the *Sentinel* called 'the greatest free show ever staged in North Staffordshire'. We stood at the nearest place to us, which was Bucknall crossroads, and I took some shots of it on my cine camera. There was a big cheer from the small crowd when the first runner, Mark Roberts, went past. One of the competitors ran into a toilet by Bailey's Garage, in Leek Road, on the northwest corner of the crossroads. It wasn't very long before the runner was back out again because after all he was in a race! Kelvin Bowers was another competitor who went past and he finished sixteenth.

Shelton Club had been going downhill financially and eventually couldn't pay its way. We were in a mess and it was decided to put the club into liquidation, but to organize a last booze-up before the liquidators came in. The drinks were free and Helen and I went along, determined to be in at the death, having been members for so long. We didn't have any more to drink than usual, though a lot of the members did! We were rather sad when it was all over.

Later, the members were called to a meeting with the liquidators in Churchill House, in Regent Road. We were told that there were insufficient assets to pay the creditors and so there was nothing for the members. I wondered whether we'd have to dip into our pockets to pay the creditors, but, fortunately, we didn't.

After the club had closed, Helen and I didn't go out for a drink for two or three weeks. Then we heard about Johnson Brothers Works Sports & Social Club from a neighbour, Beryl Eardley, who lived across the road at number 346. The club belonged to the pottery manufacturers and was situated behind Botteslow Street. It was attached to the factory and was dilapidated. Beryl and her elder daughter, Karen, used it, so Helen and I decided to try it. We went in with Beryl and Karen and sat with them. There were very few customers and I couldn't understand how the club made any profit. An organist entertained us, but it wasn't a very exciting night, though we had someone to talk to and walk home with. The club seemed reluctant to make me a member, so Helen and I just dropped in and we began to use it every Saturday night.

Beryl used to take her younger son, Kieron, with her to the club. He was four, but suffered from Down's syndrome and Helen felt sorry for Beryl, having to cope with him, so she offered to take Kieron out from time to time to help her. Helen used to take him up the park to feed the ducks, amongst other places, and did so once or twice a week for years.

Helen and I had asked around the area to see if we could find another garage, but had had no luck. Things didn't look very promising, so we tried Norman and Elsie Foster, at 7 Avenue Road, on the off chance. Helen knew Elsie from the days when they'd met in Hanley Park with their babies in their prams and Jeff and Shirley had later been in the same class at Cauldon County Junior School. Helen and I were successful with our request, but the garage was half a mile away and more expensive. We were paying the Bentleys £2.40 a month, but the new garage would be a pound a week. Also, it was in an entry at the rear of Fosters' house and it was awkward to reverse in. However, after I'd succeeded in getting our car in a time or two, we accepted the offer.

I then told Harold and Annie that I was vacating their garage, but, strangely, Annie seemed surprised and they never did move to a retirement home! Helen maintained that they'd never intended to move, but had just wanted to get us out of their garage. On 5 July, I paid Norman for the first week in advance and moved the car to his garage.

During the summer, I decorated the whole of the inside of the house and did some painting on the outside, including the gates. Also, I helped Jeff to repaper his front room walls and some parts of those in his toilet! Then, on 14 July, he and I fixed some beading on top of the skirting boards in his hall and front room to round them off and make them look nice.

On 3 August, Jeff flew from Manchester Airport to Crete with Jill, whom he was still seeing. It was the first time he'd been on a plane and they'd got no accommodation booked at the other end, so they went on spec. That meant Helen and I had no way of contacting them if something went wrong. We were worried because it was a long way away, but they came back a week later without any real mishap. Jeff told us that it had been really hot and that they'd been swimming in the sea most days. Also, they'd been to the famous ancient ruins at Knossos, which Jeff said were very impressive.

Around then, Helen and I had our bathroom carpeted for the first time. We'd long been used to having lino there and felt that carpet was still something of a luxury. But there was some material left over from a new carpet we had fitted in our front bedroom, so the workmen put it in for us.

In September, I suggested to Helen that we have the roof re-tiled because the tiles were flaking badly. I was concerned that the rain would be seeping in and rotting the timbers underneath. We looked in the *Sentinel* for roofing firms and came upon one that seemed to be genuine – A. D. Booth & Sons, of 22 Nash Street, in Knutton. One particular point impressed us, that the customer was given a month to pay if satisfied. We arranged to have a fellow call on us for a quotation and he came up with the price of £1,785. That seemed an awful lot of money as the house itself had only cost £420 to buy! He drove us to a house in Newcastle, which they'd put a new roof on. We asked the occupiers what they thought of the job Booths had done and, of course, they were very satisfied.

Helen and I gave the firm the go-ahead and in a couple of days they were round, putting up the scaffolding, a walkway at roof level and a chute for the old tiles to slide down into a skip in the road. They worked pretty quickly and the job was done in a day. The next day, the roofers arrived and again they worked rapidly and completed the job before leaving. They removed our old fired clay tiles and fitted new cement ones. We were very pleased with the speed and indeed the quality of the workmanship. It took two or three days for the scaffolding to be moved, but that was okay.

We intended to take advantage of the one month's grace, but when we got the bill, we noticed that VAT had been added. I protested, but was given to understand that if we paid in cash, the original price would stand. That meant having £1,785 in cash in our house overnight because Booths wanted to collect it in the morning. I got the money together and arranged for them to come to get it the following day, which they did, much to our relief! A few weeks later, with our permission, the firm brought along a prospective customer to view our roof.

At college, Jeff had set up a new type of course called Flexi-Study, in which the students met their tutors individually, not in classes, and did most of their work at home. After he'd advertised it, he was swamped with interest from people who wanted to join up, so Jeff had a lot more work to do, though he didn't get any extra money for it.

On 5 October, Helen and I went on holiday to St Anne's with the Hodgkisses for a few days. It was a posh place and very nice. There weren't a lot of amusements there, so mainly we walked around, but it was just nice to be there. We also had a drive into Blackpool while we were in the area.

I'd noticed that part of the main frame on the outside of one of Jeff's bay windows was rotting, so I thought I'd dig it out and put in a bit of filler. I went over on 11 October to do the job, but kept digging rotten wood out and found it went through to the inside. I carried on until I'd got all the rot out and filled the whole area up with cement. I then smoothed it down. It took me two days to do it all and then I had to put on an undercoat and a top coat of paint, but it meant that Jeff's frame had been preserved for a bit longer.

He mentioned to Jill what I'd done and she asked him if I'd do her frames as well! I think she was willing to pay me, but I said 'No' because I'd done the job as a favour to Jeff and I didn't want to spend any more time working on window frames!

Uncle Bill had been having his next-door neighbour, Mrs Poole, washing for him and, when she stopped doing so, Gill Poole took over for a few weeks. But, by then, he'd stopped changing his clothes because of the effort required. I asked him to let me take them to the laundrette, but he wouldn't hear of it, probably because he was too embarrassed about the state of them. So he never had any more washing done!

He didn't want me to do anything because he didn't want the hassle, but I did manage to clear out his fire grate a couple of times because it was clogged up with soot. Both times, I removed two bucketfuls of the stuff! I don't know how he managed to get his fire to burn and it kept going out. He'd throw a firelighter into the grate, because he couldn't bend down, then he'd toss some coal on top and finally throw lighted matches in, hoping their flame would ignite the fire lighter! Of course, most of them missed, but, occasionally, he was lucky, though he then had to hope that the fire lighter would ignite the coal!

A house by Uncle Bill's was broken into by a burglar. He forced open the gas meter, expecting to find money in it, but it was the type that was read for a bill to be sent. However, the burglar fractured the pipe and gas seeped out, which could have caused an explosion. Fortunately, though, someone smelt it the next morning and alerted West Midlands Gas.

Helen and I were still going to Johnson's Club, but the number of customers was dwindling and the organist was no longer playing, I suppose because he couldn't be afforded. Then came the news that the club was closing down, which it did in the new year (1983). As well as the club doing very little business, it seemed that Johnson's wished to make use of the room in their pottery manufacture. It was very sad for us to be customers of another club that closed.

We were visiting the Hodgkisses one day and Jack was talking about hernias that he'd got. I'd been aware for about a year of a little lump I'd got in my left groin and possibly a smaller one in my right. So I said, 'Oh, I've got one.'

Helen was surprised and said, 'What?'

Nothing further was said till we got home and then Helen brought the matter up. We had a discussion and it was decided I'd go to the doctor's about it.

So, on 21 February 1983, I went to see my GP, Dr Marley, at the Jasper Street surgery. He had a look and confirmed that I'd been correct in thinking that the lumps were ruptures. He got his note pad out and said, 'We'll have you in hospital, then.'

I didn't fancy that because I was frightened, thinking about having my stomach opened up. So I said, 'Is that necessary?'

He said, 'I can give you a truss, but it won't cure you.'

I settled for that and got one on prescription from Donald Wardle, at Unit 20, in West Precinct, Hanley. It had a belt with two pads attached to it, which pushed the lumps back into my groin. The truss felt uncomfortable and got me down, but I put up with it. I'd put it on when I got up and take it off when I went to bed at night, but I had to try to avoid sleeping on my front to prevent my hernias slipping back out. Sometimes, when I was wearing the truss, one of my hernias would come out from behind the pad, so I'd have to push it back in.

Helen and I didn't go out for a drink for a few weeks after Johnson's Club had closed, but then we thought we'd try the British Rail Staff Association Club, in Winton Square, which was known as the "Railway Club". We signed in at the door, went into the concert room and sat down. We'd have liked to have become members, but we didn't think they'd accept us because of our ages. We continued to sign in for a while, but then I filled in a form for membership. After some consideration, I was granted house membership, which was given to people who weren't railway employees. The arrangement suited Helen and me because we were then entitled to go to the club. I believe the reason why I was successful was that the club was getting fewer customers and so they couldn't be too choosy. We soon palled up with a couple who lived at 42 Raymond Street, in Shelton. They were Sam and Doris Lyth. He could crack a good joke, but she was pretty straightforward.

Helen thought that our wooden ladder was too heavy for me to struggle with now that I'd retired, so I advertised it in our newsagent's shop, at 431 Victoria

Road, which by then was owned by A. & B. Yeomans. In a day or two, on 24 March, a man who was interested in it knocked at the door. I asked for eighteen pounds for it and, after examining it, he paid me and went off with it. I'd bought it for £6 18s. 6d. in 1949 and it was still in excellent condition! I wanted to replace it with a light ladder and, the following month, saw one advertised in the *Sentinel* by Texas, at Scotia Trading Estate, in Scotia Road. It was made of aluminium and was £29.99, but it wouldn't fit in my car. So I asked Jeff if we could use his Datsun estate car to convey it home and he readily agreed.

Jeff had had a leak in his roof, which had led to part of his bedroom ceiling collapsing onto his bed. He'd had the affected area replastered, but, of course, the colour didn't match in with the rest of his ceiling. He went to Reading and London with Jill at Easter and I decided to do him a favour and put a new coat of emulsion on the whole of the ceiling while he was away. When he got back, he was very pleased.

In April, Helen and I bought a new sheepskin paint roller for ten pounds, to try out, as we'd heard good reports about them. They were being used to put paint on woodwork and walls. This was a comparatively new idea and, at first, most of the professionals didn't think much of the rollers, but later changed their minds. I found the roller was a big help on large surfaces, compared with a brush, and I did a lot of decorating with it that year.

Vale were having a good season and had been in and around the promotion places most of the time. Jeff had been to a number of away matches and, on 6 May, travelled to Stockport with over 2,000 other Vale supporters for an important match, which the visitors won 2-0. By doing so, Vale achieved promotion to the Third Division and, of course, Jeff was delighted.

I gradually started making a bit of an effort to trace my ancestors, although it was haphazard at first. The book that Jeff had bought me in 1980 said that you should start from yourself and work backwards, so that's what I did. I had a look around the house for birth, marriage and death certificates of my family and got out what there were. I found certificates of my parents' marriage and my father's birth. Then, on 7 June, I went to the Register Office, in Hanley Town Hall, and asked for a copy of the certificates of the marriage of Grandad and Grandmother Kent and Grandad's birth. An officer found the details of both and gave me a copy of them, which cost me £6.40 in total. The certificates included the name of Grandad's father, who was John Kent, and my next job was to find out information about him.

Part of one of Jeff's back garden walls was leaning over and it looked like the top of it could fall down. A professional builder might well have knocked it all down and started again, but that would have cost quite a bit of money. So I went over to Jeff's house on 14 June and spent two days with him lowering the height of the wall. Some of the bricks in it were loose and most of the rest came away easily enough with a tap with my hammer. When we'd finished, it looked nice and neat and was quite safe.

Jeff got a kitten from the RSPCA cattery, in Church Lane, Knutton, on 18 June. He was looking for a pure white kitten, but, when he was shown their collection, a little dark tortoiseshell-coloured beauty came running up to him and stole his heart away. There was nothing else he could do except to give a contribution to the charity and walk away with his prize. He called her Raedburh, which was pronounced "Radbur". Helen and I first saw her at Jeff's house in Alsager and it was a shock because I thought her colour looked scruffy and not quite right somehow, but she had a lovely nature.

On Father's Day, Jeff bought me another book to help me with my family tree research. It was called *How to Trace Your Ancestors* and written by Meda Mander. It was more detailed than the one I had and it got me more interested, but I still didn't find it very easy to know how to go about things.

Nancy and Fred had become the owners of the house next door (number 333) after Nancy's mother, Hannah Bradbury, had died. Unfortunately, Fred had been ill for a few months with cancer. He'd lost a lot of weight and looked really unwell. One day, Nancy called to me urgently over the back wall, to go round to their house as Fred was very ill. I hurried to them and Nancy explained that blood had come from Fred's seat and stained their settee. She also told me that he was on the stairs, trying to get to the toilet. I went to have a look and he was on his hands and knees, unable to move. I helped to get him to the toilet, pull his pants down and sit on the toilet seat. He said he'd be alright, but I stayed with him for a short while. Then he repeated a couple of times that he'd be okay, so I left him. Nancy rang the hospital and an ambulance arrived and took him away. He finished his days in the Douglas Macmillan Home, in Barlaston Road, Blurton, and died on 26 July. He was cremated at Carmountside Crematorium three days later.

One day when Dave Wallett called at our house, I must have told him that I was working on my family tree, but that I didn't have very much at all on the Walletts, my mother's side. He said that his mother, Cissie, had some information on it. She'd got it from Dorothy Wallett, the wife of Dave's elder brother, Stan, who lived in Caton, near Lancaster. So I wrote to Dorothy and asked her if she knew anything about the name Cadwallader, which I'd seen in connection with the early Walletts. She wrote back to me on 11 August and told me that the family had used both names until about 1800. She also said that she'd got a big family tree of Walletts, which she could send me.

On 6 August, Helen and I went to Karen Eardley's wedding at All Saints Church, in Leek Road, Joiner's Square. She married Robert Taylor, who came from Eastwood and worked as a charge hand. Karen wore white and I filmed some of the event with my cine camera. The reception was held at the Talbot Hotel, in Church Street, Stoke, but it wasn't top class. Helen and I had got Karen and Robert bathroom scales as a present, but they said the scales weren't working, although they had been when they'd been in our possession. When I looked at the equipment, only a minor adjustment was needed to put the scales in working order, which I did in a very short time. Helen, though, thought we'd better not return the scales to them, so we bought them an electric can opener instead, for £9.50!

Jeff was concerned about Raedburh getting in and out of his house, so he decided to have a cat flap fitted and acquired one. Helen and I went over one day when he was out and I sawed a square hole in his shed door to fit the cat flap in. It was a fiddly job and I kept wondering if I'd cut the hole too big, but I got the flap installed. Then we needed to get Raedburh used to it because she wouldn't have known what it was for. So I stood inside the shed and pushed her through the flap and Helen, who was outside, then pushed her back in. After a bit, Raedburh got used to it and took it up alright. That meant she could get into the house through the window of the toilet, which the shed was built onto. Helen enjoyed us pushing Raedburh in and out so much that she kept repeating the story about it to anybody who'd listen!

Helen had been building castles in the air, talking about doing French at night school. She'd taken a fancy to the idea and got a Cauldon College leaflet, with their evening classes in. To help encourage her, Jeff bought her a book on the language, called *Signposts French*, for her 63rd birthday, on 29 September, but she hardly looked at it and it was a flop. When she started thinking about it, going out at night in the rain and taking notes didn't seem quite so attractive after all!

When we called at Jeff's house, Helen would shout 'Kitty!', which was what she called his cat. If Raedburh was around, she'd come trotting up, with her tail sticking in the air. Helen would pick her up, cuddle her and dance around with her upside down in her arms, rocking her up and down, like a baby! Raedburh was very good, didn't struggle much and seemed to enjoy it. This happened every time if Raedburh was there. I used to stroke her and lift her up by her tail, so that her back legs were just off the ground. It was only for a second or two and wasn't cruel because she didn't mind.

Every now and then when we called, we used to see Jeff's next-door neighbour, Audrey Whalley, who lived at number 67. She was very nice and we used to have a chat with her.

Jeff hadn't had any luck in getting a publisher for his book, *The Rise And Fall Of Rock*, most of which he'd written in 1975. So he decided to put it out himself, which he did on 21 November, and I thought it was very good that he'd been able to self-publish it because he hadn't really got any experience of printing and publishing. He'd set up a company to publish it, called Witan Books, which sounded professional. I thought the book would be a failure, but Jeff managed to sell the 500 copies he'd had printed, although it took him over nineteen years to do it!

Kwik Save Discount Stores had a supermarket at 800 Leek Road, which was on the southeast corner with Bucknall Road. Helen and I often went for a run in the car in that direction, to Vera's, Young Harry's and the Peak District, so we started doing our shopping at the supermarket while we were out. The food was cheap and we could load our car up, but it was awkward getting in and out of the car park because the store was very close to the busy crossroads.

On 31 December, it was Vera and Harry's golden wedding anniversary and Helen and I went to a party at Young Harry's house to celebrate it. Helen supplied the two-tier cake and we had a nice time. By that time, Hans had died and Harry and Gill had acquired an English setter, which was white, with blueish-black patches and spots. They called him Jacko and he was spoiled, so he begged for food while we were eating and did more or less what he wanted.

Jeff hadn't been getting on very well with Jill for a while, although Helen and I didn't know much about it. He later told me that she went off with someone else at the beginning of January 1984, so that put an end to things.

Helen and I started to take Raedburh liver and ham and feed her when we called at Jeff's house. As we were fussing over her and stroking her, I'd get a bit of the meat and hold it above her head. She wouldn't be able to reach it, so she'd sit on her hind legs and reach up and get it out of my hand. It looked like she was begging and Helen thought it was cruel, but it was very satisfying. After a while, when we took the food in, Raedburh would sit in that position on her own in anticipation of being fed.

Helen and I heard that my Uncle Mo was ill and so I decided to visit him and Aunt Cissie. They lived at 511 Leek New Road, a semi-detached house near to Holden Bridge. I called on them several times, but I didn't go upstairs to see Mo because Cissie didn't ask me to. But, one time, out of interest, she showed me the details she'd got on the Wallett family tree from Dorothy, which roused my interest. She gave me the information, which got me going a bit on my mother's side of the family.

My truss had become dirty through use by then and it didn't wash very well. So I went to the doctor's on 22 February and got supplied with a new one. The same happened to that over time, of course, and so I carried on having them changed occasionally.

One day when I was visiting Cissie, I was about to go, when Mo's daughter, Joan Ball, who was there, appeared to be agitated and asked me to go upstairs to look at him. She didn't say why, but I thought it was to get my opinion on him and to see if I could help with any suggestions. Cissie said I didn't need to bother and I'd better go home, but Joan wanted me to stay, which I did. I went up and Mo was in a state, with diarrhoea, which was all over the bed. The women were in a flap, so I couldn't leave them and I cleaned Mo up with towels, sheets and anything else that was handy.

In the meantime, Joan had phoned the doctor, but he'd said he didn't think it was urgent. I then left when the women said it would be alright, but, after I'd gone, they phoned Mo's son, Dave. He soon went round and knew there was something seriously wrong, so he got Mo into hospital right away. I went to visit him a time or two in the Infirmary, but he didn't get better.

There was a big event in Stoke on 5 April, when Princess Diana made a visit. Helen and I were there, in Winton Square, in front of the North Stafford Hotel, to welcome her to our fair city. Shortly after the train she was on had arrived at Stoke Station at 9.50 a.m., she was whisked off to visit the Doulton Fine China works, in Nile Street, Burslem. In the afternoon, she returned to the station and Helen and I were there, but this time further along by the Railway Club, to wave her goodbye. The road was lined with people, but Diana walked along the opposite side from us, talking to the crowd, and it seemed as though she wasn't going to cross over. Then we saw an official speak to her and she gave a smile and came across. She shook hands with and talked to various people, as she came closer. Then she stopped right where Helen was standing. Helen extended her hand and Diana took it in hers. They both said a few words and Helen was thrilled. I got a close-up of the princess on my cine film and then she moved further along.

A few days afterwards, Helen and I were in Cauldon Road and met two American ladies, who were having a walk around and looking at the gardens. They were tourists and said that the gardens were nicer than those they had back home in New York. We talked about our meeting with Diana and they were impressed. They invited us to have tea with them at the North Stafford Hotel, which was where they were staying, and we accepted. We thought they might have meant a meal, but, when we joined them later, it turned out to be a drink of tea! We had an interesting conversation and Helen gave them a couple of pottery novelties each ("Whimsies", porcelain miniatures from Burslem-based Wade Potteries Limited), which we happened to have in boxes! They took our address, but we never got a letter from them.

Mo died in the Infirmary on 11 April of cancer of the colon. His funeral was on the 17th and there was a service at St. Andrew's Church, in Sneyd Street, Sneyd Green, before he was cremated at Carmountside Crematorium.

Afterwards, food was laid on at the Birches Head Hotel, in Birches Head Road, and, while I was there, Dorothy Wallett made herself known to me. She'd already got the Wallett side of the family tree done and over time gave me practically all I've got on the Walletts. She'd got as far back as the seventeenth century, when the Cadwalladers had been living in Shifnal, in Shropshire. She'd travelled around, to Wales, Shropshire, Ironville (in Derbyshire) and other places, to find all the details.

About May, Flo suggested that the four of us go to Blackpool on an advertised cheap accommodation offer at the Norbreck Castle Hotel, in Queen's Promenade. Helen and I agreed and Flo booked us up for a few days later in the month. We all travelled in our Polo and found the hotel fairly easily, but it was right up north. It was a very big place and had been built to look like a castle. We booked in at the reception and went to see our rooms. Unfortunately, ours was crummy and not what we'd expected. It looked like one of the staff rooms pressed into service! Jack and Flo's room seemed much better, but we didn't tell them at the time because we didn't want to put a damper on their enjoyment. We didn't grumble because there was a reduction in the normal price.

When we came into our room one morning after breakfast, the chambermaid was busy swilling our teacups in the sink. That didn't seem right because she was doing all the jobs in one go and may have cleaned the toilet immediately before that! I imagined that clean cups would have been brought in and the soiled ones taken out. However, the food we had was very good and we had as much as we wished.

There was dancing at night in the hotel and we had a go at bingo while we were there. The weather was cold and I was perished when we were outside. I finished up with a very bad cold.

Also, I had some trouble with my car because the engine kept cutting out, so I had to try to keep my foot on the accelerator, even when I stopped at traffic lights and halt signs. When we got back home, I took the car to Holdcroft's, who told me that I'd got some dirty petrol in the tank. They cleaned it out and the car returned to normal.

It was in the *Sentinel* on 5 June that the council was trying to get compensation from Espley-Tyas, the builders of Unity House, in Hanley, because of costly faults in it. The building had been put up between Cannon Street and Broad Street in 1973 for offices for the council. It was the city's tallest building, eighteen storeys and 240 feet high, but was called 'Fawlty Towers' by a lot of local people because of the problems with it. Some of the council's departments moved to Hanley, but others stayed in Stoke, which didn't seem to be a very good idea because it meant they were split up. Also, Unity House was an eyesore and stuck out a mile. Eventually, the council decided to concentrate most of its departments in Stoke and so a new civic centre was built in Glebe Street at a cost of £13 million. It opened in 1992 and it wasn't a bad idea to have all the council officials together in one place. Unity House became derelict and was eventually demolished in 2006, but, because the council moved a lot of their officials to Hanley and then back again to Stoke, all they did was to waste a load of money.

At the end of June, Jeff put out eleven songs, which he'd recorded at Keele University, on a cassette and it was called *Tales from the Land of the Afterglow*. It was the first half of a story he'd written, which he spoke between the tunes. He wasn't able to get it played much and so it didn't sell many copies. The second part came out in December, but, unfortunately for Jeff, that did even less well.

In July, Nancy was having the outside of her house painted by a fellow named Hughes, from Northwood. Helen felt that he should also do ours, to save me the hard work. She asked him the price and he quoted £200. We gave him the go-ahead and Ann Parrish, of number 331, hired him too. He started work and did part of the job on each of the three houses and then went missing! We couldn't make out what he'd done on any of our houses because he was supposed to put on two undercoats and a top coat of paint. Each house had varying coats on different parts at different times! So when he'd completed the job, we'd no idea how many undercoats he'd put on.

Also, he had a youth assisting him, who had the job of burning the old paint off our woodwork. I was watching him use a blowtorch on our window frames when I heard a click. I knew what had happened! The youth had let the flame touch the glass and caused the window to crack and he acknowledged the fact. When I found more windows with cracks, up to about three inches long, I thought the youth would tell his boss, but a couple of days passed and there was no attempt to replace them. So Helen and I told Mr Hughes, who wasn't very pleased, but he said that the cracks wouldn't hurt! I told him that, in the winter, they could widen and that we wanted the panes replacing. He said the reason why the cracks had occurred was because the glass was thin, but we insisted on him replacing it. When we showed him the six cracked windows, he nearly had a fit! He had to employ a glazier to do the job and afterwards we found two more cracked panes, but we didn't dare mention it to Mr Hughes because we thought he'd have blown his top!

He also put a new wooden boxroom sill in for us because the old one was rotting and the total bill was £206. Helen wasn't very satisfied with the quality of the job and told me and other people that he wouldn't be working for us again. I too thought he'd done a bodge job.

On 31 July, Jeff went on holiday to Sweden. He'd decided to drive there with his girlfriend of the time, Cath Humphries, and they were hoping to stay with two of her friends in Stockholm, which was over a thousand miles away. Their plan was to get a ferry to Hook of Holland and travel through the Netherlands, West Germany, Denmark and southern Sweden. Partly because of the distance, they were going to be on holiday for a month and most, and perhaps all, of the time Helen and I wouldn't know where they were, so it was worrying.

While Jeff was away, I painted parts of his house, but I don't think there was any message from him the whole time, so we didn't know whether he was alive or dead. Helen was more worried than me and wondering why he hadn't got in touch. She kept thinking something must have happened to him, but he returned on schedule on 30 August. I particularly remember him telling us that cars had to have their lights on all the time in Sweden, even in the day, which I suppose was to make them more visible. Also, he'd seen a wild moose, just standing right next to the main road from Helsingborg to Stockholm!

At that time, Stevie Wonder's song, *I Just Called to Say I Love You*, caught my ear and Helen liked it too, so I bought a copy of it. It got to the top of the charts on 8 September and was the last single I ever got. It wasn't all that good, really, and I can't remember him doing anything else that I liked.

The white and pink stones in our front garden were crumbling and making a mess on our path, so I took the ones which bordered it to the council destructor, in Cromer Road. To replace them, I bought some cement edgings for £14.71 and put them round the path myself.

In September, Jeff told me he was going to rent out his house to students and move in with Cath, who lived at 15 Wolseley Road, in Dimsdale. He got a lot of interest in the rooms of his house and had no trouble letting them out, but he had to get in suitable furniture, which was a fair job. He spent four days moving his things to Cath's and on the last one, 30 September, Helen and I helped him.

Jeff took Raedburh with him, but he told Helen and me that no sooner had she got there than Cath was moving her off the furniture when she got on it. So, of course, Jeff didn't like that, which caused some bother and things didn't work out properly. It turned out that Cath didn't accept Raedburh and Jeff in effect said, 'Then you're not accepting me!'

About the beginning of October, Helen and I returned to Blackpool with Flo and Jack, to see the illuminations. This time, we stayed in a boarding house, which was okay, and the lights were very interesting, particularly as I hadn't seen them for a good many years.

Jeff decided to move back to his house, but he had to give the students a month's notice before he could do so. He asked Audrey if she'd look after Raedburh till he got home and it was agreed, so he took her back on 8 October. While he was still away, Raedburh was lapping up the luxuries in Audrey's house and Jeff finally returned on the 28th.

It was around that time that Swinnerton's sold their Wood Terrace factory and moved to new premises at Unit 18, in Whitebridge Industrial Estate, in Stone. Mr John asked Helen to carry on doing the flowers for his office and so she started catching the train from Stoke to Stone to do the job, and maybe one or two other bits and pieces, once or twice a week. Jeff and I were amazed because she wouldn't normally go anywhere near that far on her own, but she seemed happy enough to do it.

One night, about eight o'clock, there was a knock on the door and a man standing outside asked for a blanket. It seemed that a youth was lying unconscious on the pavement, with a push-bike by his side. Helen produced a blanket and we went to have a look at the casualty. He certainly was out cold and we put the blanket around him to keep him warm. In a short while, an ambulance, a policeman and a policewoman arrived. The youth was taken away to hospital and the people who'd found him were interviewed. The policeman asked Helen and me to look after the bike, so I took it to the side of our house, with the idea that someone would later come for it, and the police departed.

After about a week, we'd heard nothing more and Helen was afraid in case the bike got stolen, so I pushed it up to the police station in Bethesda Street. The policeman behind the desk told me they hadn't been able to collect it because they were short of vans and that they hadn't been able to find out why the youth had been lying on the pavement.

The next day, the youth came to our house to collect his bike and I told him where it was. He couldn't remember what had happened to him on the night of the accident and he wasn't too pleased at having to go to the police station. Perhaps he thought I ought to have stored it for him, but if somebody had pinched it, whose fault would it have been?

I bought a pair of binoculars for fifteen pounds from Tung's Cameras & Hi-fi, at 38 Pall Mall, which was run by a Chinese man, Joseph Tung. After I'd had them for a few weeks, I found I couldn't focus them because the focusing wheel kept slipping. So I took them back to the shop, but the owner said I'd caused the fault! I'd always thought that the Chinese were a polite people, but he was nasty with me.

I then took the binoculars to the Trading Standards office, in an annexe to Hanley Town Hall, to see what they could do about it. One of the officers told me that they'd had a number of complaints about Tung's. The official then examined the article and told me that the focusing wheel just needed screwing up! He suggested that I go to a watch repairer's, North Staffs Watch Services, just across the road in Cheapside, at number 30, and ask the owner to do the job. I did so and the repairer screwed up the wheel in a few seconds at no cost to me! Tung mustn't have been much of an expert as he couldn't recognize that that was all that needed to be done!

On 1 December, Arthur Scargill, the president of the NUM, and Neil Kinnock, the leader of the Labour Party, spoke at a rally at the King's Hall, in Stoke. There was a report in the *Sentinel* that the police had had an anonymous caller threatening to throw two hand grenades at the platform, but that the speakers had carried on regardless! I thought they were very brave to do that!

The rally took place during the NUM strike against the National Coal Board's plan to close mines. The strike had been going on since 12 March, but was starting to fall away as more of the men returned to work. I could understand that because they had to pay their bills.

I suppose I'd expected the strike to happen because it seemed as if the government wanted to close pits and the NUM was very strong and bound to oppose it. Margaret Thatcher was very brave to take on the miners, but she had plans to deal with them and I think the government had decided not to give way no matter what happened.

The strike was called off on 3 March 1985 and the miners' defeat was pretty important because the government had beaten the most powerful union. Most of the pits were closed down after that and there haven't been many strikes since because the unions have thought they wouldn't win. It was bad that the miners were humiliated and lost their jobs and there should have been alternatives for them, but it wasn't right that workers were still having to go down into the bowels of the earth and not seeing light of day.

I was shocked when I read in the *Sentinel* on 8 January 1985 that Michelin were going to make redundant 2,400 workers, a third of the total at their Campbell Road factory. They shouldn't have been losing money because there were more cars, so more tyres were wanted, and they were a big firm, with a good name. The same month, unemployment in the country went up to

3,341,000 and there seemed no end to it, so I wondered if Jeff's job would be okay.

Around that time, Uncle Bill's house was broken into and his gas meter, in the front room, was opened up, but there was no money in it because he hadn't used it for a long while, with no longer cooking. He never heard a thing because he'd become deaf and it was noticed by John Smith when he went in one day, but, fortunately, no damage had been done.

Our washing machine was giving Helen and me some trouble in February because the agitator wasn't working properly. Fortunately, we were able to get it fixed, which cost us £19.92.

It was in the *Sentinel* on 22 February that the government had given the go-ahead to a planned £3½ million flyover, to take the "D" Road over the A 34 at Hanford. I can't remember there being a problem with traffic when I'd driven around there, but I suppose it was needed because the number of cars were increasing all the time.

About the beginning of March, Dave Wallett came to inform me that Cissie was ill and had been taken into the Douglas Macmillan Home. She was suffering from ovarian cancer, which spread to her brain. I went to see her a couple of times, but she didn't last long.

Jeff had a new girlfriend, who was twelve years younger than him, although that didn't really bother me and they didn't look much different in their ages. He'd met her at the college, where she was a part-time lecturer. She was named Rosalind Downs and lived at 10 Arnold Grove, in Porthill. Jeff brought her to see Helen and me on 10 March and they stayed a couple of hours. She was an intelligent and very nice girl and we took to her right away. She and Jeff seemed to be suited to one another and we were pleased because it meant he was settling down.

Cissie died on 14 March and five days later, like Mo, she was cremated at Carmountside Crematorium after a funeral service at St. Andrew's Church, in Sneyd Green. After the funeral, we again gathered at the Birches Head Hotel and attending were Mo's other nephews, Stan Palin and Jack Wallett. I seemed to have lost touch with the rest of that side of my family.

On 20 April, Stoke were relegated from the First Division, with seven matches still to play! They were in the middle of a ten-game run of defeats to the end of the season and only got a crowd of 4,597 for their next home match, against Norwich City, on the 24th. They won just three league and cup games all season and I felt terrible that they'd come to such a state, even though I'd long been an armchair supporter by then.

In May, Helen and I bought a new stepladder for £19.95 from B & Q D.I.Y. and Garden Supercentre, in Leek Road, Hanley. It was made from aluminium and was lighter than our wooden one, which was wearing out. We gave our old stepladder to Jeff, which was a bad move because one day, when he was using it, one of the steps collapsed and he fell to the ground, but, fortunately, he wasn't injured.

About that time, Helen and I were invited to Caverswall Castle! It had come into the ownership of Brian Milner, the son of Minnie Holmans, Ken Johns's long-standing girlfriend. Minnie and her husband, Arthur, were living there and she seemed to be the housekeeper for her son and doing some tapestry work for the castle. Helen and Minnie were fairly friendly, so we were asked over and it was quite an experience to see the castle. We went in under an archway and there was a moat, but the building was very antiquated, as I'd expected it to be.

On 24 June, the former England captain, Mick Mills, was named as Stoke's new player-manager. Although he was quite a big name, I didn't think much about his appointment and he hadn't got any experience of managing a team. It was hoped that he'd take the club back up to the First Division, but it didn't work out that way because instead they went down to the Third Division in 1990 and Mills was sacked along the way!

In July, Helen and I went on holiday with Flo and Jack to the Cotswolds. Although we'd been there twice before, we still found new places to visit. We started off south of Gloucester at the lovely small town of Painswick, which was on a hill. We had a good walk around it and it was quaint with narrow streets and a lot of very old buildings. We had a wander round St. Mary's churchyard, where there were about a hundred yew trees, which made an impressive sight. They were clipped in an annual ceremony each September on Painswick Feast Sunday.

From there, we drove up to the village of Stanton, which was northeast of Cheltenham. It was at the foot of Shenbarrow Hill and was a very quiet place, with many old houses along its long main street.

The next place we visited was Chalford, which was near to Stroud. It was in the "Golden Valley" of the River Frome and was picturesque, but had steep narrow streets. Again, there were a lot of very nice houses and there were grand views down the valley.

While we were on holiday, we also went to Little Rissington, which was a village near to Bourton-on-the-Water. In the graveyard of St. Peter's Church were buried 76 personnel (49 of them during the Second World War) from RAF Little Rissington and their gleaming white headstones made quite a picture. There was also a tall white war memorial and the whole graveyard was very well kept. We spent some time there, just wandering round and looking at the details of the airmen who had lost their lives.

Helen had had some kind of bite on her left hand, perhaps from an insect, which had developed into a blister, with red marks on her skin stretching up to above her elbow. She went to the doctor's on 9 July and was told that she'd got lymphangitis, which meant that the bite had become infected. She was given an antibiotic drug, flucloxacillin, and that cleared the problem up eventually.

We still had our coal fire and, on seeing it, visitors sometimes said how lovely it was. We'd feel a glow of satisfaction as a result. In July, we had our chimney swept by George Massey & Son, of 44 Tonbridge Avenue, in Bradeley, at a cost of £4.50, which was the old age pensioners' rate. Although the principle remained the same as in the old days, with a brush being pushed up the chimney to make the soot fall down, by then an electric-powered pipe was used to suck most of it into a bag in a machine, which was like a large vacuum cleaner. It was a better method than the old shovelling one because it reduced the number of fine particles of soot floating about afterwards.

Jeff and Ros had decided to walk the whole length of the Caldon Canal, from Froghall to Etruria, which was eighteen miles, on 22 August. So I gave them a lift to Froghall and they walked all the way back. The canal passed close to our house, so Helen and I thought it would be nice to see them when they were nearby. In the evening, we had a stroll to Etruria Staircase Locks and got there in time to meet them as they came by. We then accompanied them on the short remaining distance to the junction with the Trent and Mersey Canal, where their walk ended. They'd enjoyed the day, but were very tired and still had to walk a mile or so back to our house, where they'd left their car!

On 5 September, it was in the *Sentinel* that the wreck of the Titanic had been found in the Atlantic Ocean south of Newfoundland. The supposedly unsinkable liner had struck an iceberg on 14 April 1912 on its maiden voyage and sunk, taking most of the passengers and crew to the bottom of the ocean with it. The captain of the ship had been Edward John Smith, who'd been born at 51 Well Street, in Hanley, and the discovery of the Titanic led to calls for a memorial to him to be built in Stoke-on-Trent, but nothing came of it. The idea of a memorial to a captain who'd been blamed for sinking a ship seemed strange to me, but, of course, the tragedy had made him famous.

Helen had always looked at the Swinnertons through rose-tinted spectacles and thought a lot of Francis, the son of her old boss, Mr John. I suppose that was because Mr John was his father. Unfortunately, Francis died on 1 October, at the age of 23, having been ill for some time. Helen wrote to Mr John, telling him how sorry she was to hear about it. She received a card from him and his wife, Joan, of Outlands Cottage, in Offley Brook, near Eccleshall, dated 1 October, which thanked her for all her 'expressions of sympathy'. The letter ended with the words 'much love Mr & Mrs John' and Helen kept it for the rest of her life. We, of course, went to Francis's funeral on 4 October at Adbaston Church, near to the home of the Swinnertons, and we went back a day or two later so that Helen could see the flowers on his grave.

Jeff and Ros turned up on 6 October and told Helen and me that they'd got engaged. We were surprised, but very pleased because she was a nice girl. They showed us a green garnet ring Jeff had bought her the day before at a craft fair at Keele. A week afterwards, they had a celebration party at Ros's parents' house, which we went to. Helen took a large bouquet of flowers, which she gave to Ros's mother, Shirley. She worked as a nursery nurse on the children's eye ward at the Infirmary and her husband, Alan, was a self-employed car mechanic. Ros's brother, Nick, who worked as an optician at Ian C. Sandbach, in Altrincham, was also there, with his girlfriend, Lisa Baxter. The party was very enjoyable and we all got on well together.

At one time, low users of electricity couldn't be billed the full standing charge and only had to pay the same amount as the electricity used. One day, Uncle Bill had a bill for £7.13, which comprised £1.04 consumption and £6.09 standing charge! I thought that was ridiculous, so I made a journey to the head office of the M.E.B., at 234 Victoria Road, to complain. I was told that the rules had been altered and that everyone had to pay the full standing charge regardless of how little electricity was used. I suppose the idea was to put a squeeze on the customers.

On 28 November, John Smith came to inform Helen and me that Uncle Bill had gone into an old folks' home. It seemed that John had become concerned when he'd found Uncle in a worse state than usual one day. He'd therefore contacted Social Services, who'd taken Uncle to The Grove, a home for the elderly in St. Thomas Place, Penkhull. Helen and I went to visit him, fearing the worst, but he was sitting up in an armchair, looking better than we'd seen him for a while. I didn't recognize him at first because he'd had a bath and had his long hair cut, though they hadn't shaved his beard. He was normally clean-shaven, but the staff thought he usually had a close-cropped beard and had just trimmed it! Also, he'd been rigged out with some decent, clean clothes, after having not changed his clothes for years.

After he'd been in The Grove for a while, Uncle seemed to accept that he'd be better off there. He was being well fed and kept clean. Most of the occupants were women and some of them were mentally not quite right. There was a smell of urine and the place seemed impregnated with it. There was a television to watch and Uncle liked to have a look at the horse racing. At Christmas, they had a party and he gave them a song and a speech, although he had trouble conversing with people because of his deafness.

I visited him a couple of times a week, while Helen held the fort at home because she dreaded going to hospitals and old people's homes. I regularly took him tobacco for his pipe and bottles of Gold Label beer. I'd asked the matron if that would be alright and she'd said a couple of bottles at a time would be okay. I also took him a miniature bottle of whisky, more or less every week, which he consumed in his bedroom. All that was paid for from his own money, which he handed over to me. He gave me his pension book and Girobank account book and I got him to sign the chits when he needed money. All that was going into his bank account was a pension of £5.85 a week from J. and G. Meakin's Eagle Pottery, in Ivy House Road, Hanley, where he'd worked for fifty-odd years!

Uncle liked a flutter on horse racing and would make bets on pieces of paper for me to take to the nearby bookmaker, W Mayhew, at 267 Prince's Road. Uncle's writing on the slip would be barely decipherable, so I had to explain to the bookie what it was all about. Uncle always had the favourite to win, which saved him the trouble of looking at the form and writing a horse's name out! If he could see the races on the TV, it was all the better, even if most of his horses lost.

Jeff was writing a book about Eric Burdon, who'd been the lead singer with the pop group, The Animals, in the 1960s. Jeff had got a publisher for it, Babylon Books, in Todmorden, West Yorkshire, and had signed a proper professional contract. On 16 January 1986, he flew with Ros to Eric's home in Villa Carlos, in Minorca, to interview him. Jeff had been able to get four days off from college, but was supposed to catch the work up later. He was with Eric for six days and, when he got back, told me the temperatures had been like those in May here and that he'd had a short-sleeved shirt on during the daytime.

At the Railway Club, we'd regularly been having a singer and an organist, who mainly did songs from around the Second World War. However, about this time, they were given the sack to cut costs because there weren't enough customers, but everyone was sad.

Helen and I had a robin in our garden, which came to see us several times a day and finally became so tame that it ate food out of our hands! I started to put food on the far end of our back brick wall and stood at the other end, gradually placing it nearer. Then I put my open hand near to the bird and brought it closer until, eventually, I put some food on my hand and the robin hopped on and ate it! That happened quite a number of times and Jeff tried it successfully too.

At Cissie's funeral, I'd had another chat with Dorothy Wallett about the family tree. On 10 March, she sent me a letter with more information and a computer print-out of the main details of eighteen Walletts, going back to 1635, which was another big help to me.

Jeff had started to do some private teaching and one of his students was the daughter of Rod Fletcher, a Liberal, who was the chairman of Alsager Town Council. Jeff and Ros were invited to the annual ball and Jeff bought a suit and a bow tie for the occasion, which Helen and I were surprised about because he didn't like wearing smart clothes. The ball was held at the civic centre on 14 March, but Jeff said that the main part of the meal was cold meat and salad and that the guests had tried to do ballroom dancing afterwards to the music of a pop group, which had been hired!

On 9 April, Uncle Bill had a solicitor, from Challinors & Dickson, in Cheapside, come to him at The Grove. He altered his will entirely in Helen's favour, leaving her everything he possessed, which, I think, was justice because she'd done more for him than anyone else other than me.

In May, Helen received a bill from Staffordshire County Council for £348.52 for Uncle Bill's stay of 10½ weeks at The Grove. It was a shock to us, though we understood there'd be some payment. I showed it to Uncle and he seemed surprised, but told me to see to it. Uncle's total weekly income was £44.69 and the council was allowing him to have £11.27 of it for pocket money and the payment of the rates on his house! So the council was demanding the remaining £33.42 a week over the period and Helen and I paid them with a cheque.

With Uncle's agreement, Helen and I went into his house to clean it and sort things out. It turned out to be an unbelievable job. By the side of his bed, we found hundreds of empty crisp bags and Kit Kat wrappings. It must have been too much trouble for him to have put them in the bin. We must have taken a ton or more of rubbish to the destructor in black plastic bags, so that his neighbours couldn't see anything. While we worked in the house, we wore scarves over our mouths and noses because of the dirt, dust and a foul smell! Helen was on her hands and knees, scrubbing his red clay tile floors and I don't know how she managed it because it was a big effort. He only had one or two bits of carpet and had never updated the house.

He had no inside toilet and the one at the top of his back yard had been out of operation for years, so Uncle had used a commode in the kitchen. It was full to the brim with urine and excrement and looked as though it had been for quite some time! Uncle had told me that John Smith was attending to such things, so I'd assumed the commode was being emptied when it wasn't. We also found, under his bed, a chamber pot, which was full too! I had the job of putting the contents into a bucket, carrying them downstairs and tipping them into a grid in his yard. Also, his mattress was soaked with urine and I found a pile of screwed-up newspapers in his kitchen, with excrement in, which I put in the bin!

I went to see the local health department about moving the commode, which was too heavy for me to deal with. They sent a couple of fellows to do the job, which they did, and they only spilt a small amount of urine on the floor, which I had to clean up. Also, I got the council refuse people to come and take the mattress away, which only cost two pounds.

Anyway, Helen and I got the house cleaned out and ready to be sold because Uncle had realized he couldn't go back there. We received a letter from the county council, saying that, if the house was sold, the money from it would be taken into account with regard to Uncle's keep, at a charge of 25p a week for every £50 he had over £1,200. They also said that, if the house wasn't sold, they'd make a valuation and charge accordingly. It seemed to Helen and me that the house had better be sold, so we put the facts to Uncle and he told us to do whatever we thought was necessary.

We decided to sell his furniture, so I contacted a dealer, who advertised in the *Sentinel*, and he called to have a look at what was on offer. He refused a good condition old-fashioned three-piece suite, a decent sideboard and a lovely wardrobe and dressing table, saying there was no demand for such things. But he made me an offer for an old picture frame and photo, two or three old curtain poles, an old radio and a chest with a broken lid, which I'd been thinking of chopping up for fire wood! Altogether, he gave me forty pounds for mainly rubbish and ignored the better stuff, which stayed in the house.

Helen and I found an advert in the *Sentinel* from a property dealer, who was looking for old premises. I contacted him and he came to Uncle's house to have a look. He wasn't impressed with what he saw and told me about all its faults. He asked me how much we were asking for it and I said: 'I don't know. How much will you offer?' He proposed £1,700, which seemed to be a very low amount, so I told him I'd let him know.

Helen then saw another *Sentinel* advert, about valuing houses for ten pounds. We decided to try this and a fellow turned up at Uncle's house to give his judgement. The figure he gave was £2,000 to £4,000, which was a bit vague, but encouraging. I gave him his ten pounds and off he went.

I then got in touch with a property renovator, Joe Bott, of 12 Boughey Road, in Shelton. One of his representatives came along, had a look around and then asked how much I wanted. I told him £4,000, but I was expecting him to say it was worth a lot less. He said: 'That seems reasonable. We'll have it.' I explained that I'd have to get the okay from the owner and so I'd let him know.

The next time I saw Uncle Bill, I told him the amount that had been offered and his eyes lit up! I think the price he and Aunt Sally had paid for the house in 1947 was £213, after having rented it for years. Of course, Uncle was in agreement with the price and told me to go ahead, which I did, so that the sale was completed and he received a cheque for £4,000 at the beginning of July.

The Royal Tournament, the annual military tattoo, which was the largest in the world, came to the city on 6 July and it was the first time it had ever been on display outside London. Thousands of people lined the streets to watch it go past, on its way from Stoke Station to the arena of the National Garden Festival, which was being held on a site where Macalonie, Shelton Colliery and the part of Shelton Bar that had closed in 1978 had been. I went to Broad Street to see the parade, which had 800 personnel and tons of equipment. There were some small guns, which were rather like those we'd had in the 3rd Mountain Regiment of the Royal Artillery in the Second World War, and they were being pulled along by soldiers. The Queen's Colour Squadron was there and also passing by were other units of the armed forces, bands, native troops and a tribesman, who threatened people in the crowd with his spear! It was one of the best parades I'd ever seen in the district.

Our robin was still visiting us regularly for food, but, on 20 July, it was jerking its neck and didn't seem to be properly right. After that, it disappeared and unfortunately we never saw it again.

Jeff and Ros went on holiday to Scotland for eleven days on 22 July and while they were away, Helen and I painted the downstairs woodwork of his house to help him out and brighten it up. When he got back, he was very pleased.

On 23 August, I topped up the petrol in my car at the filling station at the bottom of Victoria Road, just the other side of the River Trent. At the kiosk, I was told to pay £9.74, even though the amount on the pump had only read £4.74. I was told I'd put another five pounds' worth in earlier. When I protested and said I hadn't, I was given a piece of paper, which was supposed to be a credit note if what I was saying was found to be true! I took it, but I wasn't very happy about the situation, so I mentioned it to Jeff. He said we should go to try to get my money back, which we did on the 26th. When we explained what had happened, I was given a five pounds' refund and got an apology for the trouble caused.

Jeff decided that he wanted to spend more time on his writing and so he made a temporary arrangement with the college to halve his job. Although that gave him more than half his net income, Helen and I were worried that he wouldn't have enough money coming in. However, he managed and eventually he and the college made the arrangement permanent.

Jeff came down on Helen's 66th birthday and gave us two tickets to go to the National Garden Festival. I'd lost touch with the area after I'd moved from Windermere Street in 1932, but it had become derelict and cost £5 million to clean up. Helen and I went to the festival the next day and although the gardens were only intended to be temporary, it was enjoyable to see them. Big shopping units and the Odeon multi-screen cinema were later built on part of the site, which became known as Festival Park, and it was an improvement on how the area had been before it was reclaimed.

I'd surrendered Uncle Bill's pension books to Social Services, at their demand, and they wanted their cut from the sale price of his house, which Uncle asked me to sort out. In October, I received a bill from them for £308.94. The outstanding charge for his twenty weeks' residence was £955.69 and his pensions accounted for £646.75, so the bill was for the balance and was paid from the sale of his house. Out of his capital from the house sale, he had to pay Social Services their proportion of the amount over £1,200, but he started to give some of his money away. Helen and I had £100 each, Vera and Big Harry £50 each and Jeff £20.

Vera and Harry started visiting Uncle and Harry took him a bet to the bookie's every time he went. In November, Uncle gave Vera, Helen, Jeff and me £30 each and I began to wonder whether Social Services would protest at his capital going down because they'd have less of it. Helen and I had already been warned not to do anything silly, like buy a car.

Uncle had a nephew, Arthur Bailey, to whom he gave his gold watch, which had been presented to him for his long service by Meakin's at his retirement. Arthur hadn't bothered much with him, but Uncle had a soft spot for him, so I was asked to get in touch with him, which I did. I told him that Uncle wanted to see him, but that he was poorly. Arthur didn't turn up, but his wife did and Uncle gave her £50.

Jeff took me to Froghall on my 71st birthday and we explored the area around the Caldon Canal. There was a short tunnel and just the other side of it was

Froghall Wharf, where the canal ended. We went on a walk from there and had a look at a track, where a tramway had been, bringing limestone from the quarries at Caldon Low to be loaded onto barges at Froghall. It was all very interesting.

In December, I paid another bill to the county council for Uncle Bill's keep. It was for £201.68 and was the difference between their £635.22 charge for a further thirteen weeks' stay at The Grove and his income of £433.54. Again, the payment came from the proceeds of his house sale.

At that time, Helen and I often had a run out to Jeff's on Thursday afternoons, but in January 1987 it became so cold that I couldn't get our car started. So for a change, on the 8th, we went on the train. The following Monday, I got the car bump started, through Jeff towing me, and then ran it to Endon to get some logs for the fire. On the Thursday, though, it wouldn't kick up, but I got a new battery and that solved the problem.

On odd occasions, I took Uncle Bill for a run in the car and I think he was glad to get out of the home for a while. He couldn't see very well and wanted some new reading glasses, so I arranged for an optician to attend to him, but I don't think his new spectacles were much use to him. So I got him a magnifying glass, but that didn't seem to help much either.

On 7 February, I went to visit him and he was in bed because he was poorly. He seemed a little strange, but I still asked him if he wanted to have a bet on the horses. He didn't seem too bothered, but I made the bet out in the usual format and took it to the bookie. I returned to The Grove, to discover that the horse had won, but, shortly afterwards, I decided to go home and told Helen how Uncle was. She thought she'd better go to have a look at him, but when we arrived, we saw some officials, who were in a panic. They said that they were sorry, but Uncle had died and they'd been trying to get in touch with us. They'd been given our address as next of kin, but hadn't been able to find it! They asked us if we'd like to see Uncle's body, but Helen declined.

Uncle had asked to be cremated, so that was what we arranged. We went to Joseph Lymer & Son, the undertakers at Trent Bridge, in Bucknall, and asked them to see to things. We then went to the crematorium at Carmountside and paid for the insertion of Uncle's name in the Book of Remembrance. The funeral, on 12 February, went off very well, with Uncle's friends from Hanley Gospel Mission (which had been in Majolica Street) and Meakin's in attendance.

Helen was the sole beneficiary of Uncle's estate and paid the undertaker's bill of £474.50 in due course. We had a letter from Staffordshire County Council, telling us that Uncle owed them £186.39 for his remaining accommodation in The Grove, but they had £111.70 cash from his belongings, so a balance of £74.69 needed to be paid. We sent that amount to them, which cleared everything up.

1. GILL and "YOUNG" HARRY POOLE, Cyril's nephew, at their WEDDING RECEPTION at the Elms Hotel, in Oxford, on 7 July 1962.

2. CYRIL, his wife, HELEN, and son, JEFF, at the wedding reception of Gill and Harry Poole at the Elms Hotel, in Oxford, on 7 July 1962.

3. The new LEEK ROAD POST OFFICE nearing completion. It opened on 12 August 1963 and Cyril, who was a postman, was based there until his retirement in 1979.

4. A still from a cine film shot by Cyril, showing JEFF with his new Dansette Conquest record player at his home, at 335 Leek Road, in Shelton, on Christmas morning 1963.

5. A still from a cine film shot by Cyril, showing BOBBY IRVINE, the goalkeeper of STOKE CITY, making a save during a 3-1 win against MANCHESTER UNITED at the Victoria Ground, in Stoke, on 18 April 1964.

6. A still from a cine film shot by Cyril, showing HELEN at Southport on a family day trip in May 1964.

7. A still from a cine film shot by Cyril, showing the arrival of BILLY SMART'S ELEPHANTS at the site of his circus on spare ground off Harding Road, in Hanley, on 4 April 1965.

8. BERRY HILL SPOIL TIP in 1965. The huge tip loomed large from the front windows of Cyril's home, at 335 Leek Road, in Shelton, but was removed in 1970-1971.

9. The double-winning POSTAL SPORTS CLUB football team, parading the Haig and Haig Cup and the Half-Holiday League championship trophy at the end of the 1965-1966 season. Their captain, BERT ASH, is fourth from the right in the front row and their centre-forward, JEFF WALKER, who scored 72 goals, is two places to Bert's left. CYRIL and JEFF were supporters of the team.

10. CYRIL and HELEN in May 1966.

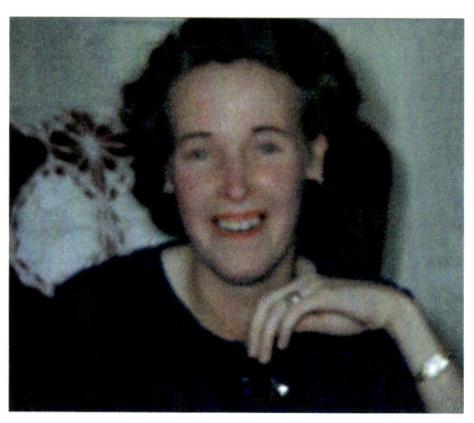

11. Stills from a cine film shot by Cyril, showing LES and JOAN BROWN at Helen and Cyril's golden wedding anniversary party at 335 Leek Road, in Shelton, on 19 June 1966. Les and Joan were close friends of Cyril and Helen at Shelton Club and Institute, in Richmond Terrace, where they were all members in the 1960s.

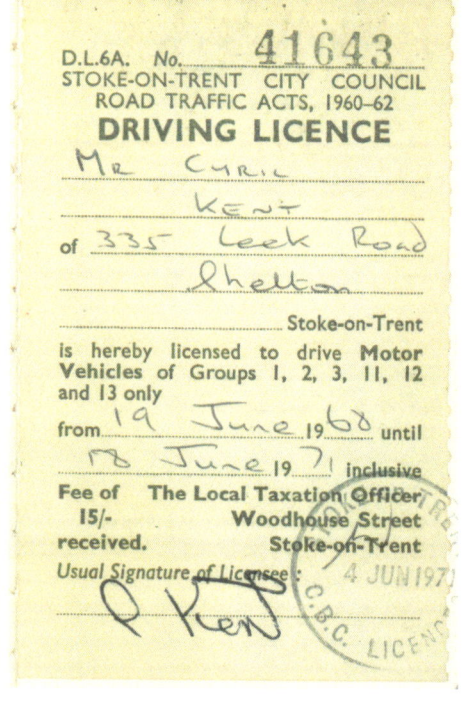

12. CYRIL'S DRIVING LICENCE, which he bought for fifteen shillings on 19 June 1968.

13. ETHEL and ELIJAH MIDDLETON. Elijah was Helen's brother, whose trouble-free driving with his Volkswagen Beetle inspired Cyril and Helen to buy one in July 1968.

14. CYRIL, having a drink of tea by his VOLKSWAGEN BEETLE in Scotland in July 1969.

15. A still from a cine film shot by Cyril in July 1969, showing the LOCH NESS MONSTER! The fraudulent beast was being towed across the loch by a motorboat and filmed for an episode of the popular television series, *Dr. Finlay's Casebook*.

16. Helen's AUNT SALLY and UNCLE BILL. When Aunt Sally died on 29 July 1971, Helen told Uncle Bill that she'd do him a Sunday lunch-time dinner for the rest of his life and she kept to her promise until he went into an old people's home in 1985.

17. A scene from the 1971 UNION OF POST OFFICE WORKERS' STRIKE. Cyril was a member of the union, which rejected an 8% wage rise offer, but was forced to accept a further increase of only 1% after nearly seven weeks on strike.

18. A scene from the STOKE CITY FOOTBALL LEAGUE CUP-WINNING CELEBRATIONS in Kingsway, Stoke, on 5 March 1972. The captain, Peter Dobing, is pictured holding the cup. Cyril shot some cine film of the team passing along Wharf Street on their tour bus, but, by then, darkness had fallen and he recorded only flashing lights!

19. JEFF in 1972. By then, he was a student at the North Staffordshire Polytechnic, in Stoke, and had grown his hair long, in the youthful fashion of the time.

20. A still from a cine film shot by Cyril, showing JACK and EDITH ELSON. Edith was Helen's cousin and they were good friends. In the early to mid-1970s, Helen and Cyril went to parties at Jack and Edith's home, at 96 Eastbourne Road, in Northwood, where there was plenty to drink!

21. MATTHEW and MANDY POOLE, the children of Harry and Gill. Cyril and Helen took Matthew and Mandy out at weekends for years in the 1970s.

22. HELEN, with LUCY and CHARLIE DEAN, at Lucy's seventieth birthday party at Scotia Club, in Scotia Road, Burslem, in May 1974. Lucy and Charlie were close friends of Cyril and Helen at Shelton Club, where sometimes Charlie would spontaneously get onto the stage and sing!

23. PAT CLARKE and JEFF, c. 1975. They had a stormy romance from New Year's Eve in 1972, got engaged two years later and broke off their relationship in November 1975.

24. HELEN greeting KELVIN BOWERS in Kingsway, Stoke, on 14 December 1975, on his return home after having run 10,275 miles to Australia to raise funds for the North Staffordshire Ladsandads Club!

25. CYRIL and HELEN at Shelton Club, probably on 10 January 1976.

26. A still from a cine film shot by Cyril, showing the start of the seventh stage of the MILK RACE (an international amateur cycling competition) in Victoria Road, Fenton, on 6 June 1976.

27. A still from a cine film shot by Cyril, showing CELEBRATIONS IN TALBOT STREET, in Eastwood, of the JUBILEE OF QUEEN ELIZABETH II on 7 June 1977. The street was later demolished.

28. A still from a cine film shot by Cyril, showing HELEN at home, with a flowering cactus, in May or June 1978.

29. AN OFFICIAL POST OFFICE LETTER OF SERVICE RECOGNITION received by Cyril at his retirement as a postman in December 1979..

30. JEFF, with his girlfriend, JILL EVANS, and her son, JASON, near Danebridge, in the Peak District, on 1 September 1980. Jeff and Jill's relationship lasted from 1977 to 1984 and Jason had lunch with Jeff at Cyril and Helen's house a time or two en route to watch Port Vale.

31. The inside of the SHELTON CLUB AND INSTITUTE LIFE MEMBERSHIP CARD granted to Cyril on 10 February 1981.

32. A still from a cine film shot by Cyril, taken from the Lichfield Street-Leek Road roundabout on 4 April 1981, showing the BIKERS' EASTER EGG RUN en route to Stoke Town Hall.

33. HELEN BEING PRESENTED WITH HER LEAVING GIFT (a gold watch) on 26 June 1981, upon her retirement as the manageress of F. Swinnerton & Son Limited. Also in the picture, from left to right, are the company directors, JOHN MORREY, JOAN SWINNERTON and JOHN SWINNERTON.

34. HELEN and CYRIL c. 1982.

35. SAM and DORIS LYTH, who became close friends of Cyril and Helen at the British Rail Staff Association Club, in Winton Square, from 1983.

36. Helen's elder sister, VERA POOLE, and her husband, "BIG" HARRY", on their golden wedding anniversary on 31 December 1983.

37. ERN and MARGARET PARKES, who became friends with Cyril and Helen at the "Railway Club", in Winton Square.

38. CYRIL and HELEN with KIERON EARDLEY at the "Railway Club" c. 1984. Kieron suffered from Down's syndrome and Helen used to help his mother, Beryl, by taking him out quite regularly for a number of years.

39. CAVERSWALL CASTLE, to which Cyril and Helen made a visit, upon invitation, in about 1985. The castle was then owned by Brian Milner, the son of Helen's friend, Minnie Holmans.

40. CYRIL and HELEN at the "Railway Club" c. 1987.

41. HELEN, CYRIL, ROS KENT (née Downs), JEFF and SHIRLEY and ALAN DOWNS after Jeff and Ros's wedding in Ullapool, Scotland, on 14 July 1987.

42. HELEN (third from the left) and CYRIL (fifth from the left) after the inauguration of their friends, GRAHAME and YVONNE JEFFRIES (both in the centre), as the mayor and mayoress of Cheadle Town Council on 4 September 1988.

43. CYRIL PLAYING THE PIANO on Christmas Day 1988 at 12 Arnold Grove, in Porthill, the home of Alan and Shirley Downs.

44. ROS, HELEN and CYRIL on 29 September 1989 in Wildboarclough, in the Peak District, where there had been a flash flood so serious on 24 May that the road was closed for over six months.

45. CYRIL and HELEN at their golden wedding anniversary party at their home on 21 June 1991.

46. GERTIE and TOM BILLINGTON, who became close friends of Cyril and Helen at the P.M.T. Employees' Social & Sports Club, in Maclagan Street, Stoke, from 1991.

47. HELEN and CYRIL, on 16 July 1991, on holiday with their close friends, FLO (second from the left) and JACK HODGKISS (far right), at Snowshill, in the Cotswolds.

48. JEFF and his new keyboard, which he bought for £1,150 in May 1992. It had 150 different instrumental sounds, but when Cyril played it, he didn't think they were true representations.

49. CYRIL'S SECOND WORLD WAR MEDALS, which he received in December 1992, over fifty years after he'd joined the Forces! On the left is The Defence Medal and on the right is the War Medal.

50. CYRIL, HELEN and Jeff's cat, RAEDBURH, in Jeff and Ros's back garden, at 65 Audley Road, in Alsager, on 12 April 1993.

51. Cyril's cousin, BERNARD KENT, and his wife, DOROTHY. Cyril and Bernard both independently produced versions of the Kent family tree. Bernard used a professional researcher, but Cyril did his own investigations, which took him years to complete.

52. Cyril's cousin, DAVE WALLETT, who was a keen photographer and bluffed his way into Stanley Matthews's eightieth birthday celebration dinner at Trentham Gardens on 1 February 1995.

53. CYRIL, HELEN and RAEDBURH in the back garden of Jeff and Ros's new house, at 8 Nelson Crescent, in Cotes Heath, in August 1996. Behind them is the garden plot which Cyril and Helen developed.

54. HELEN and long-time neighbour, NANCY CADMAN, of 333 Leek Road, gossiping over their back wall (which had been built by Cyril in 1955) in August 1996.

55. CYRIL and HELEN FEEDING A GOOSE at Martin Mere Wetland Centre, at Burscough, near Southport, on 14 July 1997.

56. CYRIL and A HERD OF DEER on 9 May 1998 at Cote Farm, near Alton Towers, where Matthew Poole was a stockman. The farm belonged to JCB Limited.

57. HELEN on holiday at LLANRWST, in North Wales, on 12 May 1998. She'd developed a breast tumour by then and therefore seemed to believe that this would be her final holiday, but it turned out not to be.

58. AUDREY and JACK PATTINSON, who became close friends of Cyril and Helen at Rectory Road Sports & Social Club, in Shelton, from 1998.

59. CYRIL as photographed in a booth in Hanley Post Office, in Tontine Street, on 1 September 1999. He went there to get a photo for a new driving licence, but misunderstood the procedure, hence the strange outcome!

60. HELEN at THIMBLE HALL, in Youlgreave, near Bakewell, the world's smallest detached house, on 6 September 1999.

61. CYRIL, HELEN, ROS and JEFF at Helen's eightieth birthday party at Jeff and Ros's house on 29 September 2000.

62. CYRIL at the ROYAL AIR FORCE MUSEUM, in Cosford, near Telford, on his 85th birthday, on 14 December 2000.

63. HELEN and CYRIL celebrating their diamond wedding anniversary on 21 June 2001 with a visit at their home from BILL and WYN AUSTIN, the Lord Mayor and Lady Mayoress of Stoke-on-Trent City Council.

64. CYRIL and HELEN outside the North Stafford Hotel, in Winton Square, at their diamond wedding anniversary party on 23 June 2001.

65. CYRIL HANDLING A PYTHON at Gentleshaw Wildlife Centre, in Eccleshall, on 1 April 2002.

66. CYRIL, HELEN and their 1982 VOLKSWAGEN POLO in Nelson Crescent, Cotes Heath, in May 2002. The car was still on the road at the time this book was published in 2012!

67. CYRIL on ST BERTRAM'S BRIDGE over the River Manifold, with Ilam Hall in the background, on 19 April 2003.

68. CYRIL PLAYING CRAZY GOLF against Jeff and Ros at Prestatyn, in North Wales, on 31 May 2003. Despite being 87, Cyril won!

69. CYRIL at the Wedgwood Visitor Centre on 31 May 2004, SHOWING HOW HE USED TO TURN WARE when he was a pottery turner.

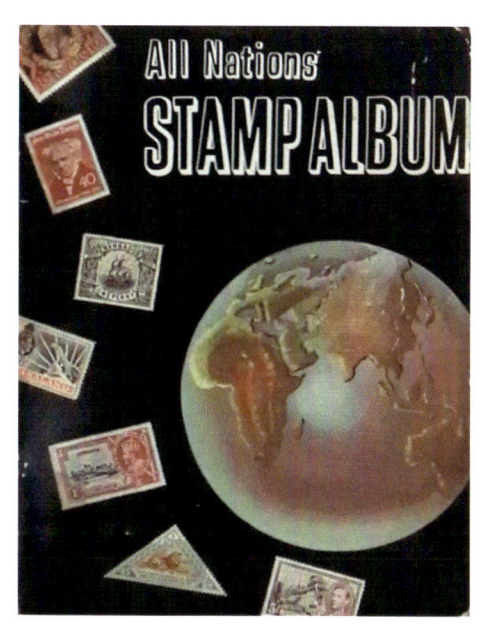

70. THE FRONT of one of CYRIL'S STAMP ALBUMS. By the end of 2004, he'd collected well over 6,000 stamps, excluding duplicates.

71. HELEN and CYRIL DANCING at the North Stafford Hotel at Dorothy Kent's eightieth birthday party on 14 May 2005.

72. CYRIL in the SECRET NUCLEAR BUNKER in Hack Green, near Nantwich, on 19 June 2005.

73. CYRIL AT HIS COMPUTER in the lounge at his home on 3 September 2005.

74. CYRIL on his ninetieth birthday trip to MANCHESTER AIRPORT'S AVIATION VIEWING PARK on 15 December 2005. Behind him is a CONCORDE airliner.

75. JEFF and CYRIL by the allotments opposite Mawson Grove, in Shelton, on 29 August 2006, being photographed for a *Sentinel* article published the following day.

76. CYRIL and HELEN, with Jeff's new girlfriend, SUE BELL, at Jeff's house on Christmas Day 2006. Ros had left Jeff two years before and Helen was suffering from vascular dementia.

77. HELEN celebrating her final birthday, at Jeff's house, on 29 September 2007, with a chocolate cake made by Sue Bell.

78. JEFF and CYRIL outside the MUSEUM OF CHILDHOOD, in Sudbury, in Derbyshire, on Cyril's 93rd birthday, on 14 December 2008.

79. CYRIL PLAYING POOL at The Junction Inn, in Norbury Junction, on Boxing Day 2008.

80. CYRIL on his MOBILITY SCOOTER in the HAMPS VALLEY on 5 July 2009. He could no longer walk very far.

81. JEFF and CYRIL in a mock First World War trench at the STAFFORDSHIRE REGIMENT MUSEUM, at Whittington Barracks, near Lichfield, on Cyril's 94th birthday, on 14 December 2009.

82. SUE, JEFF and CYRIL having an IMPROMPTU MUSIC SESSION at Jeff's house on 27 December 2009.

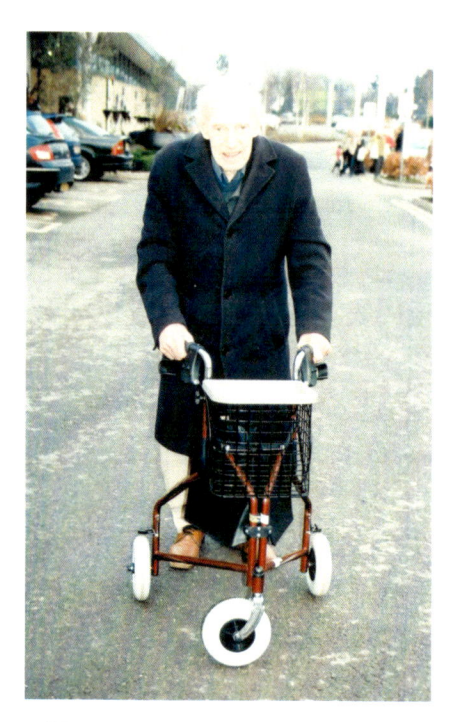

83. CYRIL using his new WHEELED WALKER for the first time, at Trentham Garden Centre, on 7 February 2010. It enabled him to continue to walk independently.

84. CYRIL and EVELYN ROYLE on 2 November 2010 at her home at 32 Mulgrave Street, in Cobridge, where she'd lived all her life. Cyril knew her as a child in the 1920s and this was their first meeting for forty years.

85. CYRIL at RADIO STOKE, in Cheapside, Hanley, during his first and last radio interview, promoting his book, *A Potteries Past*, on 28 November 2010.

86. JEFF and CYRIL on 14 December 2011, on Cyril's 96th birthday.

87. CYRIL at MISO restaurant at 161-163 London Road, in Stoke, eating his first ever Japanese meal, on his 96th birthday, on 14 December 2011.

88. CYRIL enjoying a packet of QUAVERS at the Kingsley & Froghall Station café, on the Churnet Valley Railway, on 29 January 2012 on his final trip out.

5 New Horizons

On 18 March 1987, Helen and I called to see Jeff and he told us the news that he and Rosalind were going to get married, which was a pleasant surprise. But there was a snag, which was that the ceremony was to be in Ullapool, in the far north of Scotland. Helen tried to persuade them to have a church wedding locally, but it was no use. They were adamant that their wedding would be in the part of Scotland that they both loved so much. Helen said she wouldn't be attending because it was too far to travel, but she wished them luck. It seemed strange going all that far and I just went along with her. I think Jeff was a bit hurt because it seemed he'd thought we'd agree with it right away.

Some weeks later, it came to the notice of Helen and me that a train ran regularly from Crewe Station to Inverness, carrying cars and allowing their drivers and passengers to travel in sleeper carriages. I got a leaflet from Stoke Station and we studied it. Helen liked the idea of travelling to Jeff's wedding this way, even though she was a little apprehensive about sleeping in an unknown compartment and our car being left to the mercies of the railway staff.

We drove to Crewe Station to have a look at the carriages that carried the vehicles. I had visions of open trucks, exposed to the elements and any filth lying around, but I was pleased to find they were all covered. The cost for conveying a car and its driver and passengers from Crewe to Inverness was about a hundred pounds, which wasn't bad, so we booked our trip. We told Jeff and he was really pleased.

In May, Helen decided to distribute some of Uncle Bill's money to her relatives. She gave £350 to Vera, who didn't seem very happy with that, and £50 each to Jeff, Big Harry, Ethel, Mandy and Matthew. When Ethel received her money, she said, 'Dead man's money never did anybody any good,' but she put it in her purse just the same!

The next time Helen saw Vera, she had some nasty words spoken to her. Helen was very hurt and it seemed that Vera was expecting a far bigger sum of money from Uncle Bill's estate, perhaps half. She'd put in very little effort in looking after Uncle, but she expected a big reward! After her remarks, Vera walked off in a huff. Helen and Vera had an arrangement to meet in Hanley on a Friday morning each week to have a gossip. The following three Fridays, Vera didn't turn up, so Helen came to the conclusion that Vera was avoiding her and didn't wish to speak to her. That proved to be the case and Helen was very hurt by it.

Helen and I had seen a notice in the *Sentinel* that Stoke-on-Trent was to be made into a smoke control area and we had a letter to that effect. It meant that we'd be unable to burn coal after 1991 and that we'd have to use smokeless fuel or convert to gas or electricity. Smokeless fuel was about 50% more in price than coal and it was vexing that we'd have to pay that, without any compensation, just because the council had decided there was to be a change. I got a council man to have a look at our fireplace and he decided we'd be eligible for a 70% grant towards its conversion to a gas fire. That pleased us and we decided to go ahead. A man we knew came from British Gas to measure up. He was Dennis Galley, the brother of Levi, Helen's old boyfriend. I had a look around the British Gas West

Midlands showroom in Tontine Square, Hanley, and found a fire that was suitable, which Dennis ordered for us.

Jeff's wedding had been arranged for 14 July. Only the immediate families were travelling to Ullapool for the ceremony and the reception was going to be in a marquee at Wettonmill, in the Manifold Valley, after Jeff and Ros returned from honeymoon. Helen had gone rash and bought a lovely new blue dress for the reception for £137.95 from Lucille, in Trinity Street, but she wasn't planning to take it to the wedding in case it creased in her suitcase on the journey. I had a new suit for the occasions, from Greenwoods (Menswear) Ltd, at Unit 9, in Moxon's Island, Hanley, which cost about the same amount.

The only relatives invited to Jeff and Ros's wedding reception from the Kent side were Bernard and Dorothy because Jeff didn't know any of the others. Dorothy bought a special dress for the occasion, but Bernard later declined to attend, even though we offered them a lift in our car. That meant Dorothy couldn't come either because he wouldn't let her. Bernard was so mean that he didn't even send a present and I felt disgusted that the only representative on my side let us down. Ethel also declined her invitation, though she too was offered a lift.

On the evening of Sunday 12 July, Helen and I travelled to Crewe Station, where I drove our car into a carriage, to which railwaymen fastened it securely. We came away wondering if it would be alright. We had an hour or two to pass before the train departed, so we went into the British Rail Staff Association Club, in Gresty Road, for a drink and some entertainment. Someone came round selling raffle tickets, so I bought one or two. When the draw was made, my number came out of the hat and I had to go on the stage to collect my prize, which was a tin of biscuits. Helen was delighted and I thought it was a good omen for our trip north.

Later, we left the club and boarded the train, hoping that the carriage containing our car had been hooked onto the passenger coaches. Our sleeping compartment was rather small, with two bunk beds and a washbasin, but it was okay. It was about eleven o'clock when we got into our bunks to try to get some rest. I was occupying the upper bunk because Helen didn't fancy climbing the little ladder. After a while, the train started off and it seemed to go quite slowly. We must have dozed off, though I kept waking up and each time it seemed as if we'd stopped or were moving very slowly.

About seven o'clock in the morning, an attendant knocked on our door to give us a cup of tea and told us we'd be in Inverness in an hour. Helen and I had both had a restless night, which I suppose was understandable because of the noise of the train and the lights flashing in from towns and stations. We rolled into Inverness roughly on time and stepped onto the platform to await the unloading of our car. Helen went off to get a newspaper while a railwayman backed out the cars at speed. My heart was in my mouth while I waited for him to reach our carriage, but I think he was able to reverse my car with confidence because I'd driven it in with the wheels absolutely straight. When Helen returned, I told her about the episode and she nearly had a fit because she visualized the railwayman crashing the car! It was a good job she hadn't been present.

We'd arranged to meet Jeff and Ros in Ullapool at, I think, twelve o'clock, which gave us plenty of time. I went outside the station to find out which way to turn. I walked left and came to a sign, which indicated the A 9 going to Ullapool. I went back, got in the car, drove out to the left and kept going. I drove for about twenty miles, but there didn't seem to be any mention of Ullapool and I remembered that Jeff had said we'd go over a big bridge just outside Inverness. We hadn't seen it, so I came to the conclusion that we were going in the wrong direction. At the next convenient turnoff, I changed direction and headed back to Inverness! By then, we were running a bit late, so I had to speed up a little, but, just after we got to Inverness, we went across Kessock Bridge, over the Beauly Firth, which Jeff had mentioned.

When we got to Ullapool, Jeff and Ros were waiting for us at the appointed spot, opposite The Ceilidh Place, in West Argyle Street. They were staying about fifteen miles north of Ullapool, at Avalon, in Elphin, with their friends, Russell and Bridie Pursey, who knew a couple of places where Helen and I could put up for the night. One (number 395 Elphin) was near to them and was owned by an old lady, Ina Macdonald. Helen thought this place would be nice and homely and so we went to have a look at it. It was rather shabby, but looked clean and Helen decided we should stay there because it would have been awkward to have refused it.

Jeff and Ros introduced us to Russell and Bridie and later took us for a drive to have a look at the scenery. Jeff wished to show us everything and tried to do it all in a comparatively short time. He drove us northwest to Lochinver, which was on the coast and then sped back through Inverkirkaig, along a narrow road, with very tight corners, which made me feel quite queasy! Jeff and Ros then dropped us off at our B & B, while they drove 75 miles to Inverness to pick up her parents, who'd travelled up in the day on the train. When they returned, we all had a nice meal in The Ceilidh Place.

In the morning, Helen and I drove to the Ross and Cromarty District Council Locality Office, in Market Street, Ullapool, where births, marriages and deaths were recorded and civil marriage ceremonies (like Jeff and Ros's) took place. There we met Jeff, who had Russell and Bridie and their foster children, Andrew and Wendy, with him. We then awaited the arrival of Ros, her parents and her brother, Nick, who'd flown that morning from Manchester to Inverness, where he'd hired a car! Also present was Ken Lee, a photographer for the Dingwall-based *North Star* newspaper, which was doing a report on the wedding.

We all went in for the ceremony, which was very nice, and Nick and I took photos both inside and outside. I also used my cine camera, but I was a bit limited, owing to me being in the party. We then all made our way to The Ceilidh Place, where Jeff and Ros had ordered a spread in a room on our own. It was a jolly party, which Helen and I paid for, at a cost of £157.20.

Afterwards, Jeff and his bride drove to the Far North Hotel, in Balnakeil, on the north coast of Sutherland, where they were staying for a few days before going on honeymoon to La Palma, in the Canary Islands. Nick drove off to Inverness, to catch his flight back, and took Alan and Shirley, so they could get their train. Helen and I decided to stay another day and we found a very nice B & B in the town. We had a wander round and watched the boats coming and going. We had some nice fish and chips, which we ate while we sat on a bench, looking at the harbour. While we were there, we chatted with another couple about various things, including army experiences in the Second World War. In the evening,

Helen and I went into a pub, where we had a drink, listened to the chatter and discussed one or two of the people who were around us.

In the morning, we started south, towards home. We must have stopped some place in Scotland for the night, maybe in Callander or near Oban. The following day, we arrived in the Lake District and stayed at Rachel's in Borrowdale. One day, we had a picnic by the side of a small river near Buttermere and a hen, which was pecking around, came up to us to be fed! After a day or two, we made our way back home.

On Saturday 8 August, Helen put on her new blue dress for Jeff and Ros's wedding reception and I wore my new suit. I understand Ros's parents paid for the event, apart from the Asti spumante, which Helen and I bought for the guests and which Helen liked to think was champagne. It turned out a nice day and Helen and I had no problem finding the marquee because we'd visited Wettonmill many times. It was one of our favourite spots, as it was Jeff's. We arrived in good time and were greeted by Jeff and Ros. The marquee was pitched in a field by the side of the River Manifold, where it went underground by Darfur Crags.

Helen and Vera still hadn't met since Vera had walked off, although she'd accepted Jeff and Ros's invitation to the reception. However, Helen had said to me that Vera wouldn't attend and I thought it did look unlikely. I happened to be near the entrance of the marquee when who should walk in but Vera and her family. I was nonplussed, but then Helen came over to us and the two sisters embraced, with tears falling onto their cheeks. We all moved to the table Helen and I had been occupying and it seemed that the Pooles had had some difficulty in finding the marquee. Jeff had sent a map out with the reception invitations, showing the best route to the marquee, but the Pooles had picked a shorter way, which involved very narrow lanes and a steep hill down from Butterton. I don't think they'd been in a similar situation before and it must have seemed like the back of beyond to them. Anyway, the ice had been broken and Helen and Vera were now on speaking terms.

Jeff had got a generator for the lights, cooking and music, though it turned out not to be powerful enough to cope with everything at once, so there had to be cuts in consumption so that the food didn't suffer. However, things went well and there was barn dancing to the Canalsiders, a musical group Jeff had hired. We enjoyed ourselves until well after darkness had come down. Because we were in the middle of the countryside, there wasn't a street lamp to be seen and it was really dark outside the marquee at night.

Once it had gone dark, Helen wanted to go home, though Jeff would have liked us to have stayed a little longer. We said our goodbyes and the Pooles decided to follow us because I don't think they relished finding their way out of the Manifold Valley in the pitch-black. I took our usual route, through the tunnel, to Warslow and Young Harry drove behind me. We parted company at Bottom House crossroads, where we carried straight on and they turned to Leek.

Nearly every Saturday after then, Jeff and Ros came to have a cooked dinner with Helen and me at lunch time and they seemed to enjoy the meal. It just carried on as before, with Ros coming along as well as Jeff. Helen and I were pleased and enjoyed seeing them. We'd have a chat and sometimes a brief argument, disagreeing about something, but it wasn't nasty.

One of the conditions of the council grant for our new gas fire was that our chimney should be swept before conversion, to make sure there was no soot left in it. We had this done on 10 August at a cost of five pounds. The following day, a couple of gas fitters came and put in our new fire. The bill for it came to £191, of which our 30% contribution was £57.30. We didn't know how it would compare to our old fire, but we were very pleased because it was clean and so easy just to switch on and off. I then realized what a bore it had been to clean out sooty ashes every day, get buckets of coal in from the coal house at the top of our back garden and tip some on the fire every now and then. Also, the coal fire couldn't be switched on or off – it had to be allowed to burn out, which risked the house being set alight if we went out or to bed.

The best thing of all about the gas fire was that it was more economical. When all we'd had was a gas cooker, we'd had a slot meter and paid by putting cash in it. After we had the new fire, we altered the payment method by setting up an account with British Gas, so that saved us from running out of fifty pence pieces to put in the slot!

On 30 August, Helen and I drove in convoy with Jeff and Ros to Ilam, where they parked their car. We then gave them a lift to the Travellers' Rest, in Quarnford, near Buxton, which was very close to where the River Manifold started. From there, they walked all the way down the valley to Ilam and must have done seventeen miles or more! It took them 8½ hours and they had blisters on their feet when they finished. It was dark by then, but when they finally got back to our house, Helen did their tea for them!

From time to time, I used to do jobs for Jeff and Ros at their house. One day, I couldn't find my hacksaw, despite searching for it everywhere. Then, a year or two later, I lifted their doormat and found the saw underneath! So the mat hadn't been shifted in all that time.

Jeff and Ros had us over on Helen's 67th birthday and did our tea, which made a nice change. They gave Helen a musical card, which played *Happy Birthday to You*, and I think it was the first one of those that I'd come across.

Around that time, Harry and Gill bought another newsagent's shop, at 84 West Street, in Leek. It came up for sale and they thought they'd have a go at it even though they'd been out of the business for years.

There'd been concerned talk around the neighbourhood about the safety of everyone's electrical equipment. That was because Severn Trent Water Authority had converted their pipes in Leek Road from metal to plastic. In the old days, the main pipes had been made of cast iron and lead ones had run from them to the consumers. We'd earthed our electrical equipment to the lead pipes, so that no-one would be electrocuted if there was a short circuit, but, with the use of plastic for the main ones, the earthing system was nullified. That meant some other method had to be used and Helen and I employed one of our neighbours, Fred Corbishley, of number 349, to do the job for us in November. He hammered a copper rod into our path and connected it to the lead cold water pipe. In turn, he fixed this to the electricity fuse box and then to a trip switch. Unfortunately, the wiring was rather untidy. Also, he replaced our old round pin socket, which we used for our kettle, with a double square pin one and the two jobs cost £110.40 in total.

Unfortunately, Jeff had had a disagreement with the publisher of his Eric Burdon book and decided he no longer wanted to go ahead with their arrangement, but he had to pay back £1,000 he'd had from the firm to get out of it. Also, he and Ros were planning to have their house rewired, so, on 5 December, Helen gave Jeff his remaining National Savings Certificates to help with the costs. They'd been taken out from 1967 to 1972 and amounted to £487.27.

Ros's parents invited Helen and me to a party at their house on Christmas evening, which was very kind of them. Jeff picked us up in his car and ran us back afterwards, so I was able to have one or two alcoholic drinks and not worry about driving. Alan and Shirley were nice, pleasant people and the party was enjoyable. I had a try on Jeff's electronic keyboard, which he'd taken over for the occasion, although I was well out of practice with my piano playing.

Two nights later, we went to Jeff's for another family get-together. Ros's parents were also there, along with Nick and his girlfriend, Phonda Gregory. Helen became hungry while Ros was doing the tea and sang, 'Why are we waiting?' It was embarrassing because we were guests in the house and I was vexed with her for making a scene.

It was around then that I started to write the story of my life and family for Jeff, who'd been asking me to do it for some time. He'd always been very interested in what had happened to me, but I didn't realize how long it would take to do or how much I'd write down and I never imagined that it would eventually be published!

Jeff and Ros had a conservatory on the side of their kitchen, but it was quite old and not in very good condition. Part of the frame was rotting and on 5 January 1988 I started to do some work on it for them, which took me a few days. I hacked out one or two rotten sections and put new wooden supports in, which I painted.

On 30 January, Vale played First Division Tottenham Hotspur at home in the fourth round of the FA Cup in their biggest game for years. Jeff and 20,044 other supporters turned up to see Vale beat their mighty visitors 2-1 and make the news headlines as giant killers. At that time, we didn't have a phone, but Helen was so excited about the result that she rang Jeff from our club when we went out at night, to go on about it!

A pair of robins started to visit us for food. At first, we threw bits of bread and cheese through our kitchen window for them. Then I put some outside the back door and one of them, which seemed to be the male, came nearer until it started coming inside the doorstep. It got to about our doormat one day in February, but it then panicked and flew into the kitchen. It headed for the windows, where it fluttered around, trying to get out. I managed to catch it and took it out, but it flew off. Unfortunately, it disappeared soon afterwards and I didn't see it again.

On 5 March, Helen and I went to the wedding of Beryl and Reg Eardley's elder son, Mark, which was performed at All Saints Church. His bride was Karen Porter, who came from Abbey Hulton and was a pottery painter. I filmed some of the event, but, with the increasing popularity of video cameras, my cine camera had become like something out of the Stone Age! The traffic on Leek Road was travelling slowly, as people in passing vehicles were gawping at the procession coming out of the church, and the driver of one car ran into the back of the one in front!

In April, I received a letter from the Midland Bank, at 2 Stephenson Street, in

Birmingham, stating that I was a beneficiary of the will of the late Prudence Brunt, who'd died on 17 November. I didn't know the name, but then it came to me that she must have been my Aunt Pru, who'd married a second time. Helen and I hadn't seen her in years, but had heard she'd gone into a home somewhere. I later had another letter, telling me I was to receive a fifth of the £22,315.71 my aunt had left. Then a further letter said that Aunt hadn't declared her capital to the officials of Broadway House, in Meir, where she'd lived, and their "pound of flesh" amounted to £10,701.09. After other deductions had been made, my share ended up being only £1,782.93.

Helen started to go to Zion Methodist Church, in Cotesheath Street, Joiner's Square, with Beryl and Karen Eardley. Helen had wanted for some time to attend a religious service, so that when Beryl and Karen said they were going to one, Helen decided to go along too. Beryl's purpose was to get the superintendant minister to officiate at the wedding of her younger daughter, Lorraine, and, after a few weeks, when that had been achieved, Beryl and Karen stopped attending. But Helen carried on going, on a Sunday evening, having got used to the congregation.

Jeff and Ros had had their house rewiring done, but the whole of the inside then needed redecorating. Jeff started on the job and soon afterwards, on 19 May, I went over to assist him. I said I'd help whenever he and Ros needed me, which meant I'd volunteered for a very big job. I went over more than twenty times and we finally finished the work on 23 August!

At the end of May, Helen developed lumps on her head and the skin cracked under her left eye, which became swollen, so that she was having trouble seeing through it. On the 31st, she went to the doctor's, which had moved to a new practice at Harley Street Medical Centre, on the other side of Lichfield Street from the old one. She was told that she'd got shingles and was given some tablets to take for it. The doctor was worried that it might affect her eye, so he gave her some Zovirax ointment to put on it five times a day and sent her to the Central Outpatients Department, off Hartshill Road, where she saw Mr P. Chenny, a senior house officer in ophthalmology, on 2 June. He said that her eye was okay, but told her to report back in July for a checkup. She then started to wear sunglasses to cover up the mess around her eye.

On 22 June, I went with Jeff and Ros to try to see the double sunset from St Edward's churchyard in Leek. Many years before, Jeff had read about the unusual event and had been going nearly every midsummer since to try to catch sight of it. It was cloudy at first on the night that I went, but then the sun appeared and we looked at it through my tinted binoculars as it set on the top of The Cloud, the hill in the distance. The sun was bright when it went down, but it didn't reappear from the steep side of the hill as it was supposed to have done.

Helen's shingles had improved a lot by the beginning of July and on the 6th she went to the Outpatients for the checkup on her eye. By then, she was able to see much better, which Mr Chenny confirmed and he reduced her use of the ointment to twice a day. The remaining effects of her shingles gradually went off and by the middle of July she was more or less back to normal.

I think the shingles episode had frightened Helen and she decided that we should have a phone in case of an emergency. We had one installed by British Telecom in July at a cost of £130.23 and a first quarterly hire rate for the apparatus and system of £17.25. The number we were given was 0782 (Stoke-on-Trent) 22809. We didn't use the phone much for a long time because we didn't know the numbers of many people, but having it meant that we could contact Jeff more easily. It didn't make much difference to our lives and I couldn't see the point of ringing people to talk nonsense!

On 23 July, we went to Lorraine Eardley's wedding, which took place at St. Paul's Methodist Church, in Winchester Avenue, Bentilee. She got married to Peter Jones, who came from Sneyd Green and was a lorry driver. I took shots of the wedding with my cine camera, but, just as the photos were being taken after the ceremony, the rain poured down and we had to wait inside the church until it ceased. The reception was held at Richmond Leisure Centre, into which Shelton Club had been converted and it was strange to be back there again.

My film of Lorraine's wedding turned out to be the very last one I shot. It wasn't intended to be that way, but there was nothing of note coming up that I could film and I was losing interest. Also, video had come in and cine photography seemed like old hat.

On 10 August, Helen reported to the Outpatients for another checkup on her eye. Mr A. P. Mocroft, another senior house officer in ophthalmology, decided that her shingles had completely healed up, which we already knew ourselves really, and she was discharged from the clinic.

In August, I was busy helping Jeff and Ros to finish off their decorating. While I was at their house, I made and fitted new shelves in their kitchen and pantry. They were make-do jobs, really, because I didn't have the tools to do the work to a professional standard, but Jeff and Ros seemed very pleased with what I did.

Grahame Jeffries (the son of our old neighbours, Vin and Eva) and his wife, Yvonne, were living in Cheadle, at 12 Greenways Drive. They were voted in as the mayor and mayoress of the Town Council and asked Helen and me to their parade, church service and buffet. It was a great honour, I suppose, and Helen was thrilled about it. We accepted their invitation and on the day, 4 September, we met Grahame and Yvonne and the other guests at the council offices' car park at 2 p.m. From there, led by a band, we paraded around the town and arrived at the Church of St. Giles the Abbot, in Church Street, where there was a service. We sang some hymns and a few words were spoken about the new mayor, who promised to serve the town and its people. Afterwards, we all made our way to the Catholic Guild Hall, in Tape Street, where a buffet was laid on for us. Grahame gave a speech and thanked us and then one or two other people said a word or two. Helen and I have a photo of us in the parade and another, taken by the local press, of a group of people, including us, gathered around the new mayor and mayoress. Unfortunately, because we'd been involved in the whole affair, I hadn't been able to take any cine film shots.

Jeff and Ros gave Helen a 68th birthday present of two tickets for *The Glenn Miller Spectacular*, which was being held at Trentham Gardens Ballroom on 1 October. They gave us a lift there so that I could have a drink without driving and there was plenty of old-time dancing, which suited Helen and me. The music was played by The George Thorby Military Orchestra and its members were dressed in American Eighth Air Force uniforms. Afterwards, Jeff and Ros picked us up and when Helen and I came out of the ballroom, I saw an American Second World War Jeep parked outside. It was very unusual to see one by then, so I jumped into it and asked Jeff to take my photo, which he did.

About that time, there was an announcement at the Railway Club that the concert room, where Helen and I sat and listened to the groups that played, was to be closed in future on a Saturday night because there were insufficient customers. That was a blow because there'd no longer be any entertainment. The bar would still be open, so we decided to give it a try. It had two rooms, one of which had a TV, but we went in the other. There weren't many people there, except a crowd playing dominoes, one of whom had an infectious laugh, which kept us amused. We got chatting and found one of the customers was the receptionist at our doctor's surgery, but she didn't know us because we hadn't been there very often! Also, a couple became friendly with us. Like me, the fellow had worked at Wedgwood's, so there was something to talk about. He told me he'd been awarded a medal for his services to the pottery industry and offered to bring it along, which he did. I found it of interest.

One night, a chap came in, who'd come from London to visit his son and was waiting for his train back. He told us he'd got some bagpipes and would bring them on his next visit to Stoke. He turned up again about November and, with a bit of persuasion, produced his pipes. There was a private country and western show going on in the concert room, but I asked one of the officials if he could give us a tune in there. An agreement was reached and the next moment there was a skirl of the pipes as he walked into the room, giving a rendering of the old Scottish tune, *Flowers of the Forest*, and he followed up with one or two other melodies. The episode made the night, especially for the piper!

After a few weeks, Helen and I decided to try a Sunday night at the club when they had bingo in the concert room. It turned out to be enjoyable, so we continued to attend on that night. Sunday then became a busy day because Helen was still going to the evening service at Zion Church and then we'd have to get ready to go to the club.

To get herself ready for both places, she'd colour her hair on Sunday afternoons, touching it up where the grey hair met her skin. She couldn't really see where it needed doing, so I'd help her every week and it was a bind. She used to get a dye called Brasilia, which coloured her hair black, and we'd put it on with a paintbrush. She dyed it to make herself look younger and I thought it made her hair look better. She'd first started doing it when she'd noticed she'd got some grey hair and it went on from there.

Ros had decided to set up a part-time business selling antique clothes and collected suitable ones she could find at jumble sales and in charity shops. On 27 November, she had her first stall, at the Adams Sports & Social Club, in Alma Street, Leek, and was accompanied by Jeff. Helen and I called in to see how she was doing and to give her a bit of support. It was interesting to see how she was going about it, but it was pretty quiet and stallholders were complaining about the lack of customers. It had cost Ros £11 to hire her stall, but she only took £26 during the day, which gave her a profit of around £10 after the deduction of other expenses. She carried on doing stalls after that and gradually did better, but eventually packed them in when she became too busy after getting a part-time job as an English lecturer at Stafford College in 1991.

The news came through that Swinnerton's were struggling for money. Mr John had still got Francis's desk, which was quite elaborate and attractive, and had been planning to sell it for £400. Instead, in December, he gave it to Helen, who'd asked for it for Jeff. Because Jeff had already got a large desk, it was decided that Ros would use it, which she did.

On Christmas Day, Helen and I again went to Alan and Shirley's for the evening. They had a German piano, but some of its notes were faulty. Alan, who played by ear, did very well on it and I had a go at some old tunes from a song book Jeff had bought me, but I was very rusty.

When we went out to somebody's house for a meal, Helen would always help out with the jobs. She liked to get involved and to organize things, if the chance arose. When she'd had her meal, or even while she was having it, she'd be stacking things up and tidying the dishes. She'd grab empty plates whenever she could, which was annoying while you were still eating! She'd take them away, ready to be washed, and come back and wait for other people to finish. Then she'd start washing up and I'd probably join in with her. She was harking back to Swinnerton's, trying to work in advance by doing later jobs as early as possible. Other people would get frustrated because they'd still be eating and talking when she was collecting the dishes and she'd get frustrated because she couldn't get the job done!

On Boxing Day, Helen, Alan and I went into the Boothen Stand, with tickets Jeff and Ros had bought us, to watch Stoke play Manchester City in the Second Division. The atmosphere was good, especially as a lot of the Manchester fans had plastic blow-up bananas on display, which they waved about and used to bang each other on the head! That was a new thing to us and helped with the entertainment. Stoke won 3-1, so we were all very pleased. Unfortunately, I developed back trouble the next day, which may have been caused by sitting on a cold seat in cold weather. The pain was very bad and lasted two or three weeks, but I didn't go to the doctor's because I'd been told he couldn't do anything only dole out painkillers.

By the middle of January 1989, I was more or less back to normal, but near the end of the month the problem started up again, although it wasn't as bad. A few days later, I was okay again, but, after that, I had back trouble from time to time over the years.

When Jeff and Ros came for lunch on 25 February, Helen told them she believed in reincarnation, which was strange with her going regularly to Zion Church. I didn't believe in it myself because it didn't seem to fit into reality. However, she didn't say much more about it.

By then, I'd reached 1943 in the story of my life that I was writing for Jeff. I'd filled three roughly A5-sized diaries and was onto a fourth, although I'd written only on one side of each page so that I could fit on the opposite side extra stories that came to me later. Near the beginning of Book 4, I wrote about my parents dying in 1943, but, although Jeff thought it was very sad when he read the stories, it didn't upset me because it had all happened so long before.

On Mother's Day, Jeff gave Helen a shrimp plant, with lovely salmon-coloured flowers, which she'd wanted for a while. He and I then went to find the grave of my grandparents Wallett in St. Mary's churchyard, Bucknall, where we had a good talk in the sunshine about the past and my life in the war. Afterwards, we took some daffodils to put in the vase in my parents' grave in Hanley Cemetery.

On 12 March, Jeff and I went to have a look at the old Spitfire, which had been moved into the City Museum from its display under glass in Bethesda Street. It was still a beautiful thing, all streamlined, with a design that was pleasing to the eye.

Two bouncers were introduced at the Railway Club around that time. There rarely seemed to be any trouble and so Helen and I couldn't understand why they'd been employed. During the weeks that followed, all they seemed to do was to stop people from standing in front of the bar. Later on, they must have had the sack because we just saw them a time or two more as customers. Trade had slackened and so there was less need for their services.

Helen received a letter, dated 5 April, from John Swinnerton, saying that his various firms had run into financial trouble and that he'd have to close them down. As a result, he told her that he'd got 'no alternative' except to stop her pension (from F. Swinnerton & Son Limited) from the end of the previous month. It wasn't too much of a shock because we knew his businesses weren't doing very well and it wasn't enough of a loss to affect us much. We weren't reliant on Helen's pension and I'd always believed in keeping some money in hand in case things went wrong.

On 29 April, Helen and I had a run out in our car and were approaching Cheddleton, on the A 520 from Leek, just before four o'clock. As the Churnet bridge came into view, I saw a woman standing on the pavement on the far side of the road. She appeared to be ready to cross over, so I kept my eye on her. As we got nearer, she ran across the road towards the car! Helen shouted something and I braked hard. The car stopped just as the woman collided with my side of it. A man, who'd been standing near her, ran across towards us and bent over the woman, who was lying on the road. I gathered myself together and got out of the car, not knowing what to expect. The woman was moaning a little, but I couldn't see any blood, and the man was talking to her, with little effect. He told me his name was Malcolm Ward, that he was a male nurse at the mental hospital and that he'd been watching the woman, who was a patient. He said that she was suicidal and that he'd seen the whole incident. A female witness came to us and reassured me that the accident wasn't my fault, so I felt more at ease having two people on my side.

A plain-clothes policeman (PC Cooke) happened to be passing and stopped and took charge until two officers in uniform turned up. An ambulance arrived in very quick time and loaded up the woman while the policeman took particulars from me. Helen was quiet and still and seemed shocked, so she was asked by the ambulance man if she'd like to go to hospital, but she refused. He told me to get her to a doctor if she had a reaction when she got home. I drove home pretty steadily and Helen didn't require any treatment. Later, Staffordshire Police sent for a statement from me and Helen was asked to send her version of the accident.

Jeff had finally finished his book on Eric Burdon, which was called *The Last Poet*. He published it on 13 May and went to Newcastle upon Tyne, Eric's home city, to publicize it. He was interviewed on Tyne Tees TV's *Northern Life* show and told me that he'd had to have his face powdered by a make-up woman before he went on! Unfortunately, the book didn't really catch on, maybe because Eric wasn't a big star any more, and Jeff sold more copies in North Staffordshire than he did in Eric's home area!

There was a riot outside The Alsager Arms Hotel, just along the road from Jeff and Ros's house, on 13 May. Eighty people were involved, including Leeds United supporters on their way home from Shrewsbury and Macclesfield Town fans returning from the FA Trophy final at Wembley. There were 44 arrests, but Jeff and Ros heard nothing! Helen and I went to see them the day after and we all walked along to the hotel to find there were marks all over the road where bricks had been thrown!

On 23 May, Staffordshire Police sent me a letter, saying that they weren't proceeding any further with the road accident case. I'd been confident that I hadn't been to blame and it turned out that the woman hadn't been badly injured, but I was very pleased there was no court case.

Helen and I went with Jeff to watch Vale play Bristol Rovers at home in the second leg of the Third Division play-offs final on 3 June. The first leg had been a 1-1 draw. Helen got pretty excited and, as we went in, she beat a policeman on the chest with a fist for a joke! Of course, he realized it was a bit of fun and took it well. Vale won 1-0 and the dream of promotion to the Second Division had finally come true!

Jeff had had the idea of writing a book about Vale's season if they went up, so, as soon as promotion had been achieved, he got cracking to get it out in time for the start of the next campaign. I wondered whether he'd be able to write and sell it and if he'd go into debt and get into difficulties. Also, I thought about whether he'd be liable to be sued because of mentioning people's names.

Vale had a civic reception at Stoke Town Hall on 9 June and Jeff and Ros were invited by the club so that Jeff could interview the players for his book. Jeff told me that most of the players seemed quite nervous being there, but that the manager, John Rudge, and the chairman, Bill Bell, were friendly with him.

On 30 June, I fitted a new front door to Jeff and Ros's house. The next week, I fixed two bolts on the door, painted it, cemented the surround and painted their bay, bathroom window frame, shed door, gate, gateposts and back guttering. Of course, they were very pleased, as always.

Helen had been looking in a booklet at farm holidays in Wales and picked a few she fancied. We set off on 9 July and our first try for B & B was at Llanbenwch, a farm close to Llanfair Dyffryn Clwyd, near Ruthin. I had some difficulty in finding the place, so I went into The White Horse pub in the village and asked the fellows at the bar if they knew where the farm was. They didn't, even though Llanfair was only a tiny place! However, they referred me to the home of the owner of the village store, which was closed, and he put me right. We found the farm about a mile away and the elderly, but alert, owner, Mrs Jones, fixed us up. An Australian couple were also guests and Helen loved to hear the stories they told. We had a good drive around the area and found Ruthin to be a nice shopping town, where we got most of our needs.

After two or three days, we moved on to a lovely old farm a mile or two from Caernarfon, which overlooked Anglesey. On one of our trips from there, we drove to Criccieth, a quiet seaside place, where we got a lovely ice cream and sat on The Esplanade, admiring the beautiful East Beach. We spent another day at Betws-y-Coed and revisited Swallow Falls. Also, one night, we drove into Caernarfon, but all the shops were shut. There weren't many people around, except for gangs of youths, and it seemed a rough place.

We also visited Anglesey and came to Rhosneigr. Helen told me her old boss,

John Swinnerton, owned a cottage there, so we tried to find it, though it was awkward because we didn't have an address. We asked a number of people if they knew where it was, but they weren't much use. Then we came to a post office and tried there and eventually we were pointed in the right direction. We found the cottage, which was named Glan Eifion, but were disappointed because it was on the scruffy side. We'd been told that the Swinnertons weren't in residence as they were in their villa in Spain, so we looked all around the outside of their cottage. Then we wandered around the village and saw a noisy plane take off from the nearby RAF Valley aerodrome. It didn't seem quite the place for a holiday home.

We then moved on to Benllech, which was a nice little place with a sandy beach, and later revisited Beaumaris, where we spent quite a bit of time. It was quiet, with a nice main street, a castle and a fine view across the Menai Strait to the mainland. As usual, at these places, we made sandwiches and brewed our own tea, which we enjoyed more than going into cafés.

On 16 July, Jeff and Ros went on holiday to Sutherland, Morar and the Isle of Mull in Scotland. While they were away, Helen and I went to their house and painted the new conservatory that they'd had built at a cost of £720 plus VAT. Also, we found a plague of ants in their bathroom, which we had to exterminate. At the time, the papers were on about the hot weather making ants move inside people's houses to get away from the heat, so Jeff and Ros weren't the only ones with the problem. Of course, we saw Raedburh while we were there and she seemed to like our company as well as the titbits we took her!

One day, I heard somebody shouting in the distance and had a look round to try to locate the sound. A woman was shouting: 'Help! Help!'

So I shouted: 'Who is it? Where are you?'

She said it was Ann Parrish and that she'd fallen down, so I climbed over the wall between our house and Nancy's and got into Ann's garden through a gap in her fence. I was talking to her all the time and eventually got to her. She was lying on the ground outside her house and said one of her legs was aching.

I phoned 999 and asked for the ambulance service. I explained what had happened and was given instructions on what to do, to keep her warm and so on. So I got a coat from inside her house and wrapped it round her, but it only took a few minutes for two paramedics to come. They attended to her and said it looked as if she'd broken a hip. One of them got a stretcher and they carried her to the ambulance on it. She was taken to hospital, where it was discovered that she'd fractured a hip bone. She had to have a hip replacement, which was successful, and she eventually returned home.

Jeff's book on Vale was ready in time for the commencement of the 1989-1990 season and was called *Back To Where We Once Belonged!* He described it as the *Port Vale Promotion Chronicle 1988-1989*. It was 101 pages long and sold for £3.95 at Vale's souvenir shop and quite a few of the area's bookshops. He did quite well with sales, selling 75 copies in the first hour and his whole 500 in under 2½ days, so he had to order some more from the printers. Obviously, I was very pleased about it.

News filtered out that British Rail was getting rid of some of the premises that housed its clubs and ours was one of them. We were told that our committee was going to buy the building on our behalf at a favourable price. Something of that nature had happened when West Midlands Gas had disposed of the buildings housing its clubs. The West Midlands Gas Social & Recreation Society building (the old rectory of Shelton Church), in Rectory Road, had been sold off and renamed Rectory Road Sports & Social Club. It turned out, though, that the Railway Club building wasn't bought by the members after all.

Helen and I decided to go to the local Derby match between Stoke and Vale on 23 September. It was the first time they'd played each other in the league for over 32 years. Jeff came for lunch and we all walked to Stoke together, but then he went in the Stoke End, with the Vale supporters, and Helen and I went in the Boothen End. The police were searching people going in and I suppose they were expecting trouble. I was one of those whom they searched, even though I was elderly. They must have thought I was a potential villain! I was carrying a plastic bag and they wanted to see what was in it, so I gave it to them. They had a look and then handed it back to me without saying anything, but I wondered if they were disappointed that I just had two macs in it! I don't remember anything about the match itself, but it ended in a 1-1 draw.

There'd been a serious flood in Wildboarclough, near Macclesfield Forest, on 24 May when the water in the Clough Brook had risen so high that it had destroyed a number of bridges and part of the road in the valley. The damage was so bad that the road was closed for over six months while it was repaired. Jeff and Ros took us there on Helen's 69th birthday to have a look. Although a lot of improvements had been made, there was still plenty of damage to be seen.

Jeff was writing another book on Vale, about their history, from when the club started up to the then present day. Whenever he could, he was looking things up in the old *Sentinels* on microfilms in Hanley Reference Library, which by then had been given the fancy title of Stoke-on-Trent City Central Reference Library! On 25 October, I dropped in on him there to see how he was going about it and it was interesting to see how the microfilms worked. They were only fairly small and each was wound around a reel, but they had huge amounts of information on them. It was amazing because each one had on it a copy of all the pages of the *Sentinels* for two weeks or more. After being threaded onto a blank reel, they could be read on large screens and moved forwards and backwards by hand.

On 1 November, I went with Jeff and Ros to see the film, *The Bear*, at the new Odeon cinema at Festival Park. Helen wasn't with us because she didn't like the pictures and she was nervous about being in the house on her own at night, so we went in the afternoon. It was the first time I'd been to the new Odeon and it wasn't like the old-time picture houses. It had eight different screens and looked quite posh, with paintings on the walls!

The film was the story of a bear cub, whose mother was killed, so he had to look after himself until a large male grizzly came to protect him. The movie was very unusual because there was hardly any speaking in it and the story was told from the bear's point of view. How the action of the animals all came together was marvellous.

Jeff appealed in the *Sentinel* for information for his Vale history book and one of the people who got in touch with him was Harry Lewis, my old work mate at Wedgwood's and the Post Office! He was a big Vale supporter and had a photocopy of one of their programmes when they'd played Everton in 1884! Jeff went along to Harry's house, 21 Community Drive, in Smallthorne, on 7

December to have a look at the programme and I went with him. I'd always got on pretty well with Harry and it was good to see him again.

On 23 December, Jeff went to Stoke City to get Helen and me tickets for their Boxing Day home match against Newcastle United as a Christmas present. He later told me that he'd had to queue for almost an hour and the fellow in front of him had kept being sick! Stoke won the game 2-1, although I don't remember anything about it.

Jeff was aiming to get his Vale history book in the shops before the following Christmas and I started to help him out by looking up facts in Hanley Reference Library, mainly on their microfilms. One day in January 1990, when I was there, I was asking one of the staff for something and my name was mentioned. A fellow, who was also in the library, must have heard the conversation and introduced himself as Ivan Kent. He lived in Matlock, in Derbyshire, but his family came from North Staffordshire, so we got chatting and compared notes to see if there was a connection. It wasn't clear whether there was, but he said he'd send me the details he'd got on his family tree. At the time, I was stuck on mine, so I hoped he'd got some new information that would be of use to me, but it was well over a year before I heard from him.

In February, Helen and I got a demand from Radio Rentals for £88.24 for the annual rent for our TV. We'd wondered many a time whether to buy a set of our own because they'd improved so much that they needed very few call outs, but in the end we carried on with Radio Rentals.

One day, Jeff asked me if I'd go to Birmingham with him, to help with his research on his Vale book. I agreed, so he drove us there on 23 February, but it was hectic finding our way to the Reference Library, in Chamberlain Square. Jeff even accidentally drove up a one-way street and then had to make a three-point turn to go in the opposite direction. It was interesting to see the horror on the drivers' faces as he made this manoeuvre! We had a good day out, but we didn't find much worthwhile.

I was still helping Jeff by looking things up about Vale's history for him in Hanley Reference Library. Another father and son, both named Bob Smith, were also looking into the club's history at the library. I saw them there a few times and we'd nod in recognition.

On 14 March, I was working in the library on the 1936 *Sentinel* microfilms when I saw my name mentioned in connection with the Stoke Circle Wheelers cycling club that I'd been the captain of. It seemed strange to read about something that I'd done all those years before.

Vale were doing quite well in the Second Division and Helen and I thought we'd go to have a look at them. So, on 7 April, we went along with Jeff to watch them play Newcastle United, who were in the hunt for promotion, but we brought Vale bad luck because they lost 2-1.

By then, I was going to the library regularly to help Jeff with facts for his new Vale book and I was often there twice a week or more. Fairly frequently, we were working side by side on microfilm readers looking for different things and it was quite enjoyable.

On 3 or 4 May, Stan and Dorothy Wallett called in at our house on a visit from Caton. Dorothy gave me a copy of the Wallett family tree, going back eight generations, and it seemed it was possible that there was a link to the clan of

Cadwaladr, the twelfth century prince of Gwynedd, or even the seventh century king of the same name.

Helen was still having trouble with hard skin on the bottom of her feet, so she decided to go into Scholl (UK) Ltd, at 13 Lamb Street, in Hanley. The chiropodist there cut it away and told her, 'If you stop wearing high-heeled shoes, the skin will get better.' Helen did so and, amazingly, it worked! From then on, she wore flat shoes and, occasionally, low heels to go out in and the hard skin and pain disappeared.

In June, I received my annual TV licence demand, which for years had been addressed to 'Miss C. Kent'! I'd previously tried to get it altered and told the counter clerk at Hanley Post Office, but nothing was done. I decided to have another go and this time the clerk suggested I take out a new licence, which I did, and it solved the problem.

Helen and I decided to go on a Welsh holiday again, in July. Like the previous year, Helen picked out from a booklet several farm B & B's we could try. The first place we went to was in Flint, but it was hard to find. We asked several folk its whereabouts, but they directed us here and there. Eventually, we found it up a lane, but there was no-one at home. It seemed that the proprietors had gone to a wedding and weren't due back until night time. Just then, one of their relatives came along in a Land Rover and offered to fix us up. We followed him to what looked like a smallholding, but, as we got out of the car, Helen whispered to me that she didn't like the place. A woman came to the door, took us upstairs and showed us with pride a room with a four-poster bed. As it happened, Helen didn't like them either and so refused the offer. The woman was a bit hurt, but it was no use us staying if Helen didn't like what she saw.

We then decided to try Llanbenwch, just outside Llanfair Dyffryn Clwyd, where we'd stayed the previous year. We booked a couple of nights there and Helen was pleased because the place was clean. The following day, we drove to Bala and spent most of the day there and around the lake, where we watched some lads kayaking. The weather was cold, but the next day it warmed up and it gradually got better.

After a couple of days, we thought we'd try a B & B just outside Caernarfon. It was up a narrow lane, but Helen didn't fancy walking up it late at night if we'd had a drink. So we drove all the way back to Llanbenwch and booked in there for the rest of our holiday because it was pretty good.

While we were in Wales, we revisited Criccieth and on the way back to the B & B, we passed through Blaenau Ffestiniog, which was a real dump and covered in dust. It was surrounded by mountains of slate, the quarrying of which was the main industry. We then went on to Betws-y-Coed, where we came across a couple having a stroll. In the conversation we had with them, we found out that the woman came from Blaenau and had become a GI bride.

Helen was interested in the customers in The White Horse pub in Llanfair Dyffryn Clwyd and tried to work out what made them tick. Next to the pub was the Church of St. Cynfarch and St. Mary and we gave Jeff a call more or less every night from the phone box outside it. That was common practice when we went on holiday because Helen wished to keep in touch with him because she was forever wondering if he was okay and she wanted him to know we were alright. One night, as we were walking back to the farm along the road, which had no footpaths, we were almost run down by a mad driver, who blared his horn as he missed us by an inch!

The next morning, our landlady told us of a nice place to visit, called Moel Famau, which was between Ruthin and Mold and was 1,818 feet high. It was hard to find and turned out to be the highest point on the Clwydian Hills. I asked two or three people for assistance, but their directions were vague. Eventually, I found our destination to be at the top of a pass and we pulled into the Moel Famau car park, from which there was a lovely view of the Vale of Clwyd and Snowdonia. We then went back down the road a little to a picnic area by Moel Famau Forest, where we had our midday meal on our deck chairs and then a snooze.

Later, we had a walk on a path leading upwards through the wood. As we got higher, we were surrounded by a swarm of flies and Helen was bitten on one of her legs. We kept on going higher and there seemed no end to it. Helen thought we were lost because there was nothing to see only trees, but eventually the path started to go downwards. The flies decreased and finally we saw our car through the trees. We came to a mobile refreshment vehicle and treated ourselves to a whole block of ice cream!

When we'd left the B & B in the morning, our landlady had told us she was going out for the day and had given us a key to let ourselves in. When we got back at night, I put the key in the door, but it wouldn't open. Helen had a try, but with the same result, so we checked the back door, but that was no use either. So we sat in our car and wondered how long our landlady would be or whether she'd stay overnight somewhere. After about an hour, she rolled up in her car and we told her she must have bolted the door. She gave a little smile and pushed the door open, saying that it stuck a bit!

On our way home, we called at The Mere, in Ellesmere, Shropshire, which was a nice, but popular spot. We paid thirty pence for a car parking ticket and stayed for quite a while. The ground at the side of the water was bare, from having been worn away by many shoes and boots and no doubt through the grass being eaten by the numerous geese and ducks which were wandering about. They were looking for titbits when we were there and must have got used to receiving food from tourists. We had lunch there, but when Helen went to sit in her deck chair, she dropped through it because the cloth gave way! She was wedged in between the metal and I had to pull her upright with the frame still clinging to her!

Jeff and Ros came for lunch on 21 July in a light blue and white V registration Volkswagen caravanette they'd just bought for £2,550. It had got a bed and a sink, to wash and cook in, and seemed very nice. They'd got it to tour the Outer Hebrides, in Scotland, and gave Helen and me a ride to Hanford and back in it.

They set off the following day and phoned us after a while. They'd found out that they hadn't got a plug for the sink and so had to improvise and cut up a potato to put in the hole, which wasn't entirely satisfactory! They'd arrived on the island of Barra by ferry and were stopping overnight by a beach, called Tràigh Mhór, which was the runway for the island's airport! When they'd woken up on their first morning there, they'd seen a plane come past and land on the beach.

One day in July, I couldn't find my car keys. I searched everywhere, without any luck, so I reported the loss to Hanley Police Station. A day or two later, I also informed the police in Stoke, in case my keys were handed in there. I couldn't figure out how I could possibly have lost them and kept searching. Then I thought about the plastic rubbish bag Helen and I hung on the knob of the back door. I felt something like them on the bottom of it and, when I put my hand inside, I was thrilled to find the missing articles! I then had a walk to Hanley Police Station and told them I'd found my lost property, but it was two or three weeks later before I remembered to ask Stoke Police to call off their nationwide search!

The weather was very hot at the beginning of August and, on the 2nd, Keele University recorded a record temperature of 89° Fahrenheit. The day after, the temperature reached 91.2°, which is still the highest ever taken at the university, and Radio Stoke did a stunt by frying an egg in a fry-pan on the pavement in the centre of Hanley. It took a lot longer than on a stove, but the egg did fry!

On 11 August, Jeff and Ros got back from their holiday and came to see us the next day. They said that the islands were very beautiful, with lots of wild flowers and empty beaches, and they sounded very relaxing places to live. They told us they'd discovered a hungry pregnant cat by the airport building on Barra and fed it half a tin of salmon. They'd then found out that its owner was in hospital, so had arranged to have it flown to Stornoway, on Lewis, and paid to have it spayed after the kittens had been born! Staff at Barra Airport had arranged to look after it when it returned, but the amazing thing was that the airline, Loganair, had been willing to fly the cat to Stornoway and back free!

By then, Harry Williamson, next door, had left and he and Alice had divorced, but she still lived there. She had builders in to do some big jobs, for which she had a grant from the council. I'm not sure if I ever knew the name of the firm, but Alice remembered them as being Robinsons Builders, of 27 Fairfax Street, in Birches Head. They were there for weeks and were a nuisance. They had scaffolding hanging into our airspace and actually touching our house. Then, as they were taking all the tiles off her roof, pieces with jagged edges dropped into our yard, making a mess. Even worse, one day a large piece of tile just missed Helen's head. Of course, we complained and I said I'd sue them if there were any injuries.

The builders had positioned an overflow pipe so that any water coming through it would run onto Alice's lean-to and then into our yard. I mentioned this to the boss and he said he'd attend to it, but nothing happened. Later, Helen and I made the point again, but still nothing was done. So I went to the council offices in Unity House, Hanley, and saw an inspector, who told me that they wouldn't pay the builders unless they attended to the fault. When the alterations and repairs had almost been completed and it looked as if the overflow job wasn't going to be done, Helen gave the builders a good telling off and threatened them with court action. Shortly afterwards, the job was done!

I'd noticed that our chimney seemed to be bulging, so I mentioned it to Nancy because we shared a single stack, in which our individual flues were enclosed. Nancy agreed that it needed repairing and through her we got the name of someone to do the job, Chris Pointon, of 26 Parkwood Avenue, in Trentham. In late August, he erected scaffolding and partly demolished and rebuilt the chimney. Our old clay pots were taken down and replaced by small galvanized ones at a total cost of £340. The old pots were surprisingly big and heavy, but Chris took them away because there was a demand for them.

On 3 September, I thought I'd go to see my doctor, a youngish fellow, Francis

Przyslo, about a new belt for my ruptures. The pads didn't wash very well and had become dirty. He wrote out the prescription and then told me he'd take my blood pressure. After doing it, he said, 'I hope my pressure is as good as yours when I get to your age!'

Also in September, Harry and Gill sold their detached house, Oakwood, and moved into a terraced house, 6 Westwood View, Spring Gardens, which was near their West Street newsagent's shop. The lack of space on the front of their new property meant their family were short of room to park their three cars. Helen and I couldn't understand their house move because in April local government rates had been replaced by the "poll tax" (community charge), a tax on individuals, which meant they'd be paying the same wherever they lived.

I saw an advert in the *Sentinel* about a family tree course that was being held on Wednesday mornings, from 10.30 to 12, at Cartwright House, in Broad Street. It was called *Trace Your Ancestors!*. I went along on 26 September and joined up at a cost of £12.75, even though the class had been running for a week. It ran for ten weeks and I found it interesting. The class was taught by Eva Beech and she was a good teacher. I got much more information on how to go about researching my family tree and so the course was a breakthrough.

Helen's seventieth birthday was on 29 September and she had twelve cards. Jeff and Ros bought her some chocolates, some flowers and a lovely blouse, and took us a run to Wettonmill, where we had a nice little walk. Afterwards, they entertained us at their home and Helen enjoyed feeding Raedburh.

One day, Helen and I drove to Morrison's supermarket, in Festival Park, to get some goods. I was intrigued by their system of getting their empty trolleys returned. To use a trolley, customers had to insert a pound coin in a slot on it and to get the coin back, they had to chain the trolley to a stack of others. The management didn't have to employ anyone to collect the trolleys and very few were stolen.

Jeff had been complaining about screws coming out of his garden gate and suspected that the refuse men were closing it too hard after collecting the rubbish. I offered to take a look and turned up with my tools. Things turned out as I expected. The wood around the screws had rotted and wasn't giving a good grip. My solution was to scrape out the rotten wood and pack the hole with sound pieces.

At the Railway Club, there'd been complaints from some of the members about the excessive noise of some of the groups which had played for us. The committee decided not to employ any more and just to have an organist in their place, but this was going too far and a lot of the members said they wouldn't be attending if that continued to be the case. The committee quickly reverted to the status quo!

On one of our visits to see Jack and Flo at their home in Washerwall, Jack told me that when he went for his medical for his call-up into the armed forces during the Second World War, the doctor who examined him was a friend of his employer, Frank Swinnerton (Senior). Apparently, the doctor recognized Jack and told him to get off because he wouldn't be going into the Forces. Jack told me that this was done as a favour to Mr Swinnerton because male workers were in short supply during the war!

When Jeff and Ros came for lunch on 6 October, Jeff told us that he'd got a spare ticket for the Vale Second Division match against Charlton Athletic that afternoon and he asked if one of us would like to make use of it. We decided to take up his offer and paid the cost of another admission between us so that we could have a look at how Vale were doing. They were the better side, but only managed to draw 1-1.

On 11 October, I went with my family tree class to the Mormon Family History Centre, at the back of The Church of Jesus Christ of Latter-day Saints, on Brampton Road, Newcastle, where we were allowed to use their facilities. They had local parish registers and national and international records of births, baptisms, marriages and deaths on reels of microfilm and sheets of microfiche. They were stored in sequence in cabinets and you could use whichever year for whatever you wanted if nobody else had got it. For the use of the facility, the centre asked for a voluntary contribution. While I was there, I tried to find out the date of the marriage of my great-grandfather Kent, but I didn't come across anything.

On 31 October, I walked to Stoke and caught a bus to Newcastle to do more research on my family tree at the centre. Because I'd got so much information on my mother's side from Dorothy Wallett, I concentrated on the Kents and discovered that my great-grandparents, John Kent and Charlotte Hill, had been married at St. Giles' Church, in Newcastle, on 27 June 1857. I also walked back home from Stoke, but, in the night, my right knee became swollen, painful and stiff. In the morning, I had great difficulty getting down the stairs and got Dr David Sheppard to come because there was no chance of me walking to the surgery. I was surprised how quickly he came because he was here by about 11.30! He had a look at my leg, but seemed to have difficulty in finding my kneecap, so that he could insert the needle of a syringe underneath it to take fluid out. He asked Helen for a bowl and then extracted fluid from my knee and emptied it into the bowl. After several extractions, Dr Sheppard said: 'I've had about a hundred mls!' He left me with a prescription for some medicine, an elasticated bandage to support my knee and an assurance that everything should be alright.

I could barely hobble about and getting back into bed was a problem. Helen had to lift my leg in because I couldn't manage it on my own. I had a better night than the previous one and the following day the swelling had reduced and I could get about better. Each day, there was some improvement, so a week later, I was able to walk the half a mile to Norman Foster's to pay my garage rent.

My knee gradually got better, but from time to time the problem would come on again and it gradually deteriorated. Sometimes, now, it gives a bit, almost as though it's going to give way and occasionally I get a sharp pain in it. I also get pain in my other knee, but it's not as bad as my right one.

By November, I'd finished writing the story of my life and got it up to date. It meant less work for me and it was a relief! I had a break from it, but that was short-lived because Jeff came up with questions on it and I resumed researching, mainly at Hanley Reference Library.

Jeff was interested in publishing the book, but I became concerned about all the publicity there'd be and wondered what Helen would say about me disclosing fairly intimate events of our lives. So nothing happened and eventually the idea was forgotten about.

I went to Newcastle Register Office, in Sidmouth Avenue, on 14 November and asked for a copy of the marriage certificate of my great-grandparents, which an official did for me. But I couldn't get any information from further back by going to register offices because compulsory registration of births, marriages and deaths only started in 1837.

On 1 December, Jeff published his new Vale book, which he called *The Valiants' Years: The Story of Port Vale*. By Christmas Eve, he'd sold 949 copies and, the way it started off, I bet he thought he was going to sell a million! When Helen went shopping for food in Hanley, she started going into the bookshops, especially Webberley's, in Percy Street, to rearrange their displays to put Jeff's books in the foreground, front on instead of side on, to bring them more to the notice of the public! People would see the pictures on the front covers and go towards them. Sometimes, Helen couldn't find any of his books in a shop and would tell him. That came in handy because Jeff would then ring the store and see if they wanted any more and it kept Helen on her toes as well.

After the family tree class had finished, Eva Beech invited us to her house at 56 Trent Valley Road, in Penkhull, for two hours in the morning on 12 December. She got out her records and I bought a book she'd written, *Tracing Ancestors in North Staffordshire*, although I didn't find it had much of use to me in addition to what she'd already taught in the class.

In January 1991, I signed up for another ten weeks' tuition by Mrs Beech and went to the class on the 16th, but, unfortunately, not enough students joined to keep it going and it closed after that meeting. So I was on my own again, but I decided to carry on and do my best.

I put down the Kent family tree as far as I then knew it as a chart on a piece of card, to show how far I'd got. The next step was to go to Hanley Reference Library to try to get further back. I hadn't got much idea of how to go about it, but a librarian said I should go onto parish records, which were in books that they'd got and on microfiche. I was then shown how to use microfiche to look for information. Each fiche was a small piece of plastic, which you had to put under a microfiche reader and move about according to what you were looking for. A massive amount of detail was stored on each fiche and it was all magnified by the reader to become legible. I was floundering around with it at first because it was all new to me, but I started going quite regularly to the library. I looked through births, baptisms, marriages and deaths in the books and on microfiche and found some useful information from time to time. I also spent a lot of time checking through census details on microfilms and again occasionally found something relevant, to help me piece together the Kent family tree.

Vera was taken ill in January. She went into intensive care in the Infirmary and I took Big Harry to see her. Helen didn't come along because she didn't like anything like that. We got very little response from Vera, but it wasn't very clear what had happened to her. Jeff was told that she'd had a stroke, but I was later informed that she'd had a heart attack. She'd stopped breathing and the oxygen to her brain had been cut off, so she was left with brain damage. I went a time or two to see her, but she died on the 27th.

Vera's funeral was at Carmountside Crematorium on 4 February. The procession started from her house in Greasley Road and Helen was in the first car. I was in the second with Jeff and Ros. Brian Eeley, the pastor at Zion Church, did the service and gave a lengthy tribute to Vera, but Big Harry was weeping most of the time. We then went back to his house and Helen told everybody some stories of past times.

After Vera had died, Helen and I tended to go to see Big Harry on Saturdays when we gave our car a run. We always seemed to be going up there and his lounge would be smelly with smoke from an ashtray full of fag ends! We'd then normally carry on to Young Harry's.

Helen and I had been having a problem with our hot water cylinder, which I think had developed a leak. So we got in a plumber, Charles Knight, of 20 Hillside Road, in Werrington, who said it had been damaged by frost! He removed it and put a new one in its place at a cost of £173, which I claimed back on the insurance.

Out of the blue, in early March, I received a letter from Ivan Kent, with his family tree inside. He said that if there was a connection, he'd like to hear from me. I looked at his chart and there seemed to be a possible linkup, so I wrote back to him. I'd got stuck in 1857, but his reply was a big help and gave me details that traced my family back to the village of Ellastone (which was near to Alton) in 1724.

Eventually, I got more or less everything I could from Hanley Reference Library regarding the Kents. To get further information, I needed to visit other places, but I didn't want to go too far because of leaving Helen all day, although I did go to Staffordshire County Record Office, in Eastgate Street, Stafford, and St. Michael's Church in Rocester. I asked the vicar there if I could look at the parish records, so he brought a book out, but stood over me and turned the pages, which made me feel very uncomfortable. He then expected me to give a small donation, which I did, but the little information I'd found wasn't worth the money I paid.

On 7 April, Helen and I went along to help Jack and Flo to celebrate their diamond wedding anniversary, at the Poachers Tavern, in Rudyard. We had a meal there and it was a very nice occasion.

Our cold water tank was rusting, so, in April, Helen and I got Charles Knight to put in a new plastic one. We still had our original lead pipes, but they were poisonous, so I had him replace the bathroom sections with copper ones while he was on the job. Helen and I also decided to have a new toilet at the same time and the total cost of the work was £483. Because of the danger of lead pipes, I had all the remaining ones in the house replaced over time.

In the spring, I decorated the house, as I still did virtually every year. I'd continued with the habit of doing the inside because of the smoke from the coal fire making it dirty and I carried on even after we'd converted to gas.

I mentioned to Bernard Kent my efforts to trace my ancestors. He was also into the family tree and had had somebody to do his professionally for him. I was hoping he'd give me some gems on what had happened to the family in the past, but he didn't and I don't think he wanted my information.

It took me years to do the family tree. I'd have a go at it a couple of days a week, but then other things would come up. Then I'd have another go, so my efforts were all spread out. Eventually, I wasn't getting any further and I didn't want to travel to the General Register Office, at St Catherine's House, in London, where the national births, marriages and deaths records were kept, so it kind of fizzled out.

Jeff was reading through my book and gave me some notes of things he was unsure about or needed adding to, for me to look into. I checked them out and wrote the answers in the book. That was then happening all the time until he'd gone through the whole thing.

Sometimes, when Jeff came for lunch, he and Helen used to act silly and play fight. Also, from time to time, Jeff and I used to do a bit of sparring for fun. Sometimes, we'd have *Grandstand* on the television and Jeff and Helen would each pick horses to win races. Helen more or less idolized Jeff and used to say to him from time to time, 'If you're alright, I'm alright.' I think it was pretty true.

On 21 June, it was our golden wedding anniversary and Helen had arranged a party at our house for the following night. Well before then, she'd been on at Jeff to tie his hair back for the occasion. She used to criticize him and boss me about up to a point. She was still living in the time when she'd been young and she hadn't adapted to modern circumstances, so she wanted Jeff to be perfect as in what was in her mind. Being bossy and critical was in her nature, but she hadn't been like that when I'd first met her because people try to be nice and give a good impression.

Jeff booked a photographer from *The Sentinel* to come and take pictures of Helen and me for our anniversary, but Helen told Jeff to cancel it because we weren't very keen on publicity. We were used to keeping things to ourselves. We didn't like people knowing all our secrets and Jeff had set it up without consultation, though he'd thought we'd be pleased.

We had eight guests at our party: Jeff, Ros, Big Harry, Young Harry, Gill, Alan, Shirley and Nick, Ros's brother. It was a tight fit in our house and Helen split the guests between the lounge and the kitchen. I was in the front room, with Jeff, Ros, Nick and Big Harry, and the most favoured guests accompanied Helen in the back room! Partway through, Jeff and Nick went off to St Edward's churchyard, in Leek, try to see the double sunset, which Jeff had become very interested in, and by the time they returned, Big Harry had disappeared to his local pub (The Priory Inn, in Greasley Road)! That gave Helen something to go on about, but it all went off okay.

I was kept on the go by Jeff, who was publishing two new books that year: a collection of stories about Vale, which was called *Port Vale Tales*, and the saga of Doug Moller's struggle to survive in Rockhall Cottage, entitled *The Wars Of The Roaches*. To help out, I answered quite a number of questions for Jeff in Hanley Reference Library, for both books.

The number of customers had continued to drop at our club and eventually it closed down because British Rail was selling it. Helen and I were then wondering where to go, but Sam and Doris tried the P.M.T. Employees' Social & Sports Club, in Maclagan Street, Stoke, and told us it was okay, so we joined them there after a week or two.

When we got there, they were sitting with another couple, Tom and Gertie Billington. The first week Sam and Doris had gone to the club, they'd got there early and, without knowing it, had chosen the seats that Tom and Gertie normally used. When Tom and Gertie arrived, they'd all had words about whose seats they were, but Sam and Doris didn't move. Then they'd all started talking and became friendly.

Because we all sat together, Tom and Gertie became our friends as well. They lived at 86 Newlands Street, in Shelton. Tom was pleasant and had been a foreman in the building trade, but was prone to having the mickey taken out of him, especially by Sam. Although Gertie was the boss, she felt sorry for him being put on.

The club was owned by the bus company and was up some steps above one of their offices. The room we were in was quite big and the main entertainment was an organist, Arthur Bradshaw, who was pretty good. He jazzed it up for dancing, which was the main thing, and we all used to dance regularly.

At the club, I came across the old Stoke left-half, Jock Kirton, whom I'd seen play for them after the war. He'd been pretty dour on the pitch and had played with his long shorts rolled up, which had made him look rough. I got to know him a bit at the club and we'd have a chat.

In July, Helen and I went on holiday to the Cotswolds with Flo and Jack. On the 14th, we went on spec to see Anne Kirkwood, a former Swinnerton's office girl, at her home at 9 Parkland Mews, in Park Street, Stow-on-the-Wold. It was probably Helen's idea, but I think Anne was a bit embarrassed being caught on the hop!

We moved on to Bourton-on-the-Water and got B & B nearby at Windrush Farm, on the outskirts of the village of Cold Aston. The farmhouse was quite grand and had a big lawn in front of it, with tables and chairs on, so you could sit outside and relax, but the grey stone of the building looked a bit grim.

On the 16th, we revisited Snowshill, where we stopped and sat on our deck chairs to enjoy the sun. The same day, we returned to Chipping Campden, which wasn't far away, and Jack got us an ice cream each from a mobile street kiosk because it was a pretty warm day.

We must have run out of new places to go because we then revisited Broadway and got fixed up with B & B in the village. The following day, we were having a stroll down a lane nearby and Jack was walking in front, but he seemed to be behaving strangely. He wasn't chatting and came to a stop, seeming as if he was ready to fall down. He mumbled something and we stopped. He sounded not quite right and so we decided to walk back, but, after a bit, he said he was alright. I suggested I'd run them back home, but Flo wouldn't hear of it. She wanted to carry on with the holiday regardless of whether Jack was bad or not. She was being selfish and though Jack seemed to be alright after that, we returned home later that day anyway.

We never went on holiday with them again because Helen felt it was a risk going with somebody who might become poorly. So we didn't mention going away to them again. Once, when we dropped in to see them, Jack said Flo had asked if we wanted to go on holiday, but he'd said, 'They'd let us know if they wanted to.' Helen and I didn't say anything, so nothing came of it. It was very sad and we could have continued going away with them for years. I was willing to carry on, but Helen didn't want the trouble that might have come about.

In July, the floodlights of the M.E.B. Stagefields Substation, about 150 yards away across the road, started shining into our house, which was a nuisance. So I went to the M.E.B. office in Victoria Road and told a fellow about it. He said, 'Can't you move your furniture or close the curtains?' I wasn't very happy about that and told him it wasn't satisfactory. I then wrote to our Stoke-on-Trent Central MP, Mark Fisher, on 6 August and asked him if he could do something about it, but a month went by before I had a reply.

For the first two or three weeks at the P.M.T. Club, Helen and I had signed in as visitors. We then decided we'd carry on going there and applied to become members. On 19 August, we were both issued with associate members' cards because we weren't P.M.T. workers, for whom the club was designed. We settled in after that.

On 9 September, Jeff started teaching an English class on Monday nights at the Cauldon Campus of what was by then Stoke on Trent College. This new college had been formed the previous year by the amalgamation of Cauldon College of Further & Higher Education and Stoke-on-Trent Technical College, where Jeff had continued to work. From then on, he used to come regularly for his tea before he started teaching in the evenings and would walk through Hanley Park to get here. Helen didn't like him doing that because of the risk of thugs being about. There'd been some incidents of people being attacked in the park and many of the bushes were cut down to reduce the hiding places.

Mark Fisher had sent me a letter on 4 September, saying he'd written to the M.E.B. to see if he could persuade them to do something about the lights shining into our windows. He wrote again on the 23rd and enclosed a letter that had been sent to him by Dennis Small of the M.E.B. The letter said that they'd had £20,000 of equipment stolen from their substation in seven break-ins in less than three months. Mr Small said they'd installed a video camera, which had to be illuminated by the lights, but that they'd adjusted the direction of the lights after my visit. Shortly afterwards, they were switched off altogether, which solved the problem, so I wrote to Mark Fisher on 3 October and thanked him for his help. I was surprised to get a letter back from him saying that it wasn't very often he got much thanks and that it was 'most thoughtful' of me 'to write in such generous terms'!

Roy and May Cope lived three doors away at 341 Leek Road. Roy was a postman. Unfortunately, around that time, May got knocked down by a taxi along the road. She said she was on the pedestrian crossing, but the driver claimed she was nearer to Warrington Road. She was seriously injured and was unconscious for two weeks. She broke quite a number of bones in her body and the accident permanently affected her legs, so she had to use a wheelchair after that, although she could still stand up. Roy and May had to have handrails put up at the sides of their front steps so she could pull herself up to get back in the house when she went out.

Around that time, Helen and I started dancing at Fenton Community Hall, in Manor Street, on a Friday afternoon. A girl we knew at the P.M.T. Club used to go there and we went to try it out. Helen used to go food shopping in Hanley in the morning and then we'd have our lunch and get ready, so it was a bit of a rush. The dancing was called easy sequence and it was on for a couple of hours. It was leisurely and not hectic like ballroom dancing, and was run by Jack and Freda Dawson, a husband and wife team, who lived at 113 Pacific Road, in Trentham. There was a small fee for annual membership (which was a pound per person in 1998) and Helen and I were given a membership card each.

Our friend wasn't there the first time, so we sat down not knowing anybody or any of the dances, which were taught as they went along. There was no band and the music was played from tapes. In the interval, a tape of a waltz or a quickstep was put on and we got up to give it a try. Helen was a bit shy, with it being a strange place, but that broke the ice. We gradually had a go at Jack and Freda's dances and we tried one or two on our first time there.

There was a wooden dance floor, with tables and chairs around the outside of it. We sat by a couple of women, Elsie and Barbara, who lived in Fenton, and got chatting to them. They were pretty good dancers, so we went on for one of the dances and followed them. We weren't very good, but it broke us in. We followed them in different dances for weeks, but I think they got a bit browned off with it, so we then started following another couple, Bob and Doris Rushton, who lived at 3 Hamilton Rise, in Baddeley Green. At first, we thought they were pretty good, but later realized they weren't. Helen had her idea of what the steps were and I had mine and she was getting a bit awkward in her movements, so at times she was difficult to dance with.

We started going regularly because we enjoyed dancing and there was the right atmosphere, with people of our age. We used to go up on the bus from the bottom of Victoria Road and sometimes we got a lift back. Unfortunately, Jack and Freda complicated things by having a new dance about every month and we couldn't cope with it because we'd do a new dance for a week or two and then they'd drop it and bring in another new one. It went on like that, but most of the people seemed to like it, so that was it.

We used to see Freda in Hanley and she said that she and Jack also ran afternoon classes at Blurton and Trentham on different days. We decided to give them a go as well, so for a short while we were going out dancing three times a week. The Blurton dances were in a kind of a hall and the setup was similar to that at Fenton. We went there on the bus, but I remember driving my car to the Trentham class, which was held in the ballroom and there seemed to be more room on the dance floor there. The people at Blurton and Trentham were mainly different from those at Fenton and we didn't really pal up with anybody at either. We didn't carry on for long at these new places because it was getting too much for Helen, especially with all the different dances.

On 8 December, I went with Jeff to a book fair at the YMCA, in Harding Road. He was selling copies of his new *Port Vale Tales* publication and did pretty well. Vale's Dutch midfield player, Robin van der Laan, came to sign copies and shook hands with me. I didn't think he looked like a footballer or what was fixed in my mind as such. He seemed pretty ordinary and he was nice.

On my 76th birthday, Jeff did an interview about his new book at Signal Radio, at 257 Stoke Road, and I went along with him. I hadn't known what to expect and I thought the setup was rather strange. It didn't appear to be going smoothly and the broadcasters seemed to be in a flap all the time because of technical problems!

There was a television programme on about the First World War and, after watching it, Helen asked me if I could write to somebody for information about her Uncle Wilf, who'd been killed in the war whilst serving with the Leicestershire Regiment. I wrote to the Commonwealth War Graves Commission, in Maidenhead, Berkshire, on 19 December and got a reply the next month, telling me that he'd been with the 6th Battalion and had died on 27 January 1916. The letter also said that he was buried in Humbercamps Communal Cemetery Extension, near Arras, in France.

Jeff had published Doug Moller's book, *The Wars Of The Roaches*, on 5

December and by the middle of January 1992 had sold out of the 500 copies he'd had printed. By then, Helen was convinced the book would sell millions and I thought there were business possibilities in Jeff publishing books by other people. In the end, he had a total of 1,500 copies of Doug's book printed and sold all of them except for the complimentary copies.

On 21 January, Granada Television rang Jeff because they wanted to film Doug and Rockhall Cottage for their *House Style* programme. The cottage was a lowly place and didn't really have any style, so I thought the idea was funny. However, I suppose there was a story in it because the cottage was such an unusual place. The feature was shown on TV on 18 February and it gave the book another good push.

Because Jeff and Ros didn't have a garage, they used to park their vehicles on the road outside their house, where they could keep an eye on them. However, on 14 February, a policeman knocked on their door, said that there'd been complaints about them doing so and told them that the vehicles were obstructing the highway. As a result, Jeff and Ros moved them to Fanny's Croft car park off the other side of the road, but, two days later, one of their neighbours caught three youths siphoning petrol from Jeff's Saab 99 car. I was a bit concerned about what was going to happen, but another policeman turned up, to take a statement about the petrol theft, and told Jeff and Ros that they could park outside their house after all, so it was back to square one and I was relieved.

On 29 February, Helen and I went with Jeff to watch Vale play at home to Newcastle United in the Second Division because the match was free for pensioners. Although Newcastle were third from the bottom, Vale lost 1-0, even though they had most of the play.

One day in early March, Young Harry was playing a round of golf at Leek Golf Club and bent down to pick his ball out of a hole when he heard a thud. Another golfer had teed off about a hundred yards away and the ball had come down on the top of Harry's head! He took his cap off and it was full of blood, but the amazing thing was that his head didn't hurt. He then went to the City General Hospital and had to have six stitches put in it.

One night at the club, a fellow named Frank, whom Helen and I knew, brought his Second World War medals to show us. He'd been a gunner, I think in the Western Desert, and he'd recently applied for the medals. It seemed that I was entitled to two, The Defence Medal and the War Medal, but nobody had ever informed me of that! Helen asked me, 'Why don't you apply for yours?'

I said: 'No. I didn't do anything. I don't want them things. They aren't much use.'

But Helen said, 'Go on, send for them,' and so I did.

I wrote to the Army Medal Office, in Droitwich, Worcestershire, on 12 March and they sent me a form, which I had to fill in. I sent it on the 21st, but the office warned me that they were having to deal with so many applications that I might have to wait up to a year to receive the medals! I was told that that was because there'd been a lot of publicity about various Second World War fifty-year anniversaries, which had brought memories back to people's minds. The medals were finally sent to me on 4 December, over fifty years after I'd joined the Forces!

The medals were solid cupronickel and about 1½ inches in diameter. Both had a depiction of King George VI's head on the top side, wearing a crown on the

War Medal. On the reverse of that was a lion standing on top of a fallen double-headed monster, whilst The Defence Medal showed two standing lions, protecting the crown. The War Medal was suspended from a red, white and blue ribbon and The Defence Medal was attached to a flame- and green-coloured ribbon, with two thin black stripes. They were quite nice, but there must have been millions of them around. After I'd had a look at them, I put them away and forgot about them!

Having had some information about her Uncle Wilf, Helen wanted to know if there were any medals available for him. So I wrote to the Army Medal Office for her on 10 April. I got a reply from them the following month, but they said that all the First World War medals for those who'd been killed had been issued to their next of kin. So we didn't get any further and, although Helen was disappointed, we had to leave it at that.

Jeff and Ros were planning to sell their house and a number of jobs needed doing to make it look better. In April, I helped Jeff to paint the shed and the following month, I replaced some rotten skirting board for them in their kitchen. I had to hack it out from behind their cooker and bought a length of timber, from Bands Hardware shop, at 60 Sandbach Road South, in Alsager town centre, which I cut down to size and fitted into the wall. I also replastered a small area of one of their toilet walls and dug out rotten wood from their bay at the front of their house, replacing it with bits of stone and filler. When the jobs were finished, Jeff and Ros put their house up for sale, but they didn't get much interest because it wasn't a very good time for selling.

Our back gate was rotting, so, in June, I bought some pieces of timber and made a new one. After I'd painted it, Jeff helped me to lift it onto its hinges. Unfortunately, the bottom of it dragged on the ground, so we had to take it off. I trimmed it down, but it was okay when we put it back on and it's still there now, although it's not in as good a condition as it was then.

Jeff took Helen and me to try to see a double sunset near Leek on 20 June. We got to the lay-by above Rudyard Reservoir, on the A 523, but the sun vanished into cloud. Then it reappeared, so Jeff decided to drive us on to nearby Woodhouse Green to see if anything would happen there. However, he was short on time and it got a bit hectic as he whizzed round the country lanes, to no avail because we arrived just too late to see anything! He then took us to see the Bridestones, the remains of a Stone Age burial site, at the back end of The Cloud, but I wasn't all that impressed with them.

On 12 July, Jeff and Ros went on holiday to the Scottish islands of Mull, Tiree and Coll. They went to a restaurant on Mull, The Puffer Aground, which was run by a fellow who came from Bosley in Cheshire! While they were there, they also visited Calgary, which Jeff said was a tiny place, with a beautiful beach, after which the Canadian city had been named. He also told Helen and me that Tiree was green, but Coll was rocky, even though they were right next to one another! Jeff said there was a petrol pump so old on Coll that he couldn't understand how to use it. Then when he paid for the fuel he'd had with a cheque, the lady at the store marvelled at it because it had colour on it!

Helen and I were having Saturday lunch at our house with Jeff and Ros on 8 August and I was sitting on a wooden, foldaway picnic chair as usual. Next second, it came apart underneath me and collapsed! I think the joints had come apart and I was vexed that the firm had made such a flimsy job. It could have been nasty and splintered bits of the chair might have gone into my body, but fortunately I was unhurt.

Edith Elson died from cancer on 24 August. By then, she and Jack were living in Market Drayton, at 11 Lime Grove, but Edith and Helen had become at odds over something, so we didn't go to the funeral. Helen didn't want to go and, of course, I couldn't go without her.

The following month, Bernard Kent's son, Paul, had a brain haemorrhage and was taken to the Accident and Emergency Department of the Infirmary, in Prince's Road. I went to see him, but he was all wired up and was unconscious. He died on the 12th and was buried in Fenton Cemetery on the 22nd after a service at the Church of St. Mary and All Saints, in Park Drive, Trentham. Helen and I visited Bernard and Dorothy some time afterwards, at their house, 24 Tulsa Close, in Eaton Park, and, during the conversation, Bernard said, 'Him over there,' pointing at the cemetery in the distance. He meant Paul, but couldn't bear to mention his name, I suppose.

Helen and I went for tea at Jeff and Ros's on 3 October. Jeff had bought a new music keyboard, a Technics KN 1000, which had cost him £1,150, and I had a bit of a go on it. It was marvellous because it had 150 different sounds, like trumpets, violins and flutes, but they didn't sound true to me. While we were there, Jeff put on a video that Audrey Whalley's daughter, Sara, had shot of Raedburh on her camcorder, which was a small, easily portable video recorder. The film was rather jerky, but it attracted our attention anyway because it was of Raedburh.

Stoke and Vale were both in the Second Division, which is what the old Third Division had been renamed that season after the Premier League had been set up. The teams met each other on 24 October at Stoke's Victoria Ground and Jeff called for his lunch before going to the match. It was good that the local sides were playing each other because there was an extra edge in the Derby games. I wanted Stoke to come out on top because I still supported them from my armchair, but Helen was rooting for Vale. I expected Stoke to win, because they were supposed to be the top local team, and they did, by 2-1.

In November, Jeff published a book on Captain Smith of the Titanic, which had been written by Gary Cooper – a local author, not the famous actor! The book was called *The Man Who Sank The Titanic?*. There'd been plenty of things written about the ship, but surprisingly there'd never before been published a book about its captain. I thought it might be of interest to people in the Potteries because of Smith coming from Hanley and Jeff managed to sell over 1,500 copies of it in total.

Jeff was in an Anglo-Saxon history society called Ða Engliscan Gesidas and, on 26 November, he received a letter from the national organizers telling him that they'd made him the scirgerefa (sheriff) of Staffordshire and the West Midlands. It seemed like trying to bring fiction into reality! We were used to cowboy films with sheriffs and knew they weren't real, but my son had actually been made a sheriff! I could visualize him riding down the street, looking back at all these bad men following him! So my first reaction was that it was funny, but it wasn't what I originally thought it was because the title actually meant that he became the area meetings organizer for the society.

Jeff made a cassette of ten songs he'd knocked up about Vale, called *Port Vale*

Forever. He'd decided to have a change from writing books on Vale and see if he could get anywhere with something musical. He'd recorded the tunes on his own equipment at his house and it seemed as if it was the first time that anybody had ever done a whole album about a football club. To go with the tape, he had a song book published, which had all the words and chords laid out. It was a bit like sheet music that I'd bought in the old days, except that the notes of the melodies weren't printed. Jeff was pushed to get it all out before Christmas and it only went on sale on 17 December. The songs weren't world-beaters, but they were alright and he sold 328 copies in the first five days from the cassette and songbook coming out. He gave Helen and me a copy, but we didn't play it much because it wasn't our type of music.

I was shocked to read in the papers in January 1993 that unemployment in Britain had reached almost three million and the next month it went up to 3,062,065. It looked as if we were going back to the dark days of the 1930s, so I was glad that I had a pension and didn't have to struggle for work.

Stoke and Vale were doing well in the Second Division. From 9 January to 16 February, Vale won six league games in a row to go up to second place, behind only Stoke. I was surprised to find out that it was the first time that the two clubs had ever been first and second in the same league table at the same point. It was good for the city that they were both doing well and I think it's better when they're in the same division because it creates interest and gives them two good gates. Jeff was very pleased with how Vale were doing and, of course, was cheering them on.

6 The Turning Of The Tide

On 22 March 1993, Nancy Cadman was robbed of £200 by a burglar while she was out. Helen thought she'd heard a banging noise, so she looked through Nancy's kitchen windows over the wall and saw somebody inside. Then the burglar must have gone upstairs into the back bedroom, from where he saw Helen watching him. She came in and told me what was happening. I'd already heard a thudding noise and I think the burglar had kicked the front door in to get inside. Although we didn't see him do it, he tried to get out of one of the windows, but it wouldn't open, so he put his foot in the frame and forced it open. Then he must have jumped onto Nancy's lawn because the window was wide open.

I went outside and was dodging around, trying to find out what was going on. I wondered about rushing down my front steps to cut him off from escaping and to ask whether he'd done a burglary, but I was confused and decided against it because I thought it might be a dangerous thing to do at my age. Then I saw him sitting on his motor scooter at the side of the road, so he must have just dashed down from Nancy's. I watched him ride off fairly quickly towards Milton. It seemed that Nancy wasn't in, so I rang John and Kath and told them. I suppose they or Nancy reported it to the police, but I didn't hear any more about it.

On 3 April, Helen and I went to Mandy Poole's wedding with Jon Posnett, who was from Shifnal and was a teacher at Blurton Primary School. They got married at Leek Register Office, in Fountain Street, and had their reception at The Knot Inn, in Station Lane, Rushton Spencer.

Jeff was writing another book about Vale, this time listing all the facts and figures, called *The Port Vale Record*. As usual, he enrolled me to help out by looking up answers at the reference library to queries he'd got and it helped to keep me busy.

I was dozing in my armchair about midday on 3 May and sensed somebody going past me. I thought it was Helen, but then she knocked on the window, irritated, and woke me up. She'd been gardening at the front of the house and was shouting that the gate was bolted, so she couldn't get to the back door to come in. She assumed I'd bolted it. So I went out to unbolt it and let her through, but I saw a youth standing at the top of the steps in Alice's back garden. I asked him, 'What do you want?'

He said, 'Oh, I'm looking for a ball.'

For all I knew, he might have been one of Alice's relatives. The youth stood there for a minute or so and then another one, whom I didn't see, shouted. All of a sudden, the first youth went into the next garden and disappeared.

I thought it was suspicious, so I checked our house and upstairs I found that almost all our jewellery had gone, including my mother's wedding ring and Helen's retirement gold watch. It turned out the burglars had walked past the front of our house and spoken to Helen. Then they must have got round the back, bolted the gate to keep her out, come in through the open door and walked past me while I was asleep! We told the police, but they didn't catch anybody. I wasn't particularly upset, though Helen was a bit. I had to be thankful that I hadn't interrupted and confronted the burglars because I might have got smashed up.

Mandy Morrey suggested that we contact our insurance company (Sun Alliance) and put in a claim, which we did. Our ten stolen items were valued by Goldsmiths, the jewellers, of Market Square, at £1,552.80 and we got the full compensation, which I was surprised about.

The wood was rotting in one of our kitchen windows and when it goes in one place, it all rots. So we needed it all replacing. UPVC double glazing was the thing at the time, so we decided to try it, which would save me the trouble of painting wooden window frames every so often. We came across Tailor-Made Conservatories Ltd, at Unit 3, in Castlefield Street, Shelton, and got them to do the job at a cost of £970. We paid £194 deposit on 20 May, but, one day, when the workman was on the job, the owner came down and was pestering him to go somewhere else. I said: 'Hang on! Do my job instead of mucking about!' The owner pulled his face, but he let the workman carry on and he completed it in two days.

Ros was made a full-time English lecturer at Stafford College on 21 May after having had an interview for the job the day before. She'd been part time for two years and that had been a latch lifter.

Stoke had won the Second Division championship and Vale had reached the final of the Autoglass Trophy, which was contested between Second and Third Division teams. It was played on 22 May against Stockport County and Jeff was one of around 25,000 Vale supporters who travelled to Wembley to watch them win 2-1. He'd never been there before and wasn't all that impressed with the ground, but he was back there eight days later because Vale had finished third in the league and then got to the final of the play-offs, in which they met West Bromwich Albion. Unfortunately, a second victory wasn't to be because Vale lost 3-0 and Jeff said there was a deathly hush amongst their supporters as they left to go home.

When Jeff got in his caravanette on 14 June, it wouldn't start and he found a large pool of petrol underneath it. When he had a look at how it had got there, he discovered that someone had cut the petrol pipe! He rang the police about the incident, but told me that they'd blamed it on him and Ros because they parked their vehicles at the side of the road. After that, Jeff parked the caravanette round the corner, in Oak Avenue, and he had no further trouble.

Jeff had some trouble getting the money in from shops that he'd sold his books to and the worst offender was Dillons, who owed him £721.65. He couldn't get them to pay up no matter what he did, so eventually, on 5 July, he went to their office at Berwick House, 35 Livery Street, in Birmingham, and got to see their finance director. Jeff told me that he'd asked for a cheque on the spot, which they'd refused to pay, so there'd been a big argument about it. He was told to leave the premises, but wouldn't till the director wrote him a promise that they'd pay him within the next four days. On the last day, he received a cheque from them for the full amount, but it made me wonder what the world was coming to that he'd had to do all that just to get what was rightfully his.

On 17 July, Jeff and Ros went on holiday to the Isles of Scilly, 28 miles off Land's End. They got a helicopter from Penzance Heliport and were thrilled with the ride, which Jeff said was smooth, but noisy. Harold Wilson, the former prime minister, lived on the main island, St Mary's, and I'd wondered what the Scillies were like. Jeff told me they were so small that he and Ros were able to walk round them and there were a lot of sub-tropical plants and lovely sands. They stayed on St Mary's and had boat trips out to five of the other islands, but the sun was so hot that Jeff bought a hat to protect his head and face from it.

After he got back, Jeff drove to the Football League offices in St Anne's four times in less than two weeks, to get information for his Vale book. Because it was a 308-mile round trip and he'd got so much to find, he had only a fifteen-minute lunch break in the seven hours he was there each time. He told me that most of the League's history was in dusty old handwritten books stored in the basement and that, when using them, his hands became so dirty that he had to wash them every so often!

Jeff and Ros were finding that their caravanette wasn't much use to them. Since they'd bought it, they'd only ever been away in it for four holidays and on one of those, the previous Easter, they'd stayed in B & Bs because it had been so cold! Also, Jeff was having to use the caravanette as his main vehicle, which was a problem because it consumed a lot of petrol and was cold to drive in the winter as it had a poor heater. So they decided to sell it and buy a second car. They sold it for £1,900 on 31 August, but were sad to see it go.

A new Kwik Save supermarket had opened in Victoria Road, which was quite a bit closer to Helen and me than the one in Leek Road, Bucknall. It was easier to drive in and out of and was near enough to walk to. So we started shopping there and didn't go to the Leek Road store very often after that.

Jeff and Ros bought Helen a new Pulsar quartz watch for her birthday and she used to put it on as an ornament when we went to the club on a Sunday night. She didn't really use it as a watch and didn't wear it when she went shopping, even though that meant she didn't know the time while she was out. I've still got it today.

We seemed to be taking food for Raedburh all the time, especially liver, which Helen got from the new Potteries Market. It was beneath The Potteries Shopping Centre and was generally known as Hanley Market. She used to tell the stallholder, 'This is for my son's cat,' and he'd say, 'Oh, wasting money on a cat!' I thought it was an extravagance myself, buying the best stuff for the cat, but it was fun feeding her. I was still getting her to sit up on her back legs, by offering her bits of food, and she did it most of the time!

Jeff and Ros got interested in buying a house, 12 Church View, at The Pastures, a small new development in Cotes Heath, just off the A 519 to Eccleshall. Helen and I went to the show home on the estate a time or two to look at what they'd got on offer and to see if there'd been any movement on the house in Church View that Jeff and Ros were keen on. Helen got pretty interested in it, but Jeff and Ros were finding it hard to sell their house, so nothing happened.

British Coal had been planning to have an opencast mine on Berry Hill to take out 800,000 tons of coal from hundreds of acres of land, but, fortunately, it was in the *Sentinel* on 4 November that they'd been turned down by the government. It would obviously have been a very big operation and a blot on the landscape, which we would probably have seen from our house. Helen and I had also been bothered about it because we thought it would have led to a lot of lorries, full of coal, coming along Leek Road, blowing out more fumes.

On 19 November, British Coal announced that Silverdale Colliery, the last remaining pit in North Staffordshire, was to stop mining from 3 December. It was employing 600 miners, but was reported to have been losing nearly a million pounds a month. The mine reopened in 1995 after a buyout, but closed permanently in 1998 when the high quality seams of coal ran out. I thought it was sad that the miners lost their jobs because they needed the work, but it was good that nobody had to go down such hell holes in the area any more.

Jeff's new Vale book came out on 10 December and he was very busy selling copies throughout the month, but it wasn't doing as well as his previous ones, even though he sold 577 copies before Christmas. Maybe Vale books had become too much of a good thing.

Helen bought a tape from Brian Eeley of a service that had been recorded at Zion Church. The church sold them, mainly to the congregation, to make a bit of money. Helen and I didn't have anything to play it on, but Jeff and Ros bought us a Hitachi radio-cassette player for Christmas so that we could listen to it. I think I enjoyed it more than Helen did and Brian put over the service pretty well.

The church made three or four tapes over a period of time, but Helen said: 'Don't do that again. People will be getting browned off with it. It will be a waste of time.' And she was right because they didn't sell so well as the first one.

Sam Kent had been suffering from dementia and died on 27 January 1994. I went to his funeral, which was held on 2 February at Carmountside Crematorium. Bernard and Dorothy didn't go because the two brothers weren't speaking to one another and so Sam's wife, Hilda, was about the only person I knew there.

Along with the other lecturers at Stoke on Trent College, Jeff was sent a new contract, which he received on 8 February. It said that he could be told to turn up at the weekends and sent anywhere in the world to work for the college! Also, it said that he'd have to ask permission from the principal, Neil Preston, if he wanted to carry on publishing. Of course, Jeff refused to sign it. NATFHE, the lecturers' union, that he was in, was against the contract and collected the members' copies, including his, and returned them to the principal!

Jeff and Ros gave Helen a large bottle of Youth Dew perfume for Mother's Day. It was made by Estée Lauder and was her favourite scent in later years. She used to go round the shops and try out the perfumes, so that's how she came across it. She used to get favourable comments off people at the club about it, so she felt she was picking the right thing and wouldn't use anything else. I sometimes bought her some as a present and so did Jeff. If she was getting low on it, she'd remind me to ask Jeff to get her some more for her birthday or Christmas. But she didn't wear it generally, only when she went out somewhere, mainly to the club.

I was going across Hanley Park one day in the spring, on the path towards Harding Road, when I felt I couldn't see the exit ahead as well as I thought I should have been able to, especially with my left eye. I didn't know what was happening and I was worried, so I made an appointment to go to Kenneth Wright, the optician's at 23 Regent Road, in April. I was seen by Ian Wise, who examined me and said, 'It looks as if you've got cataracts developing.' He seemed to be suspicious about it, but not sure, so I had to wait to see what happened and in any case my eyes weren't bad enough for anything to be done about them. The sight in my left eye slowly got worse and then it became obvious in my other eye. I became worried I'd have to give up driving and that everything would go down the chute, so I'd no longer be able to read or watch the television.

On 3 May, Jeff and Ros had their offer of £78,000 accepted for a house, 8 Nelson Crescent, in Cotes Heath. Helen and I had a run over to have a look at it and, though we could only see it from the outside, we were pretty impressed. It was nearly new and was a four-bedroom detached house in a nice area of the countryside. It had an open-plan front garden, but we were used to hedges and fences, so we wondered if that was quite right and whether children would play on it. Unfortunately, Jeff and Ros still hadn't sold their own house and so we had to wait to see what would happen.

Beryl Eardley died on 6 May, which meant there was a problem with Kieron being looked after, especially as Reg's eyesight was deteriorating. The family struggled on with Kieron for a while, but eventually he went into Moorside Lodge Residential Home, in Farley Road, Oakamoor, and died, aged twenty, in 1998.

Helen and I were more or less satisfied with our new UPVC kitchen windows and I fancied cutting out more of the woodwork painting, so we decided to have our lounge, front bedroom and boxroom windows replaced by UPVC and a new front door fitted. We got Stoke Insulation Services, of Bucknall Road, to do the jobs and they were using the new, internal glazing method, which was more secure than the outside fitting we'd had for our kitchen windows. Also, we decided to have Pilkington glass because it was supposed to be the best available.

Three or four workmen did all the installations on 18 May, but, unfortunately, they weren't very good. They trampled all over the plants in our front garden, but when I told them about it, they smirked and didn't take any notice. They had to prop the bay up, to get the frames out, and a tile dropped onto the new sill and made a big dent in it! I thought it would be a big job to repair and might require them to replace the whole thing because it was a single unit. But they got a piece of broken glass from the old frame and shaved the sill down with it and then planed it level, so it looked alright. It only took them a few minutes to do it and I was amazed! When they'd finished the job, a line of old paint had been left at each end of the bay, where the wood had joined the brickwork. I asked them to do something about it and one of the workmen said they'd stick on two plastic strips to cover the paint up.

We paid the company £3,080 for the whole job the day after they'd finished. We were supposed to have been given £25 for recommending them to Nancy, for whom they did some work, but we didn't get it and the strips didn't appear either. So I went down to see them. They then brought two strips along, but these were too narrow and they didn't bother again. I knocked up a letter to them on 9 June and mentioned it to Jeff, who had a look at it for me and redid part of it. Ros then typed it up and I sent it, asking them to complete the job within fourteen days and settle the £25 debt.

From time to time, Jeff and Ros bought Helen and me cassettes of different singers we liked, one of whom was Jim Reeves. For Father's Day, they got me *The Definitive Jim Reeves*, which had come out in 1992 and had two tapes of his hit records and other songs. Helen and I were really keen on it because his songs were easy to sing along with, but she kept playing it all the time for quite a while, which became a bore!

We also had three cassettes in a package, called *All the Very Best of Sing Something Simple*, by The Cliff Adams Singers, which had been brought out in 1993. Helen and I had listened to their half-hour Sunday night radio programme for years and liked to join in with the sing-along songs that were sung. So the cassettes were very popular with both of us and they had a swing. One particular song that we liked that was on there was *Tie a Yellow Ribbon Round the Ole Oak Tree*, which had originally been done by Dawn and had got to the top of the charts in 1973.

Stoke Insulation Services had still done nothing by the middle of July, so Jeff went to see them on the 15th. Then a policewoman called here and said the manager of the firm had told her that Jeff had been there with a threatening attitude. I said: 'Never! Not likely!' Helen refused to give her Jeff's address and the policewoman then drifted off. I rang Jeff and left a message. I felt shirty because the police had been, but Jeff rang back and said the manager was telling lies. He then called the police and told them the same. Nothing came of it and we never did get satisfaction from the firm.

On 10 August, Helen fell over, I think in Hanley while she was shopping, and somebody helped her up. She wasn't injured, so I didn't think much about it at the time, but she gradually became less steady on her legs.

Roy and May Cope had a sheepdog named Sally. Helen took a fancy to the dog and would go down our front steps to give her a stroke and a titbit when she went past. This happened so often that eventually I took a couple of photographs of Helen feeding Sally at the bottom of the steps.

On 8 September, Jeff and Ros signed the contract to buy their new house in Cotes Heath. Helen and I were pleased about it, as long as they could afford it, but they both had jobs. They took us to see it on the 11th and it was pretty grand. We volunteered to do jobs for them, but, with it being nearly a new house, not a lot wanted doing, so we mainly helped in the garden, tidying up and putting bulbs in.

They moved in on the 15th and at first took Raedburh out into the garden in a harness, in case she ran off, to get her used to the new place. She seemed really pitiful in it, all drooped down because of the restriction of being on a lead, but it wasn't for long. Also, Jeff mentioned the noise of passing trains on the nearby Stafford to Crewe line, but, when Helen and I went out and listened, it didn't seem all that much.

Unfortunately, there was a snag with Jeff and Ros's move. They hadn't been able to sell their house in Alsager and had decided to rent it to students, so I did some jobs for them there to help get it ready. I fixed up a wardrobe from MFI, made a platform for the kettle to sit on and maintained the garden with Helen.

That autumn, Helen and I had a problem with our drains inspection chamber overflowing. We thought the council had sorted out the problem when they cleared the blockage for us for free on 27 September, but soon liquid was leaking out of the top of the chamber again. So we got back in touch with the council and their workmen had another go on 15 November. Unfortunately, the same thing happened again and I became concerned and wondered if neighbours were putting things down their toilets that they shouldn't have been. I was relieved that the problem was eventually solved by the council's third attempt nine weeks later.

When we went to Jeff and Ros's, Jeff would ask us if we wanted a drink and Helen would say, 'Yes!'

Jeff would ask: 'What do you want? Tea, coffee, fruit juice, water or mineral water?'

She'd say, 'What else is there?' until eventually Jeff came round to whisky and then she'd say, 'Oh, yes!' She'd want pop in it, but Jeff and Ros wouldn't have any, so she had to have fruit juice instead. Jeff would ask her if it was alright and she'd say, 'Yes, it's okay.' She'd then usually have at least one more, but later Jeff would tell me that it had been almost all fruit juice. Jeff's idea was to keep her off as much whisky as possible because he didn't think it was very good for her, especially in the afternoon, and I didn't want her to get into the habit of drinking all day either.

I didn't like the idea of there being students in Jeff and Ros's house in Alsager because I thought they'd ransack the place. I was also worried that there'd be a lot of damage done, which the students wouldn't be able to pay for because I supposed that they hadn't got much money. So I thought Jeff and Ros would be left with the bill.

On 12 November, Jeff went to the house to show a student a room there that was still available to rent. Unfortunately, after he'd driven all the way there, he found that he couldn't get in because none of the other students were there and they'd locked and bolted the front door. So he wasted his time going and there were other occasions when he had to go over there to sort things out. So renting the house was a nuisance to him, really.

Jeff was writing a new book on Vale, giving details of all the players who'd been with them since the club had formed. It was a big task and I agreed to help him again. He began putting down questions for me to look into and try to answer at Hanley Reference Library, which took many a while over quite a long period of time.

On Christmas Day, we went with Jeff and Ros to Nick's house, 13 St. Ann's Road South, in Heald Green, just south of Manchester. He introduced us to his girlfriend, Claire Lawrence, and Alan, Shirley and Claire's mother and stepfather (Val and Don) were also there. Nick announced that he and Claire were getting married and Helen gave them an engagement card she'd bought because she'd had a feeling something was in the air! I thought Nick was alright, but Helen loved him because he had a big smile and was good looking. What I remember about Claire was that she was on the plump side.

Jeff and Ros had a New Year family party at their house. Helen and I were going to go, but we decided not to because it snowed. Ros's family all turned up and Nick and Claire stayed over. They slept in the lounge and both of them heard a rumbling noise in the night, which they thought was the other's stomach, but it turned out to be Raedburh snoring!

On 15 January 1995, Ros went to Haworth, in Yorkshire, to see Alan driving a steam train on The Keighley & Worth Valley Railway, which had been set up for him as a birthday present. Claire was also there and told Ros that she and Nick had been arguing about their wedding that they were planning. Claire said that Nick wanted to get married in a stately home and have champagne priced at £32 a bottle!

Jeff needed a new headlamp for his car and had got one stored in the shed at his house in Alsager. So, on 27 January, he went to get it, but discovered that the students weren't looking after the house very well. He found the cardboard centres from eight toilet roll holders on the floor and a big patch of thick coal dust in the pantry! Six days later, I went over to do one or two jobs for him and I too thought the house looked a mess.

There were strange goings-on at Stoke College around that time. Jeff told me that the principal had ordered the sale of all fiction books that weren't being used for particular classes. Also, Newcastle College had set up a centre in Burslem and so Jeff's college had retaliated and opened a guidance place in Newcastle. Then it was announced on 11 February that the college had won contracts to provide education in three prisons in Scotland!

Helen could no longer bend down to cut her toenails and when I tried to do them for her, she always reckoned I was hurting her. Some of her nails were embedded in her skin, so it was awkward. So she went to a chiropodist at Hanley Health Centre, in Upper Huntbach Street, on 27 February and carried on going every three months or so to have the job done. It was on the National Heath Service and free because she was a pensioner. Later on, she transferred to a chiropodist at Moorcroft Medical Centre, at 10 Botteslow Street, because we could get a bus from Leek Road that dropped us off close to the centre.

Helen and I still used to use horse manure to fertilize our garden and put it mainly around our roses. We still got it from Graham Reece's horses and also free from a place in Scot Hay, where we'd have a run to in our car from time to time. On 4 March, I got Jeff to go up there with me and help fill four big bags up, but there was a cold wind blowing and I don't think he was very happy about it!

When Jeff and Ros had lived in Alsager, the road outside had been busy and there'd always been a danger that Raedburh might get run over. It seemed nice and quiet in Cotes Heath, though, and Jeff and Ros's house was on a no through road, so I thought it was very unlikely that Raedburh would be run over there. However, Jeff told me that, on 26 March, she'd dashed straight in front of Nick's car as he was pulling out of their drive, but, fortunately, he'd been driving very slowly and looking out for her, so no harm was done.

On 4 April, Jeff noticed that the left-hand side of his face was swelling up and then red marks developed on his head. They started itching, so he went to see his doctor, David Carr, at The Crown Surgery, at 23 High Street, in Eccleshall, who told him it was an infection and gave him penicillin. Then it was decided that he'd got shingles and Helen wouldn't let him into our house because she thought she might catch it from him! He had it for some weeks, but didn't have any time off work.

Nick and Claire got married at Trafford Register Office, in Sale Town Hall, near Manchester, on 29 April and Helen and I drove there in convoy with Jeff and Ros. There were quite a few guests and a reception followed at Dane Lodge Hotel, at 129 Northenden Road, in Sale, but, unfortunately, it involved a noisy disco. Then Claire had an argument with one of the guests, who she said had heckled her stepfather's wedding speech! Nick and Claire renamed themselves Lawrence-Downs, which I thought was queer.

Jeff and Ros had an old manual lawnmower, which they'd used to cut the grass at their house in Alsager. Their garden in Cotes Heath was much larger and mainly lawn, so it was an altogether bigger job to mow. To help them, Helen and I bought them an electric rotary mower and Strimmer, which saved them time and gave a better cut.

When Helen and I called to see Jeff and Ros on 16 June, Jeff didn't seem right, so I asked him if he was okay. He said he'd been to see his doctor that afternoon and had been told he'd got depression, probably brought on by the shingles. The doctor had said that that wasn't unusual and prescribed Prozac, which had a reputation of being a wonder drug, but that didn't stop Helen and me from being worried about Jeff.

He and Ros decided it was too much trouble to continue renting their house in Alsager, especially because Jeff wasn't well. So they decided to make a big effort to sell it and advertised it through Halifax Property Services, of 5 Crewe Road, in Alsager, at £42,950, which was less than they'd have liked for it.

Helen seemed to have become frightened about leaving our house, in case something happened to it, and she wouldn't go on holiday. It was probably because of the burglary we'd had. I was annoyed because I was missing going away and she wouldn't put herself out for me, but it wouldn't have been much use being on holiday if she'd got the house on her mind and wanted to go home all the time.

We often had a drive over to see Jeff, Ros and Raedburh and we enjoyed visiting their house because it was a nice place. Sometimes we'd have a walk with Jeff and Ros from their home, particularly up to the duck pond in Standon, the next village. We always took some food with us, half a loaf or some cream crackers, and dished it out between us and fed the ducks with it. They nearly always came for it and it was enjoyable feeding them.

Helen and I would also have a drive to Jeff and Ros's house after we'd been strawberry picking at Bearstone Farm, near Woore, and we'd give them some of our fruit. It made a nice, little round trip and meant we could take them something as a gift.

In August, my right knee became swollen and painful again. Fluid had built up once more and I sent for a doctor because I couldn't walk up to the surgery. Dr Przyslo came down on the 29th and I was given some medicine to take. I asked if he was going to get the fluid out, but he said: 'No. It might get infected with doing it in a private home, so I don't do that.' Anyway, my knee gradually got better again.

Jeff and Ros were struggling to sell their house and so they reduced the price to £39,950. On 18 September, I painted their conservatory and shed for them, to make the house look more presentable, and finally they got some proper interest.

It took Jeff quite a while to get over the depression he had and he was off work for over two months in the autumn. The college was very good to him because, when he returned in November, he was only given a bit of teaching at first so that he could ease back in.

On 16 October, Jeff and Ros finally agreed to sell their house to a buyer, Cathy Daniel, for £35,000, as long as the sale was quick. The survey had said their house was only worth that much without £3,000 worth of jobs being done on it. Jeff and Ros signed the contract on 21 November and then got rid of most of their surplus furniture through a house clearance sale, although their estate agent, Matthew Sharp, bought their old dining table for £20 and seemed really pleased with it! Helen and I were relieved that the sale had finally gone through because having a second house was a burden round Jeff and Ros's necks.

About that time, Nancy had become concerned about her next-door neighbour, Ann Parrish, because she hadn't seen her for a while. Nancy then shouted me and told me she was worried, so I went round to Ann's house and knocked on the front and back doors. There was no reply, so I looked through the windows and the letter box, but couldn't see anybody. I didn't know what to do, but just then Dave Wallett rolled up in his ambulance. He was by chance delivering one of our other neighbours back home, so I went up to him and told him the story.

He came along and had a look around. He went to the side window and levered it open. He got through it, although to me it looked a very precarious thing to do. He found Ann lying unconscious in the kitchen and checked she wasn't bleeding. He opened the back door to let Nancy and me in and then went back to tend to Ann. I saw him bending over her and then she opened her eyes. Because he was already on a job, he sent for an ambulance, which took her to hospital. I phoned her daughter, Jean, who later came over and was incredulous that Dave had got through the window!

It turned out that Ann had fractured her other hip, so she had to have that one replaced too, but the operation went wrong and she never walked again and never returned home. After she came out of hospital, she went into The Guardian Care Centre, a residential home, at Selwyn House, in Longton Road, Trentham, and died on 31 August 1997.

Jeff took me to Manchester Airport for my eightieth birthday and we wandered right round it, watching planes loading and taking off and others landing and unloading. I hadn't been to an airport before and it was quite interesting, but it didn't seem extraordinary because I'd seen such things on the television. Afterwards, we had a nice walk on Alderley Edge, above the town.

Helen, Jeff, Ros, Alan, Shirley and I were all supposed to be going to Newtown, in Powys, in Wales, for Christmas at Don and Val's house. However, the visit was cancelled because Nick and Claire had a row with them! So Helen, Alan, Shirley, Nick, Claire and I went to Jeff and Ros's instead and had an enjoyable time anyway.

Jeff was told by the college to teach an introduction to history class at the Willfield Community Education Centre, in Lauder Place South, Bentilee. When he turned up on the first day, 15 January 1996, there was only one student, Dave Seabridge, who hadn't signed up at that point, but he was very interested, so Jeff taught him! Dave still hadn't enrolled the following week, but he eventually did and Jeff taught him as a lone student for the whole of the ten-week course!

Helen took it upon herself to buy things, mainly clothes, for Jeff whether he wanted them or not. For example, on 10 February, she gave him a green coat that he'd told her he didn't want because it was virtually the same as one he'd already got! Then she bought him a one-foot-high painted garden gnome, but he didn't like it, so she put it on our rockery. I didn't like it myself and, after she died, I got rid of it.

Jeff's 1979 Saab car was looking the worse for wear and needed replacing, so, on 24 February, Helen and I gave him £2,000 towards another car. He liked his old one and so he decided to buy another Saab. This time he had an F registration 900, which was a newer model, and paid £4,100 for it from Dennis Dickens, a car salesman in Elder Road, Burslem.

By then, Jeff was teaching a writing and publishing class on Monday nights at the college and Helen used to spoil him when he came for his tea before he taught it. She'd boil a kettle and put the hot water in a bowl for him to wash his hands with. His tea would always be ready on the table and his toothbrush, toothpaste and a glass of water would be by the sink waiting for him to use afterwards. She'd nearly always be looking out from the bay for him coming and would wave him off when he went.

On 6 April, we went to Jeff and Ros's for the evening and Alan and Shirley were also there. Helen had the idea of helping Jeff and Ros out with their garden and asked them if she could have a plot at the back. More work, I thought! Then Shirley asked for the same and it was all agreed. They were both itching to start, so Jeff worked out a plan and took measurements. The gardens were still mainly lawns, but Helen was soon on the job and I dug a corner out, up to a point under Helen's supervision. She'd direct operations for a while, but then wander off and so I'd have to use my own initiative. She decided that spring bulbs, like crocuses and daffodils, should be planted and I put them in. I think it was all because Helen was getting into the swing of Jeff and Ros's new house. We kept it up for two or three years, but then it fizzled out. By that time, Helen was struggling to bend down and perhaps it was getting too much for me, with having our own garden to do as well.

In April, Helen and I saw a notice on a lamppost that there was a proposal to turn the offices at 290 Leek Road, owned by Parkinson Engineering Services Ltd, into student flats. The building was on the other side of the road to us and very close, so we were worried that there'd be parties all night, with noise and disruption. Helen wanted to get a petition up against it and asked Jeff to write it, which he did. Helen and I then went round to neighbours collecting signatures and were pretty successful. Another neighbour did even better than us and eventually we handed the whole thing in. Also, Helen got Jeff to knock up a protest letter to the City Council Planning Department and we sent that off on the 22nd. Helen then rang John Abberley, one of the journalists at *The Sentinel*, and told him about the problem, but said she didn't want her name 'splashed all over the newspaper'. He didn't seem very interested, but, as it turned out, we received a letter from the council in September, which said that planning permission had been refused for the development, so that was the end of that.

On 6 May, Jeff took Helen and me for a ride to Newcastle in his new car, which was roomy and comfortable. It had power-assisted steering, which meant that he found it easy to manoeuvre, even though it was a big, heavy car. Helen said sitting in it was like being in an aeroplane because of the way it was laid out and all the dials and controls it had, but we both liked it.

Jeff told me that on 5 June, Raedburh went out of one of their front bedroom windows, which was open, and was walking along the sill when she fell off! He was frightened that she'd fallen to the ground, but then realized that their bay was below, so she'd only dropped a few feet and was unhurt.

On 15 June, over 200 people were injured by an IRA bomb, which caused a lot of damage in the centre of Manchester. It was at the back of my mind that it was too close for comfort to Stoke. I didn't really like the situation in Northern Ireland and kept hoping something would happen to sort it out, but I couldn't see it altering. It was a hopeless situation and I wondered why both sides couldn't get it right and settle down.

In July, the government increased the number of troops in Northern Ireland to 18,500 and I got worried in case it came to a full-blown battle over there. Even when an agreement was eventually reached in 1998, I thought the fanatics would start up again, but it's been mostly pretty quiet since then.

Sometimes, Helen would have the idea of going for a run in our car to Jeff and Ros's house after they'd gone home from having their Saturday lunch with us! So an hour or two later, we'd turn up on their doorstep, which was a bit much for them really, but I just went along with it.

On 2 August, Jeff and Ros went on holiday to Iceland, but Helen and I were worried in case their plane crashed. We were always concerned when they flew anywhere. Iceland looked a bleak place, from their photos, but I suppose it was an experience and I think I'd have liked the wide-open spaces.

Helen and I went to Matthew Poole's wedding at Bradnop Methodist Chapel, southeast of Leek, on 24 August. His bride was Jackie Knott, whom he'd met at work at Cottage Delight Ltd, a company which made jam and chutney at Basford Lane Industrial Estate, in Leekbrook. It's strange, but the thing I remember most clearly about the wedding was stroking a horse in a field by the chapel! After the ceremony, there was a reception at Jackie's parents' house at 147 Burton Street, in Leek, which Helen and I also went to.

That summer, Matthew became a stockman for JCB Ltd, at Cote Farm, close to Alton Towers. He mainly looked after their deer, which consisted of about 900 hinds and 50 stags! There were three other stockmen, but they were largely responsible for different animals. On the farm, you could walk around, with the deer all milling about. It was remarkable. If you drove to them and got out of the car, they thought you were part of the vehicle and all stood around, but if you walked up without a car, they'd run off and go nowhere near you!

The farm was run as a business, so a small number of deer were killed each week on the farm, as orders came in, and their meat was sold. The selected deer were shot with a captive bolt pistol, to stun them, and then had their throats cut with a knife. Matthew, his family, his employers and the other stockmen also ate the venison from time to time.

The stags would fight one another and even attack the staff, so every year Matthew and another stockman had to cut off their antlers. They'd run the stags into a kind of corral, lasso them and saw off their antlers with a wire cheese cutter. Matthew said the operation was painless for the stags because the antlers were dead after they'd fully grown.

Jeff was looking for photographs for his book on the Vale players, so Helen asked Young Harry if he'd got anything. He'd got a scrapbook, with pictures in, that he'd kept, so he gave it to her to pass on to Jeff, which she did. Jeff was delighted and used five of Harry's photos in his book.

Towards the end of September, Helen wasn't feeling very well because she had a really sore throat. So, on the 25th, we went to the doctor's and were told that she'd got thrush. She was given a drug, nystatin, to sort it out. It worked quite quickly, although she didn't feel up to going to Jeff's on her 76th birthday.

Jeff was interviewed by Les Scott on the *Radio Stoke Tonight* programme on 9 October to publicize his Vale book in advance. Les asked Jeff who his all-time favourite Vale player was and, of course, Jeff said it was Young Harry! Helen was so pleased about that and with how Jeff had done on the show that she rang Ros straight after to tell her.

Jeff's new book was called *Port Vale Personalities: A Biographical Dictionary of*

Players, Officials and Supporters and came out on 13 October when he launched it at Vale's club shop before the home game against Stoke that day. He got nine old players (Jimmy Todd, Albert Leake, Terry Miles, Ron Wilson, Stuart Sharratt, Mick Cullerton, Phil Sproson, Gerry Keenan and Wayne Cegielski) to turn up and sign copies of the book for supporters who bought them. Jeff would have liked Young Harry to have gone along as well, but he wasn't able to make it.

On 31 October, Matthew, Jackie and their young son, Sam, moved into a house in the grounds of JCB's farm, called Longshaw Farm Cottage West, which came rent free with his job. He bought some hens, which he kept in an outbuilding, but he ended up with too many eggs and used to give them away, so he'd give us half a dozen every time we went there. It was a beautiful place where they lived and seemed ideal for a young family, so it was a pity when they eventually left.

Helen and I had a run in our car to Fradswell on 1 November. Helen liked to relive her childhood memories and wanted her photo taken by the house where her Uncle Alf had once had his smallholding. When we'd been there before, a dog had barked and the owners had come out, so we'd explained why we were there. This time, there was no sound of a dog and nobody came out, so we concluded that they weren't in. We went through the gate and Helen stood in front of the house while I took a couple of photos of her.

Later in the month, the news came through that Big Harry had got cancer. He had an operation, which removed a lump, but, unfortunately, the doctors discovered that the disease had spread to his liver. There was nothing more they could do for him and it was just a matter of time. On the 27th, Jeff took me to see him in the City General Hospital and Harry didn't seem too bad at all. For a while he improved, as he got over his operation, and he came out of hospital.

On 2 December, it was announced that there were going to be about 200 redundancies at Stoke on Trent College, where Jeff still worked. The college was having to cut its costs by £8 million and the principal, Neil Preston, who was off sick, had been found helping behind the bar at the Dymock Arms, in Penley, near Wrexham! Helen and I read the front page story in *The Sentinel* about the job cuts and we were shocked and worried in case Jeff got the push. When he came for tea that night, Helen told him we'd got savings if he needed them and that, 'We won't let you go hungry.' However, he said he'd be okay and it turned out that he didn't lose his job.

On my 81st birthday, Jeff took me to the Jodrell Bank Observatory, near to Holmes Chapel, in Cheshire, and I remember looking at this huge disc and wondering how it worked as a radio telescope. We went into the planetarium and it was scary going inside into the darkness. There were bits of white projected on the ceiling, which were supposed to be planets and stars, and they revolved, but I wasn't very impressed with it because I'd expected something more elaborate.

Jeff bought me a new family tree book for my birthday, *Tracing Your Ancestors: The A-Z Guide*, by Pauline Saul. It went into a lot of detail and gave numerous different places where information could be found. I think Jeff hoped it would help me to fill in gaps and get back further, but it was pretty specialized and most of the places it listed were quite some distance away, so I didn't make much use of it.

Jeff had sold 853 copies of his book by Christmas, which he was very pleased about. In the new year, though, the sales were slow and he decided not to have any more copies printed once the thousand he'd started off with had gone. That meant that just over a year after he'd published the book, he had no more copies left to sell.

On 2 January 1997, Jeff and Ros found that one of their kitchen windows had been broken from the outside and discovered an orange polished stone underneath it. There was snow on the ground, but there were no footprints, so they concluded that it must have been done by a bird using the stone as a tool! They then found another polished stone on their back lawn and I said I thought they'd been fired by a catapult. Jeff discovered many more stones over the next few days and the glazier who replaced the window said that it was likely that the damage had been done by a thrown stone. Eventually, Ros heard that a lad named Andrew Lovatt, living round the corner, at 3 Briar Way, had a catapult. Jeff then did some detective work and knocked on several doors round and about and learned that a number of people had had breakages by marbles. He realized that Andrew had a perfect view of all the affected houses and rang Eccleshall Police Station. He was told that there was a lad in Briar Way who was 'well known' to the police, but that there was nothing they could do about it. Jeff then went round to the house and told the lad's father about the situation. Jeff was reassured by his angry neighbour that it wouldn't happen again!

When Helen was shopping in Hanley Market on 15 January, she spotted two teenagers who she suspected were trying to rob an old lady. She advised the woman to put her purse away and told the youths to get out of the market, which they did. She then told a security official about the incident, but, unfortunately, he said that the guards were frightened of the youths!

Big Harry had gone into Abbey Court Nursing Home, in Buxton Road, Leek. Unfortunately, he was very unhappy there and, for a day or two, refused to take his medication. Then he put a knife to his arm, threw some food over a nurse and damaged his television.

On 1 February, Young Harry rang and spoke to Helen and soon both of them were crying. Harry said his father had stopped eating several days before and was quickly getting weaker. Jeff went to the home the day after and Helen and I called to see Big Harry a few days later. He was talking to us then, but when Jeff visited him again on the 19th, Harry could hardly speak and fell asleep. Jeff said that he'd become just skin and bones. Fortunately, he didn't struggle on for much longer and died on the 23rd. His funeral was held at Carmountside Crematorium five days later and Brian Eeley gave his usual rousing tribute. Afterwards, we had tea and sandwiches at Abbey Hulton Suburban Club.

When Helen and I had a drive in the country, we used to call at different farmhouses advertising newly-laid eggs and buy some because we thought they'd be fresher than those in the shops. We got very friendly with Muriel and John Reeves, who lived at Sunnyside Farm, on the corner of the crossroads just past Cellarhead, on the Ashbourne road. We'd get a dozen eggs or so from them every two or three weeks and that went on for years. Every spring, they kept new-born lambs in an outbuilding till it was safe to let them out and Helen used to love stroking them. They were delicate and it was a thrill to see them.

In March, I was keen to get a look at the Hale-Bopp comet, which was visible around that time, but Helen didn't want me to go outside at night, perhaps because she was afraid there'd be thugs there, who'd attack me. So I tried to get the best view I could of the comet by standing in the bath and peering out of the window at it!

On 19 April Helen and I had a run out to Tissington, which was a lovely village to the north of Ashbourne, famous for its well-dressing ceremonies. There was a beautiful display of daffodils by the village pond and I made sure I took a photo of them, with Helen standing behind them.

I kept waiting for the National Health Service to get my cataracts done, but they wouldn't do them until they were 'ripe', as they called it. So I decided to pay to have them done privately and went to see Dr Przyslo on 28 April. He set the ball rolling for me to be treated in Manchester at the clinic of Surgicare Limited and for the NHS to pay the bill.

Jeff and Ros were having a downstairs extension to their house built, mainly so that Jeff could have an office in which to write his books and record his songs. On 30 May, Helen and I went to have a look at how it was going and to do some work on her plot in Jeff and Ros's garden. Unfortunately, she fell over in the extension, but luckily only grazed one of her knees.

Dr Przyslo arranged for an eye specialist, Dr Youseff, to see me at the Harley Street surgery on 13 June, which she did. She was connected to Surgicare, but didn't seem to have the knowledge of the doctors I'd seen before. I don't know why Surgicare used her. Perhaps they didn't trust the doctors in Stoke. I had to read an eye chart and she said I'd got cataracts in both eyes. She decided they'd do the worst one (my left) first, I think because, if anything went wrong, I'd still have my better eye. I was frightened of having a local anaesthetic because I didn't want my head covered up as I wouldn't be able to see what was happening. Also, I thought if I moved my head, the surgeon might cut my eye out! So I decided to have a general anaesthetic because I thought it was the lesser of two evils.

About sevenish on the morning of 25 June, I got a taxi to the Harley Street surgery and there were four or five other patients sitting in a minibus on the car park, waiting for me to turn up. The driver picked up one or two others on the way to Surgicare's clinic, which was in a big house (Parkway House) in Palatine Road, Northenden, in south Manchester, where we were put in a waiting room. There were one or two nurses about, having a chat, and eventually I was beckoned into the operating room.

I didn't have to undress. I lay on the operating table, but I don't remember having a needle. The next thing I was aware of was a nurse saying, 'Mr Kent, come on,' and then I came round. She said, 'Stand up,' but I had a job doing so because I was feeling weak and I nearly fell down. She assisted me up and helped me back into the waiting room, where the other patients were already discussing what had happened to them because they'd all had a local anaesthetic. I could feel something on my eye, but the nurse said, 'Don't touch it!' It was a white plastic protector, with holes in and padding inside, which was taped onto my head. My eye felt more or less normal, but the protector was uncomfortable.

The minibus driver dropped me off and I had a cup of tea and a discussion with Helen before carrying on more or less as usual. The nurse had told me not to take the protector off until the next day, so I did so in the morning, dreading what I might see. I kept looking through the lounge window and squinting at the letters on the signs of the buildings opposite, trying to see if my vision was any better, but it seemed blurred. I'd expected miracles and I was annoyed because it wasn't right.

I made an appointment to see Dr Przyslo and told him my eye was no better. He had a quick look and said, matter of fact, 'Oh well, they'll have to do it again.' Although it was his job not to get too excited, I thought he was insensitive treating me so casually when I was desperate. It was going through my mind that I wouldn't be able to see properly again.

I had to return to the surgery on 4 July when someone from Surgicare came to have a look. We found that I could only read the first line of the eye chart, whereas I'd managed four lines before the operation! So it was decided that I needed another examination.

It was Jeff and Ros's tenth wedding anniversary on 14 July and Helen and I went with them and Alan and Shirley for a day out to Martin Mere Wetland Centre, at Burscough, near Southport. Living there in different ponds were all kinds of ducks, geese and swans from all over the world and they were used to people wandering about. We bought some seeds for them from the shop and fed quite a few of them as we walked around. Some of them ate the food out of our hands, but one or two others couldn't wait and put their heads straight in our bags of seeds and started eating! We later rounded off the day by going back to Jeff and Ros's for tea and Helen fed Raedburh some ham as a treat.

Two days later, I made my way to the surgery in Harley Street and was taken by minibus to the Sir Robert Peel Hospital, in Plantation Lane, Mile Oak, Tamworth, for tests, with the other patients who'd been operated on in Manchester and three of them were also unhappy with the outcome! I was examined by the consultant, Mr John Bolger, and saw Dr Przyslo on the 24th for the results. He told me that Surgicare had made a mistake with all the Stoke patients who'd gone to Manchester with me and that it would cost them £10,000 to put right! He said I now needed a second lens putting in to make up for the failings of the one I'd already got! I felt angry and was worried that by messing about with my eye again it would further damage my sight.

On 30 August, Helen and I went with Jeff and Ros to the Eccleshall Show, in Sugnall Park, off the B 5026, and it was very nice. There were lots of flowers, displays of animal handling, dog agility races and some animals exhibited, including a huge sheep, which Helen stroked. There was also a Punch and Judy show, which we had a look at, and we sat on chairs outside the refreshment tent, enjoying an ice cream in the fine weather. Afterwards, we bought some chips in Eccleshall and took them back to Jeff's to eat, which made a nice end to the day.

On 2 September, I had to get to the Harley Street surgery for 6.30 a.m. and was taken by a minibus to the same place in Manchester where I'd had my operation, along with the same patients, who were having their eyes redone! I was intending to have a general anaesthetic again, but, when I got there, I found out I was down for a local one. I then had a word with one or two of the other patients and they reassured me that there was nothing to having the operation done with a local anaesthetic. Also, it would have been awkward to have changed it then, so I went ahead with it.

I was apprehensive at first, especially when the nurses covered my head and other eye up. They left a space for my bad eye, so the surgeon could fiddle about. I don't know how they did the anaesthetic because I didn't feel anything or any pain. I was lying on my back, looking at the ceiling, which was one colour and the same density, so I didn't notice any difference in what I could see when they did the operation. It took about twenty minutes or half an hour and I was fairly happy with it. Then one of the staff asked me to sit up and I said, 'Is that it?'

I was told, 'It's okay now,' meaning that they'd finished. They put a patch on again and got us all back off as soon as they could.

Again, I had to leave the patch on overnight and I was wondering whether I'd be able to see. In the morning, I was looking through the window all the time, checking it, but this time it was a lot better and I was pleased with it. My sight was about equal to that in my good eye.

Gertie Billington had her cataracts done around the same time and, like me, was sent a questionnaire about going outside the city for her operations. I think she got mixed up and said she wanted to have them done in Stoke, so she had to wait a few weeks because of the queue.

Hanley Park held its centenary celebrations on 7 September and Jeff, Ros and I went up to have a look at what was going on. There was a parade of a Victorian infantry band and cavalry, but it was a poor affair, with just a few horses, although there wasn't room for a lot of them. There were also a stuntman, who dived fifty feet into a bath full of sponges; vintage cars and a flower show and it was quite enjoyable overall.

There was a reunion of Swinnerton's office staff on 18 September at the Plough Inn, in Leek Road, Endon, and I went along with Helen because their spouses were invited. Of course, Helen was excited and dressed up to make sure she looked her best. We had a sit-down meal, which was quite nice, and I took some photos of the occasion so that Helen had something to remember it by.

On 14 October, I was once more picked up by a minibus, but this time at home, to have my right eye done. Again I was taken to the same clinic in Manchester. I was more confident this time and had a local anaesthetic because I didn't think a general one was necessary. The surgeon was Mr Khalid Khan. I went on alright, but the following morning I couldn't see very well. My sight was cloudy and the colours were dull, but a day or two afterwards I went shopping at Kwik Save, in Victoria Road, and all the different colours on the packages stood out. It was fantastic! So I was overjoyed. I went to the Harley Street surgery on the 22nd for follow-up tests and read unaided with my right eye down to the second line from the bottom. The tests confirmed that everything was alright, so I was discharged.

Jeff had been involved in setting up an organization called The Mercia Movement, to try to make things more democratic in the Midlands. Although it didn't seem likely that they'd have much success, he put quite a lot of time into it and organized the meetings, which were usually in Stourbridge, in the West Midlands. Helen didn't like him being involved and thought he'd get into trouble. She couldn't understand what it was about and called it 'Robin Hood', which in a way I suppose it was, really, because the members were quietly rebelling. That October, Jeff published a book by the movement, called *The Mercia Manifesto*, which said what they stood for and included a lot of history in it. He didn't really talk much to Helen and me about his involvement in politics; he just got on with it and he never did get into any trouble.

About that time, when Helen went shopping in Hanley, she used to see one or two Jehovah's Witnesses trying to get customers. The Witnesses had a word with her and she got to see at least one of them there more or less every week for a while. Then two other Witnesses, Gordon and Shirley Moore, knocked on our door one day and Helen mentioned the main one, Trevor Box, she knew in Hanley. Gordon and Shirley said they knew him and they kept coming to see us, perhaps once a month, and brought their magazine, *The Watchtower*, for us. At first, Helen would have a chat with them at the door, but told them she couldn't support them because she already had a church. One day, when the weather was cold, I invited them in and they carried on coming.

Jeff and Ros were having trouble getting their builder, Ian McKenna, of 23 Ribble Drive, in Biddulph, to finish off their extension. He'd been on the job since April, but kept disappearing to do other work and turning up just to do odd bits of things. Eventually, they got so fed up that Jeff wrote to him on 30 November and said his contract would be cancelled if he hadn't finished the extension by 12 December. That did the trick because the job got completed with a day to spare!

On my 82nd birthday, Jeff and Ros took Helen and me to Carsington Water, a reservoir on the far side of Ashbourne. We walked to some sculptures that had been built on Stones Island, a piece of land which jutted out into the reservoir, from where there were good views. In the courtyard, by the visitor centre, there was a Scottish pipe and drum band playing and there were also carol singers, which was very nice. Inside, there was a Father Christmas on a sleigh, whose false white beard was so big that his face could hardly be seen, and I took a photo of Helen standing next to him! Afterwards, we went to Jeff's for tea and, of course, we had a fuss with Raedburh.

Helen and I went to Jeff and Ros's house on Christmas Day, along with Alan and Shirley. When we got there, Jeff was out in the garden sorting out the many parts of their fence that had been blown down the day before by the strongest winds ever recorded in North Staffordshire, which had reached 89 miles an hour at Keele. He had so much to do, freeing trapped bushes and making everything safe, that he wasn't able to come in till it was time for us to have our Christmas dinner. Fortunately, there was no damage to Jeff and Ros's house, although others nearby had had tiles, and even ridge tiles, ripped off their roofs!

For Christmas, Jeff had bought Ros a little book, *The Secret Thoughts of Cats*, which really tickled me. There was a drawing on every page of the same cat in a different situation, but it had the same expression regardless. I was expecting some change, but, as I went on through the book, I realized the cat always looked the same – poker-faced! It made me understand that cats aren't like us. They can't see any humour in a situation.

Jeff was working on a new book, about the local football Derbies, Stoke against Vale, and I asked if he wanted any help. He did, so, in January 1998, I again got on the microfilms at Hanley Reference Library, looking for friendly matches between the teams since 1892.

The new Stoke on Trent Repertory Theatre had been built on the site of the Railway Mission and had opened on 18 November. At first, Helen and I didn't like the idea because of the extra traffic it would bring and we thought there'd be parking problems. We also thought there'd be a lot of noise, but it turned out alright and we never had any trouble at all. To win us over, the theatre gave us and other residents along Leek Road free tickets to see a play called *Ring Around* the Moon. It was a comedy and Helen and I went with Jeff and Ros to see it on 3 February. I don't remember what it was like, but the theatre was interesting. It was in one big room, with no gallery, so it was different from the theatres I was used to, like the Theatre Royal, in Pall Mall, Hanley. Afterwards, we stayed on and enjoyed a couple of drinks in the bar, which was pleasant.

Five days later, I went with Jeff, Ros, Alan and Shirley to see the *Titanic* film at the Odeon, at Festival Park, where you had to walk along corridors to the screens, which was a bit much for old folks. The film was okay, but pandered to the public by having a good-looking hero and heroine (played by Leonardo DiCaprio and Kate Winslet), who turned out to be fictitious!

Arthur Bradshaw, the organist, had been sacked at the P.M.T. Club because he'd made some kind of inappropriate remark. The club got another organist in, but he was a bit superior and things didn't seem the same. Business was going down and P.M.T. wanted to dispose of the property. So the club closed, but at least on the last night there was cheap beer.

Helen and I then went with Sam, Doris, Tom and Gertie to try the Catholic Club, in North Street, Stoke. It wasn't too bad, even though it was rather old-fashioned, but we were only there for a few weeks. The organist was the one who'd finished off at the P.M.T. Club, but there weren't many customers and he got fed up of playing for so few people and stopped coming. Interest then dropped right off until there were only the six of us in the room we went in. There was no atmosphere and it was hopeless.

Helen and I had kept the deeds to our house in an old attaché case for years, but I decided it would be much safer to deposit them with our solicitors, Beswick, Moon & Co., at 50 Broad Street. So I contacted them in April and had the deeds stored with them on the 9th.

Vale were playing at home to Middlesbrough, in the First Division (as the Second Division had been renamed), on 24 April. Jeff's old friend, Paul Lewis, with whom he sat, wasn't going to the match, so he gave Jeff his season ticket. Helen and I decided to go along with him because it would only cost us half the amount to get in. Helen got excited and was clapping, cheering and singing, and I enjoyed seeing the ground, which was a lot smarter than the previous time we'd been. I didn't think either team was very good, though, and Vale lost 1-0.

Because we were fed up with the Catholic Club, Sam, Doris, Tom, Gertie, Helen and I all decided to go to Rectory Road Sports & Social Club (which we called the "Gas Club") and it was okay there. We went into the concert room and all palled up with four people we sat next to: Margaret and Ern Parkes, whom we knew from the Railway Club, and Jack and Audrey Pattinson. Margaret and Ern ran a newsagent's at 229 London Road, in Stoke, and had a sarcastic sense of humour. Jack and Audrey lived at 3 Gresty Street, in Penkhull; Jack was a pretty tall and jovial fellow, but Audrey was little and quiet. Helen and I signed up as members of the club a few weeks after we'd started going, I think. The club had an organist, named John, and a professional drummer, called Graham. They played popular songs from pre-war onwards that we could sing along with and all of us except for Jack and Ern would get up and dance.

Helen and I hadn't been on holiday for years, but, in May, she suddenly announced that she wanted us to go away. I don't know why that was, but it might have been because she'd discovered a lump in her left breast and thought we'd go away together one last time, although she never said anything to me about that.

We decided to go for four days to Llandudno, I think to see what it was like because we didn't know it very well, having tended to go to Prestatyn when Jeff was young. We went on 12 May and stayed B & B at a place up the hill near the Great Orme Tramway, but there was an awkward path up to the house, on which we were liable to trip up. Surprisingly, on The Promenade, we came across another couple we knew from dancing at Fenton! I liked walking down the main shopping street (Mostyn Street), which was classy, and the sea front was nice too.

On the day we arrived, we drove inland to the small town of Llanrwst, which was on the River Conwy and was quite pretty. While we were there, I took a photo of Helen on the old stone bridge, Pont Fawr, over the river.

On the 14th, we revisited Beaumaris, where we liked to sit on the front and look out across the strait. Also, while we were on holiday, we returned to Prestatyn and looked at the old spots where we'd been – on the sands and where the bikes had been. We reminisced and it all brought back happy memories. I enjoyed the holiday, as I always did.

At the beginning of June, Helen told me about the lump in her breast and I was shocked. I went with her on the 4th to see Dr Przyslo, who examined her. He didn't know for certain what it was, but he had a good idea and he tried to put the bad news in a nice way. He said she should see a specialist and she decided to go privately at the Nuffield Hospital, in Clayton Road, Clayton. That was for speed and because she thought it would be more relaxed than the normal hospitals because she was still terrified of them.

Dr Przyslo arranged a visit for her to see Mr Terry Duffy on 5 June at a cost of seventy pounds. Jeff was concerned about her and ran us to the hospital in his car. Mr Duffy examined her and said he thought she'd got a cancerous lump, but that it could probably be treated with a drug, tamoxifen, which would be very likely to make it shrink and hopefully disappear altogether. However, he said he'd need to take a sample from the lump before he could say for certain. We came away with mixed feelings. There was hope, but the drug seemed too good to be true. Helen coped with the news very well and better than I thought she'd have done.

I understand that two of the other stockmen at Cote Farm had been bullying Matthew Poole and taking the mickey out of him all the time, so he'd become very unhappy. They were two mates and they'd make a cup of tea and not give him one. I think they were trying to get rid of him. So Matthew started working at Harry and Gill's newsagent's instead and he and his family moved into the flat above the shop on 8 June.

Helen was getting a bit wobbly on her legs and fell over in the kitchen in the middle of June. Unfortunately, I hurt my back picking her up because I wasn't as strong as I'd been when I was younger and she'd put on weight, so she was too heavy for me. Then, about a week later, she fell on the front steps and was helped up by a student.

On 1 July, Helen had the sample taken from her breast for examination, under local anaesthetic at the Outpatients. We were told to go back later for the results, which we did, along with Jeff, on the 14th. We waited quite a while for Mr Duffy to get to us because he was very busy and running round like a scalded cat, but he came up with good news. He said, as expected: 'There'll be no need for an operation. We'll solve it with medication.' He said she'd got cancer, but that tamoxifen should do the job. He'd given Helen a lifeline and she thought of him almost like a little god. We were given a prescription, but when we went to pick up the medicine from the hospital chemist, Helen was so excited that she dashed off to the sweet shop and forgot to sign the no charge form! She bought two bars of chocolate to celebrate.

My back pain didn't clear up, so I started taking painkillers, but then got constipation and went off my food. On 21 July, I went to see Dr Przyslo and he gave me some tablets because he thought I might have congestion in my lungs. The same day, he sent me to the hospital, where I had an X-ray on my back and a blood test. The X-ray showed no problems, but the doctor asked me if I'd had jaundice and sent me for another blood test, after which I was referred to the Outpatients for a scan on my abdomen.

I'd asked Dr Przyslo if he'd got something in liquid form or any smaller tablets than the ones he'd given me 'because I can't swallow them'. On the odd occasion I'd been given tablets, I'd chewed them, but the taste was horrible, though it was better than choking to death trying to swallow them! Helen used to say: 'It's simple. Just put it on the back of your tongue and have a drink of water and it'll be gone!' But I couldn't master doing it and she'd get het up because it all seemed so simple. I did eventually manage to get the smaller ones down after spluttering and coughing, but this time I asked Dr Przyslo if there was any alternative. He gave a little wry smile and wrote something down that would be suitable. So I got the medication in liquid form and after then I either had medicine like that or as dispersible tablets, but whenever I saw another doctor, I had to explain and the reaction tended to be one of almost disbelief!

My old iron lawnmower had done good service, but it had always been a struggle to lift it from the back path over the garden and onto the lawn. But by then, it was becoming too heavy for me to pick up, so I thought I'd buy a lighter one. I had a look at what there was and bought a Qualcast Quadtrak electric mower on 29 July, which was mainly made of plastic. It had no roller and was no great weight to pick up, so it was much better for me to use. It gave me satisfactory service and the lawn didn't get worse for the lack of a roller.

About that time, Helen and I had a combined washer and spinner for the first time, which was very handy because it saved us from having to take the clothes out of the washer and then put them in the spinner. Jeff then took our old spin dryer to the tip for us.

Sometimes, when we went to see Jeff and Ros, Raedburh ran to us when we pulled onto the drive. It was nice to know she recognized us, but Helen would shout: 'Watch her! Watch her!' Raedburh would then go round to Helen's side, with her tail up in the air, and have a stroke. Helen would then get out of the car and we'd all go inside. Raedburh would get excited and jump on the dining table, relishing the food we usually brought with us. Helen would try to scoot her off the table and then I'd feed Raedburh fresh meat by hand.

On 4 September, we were going along Nelson Crescent to Jeff and Ros's house, but Raedburh trotted out onto the road and I had to brake sharply, even though I was only going slowly. I couldn't see where she'd gone and I was worried because I might have run her over. Just then, I noticed a car behind me, so, to be safe, I got out of my car, scooped Raedburh up and put her inside with Helen. Then I drove onto the drive.

Two days later, Helen and I went to Hanley Park, where the City of Stoke-on-Trent Festival was being held and it was free to go in. There was a giant marquee, in which the main events were staged, and thousands of people turned up. The Wurzels played and amongst the other entertainments were a funfair, a Punch and Judy show, and falconry, horse and sheepdog displays. What caught my attention most, though, was someone dressed up as "Postman Pat", who'd become a well-known TV character, and I took a photo of him standing by a Post Office van.

After a couple of months, Helen said her lump was shrinking, but I wondered how she knew that. But I went along with it because you don't knock people's hopes when they're ill.

The Potteries Heavy Horse Parade had been a traditional event in the city, but had stopped being held in the 1950s. It had started up again in 1996 and this year it was held on 27 September. Over thirty shire horses were stabled in Hanley Park before the parade around the town centre and Helen and I went to have a look at them. They were quite impressive, dressed with ribbons on their necks and attached to brightly-coloured carriages, which people sat in as they were pulled along.

On Helen's 78th birthday, Jeff took us to Lichfield Cathedral and I can still visualize the three spires from the front. You don't normally see anything like that and there were ornaments sticking out of the outside of the building. I was very impressed.

In the middle of October, Helen said she'd got a lump under one of her armpits, but I couldn't feel anything. Jeff checked and he thought he could. I was concerned because it sounded like the cancer had spread and Helen was very worried about it. On the 20th, we all went to the Outpatients for Helen's scheduled checkup and the doctor, Mr Adjogatse (who was known as Mr "James"), measured the lump in her breast with a ruler. He said, 'Yes, it has shrunk,' and Helen then asked him to look at the lump under her arm. He did and said: 'That's normal. It's a lymph node!' There was a sigh of relief and we booked up for Helen's next four-monthly checkup. She was so delighted that she said she wanted to go on holiday to Scotland again the next summer if we were both still well.

Helen had become precarious on her feet and was finding it difficult to get up and down our front steps. I was getting worried about it, so I decided to have a handrail put up. I knew there was a wrought iron-working firm, G. W. Shenton, in St James Street, Hanley, and I got them to do the job for seventy pounds on 27 October. Helen then became more confident on the steps because she'd got something to hold onto, so she got up and down better.

I thought it would also be a good idea to have a handrail put up by our back steps to help steady Helen when she was going up to our back garden. I got the same firm to do that job as well, which they did for fifty pounds on 2 November. It gave her something to hold on to, so that she didn't fall down.

Helen was going hard of hearing, so we went to see Dr Przyslo on 2 November and he gave her some softening liquid for wax in her ears. The idea was that it would turn the wax into liquid and it would run out. So that cleared her ears, but her hearing didn't get any better.

Jeff's new book, *The Potteries Derbies*, came out in November. He launched it in the Waddington Suite at Stoke's new ground, Britannia Stadium, on the 21st, before their match against York City. The ground had been built at Sideway, on the site of Stafford Colliery, and had opened the year before. Jeff was helped with his launch by ex-Stoke players Terry Conroy, Jimmy Greenhoff and Jackie Marsh, who had their photographs taken with him. A week later, he did another launch, at Vale, with Young Harry and two other former players, Colin Askey and Mick Morris, signing copies of the book before the home game against Tranmere Rovers.

Jeff had been involved in the making of a video history of Vale, for which he was paid. It was called *Up The Vale!* and I let the film company, Action Sports International, use my cine footage of Young Harry playing against Brighton & Hove Albion in 1962 as part of the arrangement. In December, I was given a copy of the finished video. It was very good and I noticed I was on the credits.

I had to go for the scan on my abdomen at the Biochemistry Department at the Outpatients on 8 December. Helen was very worried about me going to the hospital, but Jeff took me, so that helped. I partly stripped off and was slid into a tunnel. I seemed to lie there for quite a while, but I didn't feel anything out of the ordinary and wasn't really worried. Eventually, the nurse rescued me and pulled me out! When the results came back, they said I was all clear, fit and healthy.

On 13 December, Helen and I went with Jeff and Ros to Little Moreton Hall, near Scholar Green, for an afternoon out to celebrate my 83rd birthday. It was a quaint place, built between about 1450 and 1580, but it showed that even the better-off people lived rather crudely in those days. There were no taps, the place was without central heating and the inhabitants had to draw their water from a well. It was interesting to see that even the higher-ups then didn't have such a good standard of living as most people do in modern times.

Jeff was disappointed with the sales of his new book. He'd hoped that, because it would appeal to Stoke as well as Vale supporters, there'd be even more interest this time, but it wasn't to be. By Christmas, he'd only sold 598 copies and thought that fans of both clubs were being put off the book because it was half about their rivals.

By then, Helen was less inclined to help with the jobs when we went out to somebody's house because she was getting older. So she was holding back, but she was pushing me to do them instead, which I did. After a while, she didn't even do that, so it was left to me until I eventually stopped too.

On Boxing Day, Helen and I went with Jeff, Ros, Alan and Shirley to see Charles Dickens's *A Christmas Carol* at the New Victoria Theatre, in Etruria Road, Basford. I don't remember anything about the play, but the theatre was nice and modern.

When Helen was shopping on 5 January 1999, she noticed that W. H. Smith, in The Potteries Shopping Centre, had got a display of Jeff's *Potteries Derbies* books along one of their shelves. She told Jeff when we went to see him and he was very pleased.

It was around then that Helen and I stopped going to the easy sequence dancing at Fenton. It was getting too much for her and the lump in her breast may have had something to do with how she felt about doing things. The dancing wasn't so easy for me at my age either and Helen didn't feel like getting ready to go any more, so that was the end of that.

Helen was self-conscious and wanted to look beautiful all the time, even by that time. She thought she'd get a wig to save a lot of trouble washing her hair, drying it, colouring it and putting it into curlers every time she went out on special occasions. I think she'd seen an advert in *The Sentinel* and she thought she'd be able to put a wig on like a hat. In February, a woman named Joan came round from the company, Natural Image, with a few hairpieces in different styles, which Helen tried on. Eventually, she picked one out, with the right fit, colour and style. It was fairly short, wavy and almost black, which was similar to how her own hair was. We paid sixty pounds for it, but she didn't wear it because she was too self-conscious, so she carried on as before! I put it away in its cardboard box in the back bedroom and it's still there!

On 23 February, Helen fell over along the road and had to be picked up by a passer-by. She hurt one of her knees and a shoulder. She wasn't seriously injured, but her balance didn't seem to be as good as it had been and was becoming a concern. After that, I went with her when she did the food shopping because we didn't think it was safe for her to go on her own, particularly because she'd have to carry a couple of heavy bags back each time. Occasionally, though, when I was unwell, she still managed to do the shopping by herself.

Helen and I went to the Outpatients on 2 March for her next breast checkup. There was more good news because the doctor, Mr Parmar, said the lump was still shrinking and had almost gone. She still had to keep taking the tablets for it, but we were very happy with the outcome.

Unfortunately, Jack Hodgkiss died of pneumonia, in Bucknall Hospital, on 26 March, at the age of ninety. It was another milestone. It didn't affect me a great deal, but I was sorry to see him go because we'd had a lot of happy times together.

When Helen went to see Dr Catherine Hobson, at the Harley Street surgery on 1 April, it was discovered that she'd got very high blood pressure (240/102) and she was given bendrofluazide tablets to take for it. I wasn't particularly concerned about it because it was therefore under control. She had to have regular checkups on her blood pressure after that, which showed that it was gradually falling. By 26 November, it was down to 130/94, which meant it was at a normal level.

On 5 April, Helen and I had our bathroom, back bedroom and landing windows double glazed with UPVC by Safestyle (UK), whose headquarters were at 1A Wharfe Street, in Bradford. The cost was £988. That completed the whole house, except for the hall and library windows, but I didn't notice any difference in the noise levels or the warmth of the house.

Jack Hodgkiss was cremated at Carmountside Crematorium on 6 April after a service of thanksgiving at Werrington Methodist Church. I don't remember anything about the funeral, but it's almost certain that Helen and I were there.

On 9 April, we were in the kitchen and Helen said: 'Look at this glass. It's all distorted.' She was talking about one of the windowpanes and it looked queer, so I went outside and found the strips at the side of the glass were missing. I discovered them placed on the garden next to Nancy's. There was a crack in the window and apparently someone had tried to force the glass out. So I contacted the police and they got fingerprint experts down, but they didn't catch anybody.

We had the pane replaced on our insurance, but also I enquired as to how I could make the house safer. The council came up with a security light, which we had fixed for free above the kitchen windows, but Helen still wasn't satisfied and wanted another one above the back door. So the council put one up there as well, but she again became afraid to go on holiday in case burglars got in while we were away. I was disappointed, but I could understand her reasoning.

By that time, Helen wasn't doing much work around the house. It was tailing off and she was becoming less and less bothered because of old age. She had less energy and inclination, so that increased my number of jobs, which was a bind, but they had to be done.

On 3 May, Helen was stung by a bee and was worried about what effect it would have on her, but I wasn't very concerned that it would be a problem. She wasn't satisfied with that, so she rang Jeff, who said she could get some antiseptic cream from a chemist. She then walked all the way to Lloyds Pharmacy, at 27 Stoke Road, but she was told that she didn't need to do anything about it and eventually she ended up back at home none the worse for having been stung!

By then, she seemed to be think that every little ache and pain she had was serious and kept telling me about them, which became a nuisance. Towards the end of May, she got a cold, which I thought was just one of those things, but she insisted on calling a doctor out on the 26th to see her! He turned up and didn't seem particularly worried, but he gave her some antibiotics, which made sure the problem was sorted out.

Helen was regularly buying turkey and chicken for Raedburh by that time, to give her when we called over, which was quite often. It got to the point where Jeff became worried that Raedburh was having too much fresh meat and asked Helen to cut down on it. She did to some extent, but she liked feeding Raedburh and at times still couldn't resist buying some for her.

On 6 July, Jeff took us to the hospital for Helen's breast checkup and when we were shown in, Mr James said, 'Ah, it's the Kent family!' Helen said she thought the lump was growing again, but the doctor told us it had completely disappeared. He said she should keep taking the tablets and come back in six months' time for another checkup. It was amazing, really. I never thought the lump would have gone like that and it took a lot of pressure off us. Helen was thrilled with the news and said, 'I shall be here for Christmas!'

When Jeff arrived for lunch on 17 July, Helen sang 'Johnny Rudge's *red* and white army' to him and laughed her head off. That was because Rudge had switched to Stoke and became their football executive after being sacked as Vale's manager. I was amazed he did it just like that. I don't know how the Vale supporters must have felt, but it was a smart move because he was given a very good wage, with apparently nothing to do!

Peter Jones, of number 325, was a gardener, with an allotment along the road, and his wife, Joan, was pretty friendly with Nancy. Helen would be looking through the window and say: 'Here's Peter. He's got some flowers in his hand. I wonder if he's got any for me.' Then he'd go next door and give them to Nancy! One day, though, he brought some for Helen and then carried on doing so regularly.

Helen and I went to Jeff and Ros's on 11 August to see the eclipse of the sun. We got there well before time and settled down on their garden chairs on their back lawn. It was interesting to see it happen and I wondered how astronomers had calculated that it would come round like that. It got darker and darker as the moon blocked out more and more of the sun and it seemed to go cold all of a sudden. Raedburh was sitting on Helen's knee, but the drop in temperature didn't appear to affect her, though, of course, she had a fur coat on! Although the eclipse wasn't quite complete, it was strange and didn't seem natural, but I don't think Helen was particularly thrilled with it. We looked at it from time to time through Jeff's filter, which was a good aid, and it seemed like a shadow crossing the sun.

On 31 August, Helen and I went on the bus to Hanley, as we usually did on a Tuesday, to do the food shopping. As I was looking for my bus pass on the way back, I must have dropped my wallet because when I got home it was missing. I phoned First PMT (as the bus company had become renamed) and the police, but I didn't see it again. About seventy pounds in cash and a number of documents, including my driving licence, were missing, so I had to get new ones and inform various organizations about the loss. It was a real rigmarole and after that, I kept my bus pass separate from my wallet to make sure the problem wouldn't happen again.

The following day, I went with Jeff to Hanley Post Office to get a photo taken to send off for a new driving licence. I was looking at the machine and trying to understand how to work it when a girl wanted to go into the booth. So I told her to go in first and I'd watch her to see how it was done. She left the curtain open, but, after a while, she got browned-off with me and drew the curtain across. I went in after she'd finished and tried the procedure, but the result wasn't what I expected. A medium-sized photo came out of the machine, with hearts all round it and the words 'I love you' printed on! Jeff and I had a good laugh about it, but eventually I got it right and got the small photo I needed.

Helen and I went for a run in the car to the Peak District on 6 September and ended up in Youlgreave, near to Bakewell, where we had a walk around. We came across a tiny cottage called Thimble Hall, which turned out to be the smallest detached house in the world. We wanted to have a look inside, but the door was locked, so we had to make do with me taking a photo of Helen outside, looking as though she was about to go in. I later found out that the house was only 12 feet 2 inches high; had got only one room downstairs and one upstairs, which were connected by a ladder, and that there was no kitchen, bathroom or running water!

On 11 October, Dorothy Kent phoned and told me Bernard had died that morning in the City General. I hadn't expected it and I was very sad. He'd been poorly and Dorothy had been looking after him, but I hadn't been able to make out what the problem was. His funeral was at Carmountside Crematorium on the 22nd and Brian Eeley took the service and gave his usual glowing tribute. Afterwards, we went to Trent Squash Club, in Birches Head Road, Abbey Hulton, and Dorothy showed me a scrapbook she'd kept which had *Sentinel* cuttings about Jeff in.

There was more bad news because Jack Elson died on 6 November. His funeral was on the 12th, but Helen and I didn't go to it because of the fallout she'd had with Edith, which was a pity because we'd been friends with him for a long time.

Not too long after Bernard had died, Helen and I went to visit Dorothy, who gave me some parchment to put my family tree on. But, when I put the details on, the ink didn't stick and it all came off. I asked at Webberley's if they'd got any special ink, but they hadn't, so Dorothy cut off some of a roll of big, wide paper, which Bernard had been using, and gave it to me. I used it to put on a chart of the Kent and Wallett family trees in pencil, in case I needed to alter it later.

On 25 November, Jeff brought it to my attention that there was a fiddle going on with my cine footage that had been included by Action Sports International in their Vale video history. I'd given them permission to use it in return for a fee, but it had come to Jeff's attention that a second company, Cavsport, was also intending to use it, without our authority, in their *Port Vale Millennium Documentary*. Jeff mentioned it to Gary Kelsall, of Action Sports, who said they hadn't given Cavsport permission to use anything from their video. Jeff and I agreed that we'd allow Cavsport to use the film and he'd get the best fee he could from them. He then rang Rob Reeves, the contact at the company, and was told that he'd got a letter from the university-based Staffordshire Film Archive, quoting £150 for the use of it and another piece of film!

Jeff sent a letter to Rod Pratt, who was running the Film Archive, to ask what was going on, but found out he'd been made redundant. Jeff then got a call from Ray Johnson, one of the directors of Action Sports and a senior lecturer in film, television and radio studies at Staffordshire University, who said Pratt must have taken a copy of my film, but that it wasn't with his permission. I don't know whether Pratt was naïve or whether he'd deliberately tried to swindle me, but it seemed that the Film Archive had got hold of my footage and tried to charge another firm a fee to use it when they had no right to do so. Ray told Jeff he'd look for my footage at the Film Archive and return it if he found it, but it never appeared! So all I could do was hope nobody else copied it.

Helen and I had been friends with Flo Hodgkiss for many years and we'd had a lot of enjoyment with her and Jack, so I was very sad when I was told that she'd died in Newford Nursing Home, in Newford Crescent, Milton, on 30 November. She was 93 and had gone so soon after Jack. She was cremated at Carmountside Crematorium on 10 December after a service of thanksgiving at Werrington Methodist Church. I can't remember the funeral, but Helen and I must have been there.

Norman and Elsie Foster had died and their daughter, Shirley, was looking after their house and their garage, where I kept my car. On my 84th birthday, their next-door neighbours at 8 Avenue Road, Joyce and Eric Barrow, called to say that the garage had been broken into. I went along and found that the lock had been cut off, probably by bolt cutters. Fortunately, there was no damage to my car and nothing had been stolen, so that was a relief. I informed Shirley, who lived in Reading, and fitted a replacement lock to the garage door.

Afterwards, Jeff took me to see the Fauld Crater, near Tutbury, which had been created on 27 November 1944 by the biggest explosion that had ever occurred in Britain. Great numbers of munitions had been stored underground, but that day there was a terrific explosion, which destroyed the whole of nearby Upper Castle Hayes Farm and killed seventy people, including six Italian prisoners of war who were working at the dump!

We walked to and partway round the crater rim. It was amazing! There was a huge hole, with trees and vegetation growing in it. It was quite an experience to see it and gave some idea of how the damage at Hiroshima must have been.

Afterwards, Helen and I went to have our tea with Jeff and Ros, who gave me a very smart gold-coloured waistcoat for my birthday. I wore it a number of times at the Gas Club and it was admired by our friends.

Helen no longer bothered to clean her glasses, which became filthy, so I sometimes cleaned them for her. She began to find it more and more difficult to read *The Sentinel* and watch the television. So it became of concern to me that her eyes weren't so good, but she didn't seem to be all that bothered about it.

Nick and Claire had invited us to go to their house, 33 Millfield Gardens, in Nether Poppleton, near York, for Christmas, but Helen didn't want to go, perhaps because she was worried about there being bad weather and leaving the house unattended. So we decided to stop at home. Jeff and Ros stayed around as well, so that we wouldn't be on our own, but then Helen made her mind up that we'd have Christmas dinner without them. Jeff and Ros were annoyed because it meant they had to have dinner on their own when it had all been set up for them to go to Yorkshire. Then, when they took us for a drive in the afternoon, Helen wasn't very cooperative and kept complaining to them, which really spoiled their day. She could be very awkward at times.

On 22 January 2000, I spotted a large fox, with a white end to its tail, at the top of the field behind our house. I watched it for a few minutes as it walked along, smelling the ground every so often. It went into a garden in Ridgway Road, came back out to where it had been before and then went into the garden again. A number of times from then on, I saw foxes in and around our garden.

At Helen's next breast cancer appointment on 8 February, we saw a different doctor, John Whiting, who said she was doing very well and he couldn't find any sign of the lump. He said that it was more likely she'd die from being run over than from the cancer because they'd got it under control, which was excellent news. As usual, we then booked in for her next checkup, as we continued to do.

On 22 February, I went to the Radio Rentals office at 2 Upper Market Square, in Hanley, and paid the annual advance rent on our television for the year from 1 March to 28 February 2001. It was £7.99 a month and £95.88 for the year, but I got a £7.19 discount for paying before 1 March. It was amazing that the cost of renting the set had only gone up by £7.64 in ten years!

Stanley Matthews died on 23 February and the news came out of the blue. Helen and I went with Jeff to watch the parade before Stan's funeral at St. Peter's Church, in Stoke, on 3 March. We stood on the corner of Wellington Road and Bucknall New Road, in Hanley, where we could see clearly and get some snapshots of the procession going past. There was a feeling of respect and it was nice to see that people thought well of him. The cortege stopped while a child from Stan's old school (Hanley St. Luke's Primary School) handed over a wreath. Helen and I then went to Upper Market Square, where Stan's statue was surrounded by wreaths and daffodils. I was shocked by his death because he was a fit fellow, but everybody has to go some time. In the back of my memory, I thought of him dazzling the fans and tricking the opposing players.

Dave Wallett, who was a keen photographer, had managed to secure a very good spot outside St. Peter's Church, in Stoke, for the funeral. He'd chained his stepladder to the railings the night before and was there early on the day to claim his place and film the cortege arriving.

Dave told Helen and me that he'd gone to the entrance of the National Garden Festival the day before it had opened in 1986, in the hope of being first in the queue. He'd got there just before midnight, but had only been able to get second spot. He also said he'd bluffed his way into Stan Matthews's eightieth birthday celebration dinner on 1 February 1995 at Trentham Gardens. He'd taken photographs of the occasion there and rubbed shoulders with many famous footballers, such as Gordon Banks, Bobby Charlton, Ferenc Puskás, Tom Finney and Gary Lineker!

He said that, when he was a lad, he'd found a frogman's outfit at Macalonie and had tried it on and got into the canal to test it out! I bet it weighed a ton and, though he was with friends, I expect it would have been difficult to have got him out if anything had gone wrong.

7 The Exit Door Opens

On 23 March 2000, Jeff told me he'd been to Shires Veterinary Practice, in Stone Road, Eccleshall, with Raedburh and tests had shown that she was seriously ill with liver damage. One of the vets, Rachel Steen, had said Raedburh hadn't got much time left and that she should be fed anything she'd eat. Jeff asked Helen and me to bring her some chicken when we next went over, which we did the following day and she had a good helping. We then regularly got her fresh meat from Hanley Market, mainly chicken, turkey and tongue, and the stallholder was amazed that it was all for a cat!

I was sad for Jeff, who was all worked up. I was concerned about him and wondered if he'd throw things to the wind and not do his job, so that he could attend to Raedburh. That was because he thought so much of her. Helen and I were upset as well, but not to that degree. Raedburh had been put on a course of steroids and did improve somewhat, but that didn't mean her liver problem had gone away.

On 1 April, Helen and I went to Sam and Doris Lyth's diamond wedding anniversary party at 10 The Brambles, in Westbury Park, Newcastle. It was all very nice, but I think they were trying to show off to people by having it at their son's house, which was big and modern and had an impressive garden.

Bill and Margaret Farmer lived near to Helen and me, at 13 Egerton Street, and we knew them to say hello to. One day, when we were shopping in Hanley, she got talking to them in Marks & Spencer, at 11 Upper Market Square. I'd gone to get a currant loaf, which she told them I really liked. Margaret said to Helen, 'Oh, I'll bake you one.' True to her word, she brought one along soon after and she and Bill started calling with currant loaves and cakes from time to time that she'd made. The cakes were always lovely, professionally done and wrapped up with a tie on the neck of a plastic bag. They even brought some lobby one time. It was very good of them to go to all the trouble, but I never knew why they wanted to do it. This carried on for a while and then Bill became unwell with dementia. After that, Margaret phoned when she had something ready and I'd go to collect it. Bill had always been on the quiet side, but I started to realize I sometimes couldn't understand what he was saying. After a while, he seemed to become withdrawn and didn't want to get involved.

Jeff had a season ticket for the Bycars Stand at Vale as usual, but the chairman, Bill Bell, decided to give Jeff's part of the ground to Wolves supporters for the last match of the season, on 7 May. The affected Vale fans were told to go in other parts of the ground to watch the game. So Jeff wrote to the club and protested and said he'd be turning up as usual because his ticket was a legal contract with the club. He did so, but the officials wouldn't let him or any other Vale supporters in that end of the ground. He had quite a few fans backing him up. He then wrote to the club and claimed recompense and an apology, saying otherwise he'd stop supporting them. He won his case because he got his money back and the club apologized to him.

In preparation for Raedburh's death, Jeff asked me if I'd make a coffin for her. I was surprised, but I could understand him wanting that to be done for her, to help give her a good sendoff into the next life. I was happy to go along with it. So,

On 18 May, Jeff and I went to Beech Cliffe Sawmills, in Beech Lane, Beech, and bought some seasoned oak. Jeff wanted something that would last for donkey's years and warships had been built from oak, but it was supposed to be hard to work, so I didn't know how I was going to do it.

Jeff and I disagreed about the dimensions of the coffin, so we put Raedburh on some of the timbers and used a ruler to measure her! It was awkward, but she took it in good part. I borrowed Alan Downs's electric saw, but it wasn't any better than my hacksaw. I did my best on the job, but the coffin was crude and didn't fit together as well as I'd have liked it to have done. I think Jeff was expecting it to be waterproof and have no cracks in it, but he seemed pretty satisfied overall.

One day, when I was at Jeff and Ros's, I noticed Raedburh's legs were wobbly as she was going across their back lawn. She was staggering, as though she was drunk. I mentioned this to Jeff, but he pooh-poohed the idea that there was anything wrong with her. She slowly got worse until she wasn't very good on her legs at all.

In May, Harry and Gill sold their newsagent's business to Matthew and Jackie and retired. By then, Harry was 65, but he and Gill still helped out in the shop from time to time.

Jeff thought the Ribena drink that Helen and I liked was unhealthy and so, one day in June, he brought us some pure apple and blackcurrant fruit juice to try. We didn't go for it in a big way, but, some time afterwards, we finished with Ribena and there was a big public outcry because the television showed children's teeth all rotted away as there was too much sugar in it.

On Father's Day, Jeff and Ros took us to Mill Meece Pumping Station, which was near to their house. It had been used for pumping water for Stoke-on-Trent, but was by then being run by volunteers in a preservation trust. One of the huge steam engines was working and it was a marvellous piece of engineering. Unfortunately, Helen was frightened of it and one of the operators had to bring her past it to join the rest of us in the main room!

Jeff felt he'd been robbed by a writer named Dean Hayes, who'd used a lot of Jeff's material in his book, *Port Vale Football Club: An A-Z*, which had been published in 1997. Jeff had produced his books first, so he must have been right. He took Hayes and his publisher, Sigma Press, to court and expected to win because it seemed a clear-cut situation, but he was in for a shock. The judge at Preston County Court ruled against Jeff when the case was heard on 19 June and so justice wasn't done.

It came to a point with Raedburh where she used her front legs to drag her body along. It was like her back legs were dead and just things to be pulled along. It seemed cruel for her to suffer like that for the sake of keeping her alive and I asked Jeff to 'let her go'.

He said: 'No! I want her to carry on as long as she can.' I couldn't bear to see her struggling and it was upsetting me, but Jeff couldn't bring himself to have her put down. He tried all kinds of things to get her walking again and even took her to the City Chiropractic Clinic, at 40 Epworth Street, in Stoke, which was where the PDSA surgery had been. The clinic was for humans, but, when Raedburh had had treatment there, she improved and started to walk again after a fashion.

Helen and I were impressed by what Jeff and Ros had told us about a B & B they'd stayed at on Anglesey, near Dwyran, called Tal y Foel. They said there was a big variety of food you could have for breakfast and the house was on the Menai Strait, with wonderful views across to Caernarfon Castle. We decided to try a holiday there and went from 16 to 22 July. It was great. The house was out of the way, but was easy to find. The landlady, Judy Hutchings, was friendly and businesslike and her helper, Margaret Williams, was nice too. They had riding stables and we saw the horses and stroked one or two of them, which made Helen's day. It was a lovely place.

We enjoyed travelling around the island and went to see John Swinnerton's old place at Rhosneigr. He'd died in 1995 and his widow, Joan, no longer owned the property. Also, we revisited Beaumaris, South Stack and Amlwch, with its quaint little harbour. We had a trip to Llandudno on the 19th and spent some time talking to the children by their paddling pool on The Promenade. Their mothers were looking and all had smiles on their faces because they were pleased somebody was interested in their children. Talking to toddlers was one of Helen's traits, but she wasn't always complimentary! While we were on holiday, we also went to Caernarfon and parked by the castle and had a wander about.

We'd been going regularly on Saturday afternoons to see Young Harry since not long after we'd had our VW Beetle and then when Mandy and Matthew had children, we went to see them as well. Mandy had a girl (Lilly, born on 18 March 1995) and a boy (David, born on 20 September 1999) and Matthew had two sons (Sam, born on 18 July 1995 and William, born on 8 August 2000). Helen always clung to Vera's family and I went along with it because I wasn't close to anyone in particular on my side.

Because of Raedburh's walking problem, Jeff and Ros didn't go on holiday that summer. One of them had to stay around the house in case Raedburh needed help, so they hardly went out anywhere together at all. Helen and I volunteered to stand in for them so that they could have a day trip from time to time, which they did. That meant they were able to go to Aberystwyth on 16 August, to celebrate Ros's birthday, and to Nether Poppleton on the 27th for the christening of Nick and Claire's daughter, Amelia.

Jeff still had over 500 copies of his *Potteries Derbies* book left and had been selling them at a pound a time since March to try to clear them out. He'd been pretty successful because he'd sold 207 books in less than five months. On 26 August, he went into London Road News, in Stoke, to see if he could get the owners to buy some copies off him, which they did. What he didn't know was that they were our friends, Margaret and Ern! The first Helen and I heard of it was at the club the following night when Ern said, 'Your son came in our shop, selling books, and he looked like a tramp,' or words to that effect. Our mates all laughed and I suppose they thought it was a joke, but I wasn't very pleased with Ern because it was humiliating. Of course, he'd had a drink or two by then, which had loosened his mouth off, but what he thought didn't stop them from selling their four books and ordering two more from Jeff through Helen and me! When Jeff delivered them, on 5 September, Margaret told him that I was a very good dancer!

Jeff and Ros invited us over on Helen's eightieth birthday for a meal. Jeff picked us up and, when we got there, Harry, Gill, Alan, Shirley and Dorothy were all there, which was a surprise. They all sang 'Happy birthday' as we walked in and Helen was thrilled. We enjoyed the meal and company and I gather Harry was impressed with Jeff and Ros's house.

I was having trouble with my left knee swelling up and, on 26 October, Dr Przyslo came out and gave me a prescription. Although Helen had already had to do the food shopping in Hanley on her own that day, she said she'd go to Lloyds, in Stoke Road, to get my tablets. But she tripped over and fell down in the entry between Cauldon Road and Avenue Road, where presumably she'd gone to check that our garage was okay. She cut one of her arms and lay there until a man helped her to get up. She had a struggle to get back because it had shaken her up and she told me that she was hanging onto the walls of the gardens before she'd reached Mawson Grove. I bet she thought she'd never get back, but there a couple passing in a car picked her up and gave her a lift the rest of the way home because of the state she was in. She didn't go out on her own again after that, except in an emergency. She lost confidence and I said I didn't want her to go down there for me again.

Raedburh was doing quite a bit better and had been walking again since the end of August. Richard Bramley, the Shires vet who was attending to her, told Jeff that her improvement was 'a medical mystery'. As time went by, Jeff became less worried about her and seemed more like his old self.

The previous year, Jeff had spent months recording, on his own equipment, twelve songs he'd written about the environment. Towards the end of this November, he put them out on a CD called *Only One World*. He fixed up a few shows to promote it, but found that his costs were greater than the money he was taking in from people who came to see him and so he didn't organize any more performances. Also, once again he was struggling to get radio airplay and so his project fizzled out.

On 30 November, the council gave Helen and me two free low energy light bulbs. I tried one of them, but the light from it wasn't very strong, so I took it out and carried on with the normal ones.

Jeff took me to the aeroplane museum at RAF Cosford, near Telford, for my 85th birthday and it was bitterly cold. There was hardly anybody there and it was a wonder we didn't get locked in. There was an impressive array of aircraft, including a Spitfire, a Hawker Hurricane and a massive Avro Vulcan bomber, which had been built for the Cold War. Nevertheless, I was itching to get back home because it was perishing.

For a change, Helen and I went with Jeff, Ros and her parents to the White Lion, in London Road, Knighton, near Woore, for Christmas dinner and everybody had fancy hats on. We all became merry and had a very good time. Other people started blowing hooters and then those gathered round each of the tables sang a song in turn!

Jeff and I kept on to Helen about having some exercise, to try to keep her going. She wasn't moving about as much as she used to do when she was in the house, so we'd ask her if she'd like a little walk, but she wasn't impressed because it would require a lot of effort. So, unfortunately, things were left as they were.

On 5 January 2001, Helen and I had cavity wall insulation put into our house and it was paid for by the council. Workmen drilled holes through the cement of our outer wall and squirted some material in. It didn't seem to take them very long to do and then they cemented over the holes. There was very little mess, just a bit of dust on the outside. The idea was to save on heating costs, but I didn't notice any difference afterwards, although there must have been.

I went for a walk with Jeff and Ros at Ilam on 20 January and we came across a chap in a diving suit, who said he was going into the River Manifold and into an underground cavern near where we were standing. He was on his own and I was concerned in case he got stuck. We watched him get into the river, step into the hole and disappear! We didn't know whether to stop there till he came up, but he seemed pretty confident, so we decided to move on, although I kept looking back to see if I could see him, dreading what might happen.

We then went along Paradise Walk, which was an ordinary path, although its name made it sound glamorous. When we got back to the steps by Ilam Hall, we saw a flash of gold in the bushes and a fellow nearby offered the information that it was a goldcrest, which I'd never seen before.

Raedburh was still knocking about and eating a lot of fresh meat, especially turkey, which Jeff was buying regularly for her. When Helen and I called over, we'd take some turkey with us and feed her with it or give her some from the fridge if Jeff and Ros had got any in. Jeff said that Raedburh had eaten 5½ slices in a single sitting on 18 February, so there didn't seem to be a lot wrong with her appetite!

On 16 March, I did our food shopping in Hanley, but when I came back, the kitchen was full of smoke and the kettle was boiled dry and ruined. Helen had put it on for a drink, but then became so tired that she couldn't be bothered to turn the gas flame off! She knew about the smoke, but wasn't bothered about that either! I told her how dangerous it was and said she shouldn't make any more hot drinks while I was out, but she didn't want to know.

That night, she tried to get into bed, but couldn't lift her legs up and got stuck halfway. She was perched on the edge and I thought I'd better try to get her in instead of risking her sliding off the bed. She wouldn't cooperate at all and said, 'Just leave me alone,' so it was a struggle, but I managed it. That was the beginning of difficulties getting her in and out of bed.

She was laid up with flu at the time and had no energy, so that was probably something to do with it, although five days later I found her sitting at the bottom of the stairs in the early hours of the morning! Unfortunately, I picked up the germ from her and it knocked me for six as well, so that Dr Przyslo put me on antibiotics. Then Jeff got the same thing and it was April before Helen started to feel properly right and got her strength back.

Jeff and Ros went away to Tal y Foel for a couple of nights after Easter while Helen, Alan, Shirley and I kept an eye on Raedburh. Jeff and Ros felt she was well enough not to need constant attention, but, unfortunately, she didn't eat very much and went off her back legs. It was tearing me apart to see her like that and when Jeff and Ros returned, I asked him if he'd thought of having Raedburh put down. He wouldn't hear of it, but, amazingly, she again recovered and started walking once more!

On 12 May, Helen and I went with Jeff and Ros to Dorothy's 76th birthday party at the North Stafford Hotel and it was a good event. Dorothy's daughter, Pam, was by then living in Hayley Green, in Warfield, Berkshire, and told me that she and Alan had got a swimming pool and a fish pond with a fountain! While we were at the party, I had a game of pool with Jeff and won, even though I'd never played before!

THE EXIT DOOR OPENS

By the middle of May, Raedburh was walking better than she'd done for a long time and was using her cat door again to get in and out, which she'd stopped being able to do. Helen and I called over to see her on the 18th and she was so good on her legs that Helen exclaimed, 'The Lord has answered my prayers!'

It was our diamond wedding anniversary on 21 June and Helen and I received a letter from Buckingham Palace, which Jeff had fixed up at Helen's request. It had a photo of the queen inside and a message from her, saying, 'I send my congratulations and best wishes to you on such a special occasion.' Helen was delighted about it. Printed on the envelope was an order for the Post Office to deliver it on that specific date.

Prompted by Helen, Jeff had also made an arrangement for the Lord Mayor, Bill Austin, to come to see us at our house. He and his wife, Wyn, arrived in his chauffeur-driven Rolls-Royce and they made themselves comfortable. I reminded him of the time when he'd previously been the mayor and had given me a lift in his Rolls when I was a postman, but I don't think he remembered it. Young Harry and Jeff were here at the same time and Bill was a Vale supporter, so I had a job to get a word in edgeways! Bill and Wyn stayed quite a while and it was all very pleasant, but our neighbours didn't mention their visit afterwards, so I don't know whether they hadn't noticed the mayor had been here or if they were jealous!

Two days later, Helen and I had a party in the evening at the North Stafford Hotel, where we hired the Frederick Room, the Garden Room and the Footlights Bar at a cost of fifty pounds. We got there in good time and I was at the entrance waiting to greet the 28 guests, while Helen waited in the room for them. As the guests arrived, I took them to the room and passed them over to Jeff, who bought them a drink. The entertainment was Eric Newton, the well-known busker clarinetist and marathon runner, who'd been hired by Jeff at a cost of a hundred pounds, and he played background music.

After a while, the staff brought in the food for the buffet and eventually somebody said, 'Come and get your eats!' Everybody queued up, chatted as they went along, got what they wanted and sat down at the tables. I was the last to fix myself up, but I couldn't see anywhere to sit down because people were arranged all higgledy-piggledy. Eventually, I pushed in on a table at the bottom of the room, where Jack and Audrey, Ern and Margaret, Doris and Sam, and Tom and Gertie were sitting. I was at the opposite end of the room from where Helen was and that caused a laugh! Jeff had said that the guests should sit at named places to eat, but Helen wanted them to sort themselves out and that turned out more or less anywhere!

After the meal, Jeff got up and made a speech about how Helen and I had met and how things had developed between us. He took it up to our wedding and our honeymoon in Coventry and he read extracts from my book from time to time as he went along. He mentioned the job that Helen had been doing when I'd met her and Jeff said she'd been 'a shop assistant' at British Home Stores, in Hanley, but Helen shouted out, 'I was a supervisor!' That brought the house down! She was indignant and thought she was being belittled to have had her job described as one of such low status.

Jeff's speech was great and it made the night, really. Afterwards, he proposed a champagne toast to Helen and me and then we cut our celebration cake, which had cost £65 from Food For Thought Ltd, at Unit 2, in Campbell Road Industrial

Estate.

Then all eyes were on Eric, but there was no proper dancing because he wasn't tuned into it. He couldn't play, say, a waltz, so we couldn't ask him to do it. He played his own type of music and we made up our own dances to it or just shuffled around. I was disappointed because I couldn't do the proper steps and Helen and I just shuffled about a bit, as did one or two others. But it was a very good night and people only drifted away slowly.

Jeff and Ros gave us a big, heavy present for our anniversary, which turned out to be a video recorder. It was an amazing gift and quite a surprise. They also gave us a copy of the classic 1939 film, *Gone With The Wind*, which was very good. It was an emotional story set in the American Civil War, starring Clark Gable and Vivien Leigh. I'd seen it a time or two, but it was nice to have a copy of our own.

Helen and I had another diamond wedding party, on 26 June, which had been arranged for us at Zion Church. A buffet was put on for us and the fifteen or so members of the congregation who turned out, and it was very nice that such an effort had been made to celebrate our anniversary.

On 30 June, Jeff and Ros were out for the day, so they'd arranged for Helen and me to go over and cat sit. We did our best, but Raedburh had got in a state again and couldn't walk properly. We fed her some tongue and beef, but most of the time she lay in her favourite spot in their back garden. We stayed with her till Jeff and Ros got back and then we went home.

The following evening, Jeff rang and told us that Raedburh had just died, at the Shires surgery in Eccleshall Road, Stone, where he and Ros had taken her after Helen and I had left. I was shocked, although I knew it was coming. Helen and I were upset, but I felt relieved that Raedburh had gone at last because she'd got in such a terrible state that it was a shame to let her live on. Jeff was devastated and I felt very sorry for him. He'd tried to do his best for her.

On the same day, I developed a painful rash on my back, which was diagnosed by Dr Joseph Hapuarachi, at the Harley Street surgery, as shingles. It was a surprise and I wondered where it had come from. My back was sore for a short while, but the shingles didn't cause me a lot of trouble. Dr Hapuarachi gave me some Zovirax cream to rub on the rash and it died down after a couple of weeks.

Jeff picked up the coffin I'd made and had an engraving done on a brass plate (at Timpson's, in The Potteries Shopping Centre), which he wanted to be fixed onto the top of it. He dug a grave for Raedburh in her favourite spot and I was amazed how far he went down. I thought he'd have dug a small hole, but it was almost like a human one because he didn't want any future owners of the house to disturb her.

He buried her on 4 July and was very upset. I screwed the plaque onto the coffin and then Jeff laid her in it. He said his last goodbyes and was crying. I then put the screws in the holes I'd drilled and I screwed the lid down tight. I then decided to leave Jeff to it and came home.

An anniversary photo of Helen and me, taken by one of the *Sentinel* photographers, was in the newspaper on 7 July, but they'd made a mistake and said we'd been celebrating our golden wedding anniversary. Jeff got this corrected for us and *The Sentinel* reprinted the item a week later, but that time reported that Helen had been a manageress for fifty years! Nevertheless, she was pretty pleased about the publicity, but I wasn't bothered really.

We had another holiday at Tal y Foel, from 26 to 30 July, and Jeff and Ros were there for part of the time. Helen and I had an upstairs room, but her walking wasn't very good, so I was worried about her using the stairs, although she managed them. Unfortunately, I'd forgotten to bring my pyjamas, so at bedtime I had to borrow one of Helen's nightdresses, which was most embarrassing!

We enjoyed just sitting in Judy and Lewis's garden by their water feature and looking across the Menai Strait, but we also revisited Beaumaris and Rhosneigr. Jeff and Ros arrived on Jeff's fiftieth birthday and we drove to Y Groeslon, a pub on a sharp bend in nearby Brynsiencyn. We had a huge meal and even Jeff, who was known for his big appetite, found it difficult to eat it all. Helen and I had gammon inside an immense Yorkshire pudding and she told the staff they'd served up too much food!

The following day, we all went to Newborough Beach, which was a vast expanse of sand overlooking Snowdonia, but Helen found it hard to walk on and it wasn't too good for me either. We discovered some driftwood to sit on, but it wasn't very comfortable because there were hard twigs sticking out of it. After soaking up the sun for a while, we walked back to the car and it was hard work.

Jeff drove us to the nearby Llyn Parc Mawr nature reserve picnic area, where we got all the tea equipment out and brewed up. I liked doing that and there was a bit of style about it. We sat at a picnic table, enjoyed our drinks and had a lovely time. We then tested the nearby bird hut, but only saw a couple of oystercatchers.

We went on to South Stack and looked down at the lighthouse. Like before, Helen and I thought, 'We're not going down there!' The path was really steep, with awkward curves, and the lighthouse looked at least a mile away, so we all had an ice cream each instead of going down and we sat contented on a bench to eat them.

We finished off at Llanfairpwllgwyngyllgogerychwyrndrobwllllantysiliogogogoch railway station and its name was a big selling point on postcards because it was supposed to be the longest place name in Great Britain. Jeff took a photo of the main platform sign and, to fit it in his viewfinder, he had to cross over to the other side of the station!

We were back at Y Groeslon that night for more big eats. The landlord was very friendly and we discovered that he collected Clarice Cliff pottery.

The next day was the last for Helen and me and we all went to Black Point, the most easterly spot on Anglesey, to see Puffin Island and the marvellous view to the Great Orme. Then I brewed up my last tea bag outside Penmon Priory and we shared a final cup. I'd brought all the tea bags from home, although I could have used those provided at the digs, but Helen had said: 'No! They belong to the landlady.' It was as if Judy and her husband, Lewis, were poor people and Helen was helping them out! If we'd actually used the tea bags, I'd have felt a bit guilty too, as though it would have been stealing! That's silly, I know.

We drove down to Beaumaris, where we said our goodbyes, and Helen and I left for home, having enjoyed a lovely few days in what sadly turned out to be our last ever holiday together.

Jeff's old teddy bear had travelled round in the back of our car for years as a kind of mascot because of an idle fancy that Helen had had. A short while after Raedburh had died, Helen brought "Ted" into the house and put him in the back bed. She tucked him in under the bedclothes, with his head sticking out on a pillow. Then she went through a rigmarole of lying him down every night and sitting him up each morning. She put a balloon in front of him, but I don't know what it was supposed to have been for. I thought it was a load of nonsense, but it could have been to do with Raedburh having died.

When we visited Jeff and Ros, Helen would go to Raedburh's grave and shout 'Kitty,' as she still called her. Helen would talk to her, as though Raedburh was there, and then say what she'd replied! Helen prayed for her every night and told Jeff, 'God's looking after her.'

Around that time, a coloured family came to live two doors away, at number 339. They were Vincent Waldron (who was known as "Danny"); his wife, Joan, and their son, Erol, whom Helen called "Hughie". I'd more or less got used to seeing coloured people by then, so it didn't make any difference to me. I don't think Helen was all that keen on the family at first, but then Danny started to come to the Gas Club and she'd go over and make such a fuss of him. I didn't like her being gushing like that and I wondered if Danny was embarrassed about it.

I was watching the television on 11 September when cameras flashed onto the North Tower of the World Trade Center, in New York, and I saw a plane crash straight into it. Then there came another plane, which did a similar thing to the South Tower. There was panic going on and I couldn't believe my eyes. Then the towers collapsed and it seemed impossible that such things could happen. It was bewildering and seemed like a movie, with special effects having been put on. I thought the towers would have been built to withstand anything, but obviously they hadn't and nearly 3,000 people lost their lives. I couldn't take it all in, but the Americans were soon planning repercussions against the al-Qaeda terrorist organization, which was responsible for the attacks.

Helen had developed vaginal bleeding and kept trying to go to the toilet. Then two protruding lumps appeared and she thought she'd got cancer, so we went to see Dr Przyslo, on 14 September. I remember her lying there and the doctor was fiddling about. She was squirming about and moaning. I could see her facial expressions of distaste, but, because her hearing had got worse, she couldn't hear what Dr Przyslo was saying! Her womb had dropped and he fitted a pessary to hold it in place. It did the trick and her bleeding stopped.

On Helen's 81st birthday, Jeff took us to Ashford in the Water, near Bakewell, which was a beautiful place, and we fed cream crackers to the ducks from the old stone Sheepwash Bridge over the River Wye. It was called that because sheep used to be washed there before they were sheared. Their lambs were put in a pen on one side of the river and the sheep were thrown in the water on the other. The sheep would then swim across to their lambs and have a good soaking on the way!

Helen and I then sat on a seat by the river while Jeff went to get us all an ice cream, but he was gone so long that we started to look for him. We found him on his way back, having walked quite a distance to find a shop and then having been stuck in a long queue! At night, there was a party at Jeff and Ros's and, on the way, we called at our house, where Helen tucked Ted up in bed for the night.

On 6 October, Jeff and Ros went to the RSPCA cattery at Rodbaston College, near Penkridge, to see if they'd got any kittens. We called at their house later and

Helen was eager to know if they were going to have one. We both missed seeing Raedburh when we called over, but nothing came of Jeff and Ros's enquiry because Jeff couldn't bring himself to have another cat.

Another war broke out on 7 October when Britain invaded Afghanistan, along with the Americans. The idea was supposed to be to get rid of the Taliban government, which was protecting al-Qaeda terrorists, but it was just ridiculous going in there. It seemed as if we stirred up a hornet's nest and we got bogged down. It made things worse and we'd got another enemy. It still isn't sorted out and I don't think it's possible to win there. Invading Afghanistan had been tried before, by us twice in the nineteenth century and by the Soviet Union in 1979 and each time the invaders eventually had to withdraw.

Helen had begun to struggle to get in and out of the bath, so I started to help her. One day, she got in, but was very unsteady trying to sit down. When she attempted to get out, after her bath, it was hard work and she said, 'I can't manage it.' I tried to help her, but it was very awkward standing at the side of the bath, pulling her up at the same time. I couldn't get her to stand, so I let some of the water out and tried again, but I still couldn't manage it. I then put one of my feet in the bath, to get more leverage, and, of course, my shoe got wet. Also, I was concerned about my hernias and that I'd cripple myself if I wasn't careful, but, after what seemed an eternity, I got her to stand up. I gave her a quick wipe down, then managed to get her out of the bath, one foot after the other, and finished drying her off.

After that, Helen said: 'I'm not having another bath. I'm not getting in there again!' Her words turned out to be true and I quite agreed with her because I didn't fancy going through that again. So, from then on, I used to give her a sponge down, once or twice a week, in the kitchen because she only made a half-hearted attempt to do it herself.

About the same time, I also started finding it difficult to get in and out of the bath and it became dangerous. I only carried on for a month or two after Helen stopped and then I started having a sponge down as well.

Jeff said that we could have a shower at his house whenever we wanted and I did a time or two. His shower was very good and it was a lot safer to use than our bath, but Helen wasn't very interested because it was too much trouble for her.

I'd had a blood test done, on 14 September, which had showed my blood to have been slightly richer in colour than it should have been. So I was told to go to the Infirmary for a liver scan, which I did on 19 November, and fortunately it found that there was nothing wrong with me. Helen was with me and we decided to get a bus to Stoke and then walk home from there to get some exercise. We managed to do it, but Helen was very tired when we got back.

One day in December, I was looking through our kitchen windows when a fox jumped on the wall between our house and Nancy's. It looked around and then silently jumped down onto our yard. It went up one of our steps and then through the hedge into Alice's garden. It didn't see me. It was a beautiful red colour and was fair-sized, probably being a male.

Another time, I got out of bed in the middle of the night and went to the toilet. On the way back, I just happened to look out of the bedroom window and saw a fox standing on the front wall, looking towards Stoke. It didn't seem as big as the first one. It glanced round several times, but didn't see me and jumped down onto the pavement. It then trotted across the road, went onto the grass on the other side and disappeared from view. A week or two later, a very similar thing happened and it may well have been the same fox.

On 8 December, Helen and I went to the Red Lion, in Market Place, Leek, where Jeff was launching his latest book, *The Mysterious Double Sunset*, in an upstairs room. As usual, I'd helped him with his research for the book, by looking through *Sentinels* on microfilms in the archives at Hanley Library for reports of past double sunsets. It was awkward for Helen to climb the stairs to the launch, particularly because it was pretty crowded, so I left her downstairs with a drink and went back down a time or two to check that she was alright. It was interesting to see what happened at the event and I took a couple of photos of Jeff and his friend, Roy Parker, who'd worked with him on the book. Afterwards, Jeff was taking people to Bosley to try to see a double sunset from there and I wanted to go, but Helen wasn't keen, so we left it at that.

The book wasn't of much interest to me, but it was very good. I didn't think Jeff would make a lot of money on it and he didn't, but he did fulfil one of his desires.

On my 86th birthday, Jeff picked Helen and me up and took us to Bosley to see a double sunset. We stood on the pavement near the Queens Arms, on the A 523, and watched it through filters he'd got. The sun was bright and it set on top of The Cloud before part of it reappeared. I watched it happen for half an hour and it was strange, but interesting.

In the evening, Jeff took us to his house for tea and Alan and Shirley came as a surprise. Then, when we were sitting down, Dave Wallett suddenly appeared, pointed his camera at me and took my photo! I was surprised to see him because Jeff hadn't mentioned anything about him coming. He seemed to ask me a lot of questions and he had a camcorder running, but I didn't know it. So he was filming the event and later put it onto a video cassette for us.

On 17 December, Helen had to go to the doctor's because her pessary had slipped and Sister Sandra Sheppard inserted a new one. Helen had no more trouble with it after that. While we were there, the sister noticed that Helen was wheezing a bit when she was breathing and said, 'I think you might have a touch of asthma.' So she gave Helen an inhaler and told her to take two puffs from it when required, but at first Helen wouldn't use it regularly. We saw Sister Sheppard four weeks later to follow up and she asked how it was going. I said, 'Well, Helen's never complained,' and so she was given a new inhaler. Once she got used to the idea of having one, she used it pretty regularly for several years. Also, she used to swear by Olbas oil, which she'd dab on her handkerchief and breathe in.

We had a Christmas card as usual from Pam and Alan Edwards, and inside was a circular letter that Pam had typed, which gave information on what they'd been doing in the past year. It was the first time we'd ever had that type of letter and Jeff and Ros also received one. It seemed as if Pam and Alan were doing very well, especially financially, through their electronic equipment company, Quartz Electronics.

Ros asked us if we wanted to go to Nick and Claire's house for Christmas, but Helen was afraid of leaving our home because of burglars, so we turned the offer down. Therefore we spent Christmas on our own because Jeff felt obliged to go to

York with Ros and it was very quiet. One of the presents they bought me was a green gilet and I wore it regularly in the winter afterwards, on top of a jumper, so that I didn't have to put a jacket on in the house to keep warm.

Jeff and Ros came back on Boxing Day and took us over to their house for tea. Unfortunately, Helen wasn't very discreet and twice told Ros she was putting on weight. I think Ros should have taken it with a pinch of salt and taken no notice, but she complained about it to Jeff. When he ran us home afterwards, he told Helen off and that led to a dispute. I said she should apologize to Ros, but she wouldn't and I couldn't make out why she was being so awkward. I was worried that Ros wouldn't come to our house again and that Jeff might then get the huff and stop seeing us, but it all blew over.

Dave Wallett had videoed our diamond wedding party at the North Stafford Hotel and gave us a copy of it, but our old rented television hadn't been designed to show videos, so we decided to buy a new one. On 28 December, Jeff went with me to Festival Park, where I bought a 25-inch screen Goodmans from Comet. Jeff fiddled about with it, but the picture was poor. So I got a couple of fellows round from the shop, but they couldn't get a clear picture either and it turned out that we needed a proper, outside aerial. I saw an advert in *The Sentinel* and a got a fellow to bring an aerial and fit it, but he just knocked a hole in the wall and pushed the cable through, instead of fitting it properly in a tube. However, that finally did the trick.

Helen liked our diamond wedding video so much that she kept asking me to put it on, so our new video recorder came in very handy. The film was worth repeating, but I got bored with it long before Helen did, even though it was better than *Gone With The Wind*!

On 5 January 2002, Helen noticed that Ted had disappeared from the back bed and was quite bothered about it. She wanted me to look for him, but I wouldn't because I thought it was all daft. We later went to Jeff and Ros's and Helen asked them if they'd seen him because 'He's my only bit of comfort.' Jeff asked her if that was because Raedburh had died and she said, 'I suppose so.' When we got home, Helen had another look for him, but still couldn't find him, so she rang Jeff again. He finally told her that he'd moved Ted for a joke and put him and his balloon on top of the wardrobe, which was where Helen then found him. She put him back in the bed and soon after told Jeff she'd thought of getting him another cat like Raedburh.

I thought it would be nice if Jeff could hit on a book that would be very successful and sell millions, but there aren't many that do that. It was a shame that he was putting so much work in for so little reward. I asked him if he'd thought of writing something that would be really popular and he said he had, about the lives of the famous pop singer, Robbie Williams, and the world champion darts player, Phil Taylor, but that he wasn't very interested in them.

After Raedburh had died, Jeff had had quite a number of dreams about her being alive and they seemed very real to him, so he wondered if she was contacting him from another world. On 9 February, he paid twenty pounds to see a medium, Gerard Smith, at the David Jones Centre, at 96A Stone Road, in Stafford. Jeff told Helen and me that the results were hit and miss, but there were no messages from Raedburh and Helen said it was all 'rubbish'.

Helen had to go to the Gynaecological Clinic at the Outpatients on 8 March for a checkup on her womb and pessary. She hadn't told Jeff anything about it because she didn't want to worry him, but everything was okay.

Jeff had decided he wanted a headstone for Raedburh's grave and had ordered one from Harold H. Leese, the funeral directors and monumental masons, in St Peter's Close, Stoke, at a cost of £145. He picked it up on 25 March and was quite pleased with it, especially the gold lettering, which had been cut on the top of it, reading: 'RAEDBURH c. 20 May 1983-1 July 2001 loving and gentle feline companion of Jeff and Rosalind Kent'.

On 1 April, Jeff and Ros took Helen and me to Gentleshaw Wildlife Centre, which was behind Fletcher's Garden & Leisure Centre, in Stone Road, Eccleshall. Jeff had got involved in helping out there and participated in the activities on the day. He lay on the ground while a Harris hawk swooped down over him for the entertainment of the crowd. That got me interested and Rob Smith, the owner, asked if I'd like to hold a snake. I consented and one of his assistants handed a python to me. It was quite large and heavy, but it was docile and they assured me that it had only just been fed! I held it and it wrapped around one of my arms. It kept moving and I stroked it to see what it felt like. I had always imagined snakes to be cold and slimy, but I was surprised how warm and normal it was. A few people were hanging around, witnessing the spectacle of man versus beast. Then I handed it back.

The Harris hawk was on a perch and I was asked if I wanted to hold it, so I did. I had to put a heavy leather glove on my left hand and wrist because the bird had huge talons, which gripped my arm. It was pretty heavy to hold and kept fidgeting around and flapping its wings in my face all the time! I stroked its beak with a finger and it was also pretty docile. When I'd had enough, I handed it back to the attendant. It was all quite an experience and something I'd not done before. I could see why Jeff wanted to go there every day.

Two days later, Jeff took Helen and me to the opening of Sproson Park, which was between Bycars Lane and Scotia Road. A plaque was unveiled by Bill Austin, who was still the Lord Mayor and was wearing a jazzy jacket. The plaque said that the park had been so named to commemorate the service of Jess, Roy and Phil Sproson to Vale. Jeff took a photo of Helen and me next to the plaque and I shot one of him with Phil Sproson, who was present. Jeff, Helen and I then went on to Vale Park, where we had a cup of tea and a chat with one or two of the old fifties' and sixties' players, including Graham Barnett, who was a chatterbox. Afterwards, we went to an upstairs room in Ye Olde Smithy, at 54-56 Moorland Road, for a buffet, but it was a scruffy little place.

From time to time, Helen became uncooperative about going out on Saturdays for a run in the car, which was disappointing, but I suppose she was tired and didn't feel like making the effort to get ready. She was getting older and couldn't be bothered to do much.

On 11 May, Ros's Vauxhall Nova was stolen from a car park in Stafford and it was never found, so she bought a replacement, a nice red Vauxhall Corsa, for £4,395 on the 29th. I had a little drive of it in Hanley, which I enjoyed, and I was impressed with how smoothly it worked as against my old Volkswagen Polo, which I still had.

A kitten had started to visit Jeff and Ros, and it was there when Helen and I went to see them on 17 June. We still missed Raedburh, so we were quite taken with it and Helen told Jeff that he mustn't 'shoo it off'. Soon after, though, it stopped coming – perhaps its owners had returned from holiday.

Helen increasingly developed different problems, for which she had to take tablets and there ended up so many that her taking them became haphazard, especially because she'd become forgetful and couldn't see properly. Sometimes, she'd get tablets out of the wrong box and other times she'd drop them on the floor and lose them. I'd try to figure out which tablets were missing and give them to her. I took a chance, but we didn't really know for sure which ones she was having and when. So we got a free receptacle to put a week's supply in and it simplified everything. There was room in each of the seven compartments to hold several tablets, so that she could have the right ones every day. I dished them out to her when they were needed and that worked fine. The first letter of each day was printed on the compartment, but there was a snag because those of Tuesday and Thursday were the same, so I had to be careful not to get them mixed up.

On 13 July, Jeff again came up with the idea of publishing my book and said he thought it would appeal to the public because of its recollections of past times. Although I was still worried about what Helen might think about it coming out, I told him that the book was his, for him to do with what he wanted.

The comedian and TV presenter, Nick Hancock, came along Leek Road from Stoke on 19 July, carrying the queen's golden jubilee baton. It was in a relay on the way to Manchester for the start of the Commonwealth Games on the 25th and had a message inside from her, which was read out at the opening ceremony. Helen and I went out to watch the celebrity go past and the traffic was all held up behind. As I got ready to take a photo of him, he smiled and waved for me.

On 23 July, Jeff and Ros went to Iceland again for a holiday. While they were there, he rang and told us he'd hurt his left leg, but he didn't tell us the whole story till he'd got back. We went over to his place on 7 August and saw him on crutches, which was a shock. He'd ruptured an Achilles tendon and his leg was in plaster. I couldn't imagine what it would be like to have the tendon snap at the back of my ankle and I wondered how it would affect him in the days and weeks to come. I did quite a few jobs for him to help out because he was struggling for weeks.

Brian Eeley finished working and Helen and I went to his retirement party at Zion Church on 17 August. He was always gushing and cracking jokes, so all the women loved him and they were very sorry to see him go. Helen was disappointed and afterwards kept asking, 'Has anybody seen Brian?' but they hadn't. I think they all expected him to come to visit them personally, but he didn't as far as I know. He'd told Helen a few times that he'd come to see her, but she never saw him again.

On 5 September, Helen and I were with Jeff at his house when she noticed a damp patch on the chair where she'd been sitting. Jeff smelt it and came to the conclusion that it was urine. That was the start of her becoming incontinent and after then he put a towel down on her chair when we visited. I started to put a cloth down on her armchair at home, but the problem slowly got worse and our bed began to get wet at times. Helen slept on the far side from the toilet, so she didn't have time to get there before she wet herself. We then switched sides, which helped a bit.

By then, Helen kept missing some of the conversation when people were talking, which had to be repeated and it got annoying. So, on 10 September, we went to see Dr Przyslo to ask about a hearing aid and he got her an appointment at the Outpatients, but it wasn't until the following May!

The next day, I saw Dr Hapuarachi about my hernias, which were getting bigger and the right one had become quite large, so I was becoming concerned about them. He said they could be done under local anaesthetic, but that there was about a six-month waiting list and he referred me to the hospital.

Jeff finally had his plaster off at Staffordshire General Hospital, in Weston Road, Stafford, on 30 September. Unfortunately, by then the muscles in his injured leg had withered and so he had to learn to walk again. He had physiotherapy to help him and it was weeks before he was properly right, but he was okay in the end.

On 5 October, Jeff and Ros came for lunch, which was the first time they'd been able to do so since Jeff had hurt his leg. He got up our steps okay and it was good that we'd all got back in the old routine.

Jeff asked Helen and me if he could have some of our hair as a keepsake. So the next time our hairdresser, Ann Cotton, came to our house to cut it, we had to tell her the story and give a little smile. She gave a handful to us and we then passed it on to Jeff. It was a bit sentimental, but nice.

Whenever I went to the doctor's in the autumn, the sister asked me to have a flu jab, but I wouldn't because I didn't want to bother. On my visit there on 6 November, I was asked the question as usual and I said: 'No. I know somebody who had it and it didn't stop her having flu!'

The sister, Beverley Cooper, said: 'It wasn't flu! It was probably a heavy cold and if you have the jab, you won't get the flu.'

So I said, 'Go on, then, I'll have one.' Ever since then, I've had a jab every year and I haven't had flu in all that time.

In old age, you're very vulnerable if you catch flu because it might kill you, but people don't like to have a needle put in their arm. I tried to get Helen to have it, but she didn't think the jab was worth having, so it was to no avail. She quoted the same thing as I'd done, about people getting flu anyway, and when Jeff tried to persuade her to have it, she still refused.

On 11 November, Helen went to Hilary Ogden's, the optician's at 15 Regent Road, for the fourth time that year, complaining about her eyes. Hilary got bad-tempered because she'd given Helen some new glasses and so thought she'd done the job. But she gave Helen another test and told us it showed that the retina in her right eye was damaged. Hilary hadn't spotted that before, but her report said there'd been 'a marked deterioration' since Helen's previous visit.

Jeff and Ros took us for a run out to Crich Tramway Village, in Derbyshire, on my 87th birthday, to have a look at the street that had been mocked up as a replica of an old town. As we were walking along, I said: 'Ooh, look at that! It looks like The Red Lion!' That was an old hotel, which had been in Church Street, Stoke, but had been demolished to make way for the "D" Road. It had been transported to Crich and rebuilt there. Jeff looked at Ros and smiled because they'd wondered whether I'd recognize it. We had a drink in there and it was just how the old pubs had been, scruffy and dull, so it fitted in just nicely.

There was a tramway down the centre of the street, with a tram on it, so we decided to have a ride. The conductor gave us tickets for an old penny each, which we'd been given when we came in. As an old-fashioned tram, it was sparse inside and the ride was uncomfortable because its wheels were metal and it had no spring. Unfortunately, it was foggy and damp, a horrible day, so we were glad to get out of the cold when we left the village.

Steve and Lindsey Purcell, Jeff and Ros's next-door neighbours at number 6, had a black cat, named Molby after the Liverpool footballer, Jan Mølby! Jeff and Ros had become pretty friendly with the cat and on occasions let him come in their house for some milk. He was a lovely animal and they let him in on Christmas Day, so we could have a stroke of him while we were there. Molby was quite friendly considering we weren't well known to him.

Jon Posnett had applied for and got a job as the head teacher at Urafirth Primary School, on the Shetland Islands, where he had a rented house supplied for his family. It seemed a long way to go for a job and everybody was surprised to hear about it, but perhaps we shouldn't have been because Jon and Mandy loved the countryside. On 28 December, two days before they left, Helen and I went to see them at their house at 28 King Street, in Leek. After they'd gone, we had a postcard or a photo from them every now and again and the scenery looked nice, but there didn't seem to be many trees about.

Vale had run into big financial trouble and had gone into administration on 16 December, but the supporters had set up a fund, Save the Vale, to try to keep the club going. Naturally, Jeff got involved and became the co-ordinator of the campaign. Helen wasn't very pleased about it and on 15 January 2003 told him he ought to be doing something better with his time. He took no notice and carried on and eventually the supporters bought the club (under the name Valiant 2001) on 6 May and saved it.

Dave Wallett still called on Helen and me every so often, but, around that time, we found out he'd got cancer in his oesophagus. Although it was very serious, the fact didn't seem to register with me somehow.

Helen was continuing to deteriorate in various ways and she even began to lose interest in Ted, so that eventually she didn't bother with him any more. Jeff was concerned that I was having an ever-increasing number of jobs to do and he was looking ahead. He said, 'Dad, you should be thinking about how to get help to make things easier.' I said I'd think about that, but that the time hadn't yet come. Nevertheless, when Helen and I went to see Dr Przyslo on 19 February, I said I thought she might be suffering from depression because she was losing interest in things. He then asked her if she was depressed, but she said she was just tired and that was the end of it!

At that time, Jeff became concerned about Helen's diet, because she was largely living on pies, cheese and white bread, and he got her some leaflets on more healthy eating. As a result, we both tried a change from white bread to wholemeal. I carried on with it, but Helen didn't want it and it was hard work trying to get her to have different things. Jeff wanted her to have more fruit and vegetables, but he wasn't very successful in persuading her to do so, though she did start having tomato sandwiches.

On 20 March, I heard on the news that Britain had invaded Iraq, along with the Americans, but the only other countries who supported us were Australia and Poland. The main reason given seemed to be that Iraq had got 'weapons of mass destruction' that its president, Saddam Hussein, had had secretly developed. I didn't like the news because we were interfering in other people's business and I was worried about what it would lead to. The war proper was won by 1 May and it seemed to be all technical, pressing buttons and guiding missiles in, but fighting continued on and off and we had soldiers there for over six years! Also, it turned out that the Iraqis hadn't got any weapons of mass destruction, so it was a waste of time, money and lives unless the real reason was to secure their oil.

Jeff took Helen and me to Wettonmill on 29 March and we had an ice cream and sat in the sun. I wondered how the River Manifold went underground, near to where Jeff's wedding reception marquee had been. He said he'd show me, so we walked to the river and came to the spot where it disappeared. We could see the river flowing and then the bed slowly went dry until the water vanished entirely. It was remarkable and I wondered where it had all gone to, but Jeff explained that there were holes in the ground that the water ran down. I was no longer steady on my legs on rough ground, so Jeff put out his hand a time or two as I walked on the stony river bed to see the river go down the last swallow hole. The day was all very pleasant.

By that time, Helen was having difficulty getting up and down the stairs because we'd only got one handrail. Jeff said it was about time we had another and kept pushing it, but Helen wouldn't have it.

On 5 April, Jeff and Ros took us for a drive to Consallforge, which was an out-of-the-way place in the nice Churnet Valley, where there was a peacock strolling about! We walked across the Churnet Valley Railway line and went into The Black Lion, where we had a drink and a meal of chips and peas. We all remarked how nice the chips were and I asked the waitress how they cooked them, but it was no different from how I did. Then, on the way back to the car, we saw a steam train, which came along just after we'd crossed the line!

By then, Helen was always on about her eyes 'all closing in', but Jeff and I couldn't really understand what she meant. Helen and I went to the Outpatients about the situation on 17 April and were seen by Mr Common at the eye clinic. He told us the problem was at the back of one of her eyes and was age related. He said there wasn't much they could do about it, except recommend a magnifying glass for reading and he booked her in to see the hospital optician. Jeff later rang the hospital and was told that Helen had got macular degeneration in her right eye and couldn't see out of the middle of it, but that she wouldn't lose her sight altogether.

A magnifying glass arrived by post from the hospital and had an adjustable handle, but it wasn't much use because Helen's eyesight was so bad. In any case, she didn't have the patience to use it properly and it would have been better if the magnifying lens had been in her glasses. Unfortunately, I'd been expecting miracles, but it was to no avail. I also tried her with Uncle Bill's old magnifying glass, which we'd still got, and she did better with it, but she didn't persist.

I mentioned the problem to Young Harry and he said he'd seen an article in a newspaper about a magnifying appliance, so I sent off for one in desperation. It was like a plastic sheet and was wobbly, but it was a waste of time because it had been manufactured distorted, so everything appeared blurred, even to me, and I threw it away!

On 19 April, Jeff and Ros took us to Ilam, where the scenery was absolutely wonderful. Ros and I walked down from the hall to St Bertram's Bridge (the stone footbridge over the River Manifold) and to the nearby weir, while Jeff took Helen to see the church. Ros and I joined them there and had a look at the carvings on the Anglo-Saxon font, which were supposed to show scenes from the life of St Bertram, who became a hermit after his wife and child had been eaten by wolves.

The hospital appointment for my hernias finally came through and, to my surprise, it was with Mr Duffy! I went to see him on 23 April and he told me I'd have to have a general anaesthetic and would be in hospital for two days, but that the waiting list was another six months to a year!

On 6 May, Jeff took us to the Outpatients for Helen's hearing assessment. As a result, she was given a hearing aid, but she didn't want to put it in and wasn't very cooperative about using it. It was fiddly to fit and I had a lot of trouble doing it for her, but she didn't seem to be able to get it in on her own. Her hearing got worse, but we carried on as best we could. It got frustrating always repeating myself and having to shout, but I kind of accepted it.

We had a scare because Helen complained that she'd got another lump in her breast. I had a feel and it seemed as if she was right because it appeared that there was some kind of growth. As luck would have it, she had a hospital checkup appointment on 27 May and the doctor, Mr Bassett, said it was scar tissue and harmless, so she was clear again and we were very relieved!

Four days later, Jeff and Ros took us to Prestatyn because Helen had said she'd like to go again and we had many memories of our holidays there when Jeff had been a boy. We went to the sea and had a little walk along the front. We then sat down on the steps above the beach, but things had altered and it didn't seem to be as good as I'd remembered. Jeff, Ros and I had a game of crazy golf, while Helen watched, and I won! Just then, a party of hikers came by, who were finishing the 177-mile Offa's Dyke Path that they'd walked from Sedbury Cliffs, in Gloucestershire, to the Prestatyn sea front. They were very excited and asked us to take their photo at the finishing point, which we did.

We then moved on to Rhyl, which was rough, and we had a drink of tea in a plastic beaker from a kiosk. After that, we went to Ffrith, which was completely unrecognizable, and we had a short walk to the sea wall. Ros helped me onto the sand, but it was awkward and I had a job to get down. We then had a meal at Offa's Tavern, at the bottom of High Street, by Prestatyn Station, to complete the day.

One day, shortly after, I was walking along Leek Road towards the pedestrian crossing, by the allotments, when a workman said to me, 'Come on, you'll be the first customer!' The Belisha beacons had been taken down and a pelican crossing had been put in. I happened to want to go across just when the job had finished and two workmen were experimenting, pressing the buttons, so I made history!

One day in June, Helen fell over on the lawn and I couldn't pick her up because she was too heavy. So I went to the front of our house and a gardener from the allotments was walking along on the other side of the road. I shouted across to him and he looked puzzled, but came over. We went to the lawn and picked Helen up between us. She wasn't hurt and seemed to be able to fall in a relaxed way, so she never suffered any serious injury when she fell.

For a surprise, on Father's Day, Jeff took Helen and me to the Anderton Boat Lift, just outside Northwich, in Cheshire, and, on the way, we went to Sandbach, which was a nice little town. We saw the Saxon crosses there, which were pretty well preserved and I was glad we stopped and had a look at them. We met Ros and her parents at Anderton, where the River Weaver and the Trent and Mersey Canal were at different heights. Some means of transfer between them was needed and the answer was a huge contraption that lifted or lowered a boat and a section of water in a container. The lift had been restored and passengers were allowed to go down it in a boat, so Jeff, Ros, Alan and I decided to try it. The boat started to drop and it gave me a funny sensation, so I wondered what would happen if one of the operators did something wrong and the container plunged down. Anyway, we got off the boat at the bottom and had a look around. It was marvellous.

Afterwards, we all went to Jeff and Ros's house and, on the way, Helen, Jeff and I stopped at Beech Caves, just off the A 519, which were crummy and being used as unofficial toilets! I'd been there when I was younger, but the caves looked different and I was shocked by the state they were in.

For a while, Helen had been complaining about her legs and how difficult walking was becoming for her, so Jeff and I suggested she should try a walking stick. We'd got Uncle Bill's two sticks, but she didn't want to bother using them. Then she said to Nancy, 'My legs are terrible,' or something like that, so Nancy gave her two sticks. However, Helen put a brave face on and pretended she didn't need a stick, but, eventually, she got round to trying one. Sometimes, she used it outside, but she was still reluctant and we had to keep on at her about it. She preferred one of Nancy's sticks, which was thinner and lighter than those of Uncle Bill, but inside the house she still managed without one.

Jeff and Ros took us on a surprise trip for our 62nd wedding anniversary and we came to Wetton, a familiar place, just above the Manifold Valley, to the east. Then we came across a banner hanging outside Ye Olde Royal Oak and I could hardly believe my eyes as to what it said: 'World Toe Wrestling Championships'! I couldn't help but laugh! It was marvellous how Jeff kept finding interesting and bizarre things that were going on and seeing them helped Helen and me have happier lives.

There was a marquee in the grounds of the pub and a mass of people milling around. Inside was a brass band, tuning up, and they played later on. They were very good. The actual toe wrestling competition started and men and women competed separately. It was interesting to see the expressions on their faces as they tried to wrestle their opponent's big toe. Everybody was drinking and there were pots of ale lying around. The spectators all seemed to be enjoying it and cheering the competitors on. Eventually, when we'd seen enough, we went off for tea at Jeff and Ros's.

On 12 July, Jeff asked if I'd like to go to the Vale open day with him and I thought that would be interesting, to see what happened on the inside. I was amazed how clean and modern it all was, with showers and baths. I'd got in my mind that there was a great big tub, with all the players splashing around, but it was so clean that it was like a dining room! I also remember looking out from the executive suites, where there was quite a view down onto the ground, and I met one or two of the old players as well.

Things were getting even more difficult for Helen to get up and down the stairs, so I finally decided to have a second handrail fitted, which I did in July. She was opposed to it, saying we didn't really need one, but gradually she got used to it and was thankful it was there. I didn't use it much at the time.

Jeff and Ros took us to Madeley, near Ironbridge, in Shropshire, on 20 August, to the replica Victorian town at Blists Hill. It had a street with quite a number of shops and works as they would have been at that time and the shopkeepers were dressed in Victorian costume. There was a chemist's, which had big glass jars, with different coloured liquids, and I also remember a locksmith's and a grocer's. There was even a Victorian policeman, who Helen seemed to think was a real one! We went into the New Inn, which was also laid out traditionally, where we had a drink.

We then went to Ironbridge and walked over the very first iron bridge, which had been opened in 1781. It was interesting to see because it had been publicized a lot and it was a lovely little humpback bridge. We looked over the side of it and saw the River Severn below.

A month later, Jeff and Ros took us out for a surprise. On the other side of Loggerheads, we came to Blore Heath Farm, where people were dressed in medieval costumes and soldiers' uniforms. Jeff said it was all to do with the re-enactment of the Battle of Blore Heath in 1459. I wandered around and had a look at the equipment. I was particularly interested in an old-fashioned gun, which was a very crude thing, with a couple of wheels and a barrel, and some cannonballs were laid out by it. I stood by the cannon, picked up a sword and put some headgear on and Jeff took a photograph of me in action!

Then the battle began and there were archers, who started firing. That seemed to be dangerous, but they judged it so that their arrows fell short of the other side. Every now and then, some girls ran onto the field and retrieved the arrows, so they could be used again. There was quite a bit of shouting going on and the two sides charged forward into battle. I was puzzled as to why they were all doing all that because there didn't seem to be any point in it, except perhaps to try to make people understand what had happened in the actual battle.

Afterwards, we went back to Jeff and Ros's house for tea. They'd just been connected to the Internet and I had a go on it on their computer, but I was fiddling around, not knowing what I was doing.

At that time, Jeff was teaching his class on Wednesday evenings at the college and, on 1 October, he came for his tea before he started, as usual. That particular night, though, he walked in with a tabby kitten, which had followed him along the pavement. He was worried about it getting run over and I wasn't too shocked at its arrival because it was typical that Jeff picked it up, with his concern for animals. Helen said, 'Get that thing out of here!' However, Jeff had found the owners' phone number on a tag round its neck and he rang them. They lived along the road, where he'd first seen it, and he returned it to them.

After Jeff had been born, I'd got a photo album to put in pictures of him and kept it going until he was eight. I'd put a few comments and dates in it, but there was hardly any information on who was who. Jeff thought it would be a good idea to write in who the various people were, so we started going through the album on 15 October and put down their names. It didn't take long and it meant that if members of the family or other people looked at it in the future, they would know who was who.

Helen was complaining about being tired, so she had a blood test at the Harley Street surgery on 24 October. We went back for the results two weeks later, but nothing wrong had been found with her. She was given a tonic to take, but it didn't make much difference.

Jeff was regularly writing pencil notes in my book, as he carefully read through it again, and was often asking me different questions. I didn't always know the answers and sometimes, to find out, I had to go to the Archives & Local Studies unit in Hanley Library, but it was laborious to get the information. I tended to put it off because other things came up to do or I just didn't feel like it, but we got it all done in the end.

I found a pair of my socks on the doormat in the hall on 20 November and was puzzled as to what they were doing there. The mystery was eventually solved when Jeff told me that he'd posted them through the letter box when he'd called earlier because Helen and I had been asleep and he hadn't wanted to wake us up. He'd borrowed them the night before when he'd been round because his own socks had become wet from walking in the rain.

On 9 December, Helen and I went to the Outpatients for her breast checkup and saw Mr Duffy. Unfortunately, this time he had bad news because he found her lump was growing again, so he changed her tablets and put her on anastrozole instead of tamoxifen. We were worried, but all we could do was wait and hope the new drug would do the trick.

Jeff and Ros bought me a portable Grundig CD player for Christmas, which was better than our existing radio-cassette player because it had all three things in one and the radio reception was superior. CDs were better quality than tapes, but not by a great deal, and Helen and I used the machine to play them quite a bit.

From time to time, Jeff bought us a CD to play on our new machine. One of the best was *Release Me*, by Engelbert Humperdinck, which came out in 2003, and we really liked it because it had most of his big hits on. So the Jim Reeves cassette that Helen had been playing for years was dropped and she then put the new CD on all the time! Jeff did very well in keeping us interested in something and he helped us fill many an hour.

Another CD that I played quite a lot was *The Centenary Collection*, by Bing Crosby, which was also produced that year. Crosby had a kind of catch in his voice, which sounded like a fault, but it appealed to me and a lot of other people. There were 88 songs on four CDs packaged as a box set. One I particularly liked was *Red Sails in the Sunset*, which had been a big hit for him in 1935 and was a sentimental song that told the story of a girl waiting for her 'true love' to come home from the sea for their wedding. Another good song on the CD was *Silent Night, Holy Night*, which was a Christmas carol that he'd first recorded in 1928 and was easy to sing along with. Of course, *White Christmas* was one of my favourites as well and reminisced about snowy Christmases in the past. It had been recorded in 1942 and was the biggest-selling single ever.

I seemed to have been waiting a long time for the date of my hernia operations to come up, but eventually the postman brought the appointment and it was for 7.45 a.m. on 30 December. Jeff picked me up on the day and I checked in at the Nuffield Hospital, in Clayton. I was shown to room 26, where I'd be stopping, and I was given a gown to put on. The room was quite nice and very different from the hospital wards. The Nuffield wasn't like a hospital. It felt more like a hotel and it was very relaxed. Mr Duffy was the surgeon and he was reassuring and said, 'We'll soon have it done!' Jeff was still with me and we said our goodbyes when I was taken to the operating theatre on a contraption, which was like a mobile table. I was given an injection and then I drifted off into unconsciousness.

When I woke up, I was told that the operations had been done on both my hernias, but I hadn't felt anything. I was taken back to my room and was amazed because I was feeling good and given a newspaper to read. At lunch time, Helen and Jeff came to see me, but I don't remember it, perhaps because I was a bit drowsy. Later, I got out of bed and sat in a chair. Then I had a meal at tea time and had no trouble with it. Afterwards, Ros came to visit me and I had a chat with her.

I stayed overnight and slept fine. I was discharged by Mr Duffy in the morning, so I rang Jeff to ask him to pick me up. When he and Helen got there, he was surprised that I was already dressed and waiting in the corridor! I wasn't in any pain. It was as though nothing had happened and I can't remember taking any tablets. The operation, which was done on the NHS, was marvellous and I've had no trouble since.

I walked to Jeff's car, but Helen clutched at me for support, as she was doing regularly by that time because of being wobbly on her legs and still reluctant to use a walking stick. This time, I pushed her off and Jeff took charge of her because if she'd pulled too heavily on me or fallen, she might have pulled my stitches out and undone the good job done. I had to be very careful and tried to impress on her not to hang on to me, but she didn't seem to understand.

Jeff took us back to his house and we decided to stop there for a night or two. It was very good of him and Ros to have had us stay with them. They fixed us up in their front bedroom and I slept well. Helen seemed to fit in with things alright, as I did. After four nights, we wanted to go home and, though Jeff wished us to stay longer, he took us back. I seemed to be alright and Jeff was satisfied with how I was doing, so everything started to get back to normal. I couldn't have wished for a better recovery and it might have been even quicker had Jeff not been holding me back a bit.

On 6 January 2004, I felt fit enough to go to Spar Stores, at 200-202 Cauldon Road, and the day after walked to Eastwood Post Office (on the other side of the Lichfield Street roundabout) and back. Then two days later, Helen and I managed to do our food shopping in Hanley, so I was pretty well back to normal by then.

When the concrete flags at the front of our house had been put down in 1959, they'd been laid wrongly. Instead of starting from the steps, the builder, Joe Davies, had begun at the back gate, which had left a gap at the top of the steps that he'd had to fill in with a bit of concrete.

The concrete fill-in had sunk over time and left the steps slightly higher, which meant Helen and I were liable to trip up. So, in February, we employed Jim Egginton, from 2 Cardwell Street, in Northwood, to re-lay the flags at a cost of ninety pounds. He started off from the top of the steps, so that the gap to be filled in this time was at the gate, which was how it should have been done in the first place. Unfortunately, he broke one of the flags, so he had to replace it with a new one, which therefore stood out. Helen didn't like it, but it was Hobson's choice.

Out of the blue, Helen started to perk up and began to do more jobs again. She washed down the front steps after the builders had finished, swept the yard and did the dishes and some cleaning, but it was all a flash in the pan because her efforts largely fizzled out after a few weeks.

One day, we were going shopping in Hanley and I wanted to go to the doctor's on the way to put in for a repeat prescription. So I got off the bus at Regent Road and told Helen to wait for me in the bus station, but when I turned up, she wasn't there! I hadn't got a clue what had happened, so I started looking around. I went up and down the bus station a time or two and asked an attendant if he'd seen her, but he hadn't. I didn't know what to do because she might have stayed on the bus and ended up in Kidsgove or Biddulph, but I decided to have a look around the town centre. I couldn't see her there, so I went back to the bus station and had another look round, but I still couldn't find her.

I thought I'd better go to the police station to see if they could help out and I explained the situation to a policewoman at the desk. She said, 'We'll sort it out,' and seemed pretty confident about it. She phoned through to their patrol in the town centre and then said to me, 'We've got her in Marks & Spencer, sitting down.'

Off I went and found her in the store, chatting to a policewoman and other people sitting next to her. I thanked the policewoman for helping and then off she went. I quizzed Helen as to what had happened and it seemed that she'd felt lost once she'd got off the bus, perhaps thinking I'd abandoned her, but she didn't really seem to know what had happened. I now think it's explained by her having been in the early stages of memory loss, which slowly got worse. I still had the shopping to do, so I told Helen to stay where she was until I got back. I was worried she'd have gone again, but, fortunately, she was there when I returned.

Helen was still complaining that she couldn't see very well and that she was having headaches. We thought we'd try a different optician from Hilary Ogden because we weren't very happy that she'd been curt with Helen on our last visit. We decided to go to Specsavers Opticians, at 8 Tontine Square, which was convenient because we could call there while we were in Hanley shopping. We went on 2 April and Helen had her eyes examined. The optician told us that she needed to go to the hospital because, as far as I could make out, she'd got bleeding behind one of her eyes.

In March, Helen had told me that she thought her lump was getting smaller, so I'd had a feel and couldn't find it at all. Then we renewed acquaintance with Mr Duffy at her checkup on 13 April and he gave us the very good news that her lump had shrunk.

Jeff and Ros went on holiday to Arizona, in the U.S.A., in April and it was a long way from home, so I was dubious about it in case they were taken ill. When they got back, Jeff gave us a good impression of the scenery, which had fantastic-shaped hills made by the elements. He said all the shops had their own big car parking areas and nobody did any walking in the towns. His photos were marvellous. They'd been to Monument Valley, which had been on some cowboy films I'd seen, but I hadn't known its name. I'd previously tried to visualize for myself how it looked and I'd imagined the cowboys and Indians charging round, but now I could see what it was really like from Jeff's pictures.

Peter Jones used to cut Nancy's hedges and one day I asked him if he knew anybody who'd do mine because I was finding it hard work. He said, 'I'll do them for you, if you like.' So I asked him how much it would cost and he said: 'Ten pounds. Will that do?' That was okay, so he came every now and then when they needed doing and I took the cuttings away in bags to the council destructor at Sideway.

Helen had to go for an appointment at Mr Common's clinic at the Outpatients on 14 May to check out the bleeding behind her eye. We had to wait for nearly two hours and then saw Mr Kotamarthi, who told us that she'd got untreatable macular degeneration in her right eye. Jeff, who was with us, said we already knew that because we'd been told so at the clinic just over a year earlier! So we'd gone to the trouble of going there for no reason at all!

Jeff took me to the Wedgwood Visitor Centre, near Barlaston, on 31 May, but it wasn't like I expected it to be. When I'd worked at Wedgwood's in the 1950s, visitors used to come round and stand next to me, but that kind of thing wasn't happening any more. Perhaps the firm had decided to have a visitor centre because tourists were wreaking havoc and interfering with the work, but it was disappointing. The factory was pretty quiet and there weren't many people around, so it didn't seem real, but I showed Jeff roughly where I'd worked.

While we were there, I had a go at throwing, but I wasn't very successful. Throwing is getting the basic shape of the item and turning, which I'd done, is getting the surplus clay off the outside, completing the shape, making it lovely and smooth and putting extra bits and pieces on when required. I hadn't really done throwing before, but I thought I could have done the basics better, especially keeping the ball of clay in the centre of the wheel, but it was wobbling all round the place.

Helen wanted manure for our roses from the horses of one of Jeff's neighbours, Julie Tomasik, of 7 Nelson Crescent, so on 4 June I asked her if we could have some. We went with her to the field off Station Road, at the edge of the village, where the horses were kept and she supplied us with a few bags. Jeff and I loaded some manure up, but I didn't take too much because it was a strain to carry and it was harking back to the old days, really. I eventually spread it round our garden, except for one bag, which I only finally put on in 2008!

One day, I saw a full-size fibreglass red elephant across the road at Jumbo Self Storage, where Remploy had previously been. It was a mobile advertising feature, on a trailer, and, because it was so unusual, it must have attracted attention. It was an eyesore, but after a while it disappeared and I was told it had been moved to 2 Beaumont Road, in Tunstall, where the firm also had premises.

By then, Helen seemed to be ringing Jeff all the time. Perhaps she was bored and got a thrill out of it. Also, she'd always be worrying about him and it was a way in which she could check he was okay, but sometimes she'd just call him and say, 'Up the Vale!' It only really dropped off when she later lost interest in doing it.

Jeff came for Saturday lunch, as usual, on 24 July, but Ros wasn't with him. He sprung a big surprise on me by saying that she'd said she was going to leave him. I was in disbelief because I thought everything was perfect with them and it seemed an ideal marriage. It was like seeing the Twin Towers collapse – impossible! I was asking Jeff questions and wanted to know what had happened. He said, 'Nothing that I know of,' so I was left puzzling over the problem and I couldn't solve it. I then thought of the implications of what could happen and he said she might want half their house. He told me it could be worth over £200,000 and I was staggered because it meant he might have to find £100,000 or more!

My mind boggled and I wondered what he'd do if he couldn't find the money.

Jeff sounded me out regarding the finances because he hadn't got a full-time job and so the situation was very grim. I didn't fancy all the messing about in the courts he'd have to do, so I said I'd help him out.

Helen was asleep in bed at the time and it was a good job she didn't know what was going on. I didn't tell her at first because Jeff asked me not to and I needed to mull it over, but she seemed to sense it. Even before then, she'd said, 'There's something the matter here.'

On 7 August, Jeff and Ros came for lunch and Jeff brought a load of literature for Helen and me to see from Social Services, regarding what they could do for old people. I had a look at it, but it seemed vague and I couldn't see how it applied to us. Also, I thought Helen might be awkward about it and not comply with what could be offered. I wondered whether if anyone came round to see us, Helen might think that she was going to be taken away or charged a lot of money. Therefore, I put the stuff away for the time being, so I could have a think about it. Helen and I hadn't got a clue about it all.

By then, Helen wasn't helping herself, let alone doing any jobs, and I had a word with her about it on 14 August. I told her I'd do all the work, but I asked her just to try to help herself, for example by leaning over and getting her own glasses from the mantelpiece when she wanted them. She said, 'Yes, alright,' but she wasn't really interested and it didn't make any difference. I gave it up as a bad job and from then on did all the work without asking her.

After Jeff had left home in 1981, Helen had wanted to continue to give him something as a gift, so she used to get him bananas or sometimes other fruit, like strawberries or raspberries. Unfortunately, at times it wasn't what he wanted and so was an annoyance to him, even more so after he'd got married. I just went along with it, even though it was a nuisance. Helen's idea was to help Jeff and Ros out, but they'd already got things organized. So I told her to give Jeff the money instead, but she wouldn't. By this time, Helen was struggling to carry any bags, so I had to haul most of the shopping home and the fruit was an extra weight for me. Jeff told me it was unnecessary to get it any more, so, in September, I stopped doing so and it was a good thing, really.

I was talking to somebody, who said: 'You ought to have an allowance. You're looking after Helen.' So I thought I'd give it a try and spoke to Social Services as I'd become a carer, but they said I couldn't have it because I was drawing a pension.

Jeff carried on about Helen not wearing her hearing aid because he wanted to see some improvement instead of her slopping about. I think she became a bit afraid because he kept on and I'd try to get it in when he was coming. That worked for a while, but then dropped off because she was awkward about it and eventually Jeff gave up.

By then, Ros had stopped coming for Saturday lunch. There was something wrong, but I hoped there was nothing serious in it, though it looked like it. Helen asked Jeff if we'd done anything to upset Ros and he said 'No.'

On 30 October, I took some rubbish to the destructor, but I couldn't get back in the house because I hadn't got my keys. So I looked through a front window to tell Helen to open the door, but she was lying on the floor in the lounge and couldn't get up. She was struggling to pull herself up by holding onto her armchair. I asked her if she was okay and I could see her nodding. I didn't know what to do. I decided to go back to the incinerator to see if I'd dropped my keys there and I tried to tell Helen, but she couldn't hear me because she was inside and didn't have her hearing aid in.

I went to the incinerator anyway, but I didn't find the keys, so I decided to call at Stoke Police Station, in Boothen Road, to see if they could help me. Unfortunately, it was a Saturday and the police were fully stretched because Stoke were at home. I asked the policewoman to ring Jeff, but there was no answer, so I then asked her to try Alan and Shirley, to see if Ros was there and had got a key. The policewoman said, 'I'm sorry, but she's gone on holiday to Italy.' I thought it was queer that Jeff hadn't told me that and I was baffled.

Anyhow, I drifted off because I wanted to get back to see what was happening with Helen. When I got there and looked through the window, she was standing up, so I beckoned her to open the door. I think she pressed the handle down and it just opened, so it seemed as if it had been unlocked all the time! I mustn't have locked it when I went out, which was most unusual. Of course, I asked Helen if she was alright and she wasn't hurt in any way. I asked how she'd got up and she said she'd pushed herself against the chair, got the seat against her back and pushed herself up from there.

Just then, Alan and Shirley pulled up. I went down to see them and said it was alright and, of course, told them the story. At that moment, a policeman and policewoman arrived in a car, too late to come to the rescue, but I thanked them anyway. Alan and Shirley then said, 'What a pity it is that Ros and Jeff have parted, that they're not together any more.' I was so staggered that I didn't know what to say and they didn't say much either. I got the feeling they were very sad about it, but they left after we'd had a bit more conversation. My mind was in a whirl, but I was thankful that Helen was alright.

I was wondering how Jeff was going on without Ros, but, when he rang me the next day, he said he was alright. He said he hadn't mentioned what had happened because Ros had told him that she was thinking things over, so he hadn't wanted to worry Helen and me unnecessarily. I couldn't really get the whole thing into my head, although I took it pretty calmly and I'd got enough to do with Helen occupying my mind. I was very disappointed that Ros had left Jeff and I'd had it in my head that things were settled and that everything was okay. They'd seemed to have everything going for them and got on better than most people do. I hoped a miracle would happen and they'd get back together again. Of course, I missed seeing Ros because she was a nice girl and we got on really well, but my faith in human nature had been shattered.

I didn't mention the news to Helen because I didn't think she'd fully understand what was going on, but Jeff told her that Ros was staying at her mother's. Helen was upset and very worried and kept ringing Jeff all the time, to see if he was alright. The next Sunday, she was so bothered about it all that she wouldn't go to the church or the club, but in time she got used to what had happened, as I did.

By that time, I was more or less doing the shopping myself and Helen was just coming round with me, but I was having to look after her, particularly because she was walking unsteadily. So I started to dump her down on a chair in Marks & Spencer while I got on with the job, but it was a waste of time her coming, really.

Over the years, Helen had said some very unpleasant things to Jeff and I was worried that he might fall out with her because of the strain he was under, but he told me that wouldn't happen. As it turned out, she rallied round and offered to help him by doing his washing (though that turned out to be unnecessary) and told him he could spend any evening with us if he was lonely. Then, on 24 November, she rang him and said, 'I wish we could go back seventy-odd years,' but she must have meant fifty!

On 6 December, I went shopping in Hanley, but when I was coming back along Leek Road, I could see some smoke in the air. As I got nearer, I became more anxious and then realized the smoke was coming from our house! The smoke alarm was making a high-pitched sound and I was in a panic then. It was funny that none of the neighbours were out. I fumbled for my key to get in and smoke was everywhere in the kitchen, but Helen was just standing about! I looked around for what was on fire and I realized it was the stove. I switched the knob off to help put the fire out and scooped up some blazing material from the grill with a shovel. I put it outside in the yard and took out red-hot embers till I eventually cleared it all.

I then had to clean up, but the smoke and remains were everywhere and the ceiling and parts of the walls were black. If I'd come in five or ten minutes later, the house would probably have been ablaze, but Helen didn't seem to realize the seriousness of it all! I could see from the remnants of the material that she'd been quick drying a pair of knickers. I'd dried clothes around the stove myself, but on the clothesmaid, well away from the flames, and I'd always kept an eye on things. It's alright if you know what you're doing, but even that was a silly thing to have done, really.

Helen had been drying her knickers *inside* the stove, but her idea had been to put them in the grill compartment because there was no live flame there. We'd both done that before, but this time she'd made a mistake and lit the grill instead of the oven, so she'd put her underwear where the living flame was! She'd kept an eye on it for a minute or two, but then forgotten about it!

I told her, 'Don't do that again,' and I don't think she did. Every time I went out after that, I said: 'Don't put any clothes in the oven! Don't make any tea!' She must have got sick of hearing it, but I had to try my best to make sure she kept out of danger.

On my 89th birthday, we went to Jeff's and found that a package, with my name on, had come in the post from Ros. Inside were some birthday presents and a card, but on it she'd written 'Cyril' instead of 'Dad', as she'd always called me. It was like I'd been downgraded from being one of the family and I was hurt. It was saying we weren't so intimate any longer, but I suppose some time had passed since she'd left Jeff.

Jeff had started seeing Jill Evans again, but I didn't think it was quite the thing. She didn't fit in as well with him as Ros had, or as I'd imagined she had. Jill didn't seem to be compatible with Jeff, although I wasn't much in her company, and Helen thought she was too old for him. As it turned out, Jeff only went out with Jill for a year or so.

Helen's memory was deteriorating by then. At first, I noticed one or two things and then there got to be more and more. The first time I'd spotted anything odd, we'd been at Alan and Shirley's, with Jeff and Ros, and Helen said something strange that didn't fit in with the conversation. We all looked at one another and it went quiet. I felt let down, but it couldn't be helped. After the initial shock, everything went back to normal and we carried on as before.

On odd occasions, Helen came up with things that just weren't right, but it gradually became more often. She started to get mixed up with things and get them in the wrong place. At the beginning, it was just loss of memory, but it was the start of dementia.

Helping Helen was taking up increasing amounts of my time and I was finding it more and more difficult to have any time to myself. I stuck into my album two 2004 British Christmas stamps, one first class and the other second, and they were the last ones I put in there. Not only did I not have the time to do any more, but also stamps were starting to be used less as firms and Post Offices increasingly printed the postage information on the envelopes. As time went on, I found it harder to do things, so from then on when I got any new stamps, I put them away in envelopes to be done at some later point, which has never come. My collection, excluding duplicates, stands at well over 6,000 stamps, with more than 4,700 of them stuck in five albums.

I went into Age Concern's office, at 6 Albion Street, in Hanley, to see what they were all about and whether they might be of any help. While I was waiting to be served, I saw a notice about a computer course for old age pensioners and fancied having a go, so I decided to enquire about it. The assistant said it was a ten-week course, to get you interested, which was meeting once a week on a Wednesday afternoon. I said: 'I haven't got a computer. Does it make any difference?' She said she didn't think so, but that I should ask when I started after Christmas. So I said, 'Okay, I'll have a go, then,' and she put my name down.

On 18 December, I had a phone call from Jeff, who said that one of his car wheels had collapsed, which was bizarre! It had happened on an awkward bend on the A 519 at Beech. I said I'd go out to him, but he'd got things organized with a rescue truck coming, so there was no need. I lent him my car while he got his repaired because he'd have been stuck without a vehicle. There was hardly any public transport from Cotes Heath and he wouldn't have been able to get to his job in Shelton without a car.

Helen and I went to Jeff's on Christmas afternoon, but I became really unwell with sickness and diarrhoea. At the same time, Jeff had to cope with Helen's disability and her demands for our Christmas presents to be opened! She also asked him a very strange question, 'You weren't at our diamond wedding, were you?' It was all a disaster!

Over the Christmas period, I rang Dave Wallett to see how he was, but his wife, Maureen, told me he'd died on Christmas Eve. I was already getting punch-drunk with recent events and I just couldn't believe it. I don't think I really understood what his illness was about and I wasn't expecting him to go.

There was a crowd of people at Dave's funeral at Carmountside Crematorium on 4 January 2005 and they were standing up inside. I think only once before had I ever seen so many, but he'd been in the hospital service and knew quite a lot of people. Also, he'd had cancer and the news would have spread around.

Two days later, Jeff, Helen and I were at Nancy's funeral at Newcastle Crematorium, off Chatterley Close, in Bradwell. She'd died on 27 December from kidney failure, but had been ill for years, so I wasn't too surprised. I wasn't terribly upset because we hadn't seen her much for quite a while, but Helen and I went to the reception at the premises of Harold H. Leese, the funeral directors, in Stoke.

8 Slipping Away

Helen had seemed to be dropping off going to the church and club and the first Sunday of 2005, she said she wasn't going. She didn't want to bother getting ready and making a big effort. That turned out to be regular and she only ever went again on an odd occasion. It was too much of a struggle for her.

I wasn't too disappointed about the club because it seemed to be going down the drain anyway. It wasn't as enjoyable as it had been because the organist and drummer had been cut out to save money and the cassettes two or three members brought weren't the same. So the atmosphere had gone and there weren't as many people turning up. Tom and Jack had died; Sam had become ill, so he, Doris and her friend, Gertie, no longer came and Audrey, Ern and Margaret didn't seem to bother as much with Helen and me. Also, Irene Whalley, with whom I'd danced regularly after Helen had started to find it too difficult, had stopped coming. She was a good dancer and Helen had called her my 'dancing partner'. The same had happened with another woman, named Freda, with whom I used to do the quickstep, so I could no longer dance with her either. It all meant that Helen and I were more or less on our own, with hardly anybody to talk to, although we had some nodding acquaintances. It was calamitous! As people dropped off, those left huddled into shrinking little groups, with big spaces in between them, so we felt isolated.

I accepted that it was too much of a bind for Helen to keep going to the church. I had to get her ready and she had to have her hair coloured before she went. Also, it was difficult getting her there because she wasn't very good at all on her legs. I had to help her down the steps and across the road. The drivers were impatient and wanted us to hurry up, even though we were on a crossing! Then we had to go down Egerton Street, which was on an incline, and Helen couldn't put the brakes on, so it was a struggle to stop her from falling over. After that, we had to cross Victoria Road and we'd only be halfway over the crossing when the traffic was given the all clear. It was even hazardous crossing Cotesheath Street because everybody was coming to the church in cars at the same time. Then I'd have to go home and hang about, waiting for the service to finish so that I could fetch her back. She was better going up Egerton Street, but otherwise it was the same palaver as on the way there.

Each Sunday, I asked her if she was going to the church and she said 'No,' but eventually I stopped bothering. It was a relief to Helen and it saved me the trouble of putting my best clothes on just to go across there. People from the chapel could have come to get her and run her back, but perhaps that's being cheeky.

On 12 January, I wandered into Age Concern for my computer course and a fellow named John Lumsdon came out. I told him I hadn't got a computer, but he said, 'Give it a try anyhow.' He took me to the back of the room, where there was just one computer, and showed me some things to start me off. There wasn't a class – it was one to one and it was free. He was a nice fellow and called me 'Cyril', so I called him 'John'. He gave me several pieces of paper with information on and he did his best, but I couldn't practise at home, so when I went the next time, I'd forgotten what I'd learnt. Sometimes the computer had been left on where the previous person had finished and that confused me. I did the whole course, but I wasn't much more enlightened when I'd finished it than I had been when I'd started! I learned more from what Jeff wrote down for me, but I thanked John for bearing with me.

For two or three weeks, Helen hadn't felt like coming with me to do our food shopping in the town and, by the third week in January, I realized that she seemed to have stopped coming altogether. From then on, I did the shopping on my own and when I went out, I tried to impress it on her not to open the door or let anyone in the house. She'd say, 'Alright! Alright!' But I was always glad to get home because I didn't know what was happening.

I'd seen notices at the doctor's about help for carers, but I ignored them because they didn't seem real. Caring for the carers! It seemed daft, but it's quite right, really, because they need looking after as well. By then, things were getting difficult with Helen, who was unsteady on her feet and had more or less stopped going out, even though Jeff was pushing her to do so. I occasionally took her for a walk to Mawson Grove or the start of the allotments, in the other direction, but it was hard work for both of us. Also, I had to help her to get up and down the stairs, so I got in touch with Social Services and a woman came round on 24 January. She asked us what we wanted and made suggestions. There seemed to be quite a number of possibilities and I hadn't realized that there were such a variety of things that could help old people in their homes. I asked what we might get, but she didn't give much away, although Social Services turned out to be very good to us. She gave me an application form and took notes and then off she went. Jeff helped me to fill the form in and then I sent it off.

Just after Jeff had arrived for Saturday lunch on 5 February, Helen made a mess of herself by the front door. She got muck all over her and was in a state. It was just when I was ready to put Jeff's chips out, so he had to have his dinner while I cleaned her up! That was the third or fourth time she'd got caught short in a few weeks, so it seemed to be another problem developing.

Nancy's sister, Kath Bennison, died on 12 February and Helen, Jeff and I went to her funeral at Newcastle Crematorium nine days later. Afterwards, Helen and I went for buns and tea at the Hopkinson, Wootton & Lovatt funeral parlour, at 15 Chetwynd Street, in Wolstanton. I happened to be sitting next to the preacher and said it was a tragedy that the Boxing Day 2004 Indian Ocean Tsunami had happened. It had killed around 230,000 people and I asked him, 'Why should it be?'

He told me: 'It's a man-made thing. You can't blame God.'

I said: 'No. It's one of those natural disasters.' But he wouldn't have it.

Because I was caring for Helen, I'd applied to the Department for Work and Pensions for an attendance allowance for her. It was available to people over 65, who needed help because they were mentally or physically disabled. At the beginning of March, a letter arrived from the DWP, saying that she was being awarded £58.80 a week, so we were very pleased about that.

On Mother's Day, Jeff took us for a run in his car and we stopped to have a look at the new Kingsley & Froghall Station on the Churnet Valley Railway. Afterwards, we went to Jeff's and he suggested that Helen and I could go to the evening Holy Communion service at St James' Church, in Newcastle Road, Cotes Heath, which we did. We were just in time for the service and, when we opened the door, the people there were surprised to see us because they weren't expecting anybody else. I suppose they only had half a dozen in the congregation each time and so they made a fuss of us. The vicar's wife said, 'It was nice of you to come.'

I said to her, 'It's a lovely little church.'

After the service, Helen and I chatted with people and said we'd come back another time if we could (though we never did) and the vicar said, 'We'd be very pleased if you did.' Then we walked back to Jeff's house for tea and Helen just about made it.

One day, Gordon and Shirley, the Jehovah's Witnesses, called and pointed at something in their magazine. Helen said she couldn't see it because of her eyes, so they brought her a large print version. They then asked her: 'Would you like to come to our church? We'll pick you up and run you back.' She decided to go and they called for us on 24 March. The church was called the Kingdom Hall of Jehovah's Witnesses and was in Ruxley Road, Bucknall. I was surprised how modern it was. It was specially built and it had an air of prosperity about it. Everything was new and modern and there were bright lights, whereas most churches tend to be dull and depressing. The people in the congregation were also different. They were all ages and bustled about as though they'd got some purpose, whereas at Zion Church they were all old folks. Everybody was well dressed and the whole thing was organized a treat. One or two people had a word with us and then Gordon and Shirley ran us home. Helen was very pleased.

On 6 April, Social Services sent a fellow to raise the armchairs in our lounge so Helen could sit down and get up more easily. To do this, he took off the runners and screwed on an adjustable metal contraption, which he put as high as it would go. Also, he fixed handrails at the top and bottom of our stairs and another outside the front door because Helen needed as many hand grips as she could have because she was at risk of falling down.

Two days later, a different fellow fitted a short rail on each side of the bed, towards the top, to help prevent Helen from falling out. She didn't like them because they made it hard for her to get in and out of bed, so she had to get in towards the bottom and then shuffle up towards her pillow, but they did stop her from falling out.

The workman also put a bath seat in, which was pretty good, but it was a lot of trouble for Helen to use and she only used it a few times. However, it was handy for me and I used it regularly. It wasn't meant for anybody who was finding it really difficult to get about. First, I had to run the water in the bath, then put the legs in it and fix the seat on top of them. The bottom of the feet had suckers and they had to be pressed down into the bath to cause a vacuum underneath. Next, I'd swivel the seat till it was hanging over the side of the bath, then sit on it and swing it back round. Finally, I had to lower myself down into the bath by pressing an electric switch, but, because it was operated by a battery, I had to charge it every so often to make sure I didn't get stuck halfway up or down.

Also, the fellow lifted our toilet seat up and screwed down a new thicker one, several inches high, in its place. The effect of this was amazing because it made it a fairly easy job for Helen to go to the toilet on her own, so I no longer had to help her and pull her back up after she'd used it.

In April, Matthew and Jackie Poole sold their shop, which I was surprised about because I thought it was a going concern. However, Harry said that by then there were a lot more outlets for newspapers and magazines, especially supermarkets, and they were springing up everywhere. So Matthew and Jackie thought they'd better get out because there'd be nothing left, but recently I've noticed newsagents are selling different kinds of things, so all wasn't actually lost. Matthew then got a job as a delivery driver for ANC International, of Unit 6, at Leekbrook Trading Estate, in Cheadle Road, Leek. He later worked for Belle Engineering Ltd, in Sheen, near to Hartington, in the Peak District, making machinery.

After I'd been out, which by then was mainly for food shopping, Jeff kept telling me, 'Mum's rung me again, several times, wondering where you were.' He'd try to reassure her that I'd soon be back, but it seemed a long time to her because she could no longer read the clock and so lost track of time. However, there was nothing I could do about it.

On 12 May, I took Helen to Specsavers, who'd moved to 2-4 Piccadilly, to see if they could do anything about her eyes, which she was still always complaining about. It was just as well we went because the optician found that there was bleeding inside her left (good) eye and told us she needed to go to the hospital urgently. We got an appointment at the emergency eye clinic, at the Infirmary, for two days later and Jeff ran us up. The clinic was at the back of the building, miles away from the main entrance, and Helen had a real struggle to walk there, even with her stick. We went through endless corridors and I thought we'd never get there! We saw Dr Syed, who said Helen's blood pressure was very high and had probably caused the problem, which was macular degeneration in that eye as well. She also said Helen had lost a fair amount of sight in the eye since our last visit and she was booked in for further tests.

That night, we went to Dorothy's eightieth birthday party at the North Stafford Hotel and had a bit of a shuffle on the dance floor, which was about all we could manage by then. Even I'd become nowhere as near as good at dancing as I once had been.

On 25 May, Jeff took us to the Outpatients, where Helen's blood pressure was taken and it had improved. She had dye injected into her and was okay with that, but, after the results had been checked, the specialist, Mr Kotamarthi, said her eye problem was probably untreatable.

Social Services sent a workman to put up a second handrail at the side of our front steps on 3 June, which was a good idea. It gave Helen something else to hold on to and it was a big help to her. It perhaps made the difference between her standing up and falling down.

Jeff drove us to the Wolverhampton & Midland Counties Eye Infirmary, in Compton Road, Wolverhampton, on 15 June for follow-up tests on Helen's eyes. She had to have another dye injection, but when the needle was put into one of her arms, she moaned so loudly that it frightened the nurses! We didn't hear anything for a while after that, but eventually we were told that there was nothing they could do for Helen.

On Father's Day, Jeff took us to the Secret Nuclear Bunker in Hack Green, near Nantwich. It was a queer place and to get there, we had to wander around a lot of country lanes. I suppose that was the original idea, in the 1950s, to build it out of the way, so people wouldn't know it was there. The concrete bunker was for the big nobs to live in, in the event of a nuclear war, until it was safe to come out. It had different objects strewn around inside it to do with the Cold War and it was very interesting. I particularly remember sitting at the desk of an old telephone exchange and wondering how it would have felt to have been stuck there, waiting for word of what it was like outside.

Helen could no longer get to the chiropodist at Moorcroft Medical Centre to have her toenails cut, so we made an arrangement for one of them to come down from time to time to do the job. Different ones came and they also cut off the thick dead skin around her toes.

One of the social workers, Vicky Veitch, came to see us on 14 July and got Helen to climb the stairs. Vicky saw Helen struggling to get up and down and so suggested that we have a stair lift. We discussed it and Helen agreed to have one and a commode, for her to use while we were waiting for the lift to be installed. I asked Vicky if she knew anyone who'd let us have a look at their stair lift and she found a found a lady at 92 Portland Street, in Cobridge, who said we could. So, a week later, Jeff took us there and we saw the apparatus. Helen had a try on it and went halfway up the stairs before coming back down. She agreed to have one and Vicky said she'd attend to it.

The day after, a fellow came with a commode, which was a chair, with arms on and a hole in the seat. Underneath, it had a bucket with a lid that lifted up. Helen said she was going to send it back and resisted it at first, but eventually she got used to using it, probably because it was easier for her than going upstairs to the bathroom. Sometimes, she couldn't make it to the toilet in time and would make a mess over herself and the carpet, so she started using the commode regularly and it was successful most of the time.

I put it in the kitchen, so people wouldn't look through the front windows and see her using it, but when she started using it frequently, the arrangement wasn't very satisfactory because the kitchen was where I made our food and we ate some of our meals. Also, Jeff complained that it wasn't very nice having his Saturday lunch by the commode and having to put up with the smell coming from it! I then took it into the lounge and put it by the sideboard and it seemed to work more or less okay there.

Jeff had the idea of putting something to identify Helen's parents' grave in Hanley Cemetery because it was just a plain, unmarked grass plot. After some discussion with us, he got a hebe and, on 30 July, took us to the grave, where he dug a hole and put the shrub in. The earth was showing, like a proper flowerbed, but the next time Jeff went there, the shrub had gone, having been run over by a council mower!

One day, while I was shopping in Hanley, I went into Boots, the chemist's, at 3-5 Upper Market Square, with a prescription. While I was there, I saw a notice to the effect that you could give them your prescription duplicate for medicines to save you going back to the doctor's to pick up a repeat prescription for the same stuff. So I signed up to save myself a journey and Boots got my regular custom. I'd hand the duplicate in (with the original prescription) and then collect the second lot of medicine the next time I was in town.

On 20 August, Jeff brought me a computer, which Jill Evans had given him for me. He tried to tell me what to do, but I couldn't grasp it at first. I kept having a try and eventually got going a bit, so I started to type my life story from my handwritten book. It was a very laborious job and Jeff said I was going too slowly to be able to complete such a big undertaking, so it was a waste of time and I stopped after tying five pages. Jeff was thinking of getting me connected to the Internet, but the cost and the slow progress I was making put me off. Also, I was by then spending a lot of time looking after Helen, so I decided to call it a day and stopped using the computer.

As Helen's memory worsened, she got increasingly mixed up and couldn't recognize Jeff at times and wondered who he was. Other times, she thought he'd got a brother, 'the other one', and she didn't know which one of them it was standing before her. We had to explain to her that there was only one son. Then, later on, she came up with the idea that Jeff had a sister and we had to tell her that wasn't true either.

I went to the doctor's on 30 August to ask for some tablets to help reduce the pain from arthritis in my knees. I was seen by Dr Julia Billingham and, while I was there, she took my blood pressure and found something wrong. She then checked my heart and discovered it was beating a bit slowly, so she said I'd have to go to hospital to have it looked into!

When Helen dyed her hair, I used to do the roots for her. Because she'd stopped going to the church and the club, it was a waste of time and too much trouble for her to carry on, so she'd finished doing it. By then, the white roots of her hair were covering a bigger and bigger area and her hair ended up all white. For a while, it was a mixture of black and white, which was disappointing because the dye had helped her to look good, but I got used to it after a while.

We knocked off our hairdresser, Ann Cotton, who used to come, because Helen didn't want the hassle of having her hair done any more. I think it would have helped her psychologically if she'd carried on with it, but she let it go. So her hair started to grow longer and became untidy, but one day I put a rubber band around it and made it into a ponytail, to tidy it up. That made it look pretty good and I got some decorated elastic bands from Hanley Market to do the job, so that Helen's hair looked smart again and was fashionable because young women were wearing them.

On Helen's 85th birthday, Jeff took us to Dove Dale and we all had an ice cream on the car park. Then we set off for a short walk, but Helen was going so slowly that the car park attendant told Jeff to drive up to the stepping stones over the river because there were few people about, which he did. We got out and he took a couple of photos of Helen and me, but we didn't stay for long because it was chilly. We then went to Jeff's for tea, but Helen thought she was going to 'Jeffrey's son's house'! Anyway, she managed to put away four whiskies over the night and we had a nice time.

Jeff took me to Professor Sanderson's clinic at the Outpatients on 17 October. I had an ECG, which I understand found I'd got small clots in my blood and so I was told to take a baby aspirin every day. I queried it because I didn't think it would do anything to put things right, but I went along with it.

Mandy and Jon Posnett and their children returned from the Shetland Islands in October and stayed with Harry and Gill until they got a house of their own in Buxton. They'd found Shetland to be a very long way from the rest of their family and their friends and had missed them. Helen was very pleased they'd come back and it meant she could see the children again. Jon got a new job as the head teacher of Hayfield Primary School, in Hayfield, Derbyshire, and Mandy went back to her old job as a teacher at Horton Lodge Community Special School, just outside Rudyard.

Helen still liked to have Engelbert Humperdinck on the CD player and occasionally she'd get carried away with it and want to dance. She'd ask me if a song was a waltz and I'd tell her whether it was or not. When we got up, she was very poor at dancing to it and I wasn't too good either. Once we used to whirl around, but by then all we could do was shuffle about and Helen didn't like going backwards or turning around. After a minute or two, she'd get tired or fed up and want to sit down and we'd be very disappointed because we couldn't do what we wanted to.

By then, we were drinking whisky every night. Jeff didn't want us to have alcohol all the time, but it had become a habit and helped to pass the time away.

On 21 November, I had to go for a further test on my heart, this time at the Cardiology Unit at the City General. I was wired up with a mobile heart tester, which I had to keep on for 24 hours, and it was fastened on with sticking plaster! I was told to be careful with it and not to pull it off in the night. It was funny and I kept touching it. I was conscious of it during the night and kept feeling it, to make sure it was still there. I went back the next day as arranged and had the monitor taken off. I was told I'd hear about the results later.

Helen's memory continued to get worse and she started to go on about things that weren't there. It was difficult to explain to her how she'd got things mixed up because she couldn't understand what I was talking about. She had things in her mind that she thought were real and so she thought what Jeff and I were saying about them wasn't. But she'd soon forget about it and get onto the next thing. Sometimes, at night, she asked if Jeff had come in, as though he was still living here. I got frustrated because I wanted to get the front door locked up for the night and I'd say, 'He doesn't live here any more, so he won't be in.'

Jeff asked me if I'd like to go out on 15 December for a surprise in celebration of my ninetieth birthday. I said I would, but asked, 'What about Mum, though?' He said he'd fixed it up with Young Harry to have her at his house for the day, so we dropped her off and she said she'd be alright. Jeff and I landed up at Manchester Airport's Aviation Viewing Park, where a Concorde was permanently situated. It was interesting to see the planes taking off and landing, but it was bleak and very cold. There was a shop, but it was very disappointing because there was little other than model aeroplanes for sale.

We then went inside the airport, to Terminal 1 Arrivals and Departures, to have a look around, but we came face to face with two policemen, armed with sub-machine-guns! We were sitting down and they were standing a few yards away. They seemed to look at me, but I suppose I was staring at them and I felt guilty about it. It was scary at first and I wondered if one of them might accidentally pull the trigger and blast us out! I hardly dared look them in the eyes in case they took it as an insult, but anyway they walked on and all in all the trip was a nice surprise.

A fellow came on 22 December to take one of our handrails down so that our stair lift could be put in. The one he removed had been there since our house had been built and was embedded in the wall, so he had to cut it off. Until the stair lift came, Helen now only had one rail to catch hold of and it was dangerous, so I went up behind her to help. On the way down, I went in front, walking backwards so that I could see what was happening, and I held onto the rail like grim death!

Jeff was very concerned about it and could imagine Helen losing her grip halfway down, falling into me and us both crashing to the bottom of the stairs. As it turned out, we managed, but, because Helen was using the commode, she didn't need to get up and down the stairs much.

Helen's bladder problem had got worse, so I mentioned it to Mrs Shirley Holdcroft, the practice nurse at the doctor's, on 30 December and she got a health visitor to supply incontinence pads. They were very small and, after a while, started to get soaking wet. So I got large ones, but Helen complained that they were too big and uncomfortable, although I insisted on her wearing them to try to stop our mattress getting wet.

The stair lift was put in on 3 January 2006 by Stannah, a firm based in Andover, Hampshire, and it was more or less straightforward. Unfortunately, Bill Farmer had died on 17 December and was being cremated at Carmountside Crematorium the same day as the Stannah workmen came. It was almost compulsory for me to go to Bill's funeral, so Jeff ran me along and looked after Helen and saw to the workmen while I was there. I'd arranged for Jeff to pick me up after the service had finished, but I waited until everybody else had gone and I was left on my own. I was there for so long that I wondered if Jeff had had an accident, but eventually he turned up, having been bogged down with the workmen and then Helen trying the lift.

I had a look at the lift and it seemed okay. I tried it under Jeff's instructions and eventually we got it more or less right. The lift had an adjustable seat, with a footrest, on a turntable and an electric motor to convey it upstairs and down again. There was a seat belt on it, but Helen and I didn't use it much because it was too much trouble.

Unfortunately, at first Helen said she wasn't going to use the lift and, when I tried to get her to do so on her own, she couldn't grasp it, so I had to operate it for her. After a while, she got used to using it because otherwise she'd have had to have tried to walk up and down the stairs. She realized it was a lot easier and quicker during the day to use the commode instead of going up to the toilet and that made it a lot safer. I carried on walking up and down the stairs and held onto the rail with both hands. Eventually, I started to use the lift as well, but every now and again walked up and down the stairs to keep my legs going and because I didn't want to be entirely dependent on the lift.

I went to see Dr Przyslo on 5 January and he told me the tests had showed that my heart was beating irregularly, which meant that I was at risk of having blackouts. He said I should have a pacemaker fitted to get my heart to beat steadily. There was a question about whether I could drive before the operation, but, eventually, I was given the okay.

Helen's incontinence and ability to get about continued to deteriorate until she could only just get to the commode in time and eventually she couldn't always even manage that. The problem was also because of her state of mind and sometimes she'd be sitting in her chair and muck would all come out. Sometimes, she'd end up doing it on the carpet and tread it all over the place without realizing it! I'd put my feet in the muck, without knowing, and also spread it around. Then, of course, I'd have to clean it all up, off both Helen and the carpet.

I needed someone to come in to make sure Helen was alright when I went shopping twice a week because I didn't know what she was doing. She might have been wandering outside or putting the gas on. Also, she used to wave to people outside when they went past and so somebody unscrupulous could have come in. That was because of her eyesight and her mental state. So Jeff rang Hanley Health Centre and spoke to Beth Weston there. She came to see us all on 26 January and said she could arrange for someone to sit in with Helen while I was out shopping.

From time to time, letters from the council, addressed to a Ms M. Smith, were delivered to our house. They said she'd been parking illegally in different places around the city and demanded money from her. At first, I wrote on the envelopes, 'Not Known At This Address', and took them to the Parking Services office, at The Regent Centre, in Regent Road. I told them what had happened, but the letters kept coming, so I got Jeff involved. He wrote them a letter, which I signed, and took it to their office, with eighteen others I'd got from them! He explained the situation and that sorted it out.

On 15 February, Helen and I had a health visitor come to test Helen's walking in the house. As a result, five days later, she was given a Zimmer frame, made of light tubular metal. It had four legs, the rear two of them with wheels, and they all joined up in a U shape. But, because the rooms were small, Helen didn't use it much and got about by holding onto the furniture. So it stayed in the kitchen, where it got in the way, and eventually we returned it.

The day it arrived, Helen refused to use it, but then fell later when I was out shopping. When I got back, I couldn't get her up and had to ask for help from a young fellow who was passing by. I thought I'd better get her to hospital to check she was okay, so I put a note in the window for Jeff because he was coming later for his tea. Helen was examined by a doctor, who said she was okay apart from a bruise, but when we got back home, hours later, Jeff turned up, worried to death. He'd been to the Infirmary, but couldn't find us there and was told we'd gone, so he'd been driving round not knowing if Helen was okay.

Jeff told me that Helen had been ringing someone else in his village with a similar number, instead of him, by mistake. The woman receiving the calls, Victoria, had somehow connected it with Jeff, who told Helen to call him through the direct dial button on our phone. But she still kept ringing the other number, which must have been annoying for the woman. It could well have been that Helen couldn't see the numbers on the phone properly because of her eyes and it carried on for some time until it eventually dropped off.

On 23 March, Jeff ran me up to the City General Cardiology Unit for my pacemaker operation, which was done under local anaesthetic. I went into the operating theatre and lay on a table, where, I think, they gave me the injection. I was awake the whole time and was aware they were messing about with me, but, of course, I couldn't feel what they were doing. I was told to keep still because I'd moved, so I did. Perhaps twenty minutes later, they asked me to get up because they'd finished! My wound was covered up with a pad and I got dressed and was then discharged. There was nothing to it and no pain unless I touched the wounded area. I've never felt any different since and it's as though it never happened, except that I've got a little implant with a battery under the skin of my chest. The only thing I'm concerned about is leaning on something and disturbing it.

Helen fell down in the lounge on 10 April. She'd got her trousers down, having tried to use the commode, and had probably tripped over them. I couldn't get her up, so I went round to Paul Jones, who was living at number 331, and got him to help me with her. We did the job and Helen was none the worse for wear.

On 20 April, we had a visit from Veronica Tinsley, of Crossroads, a care company, based in The Dudson Centre, in Hope Street, who set up an arrangement for one of their staff to sit in with Helen while I was out food shopping on Tuesdays and Fridays. The sitters started coming on the 25th and that was a big help because it made sure that Helen didn't get into any trouble, although she didn't like it at first.

I had to fill in a questionnaire for the DVLA about my pacemaker operation, so that they could decide if I was fit to carry on driving. Fortunately, on 29 April, they sent me a letter saying that they were satisfied with the standard of my fitness, so that I could continue to drive as normal.

When I went shopping, I only had two hours to get to Hanley on a bus, do it all and get back before the sitter with Helen had to go. I also had to get Helen ready before I went out, which threw me out, so I was late getting back practically every time.

Helen's memory was deteriorating even more and she often didn't know who Jeff was. When he came to have lunch with us on 6 May, she said to him, 'I thought Jeff was coming,' and on 3 June, she rang him and said: 'Hello Jeff. Is it possible to give me Jeffrey's number?' Then, on the 19th, she phoned him and asked, 'Is Jeffrey at home?'

She also started bringing up different names from the family, especially Leah, her sister, and Elijah, her brother, and asking where they were. When I told her they were dead, she went quiet, but I don't know whether she took it in or not.

Jeff took us to the Outpatients on 23 June for Helen's breast checkup with Mr Duffy. He told us that she'd got a small lump remaining, which was either the cancer or scar tissue, but that it was under control and we were very happy with that.

On 5 July, Jeff made enquiries with Social Services about Helen going to a day centre. She was just sitting in the house most of the time and wasn't having much of a life, so we wanted to get her out and doing something again. Of course, that would benefit me by giving me chance to do some of the necessary jobs and have a bit of time on my own.

Jeff made an arrangement for the two of us to visit the day centre at St. Judes, a sheltered housing block in Seaford Street, Shelton, on 10 July, which we did. It was a modern place and looked nice. When we opened the door and went into the lounge, all the old women inside looked and gasped. One of them said, 'Ooh, a man!' and they thought they were going to have a field day with me. I suppose they thought I'd liven things up if I joined and they might get friendly. In these places, the inmates were mainly women because they outlived the men. There was only one man there and he didn't seem too well. Anyway, Jeff and I had a look around and asked the staff some questions. Then we thanked them and came away to discuss it all. We decided it would be a good place for Helen to go, so Jeff got her put on the waiting list.

Helen had a book by Richard Morris about Guy Gibson, who'd been the leader of the Dam Busters, in the Second World War, and became a national hero. Some years before, she'd been obsessed with it and kept reading it. It was about his life and every so often she'd tell me about him being a womanizer. Now she became convinced she was part of his life and was his wife or mistress, but, after a while, it dropped off and she went onto something else.

By that time, Jeff had accepted that Ros had gone for good and he didn't want her to have his money and possessions if he died. So he made a will on 13 August, which left all his belongings to Helen and me jointly and he appointed me as the executor.

Jeff was asking me about the layout of the area around Windermere Street when I was young, for the first chapter of my book. Where the streets were in my mind didn't seem to be the same as on the modern maps, so, on 26 August, he took me there to have a look. It was all confusing. Things had altered and Windermere Street and Derwent Street had become no through roads, so the area wasn't like the picture I had in my mind of when I was a lad. We weren't entirely satisfied with what we saw, but it was very interesting to go back again.

Jeff got in touch with *The Sentinel* to get some interest in my book and a photographer, Alex Severn, came down on 29 August. He took pictures of Jeff and me by the allotments opposite Mawson Grove, with us walking towards him, trying to smile as we went along. I then had a phone call from Iain Robinson, one of the newspaper's journalists, who asked me questions about my book. I answered them to the best of my ability and the day after, there was a story in the paper, with a colour photo of Jeff and me walking along together. How Iain put it was quite interesting and the story was better than I'd imagined it would be.

After that, several people came up to me when I was out and said: 'I saw your photo in the paper. I'll have a copy of the book when it comes out.' There seemed to be an interest and it was very good advance publicity.

One particular stallholder in Hanley Market, where I used to go pretty regularly for cheese, said: 'It's a good picture of you. What's it all about?' I explained and she said: 'I'll have one. Let me know when it's ready.'

I also came face to face with one or two strangers, who said: 'Ooh! Was that you in the paper? I thought I recognized you. I'll tell my sister [or whoever] I've met you.' It was a nice feeling that people recognized me. Marvellous!

On 6 September, Helen had an eye checkup appointment at the Outpatients and Jeff took us along. We saw Mr Anwer and the news was better than expected because he said that the leakage in her right eye had stopped and her eyes hadn't deteriorated since her last visit.

A week later, there was a knock at the door and Helen said a child she knew was outside. I looked through the window and saw a woman, three teenagers (one of them a youth) and a girl standing there, so I opened the door. They all crowded into the doorway and made such a fuss of me. It was as though I was a long-lost relative. The woman said: 'We've brought little so and so [the girl] to see you. You remember her, don't you? She's from Joiner's Square, across the road.' All the time, they were moving forwards and pushing me back in the house. In less than no time, they were inside and sat down and made themselves comfortable. I was confused because they were all very pleasant. Helen didn't say anything, but I suppose she couldn't hear what was going on.

All the time, they were talking and one of them asked, 'Can little so and so go the toilet?'

I said, 'Yes,' so the woman and child went upstairs. By that point, I had become suspicious, so I followed them, but by the time I got to the top of the stairs, they were coming out of the back bedroom. They wouldn't have had time to have taken anything and I escorted them back down. I was in front of them coming down the stairs, which was risky, but they were female and I didn't have much time to think.

When we got back to the lounge, the youth wanted to go to the toilet, which wasn't very good, but I felt I couldn't very well refuse because it was all very pleasant and almost like they were friends. The woman then said: 'Who plays the piano? Are you going to give us a tune?' She was keeping the conversation going while the youth was on his way upstairs, but I was still very suspicious, so I made excuses not to play the piano and went up behind him. He was quicker than me and also went into the back bedroom.

I asked him, 'What're you doing in there?'

He said, 'I missed the bathroom.'

But I said: 'The door was open. You've just gone past it. You could tell it was the bathroom!' Of course, he passed it off and I got him to come back downstairs. Again, I was in the lead and I was worried in case he pushed me down, but he didn't.

They were all laughing and joking and wanting me to give them a tune, but, to get them out, I mentioned that Jeff was coming. That seemed to put them off and they said, almost in unison, 'We'll get off now.'

The woman said, 'I'll see you tomorrow,' and she and the girls kissed me on the cheek as if I knew them.

Then off they went and I said to Helen, 'We won't see them again.' I tried to think who they were, but, of course, it was all a tale and it was very convincing.

Two days later, I heard a noise by the front door, so I got up and saw one of the teenage girls outside the window. The woman and four girls were dodging about, but the youth wasn't with them. I thought I'd scoot them off and opened the door, but they crowded in the doorway again and tried to push their way in. However, I held them back and managed to keep them out. Once more, they were nice and friendly and chatting to me. One of the girls asked, 'Would you like some sex?'

I said, 'No.'

But she said, 'We can get you some Viagra if you want, to get you going.'

They must have thought that, as an old fellow, I'd need a bit of a push, but I said 'No' to that as well. I still had it in mind that they were friends of somebody I knew across the road, but I shut the door and off they went towards Lichfield Street.

I mulled it all over in my head and thought I'd ring the police, so I got on the phone and dialled 999. I told the policeman what had happened and gave a description of the woman and the girls, although I didn't think there was much to it all or anything criminal about it. A few minutes later, the phone went and a policeman said, 'We've got 'em!'

I thought, 'Flipping heck, that's really efficient!'

They'd been spotted by the camera on the island at the bottom of Lichfield Street and Detective Constable Shaun Beardmore, from Hanley CID, then came to ask me for a statement, so I told him the tale and he wrote it down. He turned out to be the son of Nigel Beardmore, an old friend of Jeff!

It seemed unfair to charge the woman and the girls because they hadn't hurt me and I couldn't really see what they'd done wrong. I just wanted the police to give them a talking to, but I was pretty naïve, I suppose, and I wouldn't have stood a chance if there'd been any trouble. Anyway, the police charged them with attempted burglary, although they all denied it. The police said the family were suspected of another burglary attempt along the road and were well known to them.

Helen fell over in the lounge on her 86th birthday, after our regular sitter, Linda Ford, had gone and before I'd returned from shopping. I tried to pick her up, but I couldn't manage it, so I rang 999 and two paramedics came. Not only did they get her up, but they checked her over medically. They were the best people to deal with the situation, so a time or two after that, when she fell, I sent for them.

Because Helen was being left on her own for a while before I returned from Hanley, Linda suggested that she do the shopping and I could stop in. I thought that might be better, even though I'd lose my freedom, so we did that from then on. There was an advantage for her because she had a car, so she could do all the shopping in an hour and then get off home. I wanted her to go to two or three different shops, but she wasn't willing to do that and just went to Marks & Spencer.

The police said they wanted to do an ID of the family who'd been in the house, but I was told, 'It's different now than it used to be.' They used to get people off the street to line up with the suspects and have the witnesses try to pick the culprits out, but by this time they'd got a little video screen, which they put a series of pictures on. Detective Inspector Jim Wood came to see me on 6 October with one of these devices, on which he put front- and side-view photos of the suspects and other people. He asked me to look through these and pick out the identification letter of anyone I thought was a suspect. The only one I spotted was the woman, Bridget Purcell, although I didn't know her name then. I couldn't tell the girls and I still couldn't pick them out when I had another try.

Social Services told me that a place had come up at Abbots House Day Centre, at 103 Abbots Road, in Abbey Hulton, if Helen wanted it, and they arranged for us to have a visit there for about two hours on 11 October. I was expecting a lot of trouble, with her saying something to upset things or flatly refusing to go, so I asked to go with her. They said she could have a meal there, to test it out, but they wouldn't let me have one.

A blue minibus picked us up and took us there. The centre was modern and there were a few old folks sitting around and one or two attendants dodging about. There was a television on, but nobody was watching it. The staff found us seats amongst the old people and brought us a drink of tea. Then they brought a list of things Helen could have in her meal and she made her choice. She ate it all, more or less, but she didn't say whether she'd enjoyed it. When it was time to go home, the minibus brought us back.

The centre was alright, but it wouldn't have suited me because I'd have had to hang around with a lot of old folks and I'm not much of a conversationalist. I don't think it suited Helen much either, because she'd have liked a lot of lively chatter and that couldn't be expected with old people. But it seemed right for her to go because it would get her out of the house and give me a break. So we arranged for her to go on Mondays and Thursdays and later Wednesdays were added on.

Helen started at the centre on 23 October and each time I had to get her out of bed, put her some clean clothes on and get her ready to be picked up by the minibus about ten o'clock. It was quite a lot of bother because sometimes she'd wet the bed and often didn't want to get up to go. She'd say: 'I'm not going there today. I don't like it,' but most of the time, I managed to get her ready and off. Once or twice, she refused to go and I had to explain to the driver and his assistant what was happening, but they pulled their faces and I got the impression they didn't like it. She got dropped back off about four o'clock and it was quite a relief for me that she was out of the house for a while. I could please myself what I did and sometimes I dozed off a bit, but mainly I did some shopping or other jobs. It all carried on for quite a while and it got her out whether she liked it or not, so it was good for her.

One day, the driver and his assistant started laughing at Helen and said, 'She's got her shoes on the wrong feet,' which was embarrassing. I had to watch that didn't happen again and so usually I helped her on with them.

By then, Helen's memory was so bad that sometimes she didn't know where she was when she was at home. Once, she told Jeff that she was visiting the house and didn't live here. Because Jeff and I were getting so concerned, we had a psychiatrist from Bucknall Hospital, Dr Fernando, come to see her on 1 November and he tested her for dementia by asking her a number of questions. She knew the name of the queen and wrote, 'Once upon a time, there was a boy,' when the doctor asked her to write a sentence, but she couldn't take away seven from a hundred and didn't know the prime minister's name. Anyway, Dr Fernando decided to send her to hospital for more tests.

Helen's incontinence had become worse still, so I started putting cardboard and pieces of newspaper under the bottom sheet of the bed to try to keep it dry. That more or less worked, but sometimes the urine went right through.

The phone rang on 20 November and Helen answered the call. After a while, she put the receiver down and said, 'No answer!' I then checked who it had been and realized it was Jeff, so I rang him. He said he'd spoken to her three times, but she obviously hadn't detected any sound!

Helen and I went to Jeff's on my 91st birthday and he introduced us to his new girlfriend, Sue Bell, who lived in Walsall, at 36 Princes Avenue, and was a principal trading standards officer with Walsall Metropolitan Borough Council. It was a shock because she'd taken Ros's place, but we got on very well together. Sue seemed to be sensible and had a responsible job, so I was pleased Jeff had met her.

Sue came to our Christmas party at Jeff's as well and did us all a very nice trifle. He seemed to get on very well with her, but it was a long way for them to travel to see each other, so I didn't think it would last very long.

On 30 December, Jeff came for lunch, but Helen thought he was still a schoolboy! Also, it was on the television that Saddam Hussein had been executed in Iraq that day for 'crimes against humanity' and Helen kept saying, 'Poor old Adam,' which really made us laugh!

By then, Helen's bladder weakness had got to the point where practically every morning the sheet on top of our bed and Helen's nightclothes were soaking wet, so that I had to wash them. It became quite a day when I didn't have to wash things from the bed!

I went to get my car from the garage on 13 January 2007, but found a double mattress across the entry and it was absolutely soaking wet, so it was a ton weight. I couldn't possibly have moved it, but Jeff was with me and he was able to shift it a fraction. I then managed to get the car out, with some manoeuvring, but I still had to run over the corner of it to get through. I phoned the council to see if they could come and get rid of it and the woman I spoke to said, 'Okay, we'll attend to it,' but nothing happened. After a week or two, I rang again, but it was another couple of weeks before they finally removed it.

I had to take Helen to the Department of Old Age Psychiatry at the City General on 6 February for tests to see if she'd got dementia. Dr Ibrahim and a nurse asked her quite a number of questions. Helen knew the day was Tuesday, but she didn't know what month it was and said she thought the year was '1960 something'! When they'd finished, the doctor told us he thought she'd got two types of dementia and said he was surprised we hadn't been to see him earlier. He then arranged for her to have a brain scan, which she did on 12 March.

I had notification from the police that I might be needed to go to Stoke-on-Trent Crown Court, in Bethesda Street, to give evidence against Bridget Purcell in her trial, which was set for 12 February. In the end, though, I didn't have to go because she pleaded guilty to burglary with intent to steal from Helen and me.

Jeff had suggested that Helen and I should have central heating put in because he felt that the house wasn't warm enough for us, but I didn't think the council would accept doing it free, so I thought it would cost thousands of pounds. That put me off and so did the likely hassle of workmen coming in when I was trying to get Helen out of bed, washed and dressed. Eventually, I accepted it needed to be done, but, to my amazement, the council said they'd grant us the total cost of the job, with no payment from us. So I thought we might as well have it done and managed to persuade Helen to go along with it, although I didn't realize the mess and disruption it would cause around the house.

The engineers from Heatex Group Ltd, of Crown Road, in Festival Trade Park, Etruria, came on 13 February and it took them two days to do the job. I'd arranged for Helen to go to the day centre each day, but the workmen were around while I was trying to get her ready and when she was on the toilet. There was a lot of confusion, with workmen coming in and going out and they had to move the furniture and get the floorboards up. When they shifted the wardrobe in the front bedroom, they found a set of Helen's false teeth underneath! They also had to knock holes in the walls to put pipes through, but eventually they got it all done.

The gas boiler was put in our boxroom and we had a radiator in each room, except for the library, pantry and boxroom. We were allowed five radiators by the council, but Jeff suggested we pay for another one, in the back bedroom, and I agreed with him. It cost £190 cash as a foreigner and one of the fellows said, 'If there's any problem with this one, don't complain to the firm.' He gave me his phone number, but I should think they were extra careful with it, so it wouldn't be likely to break down.

I didn't properly understand the controls and had to fiddle about with them. At first, I got the heating so hot that I had to have a window open to cool the house down, which was a laugh, but eventually I got the hang of it all. It was a big improvement because we could have it on round the house, so it was comparatively warm wherever we went. It was cleaner and less hassle than our open gas fire and was a lot better for Helen because there was no living flame she could get burnt on. So, unless it went really cold, I didn't bother with the fire and just had the central heating on, but we'd always got the fire to fall back on if anything went wrong.

About the beginning of March, I got a nagging pain on the left side of my back, which became murder until I started taking codeine, but it didn't really stop me doing things. So I continued to look after Helen, although Jeff did our food shopping for me. However, the pain didn't go away and at times was killing me, so I rang for Dr Przyslo and he told me to go to Bucknall Hospital for an X-ray. Jeff took me there on the 13th and I found it to be an old place, with dark rooms, which seemed like out of another world. Anyway, I had the X-ray done and was told to contact my doctor for the results, which I did. Dr Liene Bluzma came down from the surgery on the 28th and said I'd broken a rib. She asked, 'Have you fallen down at all?'

I said, 'I can't remember doing anything out of the ordinary,' and asked her what could be done about it.

She said: 'There's nothing you can do. It'll heal up on its own.' She was right because it slowly got better and the pain eased off. It was marvellous how it just improved like that!

Owing to my back trouble, I hadn't been able to drive my car, but by 31 March I felt well enough to take it out again. I asked Jeff to come with me in case I had any problem with my back, so he did. I took us on a run through Endon to Leek and back via Werrington. It was going alright, so I must have got carried away and put my foot down a bit as we went through Stockton Brook, but Jeff said: 'Hold on, Dad! You're going too fast. It's thirty miles an hour here!' I took my foot off the accelerator and slowed down, but then I started going too fast again, so Jeff told me off once more! Anyhow, I more or less settled down after that and it was nice to have got back to normal on the road.

On 4 April, Graeme Brown, one of the *Sentinel* reporters, rang Jeff and told him that Bridget Purcell had been given two years in prison, by Stoke-on-Trent Crown Court, for burglary, with the intention of stealing from my house. Graeme asked Jeff for a comment, so he said he thought it was shocking that she'd picked on old people and that Helen and I should have been given compensation. I thought the sentence was harsh for what the woman had done, but *The Sentinel* reported that the judge, Granville Styler, had said she'd been trying to 'prey on elderly people'.

The same day, Jeff bought a marvellous new car, a 2002 gold Chrysler PT Cruiser, for £6,300, from a private seller, Jeff Davies, of 33 Finchdean Close, in Meir Park. It had an unusual shape and didn't look like a modern car. It was lovely to look at and very comfortable inside, so it was a real bargain.

While I was having trouble with my back, Jeff had suggested that I contact Social Services for help, especially as Helen was continuing to deteriorate, which was making more work for me. By then, she could hardly get in and out of bed, so I got in touch with them and they arranged for St. Andrews Care Services, of Lymedale Business Park, in Newcastle, to set up a package of help. It involved sending a home helper every day from 4 May to assist Helen to wash and dress and to put the bed sheets in the washing machine and hang them out on the line to dry.

On 1 May, Jeff ran me up to the Harley Street surgery, so that Dr Przyslo could examine my rib and knees. He said I was 'doing exceptionally well' for my age and told me to carry on having exercise to 'keep moving'. When Jeff and I came out, we had a walk around the block and I was okay, so we decided to carry on, to see if I could get to Hanley Post Office, in Tontine Street, to get some cash. I did very well, except for the last hundred yards when Jeff gave me a bit of assistance. Then he got the car and ran me back home. It was essential that I tested my legs out and gave it a go because I hadn't been out walking for a while because of my back.

I'd become rusty walking and found I was getting a bit dodgy on my feet. I had to be careful in case I toppled over, so I thought I'd better start trying to walk with a stick. I tried one of those Nancy had given to Helen, although I felt embarrassed I'd deteriorated so much that I had to use a stick, but it was like an extra leg and gave me greater stability. I was pleased because nobody made any sarcastic remarks, so that increased my confidence. I then carried on using it, so I'd turned a corner.

On 5 May, Jeff told me that Ros had asked him for a divorce. That was worrying, but I wasn't surprised because it was over 2½ years since she'd left him.

Six days later, Jeff took Helen and me to the Memory Clinic at the City General for the results of her brain scan. She was asked more questions to test her memory, but she still didn't know what month it was, although she knew where she was and the names of the city, the county and the country. Despite that, Dr Ibrahim said the scan had indicated that she was suffering from vascular dementia, caused by a series of minor strokes, which didn't mean a lot to me. He told us there was no treatment he could give and that it was likely to get worse, but he recommended that she take aspirin to try to prevent any more minor strokes. I wasn't really aware of the implications, but at least she was still with us.

Jeff was keen to get Helen a digital hearing aid because he thought it would help her to hear what was going on. Alan Downs had had one and he'd said it was much better than his ordinary one. So Dr Przyslo fixed Helen up with a hospital appointment for 18 May. When we got there, they discovered that she'd got wax, which was cleared out, but nothing was done about the hearing aid, so Jeff rang Dr Przyslo to try to get it moving.

From time to time, Jeff cut Helen's fingernails, but it was a hard job because she kept moving about and complaining that he was cutting her flesh. The nails were getting in a state because they were filthy and it became a regular task to clean them up.

About 24 May, a fellow knocked on the front door. I opened it and he wanted to come in to use the phone, but I said: 'No. There's one along the road.' He didn't like that and was complaining as he went off, but I thought he was a con man. Jeff got me the number of the Staffordshire Police Crime Prevention Unit, so I rang them and, on 4 June, a fellow came to fit a chain to the door. I was suspicious because the police hadn't given me any notification that anybody was calling, so I asked him, 'Who's paying for this?'

He said, 'The police.'

It operated through a flat piece of metal in the middle of a chain of links. When turned on its side, the metal piece slotted into a gap on the fitting on the door. So when I opened the door, the chain couldn't be undone. With the chain on, the door could only be opened a few inches, which meant I could talk to people, but they couldn't get in. It was very good, but I think it should have given a bigger gap to talk through.

In the early hours of 8 June, Helen slid out of the bed and I tried to get her back in, but it was hopeless because I hadn't got the strength to do it. She was lying awkwardly and I didn't know what to do, so I thought I'd ask the fellow next door, Peter Wood, to help. He'd bought the house after Nancy had died and he seemed pretty friendly. I put my dressing gown on, over my pyjamas, and knocked on his door. He got out of bed and I explained what had happened. He said: 'Hold on. I'll be round just now.' He put his trousers and shirt on and came round. I led him up to the front bedroom and he said: 'Leave it to me. I know what to do.' He got round the back of Helen, put his arms under her armpits and lifted her onto the edge of the bed. He must have been pretty strong to have done that, but she was precarious there and we pushed her back into bed between us. Helen didn't respond much and acted as though it was just part of life! I thanked Peter and then off he went.

One day, I went into Lloyds Pharmacy, at 29 Derby Street, just across from the doctor's, with a prescription. It was a one-off job because I didn't fancy walking up to Boots. When I handed it in, the assistant said: 'There's a queue waiting for medicines to be dispensed. Do you want to have it delivered?'

I said, 'Ooh, ah!'

They duly delivered it and thereafter all I had to do was pick up the phone and tell them what I wanted and it saved all the hassle. It's never cost me anything because I'm over 65 and the only snag is that I have to make sure I'm in because they won't bring medicines a second time.

I'd given Jeff £1,000 towards his new car and accidentally went £129.29 overdrawn on my current account with Alliance & Leicester because I wasn't used to taking such a large amount of money out. So it came as a surprise when I got a statement saying I owed them £75 as a penalty. I just couldn't make it out and mentioned it to Jeff. He got in touch with them and protested that it was outrageous because I hadn't been overdrawn in the whole of the thirty years or so I'd been with them. But they stuck to it, so Jeff knocked up a letter for me, threatening to close my account if they didn't cancel the charge, which I signed and he posted on 13 July. They still didn't refund me the money, so I closed the account and transferred my funds to The Co-operative Bank. If the charge had been reduced to £10 or £20, we'd have got back to normal, so Alliance & Leicester lost my business because they were heavy about it. That was surprising because, at the time, there was a controversy about banks overcharging their customers, which was all in the newspapers and there was an ongoing inquiry into it.

Helen was wetting the bed so much and so often that it became nearly impossible to get the mattress dry. So I got a big, waterproof, plastic sheet, like a bag, from Wardles Hearing and Care Centre, at 51 Upper Huntbach Street, and put the mattress inside it. The sheet was quite useful in helping to keep the mattress dry.

At night, Helen used to put her false teeth into a bowl to soak, but by this time, she'd got into the habit of taking them out and just putting them on the hearth whenever she felt like, without even a handkerchief underneath. Jeff and I kept telling her not to do it, but she just carried on and they kept getting dirty. Eventually, she didn't bother to put her teeth in her mouth at all because she could eat without them.

Around that time, Helen started occasionally to wander around in the house with her trousers and knickers down. I was surprised and upset that it had come to that, but it couldn't be helped. I think it happened because she decided she wanted to go to the toilet and then forgot about it or had used it, but then forgot to pull her clothes back up afterwards. It was dangerous because there was a risk she'd fall over, so I pulled her trousers and knickers back up when I saw her with them down.

Helen kept coming up with more things that weren't right and sometimes she didn't know who I was. On other occasions, she thought Jeff was dead, so when he came to visit, she was really excited to see him! Then she started shouting upstairs to see who was there, but it was all part of her illness and I took no notice of it.

The Memory Clinic at the City General had given Jeff and me a booklet on what to do next because of the state of Helen's mental health. Jeff suggested we go to see a solicitor to fix up enduring power of attorney. I was very vague as to what it meant, but I gathered later that it was giving us the power to deal with Helen's affairs if she got in such a state that she couldn't manage them. So, on 7 August, Jeff and I went to Woolliscrofts, at 6-10 Broad Street, to see Ray Basnett because he was Jeff's solicitor. Ray said he thought we should go for joint power, so that we could both deal with her affairs. He also suggested that, while we were at it, I should give Jeff the power to take over my affairs if anything happened to me. The advantage was that that would save him the time and trouble of contacting a solicitor again if I ended up like Helen, so I thought it was a good idea.

Helen made a real bloomer on 11 August by putting my walking stick on top of the stove when it was still on! After a while, the stick began to smoulder and I just happened to wander into the kitchen and saw smoke coming off it. I quickly pulled it away, turned the stove off and put the stick under the cold water tap. It was okay, except for a black mark, which had been left on it. If I hadn't been in, it might have had the house afire, but there wasn't much I could have said to Helen because by then she wouldn't have understood how dangerous it was.

Three days later, Jeff and I went back to Ray Basnett's office and signed the forms. Then we came home and got Helen to put her signature on the appropriate document as well. When Jeff looked at the papers again, he said: 'There's something wrong here. We've signed in the wrong places.' So I'd finished up having future power over his affairs instead of him over mine! We had to go back up to the solicitor's and he apologized for putting the forms in the wrong order and we had them altered. It all cost me £65 plus VAT, but we put the papers away and didn't take it any further.

Jeff said he thought I should get my book up to date with more stories because nearly seventeen years had passed since I'd finished writing it. He was right, but I found that I didn't have the inclination to do it because I was having to spend so much of my time looking after Helen, which was very tiring. So I asked him if I could tell him the stories and he could write them down, which is what we agreed to do. We started on 18 August and carried on doing so right up to date.

The minibus driver and his assistant from the day centre complained that it was dangerous getting Helen down and back up our front steps, so I told Social Services. They took a note of it and, some time later, we were informed that Stannah were coming to fit a step lift, which they did on 1 September and it was pretty straightforward. It was okay, but at first Helen said she wasn't going to use it. The day centre staff weren't very pleased about that because it would be a lot safer and save them struggling up and down the steps with her. They then kidded her up as to how nice it was, so she couldn't do much else except get in it.

It was similar to the stair lift, but it was protected against the weather by a cover that kept the rain off it. I had to learn how to operate it myself because of times I'd need to get Helen down and back up the steps. So I kept fiddling about with it, but pressing the wrong buttons because it was new to me. Eventually, though, I mastered it, except for one occasion when I sent for an engineer. That time, I couldn't get it going, but I was doing the wrong thing. The engineer came from Birmingham and just turned a switch on and it started up okay! A day or two later, I got a letter from Stannah, charging me seventy or eighty pounds because it was my own fault. I mentioned it to the council and they fixed it up so that Helen and I didn't have to pay!

Jeff took Helen and me to the Outpatients, on 11 September, for her six-monthly breast cancer checkup. Mr Duffy examined her and told us that the lump was the same size as before and so the medication was still working okay. We said, 'We'll see you in another six months, then.'

But he replied: 'Oh, no. I'm retiring in the new year.'

We all said how sorry we were that we wouldn't be seeing him again and we thanked him for all the good work he'd done. He was a real charmer and Helen had always adored him.

When Jeff came for lunch on 15 September, Helen thought there were two Jeffreys, one being her son and the other being Jeff! Then, for a bit of fun, he shouted to her from the kitchen: 'Come on then. Let's go the Vale.' She obviously thought he was serious because the next minute she'd gone out of the front door, with her walking stick, and Jeff had to get her back in!

We went to Jeff's for tea on Helen's 87th birthday. Sue was there and had made Helen a chocolate birthday cake, with seven candles, which she blew out. We enjoyed ourselves and Helen had a number of whiskies! The only snag was that I'd taken my cine projector to show some old films, but I found out that I hadn't got a bulb and so we didn't see anything.

On 10 October, the driver from the day centre told me that Helen kept pulling her trousers and knickers down, but, of course, there was nothing that I could do about it. He also asked if he could bring her back earlier because she was getting restless after a while. I couldn't really refuse, although it cut down my time to do the jobs.

On 3 November, Jeff told me that Ros had said she wanted the money from half the house. I was staggered to think that he might have to sell his home to be able to pay up and on top have all the hassle of finding another place.

From time to time, Jeff gave me a lift to my garage to get my car, particularly if he'd been for lunch on a Saturday and was going that way to watch Vale. On 17

November, he was still at our house when I returned from a run and he drove to my garage so that he could bring me back after I'd put my car in. He was amazed to see I still reversed in successfully and said it would even be a very tight manoeuvre for him!

At long last, on 13 December, I took Helen to the Outpatients for an appointment for her to have a test for a digital hearing aid. She didn't get it then, but a mould was taken of her right ear so that one could be specially made for her and we were told it would be much better than the one she had.

Jeff bought me a three-CD box set for my 92nd birthday. It was called *Hits from the Blitz: Songs from the War Years 1939-1946* and had come out in 2005. It had all kinds of different singers on it and I put it on quite a bit. One song I liked from it was *Mairzy Doats*, by the Pied Pipers, which had been written in 1943 and had trickery in the words. That's what made it because there wasn't much of a song, really.

Most of my other favourite songs on the CDs were sung by Vera Lynn, including *A Nightingale Sang in Berkeley Square*, which she'd recorded in 1940. It had a nice tune and I associated it with the war. *White Cliffs of Dover*, which came out in 1942, was very nice too and looked forward to the end of the war when good times would come. There was also her version of *Lili Marlene*, which was a German song that had been heard by British soldiers on their radios in North Africa from 1941 and had been taken up by them. It was a sentimental story about a soldier having to leave his sweetheart behind and go to war.

Helen and I were at the hospital again on 21 December for a checkup on her eyes. This time, she couldn't read the chart at all, not even the big top letter. The doctor put some drops in her eyes and tested her again, but she did no better. So he said: 'It's too late now. There's nothing we can do.' It seemed that what she could see from her good eye was by then no better than from her other one, but we were told it wouldn't be likely to get any worse.

Jeff went with Sue, to meet her father, Roger, for the first time, on the Sunday before Christmas, but they found him lying on the floor of his bedroom in his house, 34 Burnaston Road, in Hall Green, Birmingham. He'd had a stroke and Sue was informed that there wasn't anything that could be done for him. She had to be with him at Selly Oak Hospital, in Raddlebarn Road, Birmingham, so she wasn't able to come to our family party at Jeff's house on Christmas Day.

Helen was increasingly wetting herself on her chair in the lounge and so I started to put a plastic bag on the seat, with *Sentinels* on top to soak up the urine. I had to do this once or twice a day and it stopped the chair cushion getting wet.

Sue's dad died on 13 January 2008 and she started to get rid of his belongings, so Jeff brought me a new cardigan, which I had, and a couple of pairs of his shoes. They were good ones and practically new. Jeff told me they were size 8½, but, because I usually take nines, I expected that they'd be too small. Anyhow, I thought I'd try them and, as it turned out, they were a very good fit. I decided to use them for best, but I haven't been out to any smart places since, so they haven't had much wear and it's unlikely I'll ever buy any more shoes.

I took Helen to the Outpatients on 15 January, so that she could have her new digital hearing aid fitted. Jeff tested her hearing with it when we got back home and thought there was a big improvement, but I didn't think it made much difference, although that may have been because I was getting no cooperation from her. She'd get fed up of replying when I was checking what she could hear and would stop answering. She'd given up by then, really, and she kept pulling the hearing aid out, just like she'd done with her old one.

On 25 January, I found the washing-up liquid top on the windowsill and I asked Helen how it had got there. She said she'd had a drink, but that, 'It didn't taste very nice.' I told her that she hadn't ought to drink it because it could be poisonous. She nodded her head and agreed and there was nothing else I could do about it.

Jeff said he was going to clean out the debris from my bay guttering, but I thought: 'Well, I'll do it while I'm at it. It won't take long. It'll be one less job he's got to do.' So, on 8 February, I got on the next to the top rung of my stepladder, to see where the rubbish was, and cleaned it out. When I told Jeff, he said it was dangerous for me to do things like that at my age and that if I fell off and hurt myself, I wouldn't be able to look after Helen, which would complicate things even more. I quite agreed.

Four days later, Jeff and I discussed how whichever of us died first could give a sign from the afterlife to the one who was still living. We were on it for quite a while, but there was no end agreement on how to do it, so we left it for another day. I think it's a waste of time looking into the afterworld because the facts don't suggest there is one.

Helen used to climb up the steps into the minibus to go to the day centre, but, by then, it was getting awkward for her and it looked as if she might fall. So the driver suggested that she try the lift attachment he'd got at the rear entrance to the bus. They tried it a time or two, but it wasn't very satisfactory because it didn't seem to work properly.

Looking after Helen was getting too much and very time-consuming, so I thought it might be the time to give my car up. To get it, I still had to go to the garage in Avenue Road in all kinds of weather and by then I was having difficulty in walking along there. Also, I couldn't last too long without going to the toilet. I mentioned my idea to Jeff, but he thought it might be advantageous for me to keep the car because it helped me to get bulk food items in and meant I didn't need to carry them back on a bus. Also, he said it meant I'd still have the chance to have a run in it for a break. So I didn't make a firm decision and decided to think about it.

When Helen tried to get out of bed in the morning on 23 February, she slid onto the floor and I couldn't get her up because she'd got one of her legs jammed under the wardrobe. I phoned the paramedics for assistance and they got her up. She seemed alright, but the following morning she slid out of bed again. So things were getting desperate and Jeff rang Social Services and arranged for them to send somebody to help me get Helen in and out of bed.

The first night (the 24th), Jeff got a phone call from Care Homes Stoke Ltd (of Unit 2, Trent House, in Dunning Street, Tunstall), saying the carer, Wendy Mottram, had been banging on my door, but couldn't make anybody hear. Jeff was then worried that something had happened to me and rang me straightaway, but everything was alright and Wendy had obviously gone to the wrong house. Jeff found out she was at Leek *New* Road, so he put her right and gave her directions to my house. She then came along and got Helen to bed, so that was a satisfactory end to the night. Wendy came again in the morning and got Helen up after a bit of a struggle.

After that, Jeff made a permanent arrangement for two carers to come and get Helen up and put her to bed each day. However, that was awkward because they could only provide help at set times (10.45 a.m. and 8 p.m.), but Helen wanted to get up and go to bed when she felt like it. Also, after she'd been put to bed on the 25th, I heard noises from upstairs, so I shouted up and asked Helen if she was alright. She made some remark, so I decided to go to see what was happening. She was standing looking through the window, so I had to get her to lie down in bed again!

Unfortunately, the carers weren't able to get Helen out of bed on 1 March, so I rang for an ambulance. The crew got her out and downstairs and then checked her over, but found nothing wrong. However, she didn't have anything to drink or eat and acted strangely. She wasn't speaking and just sat there. When Jeff came in the evening, he got her to have a drink of tea and a sandwich, but decided it would be best to ring for a doctor because there seemed to be something serious going on with her health. Before the doctor had got there, the carers came, to put Helen to bed, but they were so concerned about her that they called for the paramedics. Just after they arrived, the out-of-hours doctor (Dr Unyolo) came and they gave her a check over. Everybody was talking at once, so all I could do was to stand there and wait for them to decide what to do. They discovered that she'd got high blood pressure, an irregular heartbeat, a high temperature and probably an infection, so they sent for an ambulance. We ended up at A & E (the Accident and Emergency Department), but the staff weren't very clear about what was wrong. She was kept in all night for observation and so Jeff, Sue (who had joined us) and I went home.

Sue and one of the carers had said they could smell gas in my house, so I rang the National Gas Emergency Service when I got back. A fellow came out and found the central heating boiler had a leak, so he disconnected it. Fortunately, I had my gas fire and the weather wasn't particularly cold.

The next day, Jeff, Sue and I went to the hospital to see Helen. She was sitting up, talkative and more like her normal self. She knew it was Mother's Day and Jeff gave her a box of chocolates. The staff told us they'd found her a bed at Cheadle Hospital, in Royal Walk, Cheadle, where they were going to take her for physical rehabilitation. I was hoping that would do the trick and I never gave it a thought that she wouldn't come back home.

I went with her in the ambulance and they took her to Ward 1, where she was examined. I went into a lounge for the patients, where Jeff and Sue joined me, and a fellow was sitting at an organ, playing all the old wartime songs and jazz. Every now and then, he sang a few words and he told us he came every Sunday to give the patients a treat. After a while, the deputy manager, Jane Wardle, came to us and said that Helen would have physio, with the idea of getting her more mobile and hopefully back home.

The following day, a fellow came from WarmSure, the servicing and repair company, of National Avenue, in Hull, to look at my central heating boiler. He opened it up and said: 'I've got it. They haven't tightened the nut up.' So he got his spanner out and did it, but the gas was still leaking. He had another look and said, 'Oh, they haven't put the flipping washer in,' or words to that effect! So the installers had done a sloppy job and I might have been gassed! Anyway, he put a washer in and that solved the problem.

Jeff asked if I'd like to stay with him, but I wanted to be at home. I seemed to be alright on my own and I wasn't all that upset, so I managed to sleep well.

The hospital seemed to be alright. It was comfortable and there were armchairs and a television in the lounge. One or two of the patients were chatty and Helen didn't seem to settle in badly, considering her character. During the day, the nurses took her into the lounge and at night they returned her to the room which she shared with three or four others and where she had a bed. It would have been nice to have had Helen at a local hospital instead of having to go to Cheadle to see her, but that's how it was.

At first, Jeff and I visited her together, but it got too much for him, with working, so I carried on going each day and he went about every other day. It was daft walking along to Avenue Road each day for my car to drive to see Helen, so I decided to leave it parked outside my house and carried on doing that.

Most of the time when I visited her, there wasn't much response and she was still often confused about things, but occasionally there were flashes of the old days. She was having physio and part of the treatment was her exercising her legs. The physiotherapist said Helen could do with more exercise, so if Jeff and I could help, it would be appreciated. As soon as we arrived, we got Helen to lift her legs up and straighten them, which she did most times, but she didn't manage many attempts before she gave up. I don't suppose it helped a lot and it was like bashing our heads against a brick wall.

Helen seemed to be taken up by one of the other patients. When I went to see her on 6 March, she was sitting in the next chair to him and they held hands while I was there! I don't know if she thought he was me. I looked at them, but left it at that because it was harmless and it would have been daft to have made a scene. It wouldn't have helped her and she seemed happy with it. Another time, she put her head on his shoulder and went asleep, which was a bit embarrassing. I said, 'You're not supposed to do that,' but she didn't do anything about it and I suppose she didn't understand.

While all that was going on, I was told, probably by the Victim Liaison Service, that Bridget Purcell had been let free from prison, having served less than a year of her sentence, but that, shortly afterwards, she'd been taken back in because she'd broken the rules of her release.

One or two of the nurses at the hospital were okay and very pleasant at times, but things seemed to go downhill and they weren't as nice later on. Jeff and I went to see Kath Ramage, the matron, on 20 March to discuss Helen's lack of progress. All the labour in trying to get her right had been wasted because she'd slowly deteriorated since she'd been in the hospital. Kath said a lot, but half the time she was talking down to us, so we didn't get much satisfaction out of her. She suggested it was time for us to think about what to do with Helen and it seemed we'd got to the stage where they couldn't do much else for her. I suppose the hospital wanted to get rid of her by that time because she'd been in a considerable while for the job they were supposed to be doing. Kath told us Helen could return home, with added assistance four times a day, or she could go into a permanent home. We said we'd think about it.

I'd been every day to see Helen, but I couldn't manage it on the 26th because my back was killing me, so I rang my surgery. Dr David Loughney came to see me and prescribed some tablets to relieve the pain. I didn't feel up to visiting Helen after then, so Jeff took over the job and did the best he could. He told me that the staff had become almost casual in their treatment of her and he kept asking for different things to try to help her, but it seemed they thought it was a bore or resented it.

On 28 March, Jeff told me that Helen was having difficulty in swallowing food and she could only take purée. Things were looking very serious because no food meant no life. It was all too much for me to take in because the situation was getting desperate and my mind was in a whirl.

Four days later, Jeff said he'd been told that the hospital was giving up Helen's physio because it wouldn't help any more. By then, she was slipping off the chair she was in and so the physiotherapist had said that if she couldn't sit, there was no purpose in trying to get her to stand up. It was disappointing, but to be expected the way she was deteriorating.

Jeff kept me well informed, but, the way he described things, it seemed as if Helen was slipping away, though I didn't really think of it like that. He said she was by then lying down all the time because he'd been told she wasn't safe sitting on a chair. That was a bad sign, but it was just how things were and what will be will be.

I had a phone call from Jeff on the evening of 6 April. He said an ambulance was taking Helen to A & E in Hartshill because she was in a serious condition. He said he'd call for me and take me there and I agreed to go, even though I was struggling with my bad back. When we got there, she was in the Resuscitation Unit and things seemed to be chaotic. Everything seemed all mixed up and nurses kept coming in and going out and talking. I looked at the machine Helen was wired up to and then a doctor, Magnus Harrison, took Jeff and me into a quiet room. He seemed to be talking mainly to Jeff and using technical terms, so I didn't really understand what he was saying. Jeff then told me the doctor had said he'd be surprised if Helen lasted the night.

I seemed to accept it, as if I knew it would be like that. Deep down, I'd realized that the end was coming, but I don't suppose I'd showed it. I felt helpless and didn't know what I was going to do, but I was kind of settled with it. I went to the toilet and Jeff came with me to see I didn't fall down. I washed my hands and we then went back to Helen. I touched her arm, but she recoiled and groaned because my hand was still cold from washing. About midnight, I decided to go home for a rest and Jeff ran me back. It was strange, but I didn't seem to have had any problems with my back. Perhaps it was because I'd been sitting in a chair, resting, or maybe I just hadn't noticed it aching.

In the early morning, Jeff rang from the hospital and woke me up. He told me that a nurse had called him and suggested he go over to the hospital because Helen wasn't doing very well. Sue picked me up and took me there and Jeff told me that Helen's condition was critical. We all sat there for quite a while and encouraged her to hold on. Jeff, Sue and I held Helen's hands, but we were also watching the indicators on the machine to see what was happening to her. The nurses came in occasionally to check on the instruments, but everything was pretty quiet and I was anticipating the final moments.

The figures gradually went down on the machine and Helen was slipping away.

Jeff and I kept having a word with her, to try to keep her going, but she wouldn't have realized it. It was a waste of time, but we kept on trying, to see if we could rally her round, hoping for some miracle cure. We were watching and listening and Helen just drifted away around 11.30. It was merciful and she can't have suffered any pain. A nurse as good as pronounced her dead and switched off all the electrical apparatus that had been monitoring her. And that was the end.

We'd already given up hope, so it didn't seem much different when Helen had died. I felt sad and numb and I didn't know what I was going to do next. Jeff, Sue and I sat there for a while and then they asked me to go back with them to Jeff's house. I just wanted to leave it at that, so they ran me home. We had a few words there and then I waved them off. I sat down and went over the events of the day in my mind.

Later in the day, Jeff and Sue returned. Jeff had been back to the hospital and picked up Helen's wedding ring. He brought it to me and I gave it to him as a keepsake. It would have passed to him anyhow, so I thought he might as well have it. I thought somebody might rob Helen's grave at some time and take it, so we'd know where it was with Jeff having it.

We phoned a few people to tell them the bad news and Jeff visited one or two of my neighbours. Then he took Sue for a walk around Hanley Park to reminisce to her about when he'd played there as a child. When they came back, he asked me if I wanted to stay at his place for a bit to get over the trauma, but I said: 'No. I'll be alright on my own here.' I wanted to be alone for a while, I suppose.

Jeff got bereavement leave from the college and the next day took me to Festival Park to look for a replacement fridge because mine had conked out. I decided on and bought a Proline fridge-freezer from Comet for £159.99 and then Jeff put me in the restaurant at Sainsbury's supermarket, in Etruria Road, Hanley, with a pot of tea, while I waited for him to do our food shopping. I felt guilty and ashamed doing these things because I should have been crying and moping, but the activities broke the day up and relieved the tensions.

The following day, I rang Lily Birch, one of the leaders at Zion, about having the funeral for Helen at the church. Helen had said she'd like the service to be done there and Lily agreed and offered the church free for the reception as well. Helen would have liked Brian Eeley to have taken the service, but Jeff couldn't get hold of him, so we went along with the superintendant minister, Richard Parkes, doing it and we decided Jeff would do the talk about Helen.

I thought how discreet and efficient Williamson Brothers Ltd., of Birch House, in Birches Head Road, had been during the many funerals I'd attended organized by them, so I went for them as the funeral directors. Robert Williamson came down on 11 April and was very courteous. We chatted about the arrangements and the funeral was fixed for the 18th.

Helen's death certificate said she'd died from sepsis leading to pneumonia, brought on by her dementia, but I think the pneumonia was the main thing. Jeff and I decided to go to see her in the hospital morgue on the 11th and Sue was with us. Helen looked quite peaceful, but the situation didn't seem to be real. We stayed a while and then left.

Jeff picked Helen's going-away outfit and took it to the undertaker's for her to be dressed for the funeral. Jeff and I went there the day beforehand to see her and we stopped a while. She looked very nice and Jeff took some photographs of her. She was lying in a lovely golden oak coffin, which had gold handles on and had been chosen by Jeff. He and I had each got a lock of our hair and put them in her hands. It was all going through our procedure and I'd more or less got into a routine with it because it had been going on for days.

On the morning of the funeral, the undertakers came and put no-parking cones along the road, so their hearse and mourners' car could get in. Jeff attended to some things and then he and Sue joined the other main mourners (Harry, Gill, Dorothy and Helen's niece, Helen Sargent) at my house. We all got in the car, except for Jeff, who walked in front of the hearse to about Egerton Street. He then got in with us and we went around the Victoria Road roundabout to the church, which seemed to be pretty full.

The service started and partway through, Jeff took over from the minister and made a lovely speech, which lasted about twenty minutes. Afterwards, the minister carried on and the service finished with prayers and a couple of hymns. Then we had the lid taken off the coffin for anyone who wanted to have a last look at Helen. Jeff and I went up to give her a kiss and say goodbye. The lid was then put back on and she was never to be seen again.

After the service, the other main mourners and I got back in the car, which proceeded into Victoria Road and then Leek Road. Just past Egerton Street, Jeff got out and started walking in front of the hearse again. The parade stopped outside my house for about a minute as a mark of respect and so that Helen could be connected to it in some way or another. We started off once more and Jeff got back in the car just after we'd passed Mawson Grove.

We arrived at Hanley Cemetery, where the undertakers took the coffin to the open grave, which was where my parents were buried. There was room in Helen's parents' grave for her, but she'd said she wanted to be buried with me and I wanted to be laid to rest with my parents.

We had a little ceremony and then the coffin was lowered into the grave. The minister came round with earth, in a wooden box, for the mourners to throw down onto the coffin. I got some and Jeff did too and we threw it in, as did some others. Sue had brought along a number of red roses, which she handed round. I put the first one in and Jeff and other people followed. I got the spade and shovelled some earth down onto the coffin and then Jeff took over. I went back to Zion with the other mourners for the reception, but Jeff carried on shovelling. He'd been intent on filling the grave in on his own, but the earth was really soggy and he was helped by one of the gravediggers. Eventually, he stopped because he had to get back to the church for the buffet and the gravediggers finished the job off with their mechanical digger.

The buffet went down very well. People were chatting and it was very friendly all round. Ros had been to the funeral and attended the buffet, which was a very nice thing to have happened. Jeff had got a book of remembrance, in which the names of 63 people had been entered and most of them had made comments. Jeff and I thanked everybody at Zion for their help and letting us have the room and meal free and we gave them a hundred pounds between us for being so kind.

Jeff, Sue and I went back to the cemetery, to have a look at the flowers and they were very nice. Jeff asked if I wanted to go to his place for a meal, but I said: 'No. I'll be alright.' It had been quite a day and I wanted to be quiet and on my own.

9 Just As Usual

The day after Helen's funeral was a Saturday and Jeff came down as normal. We had our usual chips and peas at lunch time and then he put back up my bay guttering bracket, which had come loose. Afterwards, we drove down to Empire Service Station, in Stoke Road, and he checked my car tyre pressures before I went off for a little run.

My back had improved quite a lot, so, on 21 April, I was able to take my car to Kennerley's Cauldon Garage, in Cauldon Road, because I'd been having a bit of trouble with it. I'd been using them for years to service and do repairs on my car. From there, I then managed to walk to TJ's Barbers, in College Road, for a haircut.

Five days later, I went with Jeff to visit Helen's grave, despite the ground being very uneven. I was afraid I'd fall down, but Jeff gave me a hand to steady me. We stopped a while reminiscing, but it was surreal. I didn't go there on a regular basis afterwards because I felt it was unsafe to go on my own, with the risk of falling, but I went a few times with Jeff. He visited the grave regularly and tidied it up, but we decided to wait to see how the earth would settle before putting anything permanent on there in memory. I'd gathered that it would be a waste of time having a gravestone there less than twelve months after the burial.

There were plenty of official things I had to attend to after Helen had died, but Jeff helped me quite a lot in dealing with them. I paid Williamson Brothers £1,856.48 for handling Helen's funeral and one of Jeff's friends, Geoff Milward, of 110 Mow Lane, in Gillow Heath, came in as our adviser on what to do with Helen's assets. Also, he said my will was obsolete because it was leaving everything to Helen and so he suggested I make a new one as a priority. It was agreed he'd put it together for me and it was understood that I'd leave everything to Jeff.

On 10 May, Jeff and Sue took me to Stoke on Trent Film Theatre, in College Road, to see *There Will Be Blood*, which was about prospecting for oil. The film began with an almighty crash, which frightened the wits out of me and would likely have killed somebody with a nervous disposition! The film was alright and it got me out for a change, but the overall volume was too loud for such a small room.

Peter Jones, who'd still been doing my hedges, had had a slight stroke and I gathered that he wouldn't be able to continue to do the job. Also, I was struggling by then to do the rest of the garden, so Jeff enquired about getting a gardener, to save me doing all the heavy work. He came up with Paul Berry, of 100 Stoke Old Road, in Hartshill, who came to see us on 13 May. He seemed to be satisfactory, so we fixed up for him to come once a month for two hours at a cost of thirty pounds.

I felt alright, but couldn't do things as quickly as I once could and I soon got tired. So I got a cleaner through Age Concern for two hours a fortnight at eleven pounds an hour, starting on 21 May. One or two different ones came and then Phyllis Dimond became the regular. She was very chatty and wanted to know all my business! She was always rushing about, but was pretty good and even climbed up to put new hooks in my lounge curtains. It was nice to know that I could get a decent job done at a reasonable price.

I decided to have a trip to see Dorothy in her ground-floor flat, 6 Etruria Locks, in Kilndown Close, Etruria, where she'd moved to from Eaton Park. It was too far to walk, so I drove there on 21 May. From her lounge, she had a lovely view of the Caldon Canal, which looked like a little river. It was a pleasant visit and broke the day up.

I was feeling okay in spite of Helen's death. It was marvellous that I didn't get a bit morbid and I seemed to settle down easily enough. It was a relief to have got rid of all the washing of the bed sheets and her clothes and I didn't have to spend most of the rest of my time looking after her, so I wasn't left with a lot to do. I only had to look after myself, but I did keep thinking Helen was sitting beside me in the lounge and I still do occasionally even now. Also, it was disturbing when I got out of bed in the middle of the night to go to the toilet because I'd glance over to where she'd have been lying, but there was nobody there. It was a shock each time, but it all happened in a second and I then carried on as normal. It continued to happen on occasions for a couple of years.

On 7 June, Jeff told me that he'd had a lawyer's letter telling him that Ros wanted a divorce. It wasn't a total shock to me because it was expected in the circumstances. I accepted it for what it was, a bit of movement at the end of their relationship. The lawyer, Julie Wain, of Hand Morgan & Owen, at 17 Martin Street, in Stafford, had threatened Jeff, saying, if he didn't give Ros a divorce, they could take him to court on the ground of unreasonable behaviour. That seemed a cheek considering that Ros had left him in the first place and was committing adultery and living with this bounder, Phil Cumming, at 12a Garden Street, in Stafford. Ros was claiming half the house, so I decided I'd help Jeff out with money. He asked, 'How much can you give me?' I said I could give him £50,000 and he was very pleased. He then told me he was fixing himself up with a solicitor to see to the divorce proceedings.

Jeff and Sue took me to Ilam for Father's Day. We had lunch in the tea room and then sat in the grounds, gazing across at the hills for getting on for two hours. We picked out people on Thorpe Cloud with Jeff's binoculars and it was very enjoyable in the warm sun.

When Helen had stopped using the bath, the idea of having a shower had come up and eventually I'd got in touch with the council to see if we could get a grant towards it. Although Helen had died in the meantime, the council did an assessment and decided it could be done for me instead and I wouldn't have to pay anything, even though the cost of putting it in was £6,760.88. That was very good of them.

The job started on 25 June and the old bathroom furniture was stripped out and dumped at the front of the house for the time being. The cast iron bath had to be broken up with a sledgehammer because it was too heavy to carry downstairs, but it was brittle, so it was done fairly easily. The tiles were taken off the walls and the bathroom door was replaced. Fitting out the new shower room wasn't straightforward and different workmen came at different times to do different jobs, so that it was 30 July before everything had slotted into place. A new ceiling was put in and plasterboard was fixed on the walls. A waterproof floor was fitted and the ends of it were sealed a few inches up the walls. A grid was positioned in the middle of the floor to take the water away and a new toilet and bigger washbasin were installed. The actual shower was put on one of the walls and an air extractor was fitted.

New tiles were being put on the walls, but I was allowed only two colours, one of which had to be white. Jeff and I had picked yellow and two different greens to fit the pattern we wanted, so I had a talk with the contractor, Craig Rollings, of Vale Lodge, in Brindley Lane, Baddeley Edge, who said it would cost an extra £120 to have them, which I did.

On 29 June, Jeff and Sue took me to The Trentham Estate, which had replaced the old Trentham Gardens. There was a shopping village and it was okay. We had a stroll round to the lake side, where a miniature railway started and we waited for the train to come back. It was very pleasant.

Geoff Milward turned up on 10 July with my new will, which he asked me to sign. I did so and that meant that Jeff would get everything I'd got.

When my new shower room was finished, it was very nice. Soon after, the council came and put me a seat in because I had to be careful in case my legs gave way while I was having a shower. I used the seat most of the time and I was alright showering, but it gradually got harder work for me.

On 3 August, Jeff, Sue and I went to the new Trentham Monkey Forest attraction, which was part of The Trentham Estate and had about 140 Barbary macaques living in a wood. It was quite a walk from the entrance till we came across the sight of a monkey. There were a fair few people around and we sat down where the monkeys were fed. I was surprised that was done because the environment was supposed to be similar to that where they came from, in the Atlas Mountains of North Africa, and so I'd thought they'd be self-contained and feed on what they could find in the trees. They'd been brought in from existing parks in France and Germany and seemed pretty healthy.

We waited for feeding time and eventually a girl came along with food, which she threw into the grass arena. The monkeys had congregated there, I suppose because they knew what time it was. There was such a scramble for the food, but the leader had his share first. The youngsters kept trying to nip in and every now and then there'd be a scuffle, but it soon calmed down. When all the food had gone, the monkeys started moving away. We took some photographs, but they didn't come out too well because the monkeys seemed to be camouflaged and it was a dull day. The monkeys were a letdown, really, but perhaps I was expecting too much.

A week later, Jeff and Sue took me to Tittesworth Reservoir, where I had a short walk with them. I then went to the visitor centre while they walked all the way round the reservoir, but they were so long coming back that I had another stroll in the meantime!

I heard that Sid Asher had died on 21 August, which meant going to yet another funeral, on the 29th at Newcastle Crematorium. Harry and Gill were there and Jeff and I sat with them and afterwards at the reception at the Borough Arms Hotel, in King Street. The vicar's speech didn't mention Leah (Sid's first wife and Helen's sister, who'd died in 1957), which was rather funny. Sid and I weren't very close, but Helen and I used to visit him and his second wife, Mavis, occasionally and kept in touch.

I'd often wondered what it was like on the southwest side of the Wirral and Jeff and Sue took me there on 13 September. I was expecting it to be something like

New Brighton, but it wasn't how I thought it would be. We arrived at Parkgate, which wasn't very glamorous because it faced marshland, although that was a nice wild area. We had a meal in Parkgate Coffee Shop, where Jeff got excited and said, 'There's a heron there!'

I had a look and could see that there was something there, sticking up out of the marsh, but it didn't move at all. Then Jeff went to the counter to pay and the thing moved, so I shouted across to him, 'It's walking!' So he was right after all and it was a live heron. It was interesting to watch it, although the other customers didn't seem to be very bothered about it. The heron moved about a bit and then flew off to another spot nearby.

We then called at Thurstaston, further down the Dee Estuary, but there wasn't a lot to see there. We sat on a bench above the river, with some greenery around, and looked across to North Wales and out to sea.

We went on to West Kirby and sat by the boating lake, admiring the view and having an ice cream. A passing dog made a dive for mine, but I snatched it back, almost out of the dog's jaws!

At Hoylake, I had a little walk on the beach, but we didn't stop long because there was nothing outstanding there. Also, I'd been thinking I'd like to see New Brighton again because I hadn't been since Helen and I had taken Jeff when he was a lad, so we moved on to there.

New Brighton was very disappointing. It was rundown, although there were some new buildings. We went to see the River Mersey and the fort, which was shut. The lighthouse was out of view, but I'd seen it as we drove up. A boat came down the river and we took one or two photographs before we decided to find somewhere to eat. We came across a likely-looking pub called The Harvest Mouse, at 164 Pensby Road, in Heswall. It wasn't very glamorous, but the meal was okay, so it rounded off a very nice and interesting day.

A few days later, I had a phone call to say that Bridget Purcell had been released from prison. I wasn't really bothered about it, but I wondered if she might try to take her revenge somehow or other. Then, shortly afterwards, I was told by the police that her daughter, Margaret Delaney, had been charged with attempted burglary at my house and that I might be needed at court. However, in November, I received a letter from the Crown Prosecution Service, saying that there wasn't enough evidence to convict her. Jeff later made enquiries and was told by North Staffordshire Magistrates' Court, in Baker Street, Fenton, that the case had been discontinued on 26 November.

I started to sort Helen's things out, but Jeff said he wanted to look at everything before I threw it away, so I left it. When it came to it, he couldn't bring himself to get rid of anything, so he'll have to sort it all out when I've gone!

Geoff Milward came down again, on 25 September, and it was decided that he'd handle the probate. He also gave me more advice about Helen's investments. The economic situation was up in the air and I didn't know what to do. Geoff didn't really know either. He dealt with some of Helen's savings and I reinvested them. It went pretty well and, because of the risk with the economy, I just tried to make them safe with short-term investments.

On 12 October, Sue drove Jeff and me to the West Midlands Safari Park, in Bewdley, where we saw a variety of animals, including tigers, lions and rhinos. There were also some wild dogs, but they were lying down, so we didn't see them moving about. I'd wanted to see them standing up because Jeff had said they were pretty big. Unfortunately, there were those many cars that the road became gridlocked and so we had to stop for ages to look at things, even when we didn't want to. It was the first time I'd been to a safari park and it wasn't quite how I'd thought it would be. I'd imagined there'd be a big area you drove through, with animals, like monkeys, jumping on the cars, tearing the windscreen wipers off!

After we'd driven round, we walked to a reptile section, where Mark O'Shea, the star of Channel 4's series, *O'Shea's Dangerous Reptiles*, was the consultant curator. He did a talk on large snakes and Jeff had a word with him afterwards. Then we carried on to look at the hippos in their lake, but we didn't see them close up like you do on television. I was disappointed with the park overall because the animals weren't right by us, although perhaps we'd been in the wrong place at the wrong time.

My kitchen didn't look right because of the black stains on the ceiling and walls, which remained from the fire that Helen had started in 2004. Chris Allen (of 18 Woodland Avenue, in Norton), who'd supervised the decorating of my shower room, which I'd been pleased with, said he could do the job. So I thought I'd try him. We agreed on £370, on 14 October, but he asked, 'Have you thought of claiming for it on the insurance?' I said I hadn't because it had happened some time before, but I decided to try to anyhow.

I got on the phone to More Th>n [sic], the insurance company, and the man who answered said it would be okay. I told him the cost would be £370, but Chris was standing by me listening and butted in and said '£550'! I didn't think about it and repeated what he'd told me and the company just accepted it! Chris said I could have the excess from the policy, but there wasn't one.

Chris then did the job, in yellow, and it really smartened the place up. When he'd finished, he said, 'If you pay me now, you can have the insurance cheque,' but Jeff had told me not to give him any money before I'd got the cheque through.

'Many a slip between cup and lip,' the old saying goes, so I said, 'I'll pay you when the cheque comes.' He seemed alright about it and I phoned him when the money arrived. I wrote him a cheque for £550 and said, 'Call it quits.'

Jeff had noticed that there were a lot of items on my back bed, getting all mixed up, piled on top of his teddy bear. Ted was still there from when Helen used to sit him up in the day and tuck him up at night. It looked like he might eventually get damaged, so Jeff decided to take him home and have him in his office, where he'd be safe.

I saw an advert on a bus, saying that old age pensioners could get their electric blankets checked by the fire brigade. So I phoned them and asked them to check that mine was safe. A day or two later, they came down and gave me a new one and a plug for free.

Jeff and I went to the probate department of Stoke-on-Trent County Court, in Bethesda Street, on 11 November and met Geoff Milward there. We saw an official and it didn't take long to get the business sorted out. It meant I was in charge of all Helen's affairs and it told everybody I was the rightful person to deal with them.

The lounge carpet was old and all mucky, with the problems Helen had had, so I needed a new one. Jeff and I went to have a look at what there was and I bought a buff-coloured one from Carpetright plc, at Unit 2a, in Festival Park, for £315. They fitted it on 19 November and it had a thick pile, so you sank into it.

On the 21st, Jeff told me he'd had a letter from Ros, saying her father had died suddenly three days earlier from a rupture in his aorta. It was a shock because Alan had been fairly close to us and it was very sad. On the day of his funeral, 1 December, Jeff picked me up and drove us to Newcastle Crematorium for the service. There was a decent crowd there. The minister, Reverend John Palmer, recited a poem Alan had written, *Lament for Pitgreen Fields*, which was very nice. Outside, afterwards, Jeff and I had a chat with Ros and she asked if we were going to the buffet at The Wulstan, in Dimsdale Parade East, Wolstanton. We did and stayed till most people had gone. Then we said goodbye to Ros and went to have a look at the floral arrangements at the crematorium.

Jeff and Sue took me to the Museum of Childhood, at Sudbury Hall, in Sudbury, Derbyshire, for my 93rd birthday. It had a lot of, mainly simple, things that children used to play with and some of them brought back memories. I remembered the hoops and the museum had both varieties that I'd played with. I also remembered a wooden spinning top they had, with a piece of string tied to a stick. The idea was to throw the top on the ground and pull the string with the other hand, so that the top would go spinning round. I tried it at the museum, but it was an utter failure and I was very disappointed I couldn't do it.

A fellow came along and organized us and other visitors into a group and told us to go into a room. It was a replica of an old school, where we all sat down. It was cramped and the desks were small, so you couldn't get your knees underneath. The fellow came in and shouted 'Quiet!' I offered him my walking stick so he could get attention, but he wasn't amused! He went round the classroom to all the people, who were acting the roles of children, and asked them how often he used the cane.

They kept saying, 'All the time,' but Jeff said 'Never!'

The fellow was pleased with that and said: 'Quite right. I only have to show them the cane. It quietens them down!' When he finished, we all gave him a clap and it was nice to go back and see something similar to how it had been in the past.

When we got back to Jeff's, there was a present in a big box, which turned out to be a DVD player, and Jeff had also got several film discs for me. We tried out one of them, *Animal Farm*, a 1954 cartoon, in which the animals revolted against their farmer. It was based on George Orwell's book, but there didn't seem to be much of a story and it didn't appeal to me.

Another DVD Jeff had bought me was *Tiger: Spy in the Jungle*, which had been made by the BBC. The commentary had been done by David Attenborough, who was pretty good at it. The film was about four tiger cubs and their mother, who was bringing them up. The cameras had been carried on elephants' tusks or disguised as logs and put in nearby spots, so they got right up close and the photography was beautiful. The elephants and the tigress more or less ignored each other and the log cameras weren't seen as being a threat, so things were filmed about the world of tigers that had never been seen before.

I received a letter on 18 December saying I'd been speeding at 39 miles an hour in a 30 zone on the A 520 at Cellarhead on the 9th and I was shocked because I didn't remember driving too fast. There was a sixty pounds' fine and an endorsement on my driving licence, the first I'd ever had. An alternative to paying the fine was attendance on a speed awareness course at the same cost and there was a choice of one or two local venues, which I wasn't familiar with. After some consideration, I decided to pay the fine because I didn't fancy driving round to try to find one of the places where the classes were and then walk to it. So I sent off a cheque to the court and had the three points put on my driving licence.

I went to Jeff's for Christmas and stayed two nights. Sue was stopping with him for a few days and was with us the whole time. On Boxing Day, we all went to Norbury Junction and had a bit of a walk along the Shropshire Union Canal, but it was very cold, so we soon went into The Junction Inn for a drink. There was a pool table, so we all had a game and Jeff was competing against Sue and me. Sue thought Jeff would be so superior that it was agreed we'd have two shots to his one. I was sluggish to start off with, but got more used to it after a while. Jeff was a lot better than us, but, with having double the shots, we won. It was different from normal and we had a nice afternoon.

That night, we had a DVD on that Jeff had bought me, *Letters From Iwo Jima*, a film from 2006 showing the Japanese side of the Second World War battle story and it was pretty good. It was different from the normal war films and showed the Japs to be more or less the same people as us. When I was in the war, I hadn't given a lot of thought to what the other side felt and we only knew what the top brass told us.

Two days after, Jeff rang to tell me that Ros's mother, Shirley, had died of cancer on Boxing Day and it was a shock, especially as it was so soon after Alan had passed away. Bad news seemed to be coming all at once.

On 6 January 2009, Jeff did my food shopping because he was concerned that the pavements were too icy for me to walk on. While he was doing so, I cleared all the snow off my front steps, so that I could get up and down. I then found it wasn't too bad on the pavement outside, so I gave my car a run and Jeff was pleased that I could still do those things.

Six days later, we attended Shirley's funeral at Newcastle Crematorium. Again, we went to The Wulstan afterwards and some of the mourners showed a lot of interest in my book. Two women kissed me and I'd never thought it would be like that if I wrote my life story! However, when Jeff and I left the pub, I said to him, 'Now there's only me and you left.' We were the only ones of real importance still around and it was one step off the end of the world. Helen, Alan, Shirley and Raedburh had all died and Ros was no longer in our circle. It made me feel lonely.

When Jeff took me out, he found it difficult to park his car without me having to walk a distance to wherever we were going. So he contacted the council's Parking Services department and got an appointment for me to have an assessment at Fenton Local Centre, at 5 Baker Street, to see whether I was unfit enough to warrant having a disabled parking card, known as a "Blue Badge". Jeff took me there on 26 January and, unknown to me, the interviewer watched me walk in from outside. She could see I was a genuine case and seemed to push my disability as far as she could to get me a card. I filled a form in and one of the questions asked how far I could walk without stopping. I put down a hundred yards, but she said it was only thirty to forty. Just over a week later, I got the "Blue Badge" and its number was P45/09/SKX073818.

I first tried the badge out at The Co-operative store in Werrington Road, Bucknall, and drove to where I thought the disabled spaces were, but, when I got out of the car, I noticed it was reserved for mothers and children. I left it at that, but then I saw that the disabled spaces were nearer to the store entrance. Anyway, it gave me confidence to use them, although I felt guilty about it because there were people worse off than me.

The police had taken for use as evidence the trousers and shirt I'd been wearing when Bridget Purcell's family had forced their way into my house. I finally had a letter asking me to pick up my togs from Stoke Police Station, which I did, and the next day I put them in the washer!

Jeff and Sue took me to the Film Theatre on 21 February to see *Australia*, but, like on my previous visit, the film began with a crashing noise. I'd been dreading going in and was glad when the movie had finished! Nowadays, there's a mania for noise and everything is made as loud as it can be.

I was suffering from constipation at that time and rang the doctor's for help. I was told that I needed to drink more water and eat more fruit and veg. Jeff said the same thing, so I gave it a try and it seemed to do the trick. I'd been drinking whisky at night, but instead I started to have apple juice, which tasted nice. So I dropped alcohol off altogether.

Helen and I had seen the wonderful display of snowdrops and daffodils in St. Oswald's churchyard, in Ashbourne, a number of times, but I hadn't been there for many years, so Jeff and Sue took me on Mothering Sunday. However, we were disappointed because not many daffodils had come out, so we had a look in the church, which was interesting.

Jeff then suggested we have a look at where the all-in Ashbourne Royal Shrovetide Football match takes place every year on Shrove Tuesday and Ash Wednesday. I was surprised to find that it begins in a car park, where there's a brick plinth that the ball is thrown from to start the game. Each end of the town tries to score a goal against the other on posts three miles apart and there are hundreds of people involved. Injuries are plentiful and Jeff said windows of houses and shops are boarded up to try to prevent damage!

After Ashbourne, we went on to Carsington Water. The visitor centre was queer because the restaurant was upstairs and there was only a small lift, which was hazardous. Anyway, we had a cup of tea there and sat by the window, overlooking the reservoir, where we could see the windsurfers. It intrigued me that they went remarkably fast and then suddenly seemed to fall in the water. They had to get their sails back up and then returned to where they'd come from and I couldn't understand how they were doing that. It was all most interesting.

On 4 April, Jeff and Sue took me to the Odeon to see *The Damned United*, which was a film about the problems Brian Clough had had when he'd managed Leeds United in 1974. The film confirmed that Clough was a big head, but a good manager and the volume was more to my liking than that at the Film Theatre!

The day after, we all went to St. Oswald's churchyard again and this time the daffodils were brilliant. We then carried on to Milldale, where we sat by the River Dove and had an ice cream before having a nice little walk along the river.

I was restless in bed in the early hours of 18 April when my left thumb and, to a lesser extent, forefinger went numb. I kept rubbing them, thinking that the blood must have run out because of how I'd been lying on them. They didn't go any better, but I suffered the numbness and went back to sleep off and on. When I woke up, the numbness was improving and it gradually went. However, when I had my breakfast, I noticed I'd got a tickle in my throat. It was as if something was catching or there were sharp edges on my food and I tried to clear it. Also, I found I was biting my lip from time to time.

I phoned Jeff to ask him to get me some food in, but he noticed I'd got a slur in my speech. I'd realized there was something wrong, but it seemed to be just one of those things. Jeff suggested he ring a doctor and the next thing I remember was an ambulance coming, which had got here pretty quickly. It took me to A & E and Jeff met me there. I had to get undressed, put a gown on and get on a bed. I was given some tests and then moved to Ward 10, one of the stroke wards in the Infirmary. The doctors seemed to be debating whether I'd had a mini-stroke, but eventually they decided it was a stroke and kept me in.

The ward was busy and there was a lot of conversation. The building was old and so was the equipment and sometimes it didn't work. I felt shy and didn't like to get out of bed because people would be watching, so the time or two I wanted to go to the toilet, I asked for a bottle. The next morning, I walked to the toilet and got there and back alright. That broke the ice, so after then, I walked up and down the ward a bit, but there was obviously a limit to where I could go. I went into the television lounge a couple of times, which was a small, cramped place, up three steps, but the reception on the TV wasn't much good.

The following day, I was told I could go home after my tea and I was very pleased. I was given dipyridamole, a medicine to try to stop me having another stroke, and simvastatin, to lower my cholesterol level. Because I wasn't able to swallow tablets, I was put on liquid medicine and dispersible tablets. Jeff was with me and I walked out to his car. Then he took me home and it was nice to be back. Life then carried on more or less as normal.

The stroke hadn't seemed to be too serious, more that there were niggling little things. Over time, my speech, eating and lip-biting problems more or less cleared up, but Jeff was concerned about knowing whether I was alright at home or not. So we arranged that I'd ring him the last thing at night and he'd call me the first thing in the morning. That worked alright for a while, but then I kept forgetting to ring him, although we persisted until eventually I almost always remembered.

On 4 May, I went with Jeff and Sue to Foxfield Railway, in Blythe Bridge, and it was interesting to get back on an old-fashioned steam train, even though it wasn't a very elaborate thing. The carriages were second-hand and weren't plush like they used to be. They were hard to get into because they were high off the platform, so Jeff and a porter helped me on. After a short wait at Caverswall Road Station, the engine gave a little whistle and the train started chugging along, but it was very laborious and we went along at a snail's pace. The countryside was rough, with a lot of shrubs, and after about three miles we came to a stop. With assistance, I got down a ramp onto Dilhorne Park Station and had a look around. Then we all got in again and the train made slow progress back to Caverswall Road Station. We had a look at the railway furniture they'd got, which was all crummy, but perhaps I was expecting too much because they were doing up old stock.

I'd been banned from driving for a month while I was recovering from my stroke and Jeff did my shopping for me. Then, on 20 May, after my time was up, I gave it a go again. I took my "Blue Badge" out and parked on double yellow lines in Goodson Street, Hanley, so I could do my shopping in Marks & Spencer. I did alright, so, three days later, when I was running short of the toffee that I liked to eat, I drove back to Hanley, parked in Percy Street and called into Mr Simms Olde Sweet Shoppe, in Tontine Street, to get some more. I don't know whether I parked in a disabled space or not, but it didn't take long and then I drove off.

I decided to get rid of the garage I'd been renting from Shirley Foster because there didn't seem to be any purpose in keeping it on, even though it was only costing me two pounds a week. I was still parking my car outside my house and I didn't think I could walk all the way to the far end of Avenue Road any longer. Shirley wasn't there much, so I wrote a note and put it in an envelope, with a cheque for the sixty pounds' rent owing up to the end of the month, and pushed it through the door.

I went with Jeff and Sue to Hulme End, in the Manifold Valley, on 28 May. Sue had brought along a mobility scooter, which she'd had for her father. She fixed it up, gave me the instructions on how to drive it and we set off down the Manifold track, with Jeff and Sue walking behind me. I found it tricky to start with because the track had a curved surface and the vehicle had a small wheel base, so it was liable to tip up. The scenery was nice and things went very well for a while, apart from cyclists overtaking. Then, just before we got to Ecton, the vehicle stopped and we discovered that the battery had run down. We tried to get it going again, but we couldn't, so there was nothing for it except for Jeff and Sue to push me until we came to the road again, which went into the tunnel towards Wettonmill. We stopped there and Sue walked back to get the car.

When she returned, she and Jeff dismantled the scooter and stacked it away in the boot of her car. Sue said she'd see what she could do about the battery and I offered to buy a new one if it needed one. We then went to the Manifold Inn, in Hulme End, and had something to eat to finish off our day out.

On 3 June, I forgot to ring Jeff, but he called me before I went to bed and asked how I was. I said, 'Alright, but my eyes don't seem to be functioning properly.' After I'd got up that morning, I'd found I couldn't focus my eyes on the right-hand side of lines of letters when I was trying to read. They seemed to go distorted, so I was fiddling about, trying to join the words up to the next line down. Jeff thought I should go to hospital to get the problem checked and rang for an ambulance, so I was taken to A & E again. I met Jeff and Sue there and went through more or less the same procedure as before, ending up back in Ward 10!

A nurse asked me if I'd volunteer to help them test a new system by giving stroke patients oxygen. I didn't understand it properly, but I said I would do. So they brought this apparatus and wrapped a tube around my head. At the end of it were two points, one under each nostril, which blew the oxygen up my nose. The hospital wanted me to use it for three days, but it wasn't very comfortable and I had to undo it to go to the toilet, so I left it off after a while.

I had more tests, which showed that I'd had another stroke, but my eyes improved as I went along. My reading became better and better quite quickly.

On the second night I was in, I wanted to go to the toilet and searched for my walking stick, but I couldn't see it anywhere. Another patient was looking at me, so I told him about it and he helped me try to find it, but we had no luck. I managed to go to the toilet without it and then went back to bed. I mentioned it to the nurses the next day and they had a look around, but there was still no sign of it, so I gave up. The physiotherapist said they'd make another one for me and measured up. Later, she brought me two new ones, but they weren't varnished like the one I'd lost!

I had to wait another two days before I had the final assessment, which was to check if I could make a cup of tea. Then two doctors came round and one of them said, 'He can go.' I said goodbye to one or two people I'd got acquainted with and Jeff and I walked to his car, where Sue was waiting. We then went shopping at Sainsbury's, in Hanley, so that I could get some food in.

The hospital replaced one of my medicines, dipyridamole, with clopidogrel, but the new one wasn't available in liquid form or as a dispersible, so I had to have tablets. Fortunately, they were very small, so I managed to get them down with the aid of food. That was the first time I'd ever swallowed any regularly and it was easier than I'd thought it would be!

My smoke alarm at the top of the stairs was giving a cheeping sound, to say that the battery was running out. I decided to phone the fire brigade because they'd volunteered to fit a new battery for me when I needed it. Two firemen came on 10 June, took the alarm out and fitted a new one, with a ten-year guaranteed battery. I said, 'That'll see me out,' but later that day, I could hear the same noise going on, though strangely it was coming from downstairs. I couldn't understand it, so I called the fire brigade again and two different fellows came down.

They had a look around and one of them suddenly said: 'I know what it is. What did you do with the old alarm?'

I said, 'I put it in a bag by the back door.'

He had a look and there was the problem! He said: 'I'll put it in the bin outside. You won't hear it again.' So he did and then said, 'If there's anything else you want, let us know.'

I asked, 'Do you change light bulbs?' They laughed and left!

Two days later, I heard the cheeping again and I knew what it was straight away. Paul Berry was here, doing my garden, and he got the alarm out of the bin and took the battery out of it for me. That put a stop to it and it's what the firemen should have done in the first place!

I went with Jeff and Sue to Rudyard Reservoir on 14 June and it was interesting to see the changes since I'd last been there perhaps thirty years before. There were a lot more people there, but the old amusements had gone.

Two days afterwards, I decided to go to Hanley on the bus and back for the first time since my second stroke to see how I got on. I walked from the bus station to the post office in W. H. Smith, but it was very tiring, so I got a taxi back. By then, I'd had enough.

On Father's Day, Jeff took me to Gladstone Pottery Museum, in Uttoxeter Road, Longton, and it was a scruffy hole. It still had three bottle ovens and didn't look a very nice place to work at, even in the present, but it did show the visitors how bad it had been to have worked in the pot banks in the past. It was similar to how Taylor Tunnicliff & Co. Ltd., Mintons Ltd. and A. G. Hackney & Co. Ltd., where I'd worked as a turner, had been and I could imagine myself having fitted in there. I was glad I didn't have to do that kind of work any more, but I enjoyed the visit.

I had to go to see Dr Christine Roffe, at the Department of Geriatric Medicine at the Outpatients, on 22 June. She said my irregular heartbeat had probably caused my strokes and that she'd replace my clopidogrel tablets with warfarin to try to stop any more strokes happening. I said, 'Oh, that's rat poison, isn't it?' She gave a little smile and I started taking it. She said they'd check the situation regularly, so each week I had to report to the hospital for a blood test.

She did a quick test of the outer edges of my vision by putting her hands to the sides of my head and it seemed alright, but the test wasn't very scientific. I wanted to drive my car again, so she told me to have a test done at an optician's.

On 5 July, Jeff and Sue took me to the Manifold track at Weags Bridge and got me on the mobility scooter. We set off and turned up the Hamps Valley, but after about 1½ miles the motor cut out. We carried on, with Jeff and Sue pushing me and sometimes the scooter running for a short while, until we got near to the café at Lea House Farm. Jeff then turned back to get the car while Sue and I relaxed and had an ice cream and a cup of tea in the café garden.

I had to go to the City General Cardiology Unit on 8 July, to have an ECG tape recorder fitted. I had to keep it on all night and I took it back to the hospital the next day for them to process the information.

After I'd had my ECG recorder fitted, I went to Specsavers and they put me under a machine, which tested my eyesight. I had to press a button every time I saw something come on the screen and the machine printed out the results. They showed where I'd missed out, which was mainly in the top right quarter, so I didn't think my eyesight would be good enough for me to drive again.

Jeff and Sue took me to the Port Vale open day on 12 July. Before we went into the ground, we had a look at the new Roy Sproson statue, which had been brought along for people to see, even though it wasn't about to be erected. Also, we had a chat with the chairman, Bill Bratt, which was a minor privilege. We then went to the top of the Lorne Street Stand and admired the view of the beautiful ground.

The next day, Jeff took me to see Dr Roffe for my checkup and I gave her the printed results from Specsavers. She wasn't surprised by them and told me I'd got no vision on the top right-hand side. She said, 'You won't be able to drive, but I've occasionally seen patients recover, so you can try another eye test in three months.' I'd expected that outcome, but it was disappointing. It meant I hadn't got the same freedom as I'd had before and I couldn't any longer go where I wanted when I wanted to.

My old next-door neighbour, Brian Cotton, had died on 2 July and I somehow couldn't imagine it had happened. Jeff took me to his funeral at Shelton Church on 14 July and outside I spotted his ex-wife, Joan Wilding, who was using a wheeled walker. I was shocked about that as well because she seemed so young. We had a chat and the old days in Leek Road came into it. After the service, Jeff and I went to Hanley Cemetery, where Brian was buried, and we then attended the reception at the North Stafford Hotel.

On 20 July, Jeff and Sue went on holiday to Galloway, Northern Ireland and the Isle of Man, but while they were away my back started playing up and became very painful, even when I took painkillers. I had to get Dr Hapuarachi in, who fixed up for me to have an X-ray. I wasn't able to walk up the stairs and from then on relied on the lift to get me up and down.

When Jeff and Sue were on the Isle of Man, they looked around and found some of the places I'd been in the 1930s, including remains of Cunningham Holiday Camp. It was interesting to know what had happened to it and I visualized being there when they were talking about it. Also, they gave me some picture postcards of the horse-drawn trams in Douglas and they brought happy memories back.

I went to see Dr Roffe on 10 August for a checkup and she was happy with how I was doing. She told me to come back in a year's time and said that in the meantime I could go to Shelton Primary Care Centre, in Norfolk Street, for my blood tests to save me going all the way up to the hospital, so I did. Even that was a bind because of the problem with my back and having to get ready and get a taxi there. So I complained and after that a nurse came down to take the sample.

I started to get constipation and Jeff said it was being caused by the painkillers I was taking, so I knocked them off. That got me going to the toilet again, but I seemed to have a never-ending problem – pain or constipation or both.

Jeff and I both thought I needed help in the house because of my back trouble, so he got in touch with Social Services. On 13 August, one of the social workers, Jannette Ryan, came to see me. She wanted me to have some carers coming in to help, but it didn't seem right to me to do that. I didn't want anybody coming in the house, so I said I'd think about it and it was left at that.

Jeff recommended that I go to see Dr Christine Kusiar, a chiropractor, about my back because she'd done well to get Raedburh back on her legs in 2000. So, on 13 August, he took me to Christine's surgery, in Epworth Street, Stoke. I had to stand on a piece of apparatus, which was then tipped up, like a bed, so that I was lying face down on it. She pushed into my back, I think to try to straighten it out, but it was very painful. I wasn't very impressed with the treatment, but I thought it would be worth suffering if it would help. I should have paid her £40, but she charged me £25 and gave me a free ice pack to put on my back.

My X-ray appointment finally came through for 14 August, so I got an ambulance to the Outpatients and went to the Radiology Department. After they'd taken the X-rays there, I was told that they'd send the results to my doctor.

Two days later, Jeff and Sue took me to the Ramblers Retreat café, at the foot of Dimmings Dale, which was in a lovely spot. We sat in the garden and had an ice cream and a drink of tea while we looked out at the woods in the valley. Then we went on to Kingsley & Froghall Station, on the Churnet Valley Railway, and sat on a bench to see a train come in, but unfortunately it was pulled by a diesel and not a steam engine.

Jeff took me to my follow-up chiropractic appointment on 20 August, but Christine was on holiday, so I was seen by her brother-in-law, Bill Kusiar, and he had a different approach. He rubbed cream on my back and sore hip and ran an electrical instrument over my skin, from side to side. It was called ultrasound treatment and it wasn't painful. My back was improving by then, so Bill told me I didn't need to return the following week unless it was particularly bad.

Three days afterwards, I went with Jeff and Sue to Kidsgrove and they set up the scooter for me. We then went on a path, which followed the route of the old Loop Line up to the site of Newchapel & Goldenhill Station. Part of the path was a bit rough and I was jogged about, which started my back aching. The battery failed again partway back, so Jeff and Sue pushed me, which wasn't too bad because it was downhill, and, after a while, the scooter got going again and completed the journey.

On 26 August, I felt fit enough for Jeff to take me to Sainsbury's, in Hanley, to do my food shopping while he was doing his. I got round with the trolley okay and we went regularly after that, except for times when I had more back trouble. It was easier than me going to Marks & Spencer because Jeff took me from door to door and I didn't have to do any lifting, so it was a big help.

I still hadn't heard anything about the results of my X-ray, so Jeff rang the Harley Street surgery on 3 September and was told that I'd had 'an extensive fracture' of one of my ribs on my left-hand side. I was shocked when he gave me the news and I tried to puzzle out how I'd done it.

Three days later, Jeff and Sue took me to Stapeley Water Gardens, on the A 51 just south of Nantwich. I got on the scooter and we went round and looked at all the specimens they had, which included animals, fish and insects. We were there when their red piranhas were fed, but it was a letdown and not what I'd expected. I thought there'd have been a lot of action, but I don't remember much happening.

A week afterwards, we were off on our travels once more, this time to North Wales, despite me having trouble with my back again. We took a minor road off the A 5151, through Gwaenysgor, and had a picnic in a pull-in on the hill above Prestatyn. There was a marvellous view of the town and the coast from there, and the North Hoyle Offshore Wind Farm, five miles out to sea, looked as though it was hanging in the sky!

We had a brief look at the seafront and then went on to Llandudno. We'd planned to get a tram to the top of the Great Orme, but the driver said it wouldn't be suitable for me because it had got high steps and there was a changeover halfway. It was disappointing, but we got the scooter out of the car boot and went along The Promenade to the paddling pool, where I'd been with Helen in 2000. I must have put my foot down and got so far ahead that I couldn't see Jeff and Sue when I turned round, but after a short while, they came in sight, waving. We then sat outside the café by the pool and had a cup of tea and an ice cream in the sun and it was lovely.

After that, we paid £2.50 to go onto Marine Drive, which went round the bottom of the Great Orme. I was surprised that it was a one-way road and in places it was so close to the cliff edge that it felt as though we might drop into the sea! Also, we drove up to the top of the hill and there was a very good view from there, over part of Snowdonia and Anglesey. Then, to finish the day off, we had something to eat at Buttercups Bistro, at 155 Upper Mostyn Street, and it was okay.

My back became very painful again and I was struggling to look after myself, so I decided I needed some help after all. Jeff rang Jannette Ryan and she recommended me having three visits a day from carers: one in the morning, to help me get out of bed, have a shower and get my breakfast; a second about midday to do my lunch and make me a sandwich for tea time; and another at night to see me to bed. She said the latest they could put me to bed was 9.30, which was rather early, but, of course, I couldn't have everything exactly how I wanted it. Jeff and I didn't really know what was needed, so we decided to try that and, if necessary, alter it as we went along. The only problem was that it took three weeks to get it set up.

Because my back was so bad, Jeff booked me another chiropractic appointment for 17 September when I was seen by Christine. I went back five days later, but couldn't lie face down on the "torture couch" because I couldn't bear the pain, so she said she couldn't treat me properly. Anyway, she got me on the couch and pushed hard into my back and sides, which really hurt me.

I didn't have any more sessions with her after that because she said she didn't want to take my money off me without treating me properly and I didn't have any faith in the treatment, which seemed cruel. As it turned out, my back gradually started getting better again.

Around that time, little lumps of excrement started to drop out of me from time to time, which may have had something to do with all the painkillers I was taking. It was embarrassing and I had to look everywhere I was going in case I trod in a piece, which I did occasionally, and then made a mess.

So that the carers could get into the house without me having to get up to let them in, especially in the mornings, it was decided that I should have a key safe fitted outside. One was fixed free by Staffordshire Housing Association, of 2-4 Woodhouse Street, on 5 October and the carers (from Care Homes Stoke, who'd moved to Furlong Road, in Tunstall) started coming two days later. The first carer, Kelly Bentley, was half an hour late, so I got up and then she arrived a quarter of an hour after that. Then that night, another carer, Deb Docherty, came to put me to bed at eight o'clock, but I just had her help me undress and I stayed up till about eleven as usual. I carried on doing that afterwards, so I could still go to bed when I wanted to.

The times that the carers arrived were a bit haphazard and they were often different people. Sometimes I'd be lying in bed, wondering what time they'd come and on odd occasions I'd get up before anybody turned up. I cancelled a visit once when the carer was 1¾ hours late, but it more or less settled down eventually. After a few weeks, I started to have a pretty regular carer in the morning, Annie Clews, who was very good and almost always came within ten minutes of 8.30, which was a convenient time for me.

Having carers has been a very good thing, especially as a matter of safety. Helping me get out of bed has been important, to prevent me from falling down, and then they've seen me safely into the bathroom to go to the toilet and helped me have a wash or shower. Helping me get dressed and undressed has also been important to make sure I haven't overbalanced. And then they've done little jobs for me, like making me a cup of tea and my breakfast, which has saved me the bother. It would have been a struggle to have tried to carry on doing everything on my own, so I think it's helped me to stay in my home.

On 11 October, Jeff and Sue took me the Roaches Tea Rooms, which were just below Hen Cloud, and we had a drink in their conservatory. The sun was streaming in and it was quite warm. It was a nice place and there was a beautiful view of Tittesworth Reservoir.

About 1.30 in the morning on 14 October, I was in bed when I heard Jeff shouting: 'Dad! Dad! Are you alright?' I didn't know what was happening, but I said I was okay and he came upstairs. I had an emergency alarm, which was (and still is) connected to the council's Lifeline control centre, and I was wearing the alarm button round my neck. I was bemused, but I must have accidentally pressed it, so the centre (which was in Dewsbury Road, Fenton) had rung Jeff and told him it had gone off. He'd been worried and rung me, but of course had got no answer from the phone downstairs, so he'd driven over. I apologized for getting him out unnecessarily at that time in the morning and after that I took the alarm off when I went to bed.

My home care was costing £128 a week, but I'd applied for an attendance allowance to help me pay towards it. I was awarded £47.10 a week and got my first payment on 21 October, backdated to 14 August when I'd put in my application form.

I'd been wandering round the house in old shoes for a while, but Sue felt sorry for me and bought me a new pair of slippers, which she gave me on 25 October. We then went out with Jeff to Tittesworth Reservoir Visitor Centre, where we had a drink and an ice cream in their café. We sat by a window and gazed out at the wonderful countryside, including the reservoir. While we were there, Jeff read to me some of the pages of my book he'd typed up, to get my comments. It was taking a long time for us to finish the book and it was looking tight for Jeff to get it out for Christmas, so we decided it would be better to leave it till the following year rather than rush it and risk getting things wrong.

Three days later, Social Services brought two walking frames for me to use round the house. One was a trolley, like a mobile table, with two shelves and four wheels. It turned out to be handy to help me walk short distances downstairs safely and to transport food from the kitchen to my seat in the lounge. The other was a Zimmer frame, with two legs and two wheels, but I didn't find it much use because the other one was doing the job better.

Late at night on 28 October, I couldn't find my case with my keys in anywhere, so I wondered if it had dropped out of my pocket when I'd got out of Jeff's car in the afternoon. I'd got my pyjamas on, but put a jacket on top and went out with my torch to have a look for the keys along the road. I couldn't see anything, so I checked the pavement on the way back, but there was nothing there either. Finally, I had a second look in my trouser pockets and there the case was, having been there all the time!

On 2 November, Jeff, Sue and I were off on our travels again and had a look at Croxden Abbey (which was near to Alton) from the car. We then went on to Doveleys Garden Centre, in Denstone, but it was near closing time when we got there. We had a drink in the café, but the staff were mopping up with a bucket of water. I got up to go to the toilet, but my stick went from under me when I put it down because they hadn't dried the floor properly. I managed to get the stick under control, but told one of the staff off about it because I could have slipped over and been injured.

Eight days later, Lou Brady, of Disability Solutions (a charity based in The Old Wedgwood Johnson Buildings, in Pelham Street, Hanley), came down to see if she could get me an increase in my attendance allowance. We filled another application form in, but I didn't hear anything for over two months. Then I got a letter telling me that my allowance was being increased to £70.35 a week from 5 April 2010.

Afterwards, Jeff drove me to Cheapside to look for the building where I'd done my Trinity College of Music piano exams in 1929. I remembered that it had been called Gordon Chambers and when we got there, I spotted it straight away. Going there brought back memories, especially of wondering whether my hands would get too sticky through fear while I was playing, but fortunately they hadn't.

On 27 November, Dr Przyslo came to see me about my involuntary motions and told me to have a sachet of Fybogel (fibre) powder every morning and night. I said: 'That seems a lot. It might give me diarrhoea.' But he told me it would work itself out in time, so I carried out his instructions and the problem gradually got better. It eventually stopped altogether, so I finished taking the powder. Unfortunately, the problem returned the following spring and from then on I took Fybogel whenever I needed to.

Jeff and Sue took me to the Biddulph Grange Garden tea room on 29 November. It was in a big Victorian house, at Biddulph Grange Garden, in Grange Road, Biddulph. When we'd been out before, Sue had had a nice-looking type of coffee, called a cappuccino, so I thought I'd try one. I really enjoyed it, so I had one a time or two on our afternoons out after that, but then it didn't seem to taste as good and I went back to having tea most of the time.

The next day, Jannette called to assess me and wanted me to do more for myself, so we agreed to cut out the lunch-time visit, which suited me as well. She also wanted me to make my own sandwiches for my tea, but standing up and doing them made my back ache, so she decided that my morning carer would carry on making them. Then my back started aching less, so I got round to doing them myself again after all.

On 8 December, Ben Wain, a physio from Longton Cottage Hospital, in Upper Belgrave Road, Normacot, called and gave me two exercises to do each day, to try to straighten my back and keep me moving. When he came back, three days later, to check how I was doing, I said I couldn't do one of them, so he gave me another instead. After a while, I didn't do them very often because I kept forgetting, so they didn't have much effect.

Jeff was still trying to find things out for my book and on 10 December, he discovered that Stan Palin and his wife, Mollie, were still alive and living at 9 Ashmores Lane, in Alsager, where they'd been for many years. I'd lost touch with them a long time before and I was very surprised that they were both still there.

Jeff also ended up talking to Ray Skerratt, the youngest brother of my childhood pal, Lenny. Ray told Jeff that his sister, Evelyn, was still living at 32 Mulgrave Street, in Cobridge, where she'd been when I was a lad, which was amazing! Unfortunately, Monty Royle, her husband and my old friend, had died many years before.

The day before my 94th birthday, Jeff and Sue took me to the Roaches Tea Rooms for Sunday lunch. We were in the conservatory again and got talking to three people on the next table, whom I recognized from the previous time we'd been. One of them was a lady of 91 and, as a joke, I asked her, 'Have you got a boyfriend?' Everybody laughed!

On my birthday, I went with Jeff and Sue to the Staffordshire Regiment Museum, at Whittington Barracks, near Lichfield. It was a damp day and there was hardly anybody there. Because the scooter wasn't really suitable, Jeff got me a wheelchair and I propelled myself around. Inside, there were exhibits of uniforms, badges, helmets and so on. I tried on a helmet and it just suited me!

Outside, there was a mock First World War trench, which had sandbags on the top and was impressive, although we couldn't imagine what it would have been like in the actual situation when it would have been soaking wet and muddy, with bullets flying around.

Afterwards, we went to the nearby Whittington Arms and ordered some sandwiches, but the staff were very slow doing them and kept coming up with excuses for the delay. It must have taken about an hour before we eventually got them!

We then went back to Jeff's and I opened my presents. One of them was a big box of CDs, with all the films that Laurel and Hardy had ever made, which I was very pleased about. We tried one of the movies, *The Music Box*, which I still remembered from the 1930s and I was glad that I found it just as hilarious as I'd done then.

On 23 December, I went to Jeff's for a week and got on pretty well, especially as his house wasn't geared up for my needs. Sue joined us on Christmas Eve and we tried three more Laurel and Hardy films. We expected a similar amount of laughter as we'd had with *The Music Box*, but they weren't very good and we hardly made a murmur. I was bitterly disappointed because I'd thought we were in for a real treat.

Jeff and I went to the cemetery on Christmas Day, to remember Helen, while Sue did the dinner. Later, we opened our presents and Jeff had bought me a new CD/cassette player/radio because my old one wasn't playing CDs properly any more. At night, we had *Calamity Jane* on, which was a DVD of the 1953 musical that Jeff had bought Sue. But it had a very neat and tidy Wild Bill Hickok, which was far-fetched, and the film wasn't all that good.

On Boxing Day, we went to The Junction Inn, in Norbury Junction, just like we had the previous year, and again we played pool, but I only managed most of one game because I didn't want to risk straining my back.

The following afternoon, we had on *The Square Peg*, a DVD of the 1958 Norman Wisdom film, which Sue had bought Jeff. He thought it was funny, but I wasn't very impressed with it because it was all so ridiculous!

After tea, Sue, Jeff and I knocked out one or two tunes. She played her melodeon and Jeff and I tapped out time on one or two small pieces of percussion that he had. It didn't sound very impressive, but we had a bit of fun doing it.

I had a talk with Jeff about my car and said: 'It's no good to me now. Do you want it?' He decided to have it and use it to knock about in because it was cheaper to run than his own car and he's kept it ever since.

Jeff brought me back home on the 29th and it had all been a nice change for me, but about a week later my back started playing up again. Because it got worse, on 8 January 2010 I decided to send for Dr Przyslo, but he couldn't find anything wrong. He said my bones would be crumbling because of my age and prescribed calcium tablets, which I've taken ever since.

For two or three weeks, I'd been breathing more heavily and my legs and feet had swollen up. Although it wasn't stopping me from doing anything, the condition was frightening and I wondered if it might be serious.

Jeff was worried about me, but we went for a run in the car with Sue on 17 January, even though I didn't feel right. We went to Buxton and there was plenty of snow at the sides of the road once we got up into the hills. We then came back on the B 5053 through Longnor, where Jeff got us an ice cream each, which we enjoyed even though it was cold and there was snow and ice around.

That night, Jeff suggested I get the emergency doctor in to have a look at me, but I said I'd ring the Harley Street surgery in the morning. I did and, after I'd been examined at home by Dr Ashwini Nayak, I was taken off in an ambulance to Ward 21 of the Infirmary! I had a blood test and an X-ray and then a consultant, Dr George Varughes, said I'd got heart failure. I didn't hear him say that, but Jeff, who was with me, did and was stunned, thinking he'd misheard what had been said. The doctor said fluid was building up in my body and that they were going to try to drain it from my lungs and legs. So I was given water tablets, which kept making me urinate. I'd also got pneumonia, although we weren't told at the time, and I was given antibiotics through a drip fixed in one of my arms. I was then taken by ambulance to Bay 3 in Ward 84, in the Springfield Unit, at the City General.

My medicines seemed to work quite quickly because I stopped being breathless and the swelling in my legs and feet went down, but on my second night in the new ward there was a rumpus! I heard raised voices from the direction of Bay 4 and they got worse until a woman shouted and was nearly screaming. Then a man shouted 'Get out of my house!' and something that sounded like 'Murder!' I think he got hold of the woman, but I couldn't see what was happening because it was round a corner. I had a look around to see if there was anything I could defend myself with if things got out of control, but I couldn't see anything useful. The noise kept going up and down and, after about three-quarters of an hour, three policemen strolled past. Everybody gave them their version of what had happened and then the noise gradually died away.

When Jeff visited me on 21 January, someone was shouting out from the Bay 4 direction and I recognized the voice as being that of the man involved in the rumpus. So Jeff went to have a look and found out that it was one of the patients.

Jeff had found a CD player in the ward and brought me a few of my CDs from home to play on it. He plugged the machine in and put on one of my favourites, *Hits from the Blitz*, which turned out to be appreciated by other visitors.

The same night, Jeff was told by the ward sister that they'd stabilized me. She also said that I wouldn't be having any more tests because people could live okay with minor heart failure if they were given the right medication. So the condition turned out not to be as serious as Jeff had first thought.

On 25 January, a physio tested me walking and getting up and down from the toilet and then the doctors decided I was fit to go home the next day. That night, a girl named Lydia, who'd been a number of times with a group of people visiting Jack, the patient on my right, gave me a kiss and waved goodbye to me as she left.

The following afternoon, Jeff came for me and I walked to his car, with the aid of a walking frame from the ward. With me, I took three new medicines: ramipril (to stop my heart failure), frusemide (to make me pass water) and Sando-K (to give me extra potassium). I wondered if I was still up to looking after myself, but I managed to do my food shopping with Jeff after we'd left the hospital and I settled back in okay at home.

Jeff had been on to me about having a wheeled walker because he thought it would help me get along on my own, which I wasn't doing outside any longer. So he, Sue and I went to Ableworld, at 430 Leek Road, in Joiner's Square, on 7 February and had a look at the models that they'd got in. We didn't really know what we were looking for and it was hard to make a choice, but eventually I decided to buy a £49.95 solidly-built Tri-Wheeled Walker, with brakes and a bag for groceries. We then went to the huge new Trentham Garden Centre to try it out and I did okay. I've used it from time to time since and it's given me confidence to walk on my own.

Jeff and I went to see Sarah Bardsley, the manager of the Harley Street surgery, on 9 February. We had a chat with her and agreed to pay eighteen pounds for photocopies of my medical records for use in my book.

I was supposed to be having a shower every morning, but it was a bore and I didn't really get very dirty, so some days I didn't bother. It meant I was paying for care that I wasn't always having, so I decided to cut down on it. I rang Jannette and it was agreed that I'd have two showers a week and cut the visits down to half an hour on the other days.

On 13 February, I went for a walk along Leek Road with my wheeled walker and it was nice to be out. I got to Egerton Street and then turned back. I did very well and felt confident because Jeff was with me, but I'd had enough when I got back. On occasions when Jeff came over, I repeated the little walk and was always okay, but I got more tired as time went by and didn't go so far.

I also had a trot around with the walker when Jeff, Sue and I went to Tittesworth Reservoir on 28 February. I did about 150 yards and then we all went into the visitor centre for refreshments.

Jeff told me that he'd had a letter from Ros's solicitor on 3 March, saying that Ros would accept £75,000 to settle their affairs. Jeff said he could agree to that and it was pleasing that things were moving on for him. He asked if I could get the money ready that I'd said I'd give him and so I gave notices of withdrawal of savings from two of my accounts.

On 14 March, Jeff and Sue took me out for the afternoon. We decided to have a look at the field near Rudyard where I'd camped when I was a teenager. It was on the right of the A 523, coming from Leek, just before the turn to Rushton Spencer. A house, Fresh Water, had been built on the land and the field had been landscaped, so it didn't look the same, which was disappointing.

We carried on to Hulme End and went to The Tea Junction tearoom, which was in the old engine shed at the end of the dismantled Leek and Manifold Valley Light Railway. My wheeled walker came in handy because we had to walk to the tearoom from the car park and it meant I could get there and to other interesting places. The tearoom had been very well done and they were showing a video of the Peak District on a big television screen on one of the walls. We watched it while we had a drink and saw beautiful shots of the surrounding countryside.

The finding of the Staffordshire Hoard of Anglo-Saxon gold in 2009 had caused a sensation and there'd been a lot of publicity about it. Quite a number of items from it had been on display at The Potteries Museum (as the City Museum had been renamed) from 13 February to 7 March. There'd been long queues every day to see it and I hadn't fancied being in the middle of all those people, so I hadn't gone. A smaller display stayed there afterwards and Jeff took me to see it on 21 March. There was hardly anybody there and we just walked in. The staff were very helpful and loaned us magnifying glasses, but I was disappointed because the Hoard wasn't as elaborate as I thought it would have been. There was dirt on it and I thought they could have given it a brush, but maybe that would have risked damaging the precious stones in it. It wasn't shining very much, but I supposed it would be brilliant when it was cleaned up.

On 31 March, Jeff told me that he might lose his job at the college, which was £4,800,000 in debt. I started worrying about whether he'd have enough money, but he appeared to be taking it well. I hoped things would turn out okay, but there seem to be redundancies all the time now, so where is it going to end?

On Easter Sunday, I went for a run with Jeff and Sue to the Cheshire Workshops, in Barracks Lane, Higher Burwardsley, on the Mid-Cheshire Ridge. They made and sold a large variety of candles there, but my back was aching a bit, so I had a cup of tea and a cake in the café instead of looking at them. On the way back, we went past Beeston Castle, but it was a ruin and looked more like a jumble of rocks. Then we had a lovely tea at Jeff's.

Jeff and Sue took me to the cemetery on 7 April and I got down to Helen's grave with their help. It didn't seem two years since she'd died. Things went in and out of my head, but I felt okay. Jeff had put quite a lot of flowers in the grave and it was looking nice, so I wondered if we'd need a headstone.

I went with Jeff and Sue to try out Biddulph Grange Country Park, off Grange Road, in Biddulph, on 25 April, but we found the entrance to the disabled car park padlocked! That meant we couldn't do anything there, so we went to Astbury Meadow Garden Centre, in Newcastle Road, Astbury, just southwest of Congleton, and had a cup of tea instead, which wasn't quite as exciting!

On 3 May, we all had another trip to Kingsley & Froghall Station and this time there was music from the 1940s playing in the café, which was very nice to hear. It brought back memories and I sang along to some of it. While we were there, there was a terrific hailstorm.

For a change, Jeff and Sue took me to Tunstall Park on 23 May. I hadn't been there for a long time, but I walked to the lake, with the aid of my wheeled walker. We sat down on a bench and had an ice cream because it was hot. We noticed a goose distracting a swan on the lake from its goslings by going up close to it so that the swan chased it and the goose kept performing the same trick. It was intriguing to watch and it was still going on when we left.

Six days later, when he came for lunch, Jeff told me that he'd had a letter from Stafford County Court telling him that he'd been divorced on the 27th! I was relieved and Jeff handled the news very well.

When he left, he found a parking notice for seventy pounds on my car, which he'd left outside my house! When he looked, he found that my parking permit had run out 2½ months before. I was trusting him to deal with such things, but he'd thought the permit was permanent. He appealed to Parking Services about it, but they weren't at all sympathetic and so I paid £35, which was the amount required for an early settlement.

On 13 June, Jeff and Sue took me to Crewe Heritage Centre, which was off Vernon Way, just north of Crewe Station. Just inside the entrance of the main exhibition area was an old bench with 'Prestatyn' painted on it. It must have come from Prestatyn Station and it brought back memories of when Helen and I used to take Jeff on holiday there, so he and I sat on it and had Sue take our photo. There was also a railway stamps exhibition and part of a diesel cab, which we went in. We then walked on to Crewe North Signal Box, which had a café, a viewing window of the junction of the railway lines from North Wales, Liverpool and Manchester, and a signals and points power room, with wires everywhere, which was pretty interesting.

On the way back home, the heavens opened and the rain was so heavy that we all sat in the car outside my house for over half an hour before it eased off enough for us to get out!

Sue was a morris dancer and performed with Glorishears of Brummagem, an all-women group, who were from around the Birmingham area. Jeff had been out to see her dancing a time or two and joined the group as a musician, playing different types of percussion. On 19 June, they performed at the Lichfield Festival, so they were doing quite well.

The following day, Jeff, Sue and I went to the Roaches Tea Rooms for Father's Day lunch, but the service was pretty slow. Afterwards, we sat outside in the sun and there were two black and white cats, which kept coming for a fuss. Then one of them caught a mouse and left it by a nearby table!

Because it seemed very likely that Jeff would lose his job at the college, he'd asked for voluntary redundancy, which meant he'd get better conditions. On 25 June, he got the news that his application had been successful. I wondered if he'd done the right thing, but there didn't really seem to have been anything else he could have done.

Two days afterwards, I went to Jeff's to watch England play Germany in the second round of the World Cup finals. There was a controversy because England had a goal disallowed when the ball was over the line, but it didn't matter at the end because they lost 4-1 and were well beaten. I was also at Jeff's for the final, on 11 July, which Spain won 1-0 against the Netherlands, but it was a bore and I fell asleep twice while it was on!

A week later, Jeff and Sue went on holiday to Wester Ross and Jeff rang and told me about places they'd been to on the way, like Balloch and Fort Augustus, which I remembered from previous holidays of my own. They'd walked up the side of the staircase locks on the Caledonian Canal at Fort Augustus and seen four boats sail out into Loch Ness, but there was no plague of flies there like there had been on our family holiday in 1969!

Jeff told me that he and Sue had walked over the Skye Bridge, which had been opened in 1995, and he said the views of, and from, it were amazing. I tried to visualize the gap between the mainland and the island from the memory of my visit there with Helen in 1973 and to imagine it with the bridge added. When I saw Jeff and Sue's photos later, the bridge looked quite impressive.

Jeff later rang to tell me that they'd visited Plockton, Gairloch and Inverewe Gardens. I was pleased to hear about them and I had happy memories of them too.

On 31 July, Jeff rang and said he was in Muir of Ord, where he'd found my wartime army camp, which was overgrown, and only the old concrete bases were left. Soon after, he called again and told me he'd been into the Lovat Arms Hotel, in Beauly, where our officers had stayed when we were there, but the building that had been the mules' stables had burned down and a new garage stood in its place. However, Jeff and Sue had discovered that there was a plaque outside

Beauly Priory commemorating all the soldiers, like me, who'd trained there during the war. It was very interesting to hear about it all and I was very pleased that Jeff had rung me with the news.

Jeff had to go to see David Moore, his solicitor, at Bailey, Wain and Curzon, at Springfield House, in Baker Street, Fenton, on 2 August to sign the Land Registry form to put his house into his name alone. Ros had already been paid the agreed £75,000, so it was then all over, thank goodness!

I hadn't been very happy with my gardener, Paul Berry, for a while because he'd kept doing short time and not tidying up properly, which was giving Jeff another job. Young Harry volunteered Matthew for the work, but it didn't seem fair to expect him to do it because it was a big and regular job. So I looked in *The Sentinel* and tried John Goodwin, from 3 Heron Close, in Packmoor, who'd advertised his services. John seemed to do a good job and kept more or less to the time he was supposed to be there, so I kept him on.

I could see wasps around one of my kitchen windows, so Jeff had a look on 7 August and found them flying in and out from my tiles, so there must have been a nest. I rang the council, but was told it would cost £58 for them to do the job. Jeff sprayed insect killer into the nest, but it wasn't successful, so I decided to wait and see if the wasps were still there after the winter. As it turned out, I had no further problem with them.

On 8 August, I went with Jeff and Sue to Blaze Farm, which was on the A 54 in Wildboarclough. The place was scruffy, but we sat at a table outside in the sunshine and had one of their Hilly Billy ice creams each, which were nice.

Jeff rang on 12 August and told me that my sister-in-law, Ethel, had died that morning. I was sorry to hear about it, but I hadn't seen her for a long time and so the news didn't upset me too much. Her funeral service was on the 24th at St. John's Church, in Greasley Road, and she was buried afterwards in Carmountside Cemetery. I thought it would be too much of a strain to go, so Jeff represented me.

On 16 August, Jeff took me to the City General Cardiology Unit for a checkup on my pacemaker. My battery was checked and then I heard something being mentioned about 2½ to 3 years, so I thought, 'It looks like I've had it.'

I didn't have time to panic before Jeff realized I'd got mixed up and he said to me, 'That's the length of time that the battery's got left!' I was very relieved!

Six days later, I went with Jeff and Sue to the Tern Valley Vintage Machinery Trust annual show, in Sugnall Park, near Eccleshall. Because of the size of the show, I used the mobility scooter to go round it, but it still took us 2½ hours to see the surprisingly large number of stationary engines, steamrollers, tractors, old army vehicles and vintage cars, lorries, buses, motorbikes and caravans that had been assembled.

On 24 August, Jeff and I did our weekly food shopping at Sainsbury's, but when we got back to my house in the evening, my key wouldn't open the front door. We were fiddling about for many a while before Jeff decided he'd try to get in through my back door. He climbed over two neighbours' walls and opened the door, but unfortunately found the next door, to the kitchen, was bolted! He then disappeared and came back with a fellow whom I didn't recognise. He turned out to be one of my neighbours, Angelo Pezzaioli, of number 331. After a few minutes, Angelo had prised the door open and discovered that the problem was a screw out of alignment. I was very relieved to get back in and, the next day, he returned with a new screw of the right length and repaired my lock. He wouldn't accept any money and said, 'If you're in trouble, let me know.' I thought how lucky I'd been that he'd done all that for me for nothing because I'd have had to have paid a lot of money if I'd called out a locksmith to do the job at that time of day.

Jeff asked me if I'd like to go to the seaside with him and Sue for a night for a break. The last time I'd been away was in 2001 and I thought I'd finished going on holidays. He booked up the digs at Sandy Brook Farm, in Wyke Cop Road, Snape Green, just outside Southport, and off we went on 3 September. When we got there, we had a picnic in the sun in their garden, with hens, a cock and ducks wandering about.

We then went to Formby to try to see red squirrels in the pine woods behind the sand dunes. We didn't see any, but we did get the scooter stuck in deep sand a time or two, so that Jeff and Sue had to carry it till we got on firmer ground!

At night, we went to Sorrento, an Italian restaurant, at 29 Three Tuns Lane, in Formby, and had a pizza each. It was quite an experience because it was the first foreign restaurant I'd ever been in, but I was on safe ground because I'd been having a pizza with Jeff for lunch on Saturdays for a while. Afterwards, he drove us along the sea front at Southport and we saw green lights flashing in the sky. We later found out that they were lasers in Blackpool, whose illuminations had just been switched on by Robbie Williams, who, like me, was from Stoke.

The next day, we went into Southport and Sue drove us along Lord Street, which I'd wanted to see again. It was still very wide and high class. We then got a tram to the end of the pier and went into the Pavilion, where the National Museum of Penny Slot Machines was. It was a novelty to see and remember how the machines had looked in the old days. We then caught the tram back and went into Southport Model Railway Village, which was interesting and a bit like the Land of the Little People that used to be in the town. We also had a look at the fairground, New Pleasureland, and some of its rides were hair-raising!

At night, Jeff decided I was ready to go to a Mexican restaurant he knew, Fuego's, at 3-5 Stanley Street. I had no trouble eating the meal, which didn't seem all that different from English food, and Jeff played along, on a couple of small drums that were lying around, with the music coming out of the speakers.

It was a lovely break and it was interesting to do things I hadn't done before. We all thought I'd done very well overall and better than expected.

Jeff took me to the Outpatients on 27 September for my annual stroke checkup. I was seen by Dr Sanyal, and not Dr Roffe herself, so they must have thought I was doing alright. It all went okay and I was happy to get a copy of the follow-up letter Dr Sanyal wrote to my surgery saying, 'I am pleased to say he is doing very well.'

On 1 October, Jeff noticed that the council had charged me for home care when I'd been in hospital and on holiday and on special occasions when we'd cancelled it. So he got on to them about it and eventually managed to get me the money refunded.

I didn't seem to be able to read very well and thought there was a problem with my eyes. Jeff thought the difficulty was because the light was so poor in my lounge because I'd had to replace my old 150-watt bulb with a 20-watt low energy one. He took me to Specsavers for an eye test on 12 October and was proved right because the optician's report said there'd been 'No change' in my sight since my last visit. That was very good news, but it didn't help with my reading.

Jeff was spending a lot of time working on my book, trying to get it finished off. On 31 October, he took me to different places for me to identify so he could take photos of them. The old Majestic Ballroom and Theatre Royal buildings were still standing in Pall Mall, the Coronation Working Men's Club was still there in Mulgrave Street and the Cobridge Picture Hall premises remained in Waterloo Road, but Cobridge Post Office and the James Macintyre & Co. Limited factory, in Burslem, had been demolished.

We wanted a photo of my old pal, Lenny Skerratt, for my book, so Jeff took me to see Lenny's sister, Evelyn, in Mulgrave Street, on 2 November. I hadn't seen her for over forty years and she made such a fuss of us.

Jeff finally finished his work on the first half of my book and got 300 copies of it run off by Hanley Print Services, of Shelton Enterprise Centre, in Bedford Street, Shelton. We'd decided that we'd get it out in two parts because of the large number of words and we called this first book *A Potteries Past*.

Jeff had fixed up for us to launch the book at the New Vic Theatre, in Basford, on 27 November. It snowed overnight, but I got down my steps okay and into Sue's car. Jeff had set us up at a couple of tables upstairs in the theatre and I was sitting there with all these people milling around. It was exciting and I felt rather important because people came up to talk to me and have their copies of the book signed. People took photos of me with my book and Richard Ault and Fred Hughes interviewed me for *The Sentinel*. Afterwards, Jeff drove us on what seemed a grand tour of Newcastle and Hanley, so that he could sell copies of the book to shops there.

The next day, Jeff and Sue took me to Radio Stoke, in Cheapside, so that Terry Walsh could interview me about my book on his *Good Times* programme. He gave me some headphones, but I found them confusing to use. He was facing me and asked quite a number of questions, which I had to answer on the spot. My interview seemed to go down alright and I didn't muck it up as much as I thought I would have done. It was interesting to do and I got actual experience in the studio.

The day after, there was a very nice write-up in *The Sentinel* about the book and me, which was spread over nearly three-quarters of a page, and two photos were included. It was quite something to see myself in the newspaper and I felt important when people mentioned it afterwards.

On my 95th birthday, Jeff took me to the National Brewery Centre, in Horninglow Street, Burton upon Trent, but it was perishing, which was a pity because there seemed to be a lot of things of interest. The museum was supposed to be mainly indoors, but they had the doors wide open, so it was like being outside. It was so cold that before long we decided to go, but we couldn't get out because the exit door was locked. Jeff bumped into a workman, who went off and found someone to let us out! It was a relief because I had visions of us having to stop there all night in the cold.

By Christmas, 135 copies of my book had been sold, which didn't seem many, really. However, there were obviously people who wanted to read about the life of an ordinary working-class fellow like me, which, in a way, was remarkable.

I went to Jeff's for four days over Christmas and, of course, Sue was there. It was nice and cosy and a change from the usual routine. We watched the 1981 First World War movie, *Gallipoli*, on DVD, which Jeff had bought me, but I didn't think there was enough action in it. Then we had another DVD film on, *How the West Was Won*, which had come out in 1962, but it didn't seem in the same class as the usual cowboy films. Also, we saw a Channel 5 programme, *There's A Hippo In My House!*, about a couple in South Africa, who had a hippopotamus called Jessica living with them! Even though she was very tame, it was ridiculous, really, having such an animal around, causing damage in the house.

One of the things Jeff bought me for Christmas was a table lamp and, when I got home, he fixed it up for me in my lounge. It was quite bright and concentrated the light on the print of what I wanted to read, so it was no longer blurred because of my lounge being dull. The optician turned out to be right about my eyes having not deteriorated and I'm reading properly again now.

There was a very interesting two-part drama on BBC Two on 6 and 7 January 2011 about the sinking of the British troopship, RMS Laconia, by the U-156 German submarine on 12 September 1942. The Germans were supposed to be butchers and villains, but the U-boat commander, Werner Hartenstein, was kind-hearted and rescued as many survivors as he could, ending up with a crowd of people on deck and four lifeboats in tow. He radioed for assistance and put a Red Cross flag on deck, but was attacked by an American B-24 Liberator bomber. Hartenstein then had to cut the lifeboats adrift and order the survivors into the sea so that his boat could dive to safety, but he was awarded Germany's highest military honour, the Knight's Cross, for his efforts. I hadn't known about all that till I saw it on TV because those kinds of things were kept hush-hush, especially during the war.

My cousin, Stan, rang me up and invited me to visit him in Alsager, so Jeff took me on 14 January. It had been many years since I'd seen him and it was nice to renew his acquaintance. He hadn't changed much from how I remembered him, even though his wife, Mollie, had died, on 1 November. We had a good chat about the old times.

There was a scare about my car on 18 January because the mechanic that Jeff used, Roger Chadwick, at The Hollies, in Station Road, Cotes Heath, thought it would cost £400 or more to get it through the MOT. I felt a bit sorrowful because it looked as if it would be sensible to scrap it, which I knew would have to happen some time. But Jeff rang Kennerley's Cauldon Garage and was quoted £189 to have some welding done to fix it up, so we agreed to that. It was a nice feeling that it would still be around because it had been a good servant and brought back happy memories of many trips I'd made in it with Helen.

On 20 January, I read on the front page of *The Sentinel* that there'd been a murder in Birches Head and then saw a name that caught my attention – Bridget Purcell! She and another woman, Stephanie Stubbs, had been charged with stabbing William James Anderson to death with a knife at 21 Chorlton Road, on the 16th, and they were remanded in custody by Stafford Crown Court. I thought of what might have happened when Purcell had forced her way into my house in 2006.

On 1 February, Jeff gave me a copy of *The Sentinel's* old times paper, *The*

Way We Were, which had come out three days before. He'd fixed up for them to do a six-part series of stories from my book, with photos, and it was a thrill when I saw that I'd got a double page. It isn't very often anybody has a write-up like that and I wondered if I was worthy of it, though I was very pleased.

Soon after, Jeff and I heard from a lady named Margaret Rowley, who'd seen the piece, and she was the elder daughter of my cousin, Wilf Wallett. I hadn't seen him since I was a lad and she said he'd died in 1977. She told me that my maternal grandparents, George and Ann Wallett, had had eleven children and not nine, as I'd thought! I hadn't previously known about William, who'd been born in 1898, and Reginald, in 1901. Margaret also said that my Uncle Bram had deserted from the army in 1920 and that he was still listed as missing the following year!

It's amazing how people find things out! On 14 February, Jeff was contacted by Rose Brooke, who said she wanted a copy of my book. She was the youngest daughter of my old friend, Jack Green, who'd died in 1963! I was very pleased to have heard from her and to know that she remembered me. She was still living in Blackpool and told Jeff that her mother (and Jack's wife), Rose, had died in 1995. She also said that her older sister, Pat, had moved to Ainsdale, near Southport, but that her eldest sister, Mildred, was living in Bentilee and had already bought one of my books!

My kitchen fluorescent light stopped working and I didn't have a replacement, so the day after, 15 February, I rang my neighbour, Angelo, to see if he knew a good electrician. He said, 'I'll be round in five minutes,' but he was here in about two! He pulled the starter out, had a look at it and thought he might have one, so he went home to check. Before long, he was back with one and fixed it up for me for free. It was marvellous and my luck was really in because he wanted to buy a second copy of my book, but for shame I couldn't make him pay for it!

There was very bad news on 24 February because Sue was told she was being made redundant from her job, but I think she was expecting it might well happen. I wondered if she'd get another one or whether she'd have to sell her house to try to get by.

Four days later, there was a body blow because Sue was told that she'd got leukaemia and she'd have to spend a long time being treated in hospital, although it seemed that she could be cured eventually. Jeff was with her at the time and they were very upset. I wondered if she'd pull through because having leukaemia seemed like a death sentence. I also wondered how Jeff would take it, but he coped wonderfully well and went to see her in New Cross Hospital, in Wolverhampton Road, Wednesfield, every day, except for a time or two when she was too ill to have visitors. Also, he did a lot of jobs for her while she was in the hospital.

Sue started to have chemotherapy on 3 March, but she soon got cellulitis in her right ear and developed blisters over most of her body. The hospital didn't seem to be clear as to what had caused the problems and put her in a room on her own because they thought she'd got an infectious disease. For a few days, Jeff had to put on a protective apron and gloves when he went into her room! He became very worried about her because for a short while he thought she was more poorly each day than the last. When the worst of it was over, she spent a lot of the time sleeping and it was 30 March before the hospital let her out for a week's break.

On 13 March, Jeff took me for a trip out to Trentham Garden Centre and we had an ice cream there. We bumped into one of Jeff's old students, Caroline Johnson, who told me that he was a 'fantastic lecturer' and she shook my hand and congratulated me on my book!

Sometimes when I'm food shopping, I see something that catches my eye and think I'll try it. I have pre-cooked meals at lunch time, but I don't know whether some of them are English or foreign food because I don't particularly read the labels and sometimes the meals are too hot or irritate my throat.

I'd been able to feel a scab on the top of my head for a while, but it wasn't painful. Eventually, I decided to get it looked at and, on 23 March, Dr Timothy John, from the Harley Street surgery, came down and examined it. He didn't know what it was, but said it wasn't cancerous and I should see how it went on. During that night, the scab came off and the skin was smooth underneath, but the scab grew again. It's since come off a time or two, but has regrown and is still there. However, it isn't on my mind because nothing has ever become of it and I've got other things to worry about.

Jeff came to see me on 3 April and Sue was with him. He'd told me she'd lost all the hair on her head because of her treatment, so I was prepared for it, but she bore up very well and was very brave about it. We went to Central Forest Park, where I'd never been before. We pulled into the car park off Chell Street and had an ice cream while we watched the geese and ducks in action on the lake. The park was like countryside, with miniature mountains, and was a big improvement on the wasteland that it had been before it had been reclaimed. After a short while, we moved on to Westport Lake, which was a big expanse of water that helped to beautify the city.

On 7 April, it was three years since Helen had died. I no longer thought she was next to me in the bed when I woke at night, but sometimes I still had it on my mind when I was downstairs in the day that she was asleep in her chair in the lounge. When that happened, I tried to be quiet, so as not to wake her up, but when I turned my head, I realized and could see that she wasn't there. It was a bit annoying, but it didn't upset me.

Sue had started her second chemotherapy treatments on 6 April, but was allowed out of hospital four days later because she was doing well. A week afterwards, I went with her and Jeff to Hulme End, where we sat round a bench in the sun and enjoyed an ice cream in a dish each from The Tea Junction. On the way home, we thought we'd switch the car radio on and listen to how Stoke were doing about twenty minutes into their FA Cup semi-final against Bolton Wanderers at Wembley. I didn't fancy Stoke's chances, but, to our surprise, they were already 2-0 up! Even then, I wondered if they'd make a mess of it and let Bolton back into the match, but they ended up winning 5-0, which was marvellous!

A week later, Jeff, Sue and I went to Deep Hayes Country Park, which was between Longsdon and Cheddleton, on the site of the old reservoir. We sat on a bench in a beautiful spot above Cumberlidge Pool and watched the ducks wandering about, boldly trying to get titbits from the visitors.

On 3 May, Jeff and I picked up from *The Sentinel* offices our copies of the latest edition of *The Way We Were*, in which was printed another of my book stories. Jeff pointed out to me that in the paper there was a letter from an Alan

Walker, of Trentham, about the gas explosion that had occurred on 6 August 1939 at 56 Derwent Street, in Cobridge, where I'd been born. Alan had included a cutting from the following night's *Sentinel*, which had reported it, and an attached photo showed the front of the house and that of number 54 to have been completely collapsed, although, miraculously, no-one had been seriously injured.

Sue went back into hospital on 3 May for her third chemotherapy treatments, but because she'd complained of having heart palpitations, it was decided to investigate them before going any further. So she was allowed out the next weekend and, on the Sunday (the 8th), she treated Jeff and me to lunch at the Ramblers Retreat. We had a lovely meal, but there was so much food that there was hardly enough room to put it all on the table, although we managed to eat most of it. Afterwards, I went to the disabled toilet, but when I caught hold of a manouevrable handrail, it came loose and hit me on the top of the head! Fortunately, it didn't do me any damage, but Jeff complained about it. A few minutes later, one of the co-owners, Gary Keeling, came over and said he'd fixed it and he told us all about the history of the Ramblers Retreat.

On 14 May, Jeff came down to watch the FA Cup final, at Wembley, on television with me. Stoke's opponents were Manchester City, who had a lot of expensive players in their team, so I didn't hold out much hope of Stoke winning and therefore wasn't too disappointed when they didn't. The match was alright, but it wasn't very exciting. Manchester were in a different class, but only won 1-0. Stoke didn't do too badly, but I'd expected them to bustle Manchester out of their poise and they didn't.

Jeff thought it would be a good idea to copy all my cine films onto DVDs because they'd then be much easier to watch and so that we'd got duplicates in case any of the originals were ever damaged. He decided to have them done by a company called Images4life Limited, who were at 6 Wychwood Park, near Weston, in Cheshire. He told me that their premises were on the same private housing development where Phil Taylor lived, which had a security guard at its entrance! I couldn't imagine the films being any different on DVD, but Jeff had a title put on each film and it all looked very professional. It was amazing because my 131 cine films were stored in two cardboard boxes whereas they'd been put on only six DVDs, which fitted into two small plastic cases! The whole job cost £639.06, but Jeff seemed to think it was worth it, partly because he thought there were enough scenes of general interest to make a DVD to sell.

On 31 May, Sue was told that her treatments had been successful and that she'd no longer got any leukaemia. I was very thankful about that when Jeff told me, but she wasn't able to leave the hospital for another twelve days because her blood levels were so low that she might not have been able to have fought off an infection if she'd picked one up.

Jeff had got in touch with some of the old Postal Sports Club footballers from the 1960s to find out things for my book. I was surprised that he tracked them down, but he seemed to be good at doing things like that. On 11 June, he went to see Dave Lovatt, at 29 Laburnum Grove, in Blurton, and then came to my house with photographs and newspaper cuttings of the old teams, which were very interesting. Dave had been a good footballer and was a nice lad.

On 25 June, Jeff and I were having our lunch at my house when Ted Green, the old postman and Postal centre-half, knocked on the door. Jeff had been talking to him about my book and he'd decided to pay me a visit. It was a surprise, but we spent nearly two hours reminiscing about the old times. The only bad thing that came up in what Ted said was that Bert Ash, the old football team captain, had died, which I was surprised about.

Jeff had told me a time or two that he'd had itching on occasions for years, but it didn't seem to have bothered him too much. However, around this time, it got worse, so he had a blood test. It showed that he'd got a rare blood disorder called polycythaemia vera and he was told that he'd have to have blood taken out from time to time at Staffordshire General Hospital, which would, hopefully, reduce or stop his itching. We'd had enough with Sue having all her treatment, without anything else going wrong, so it was a bit of a blow, but Jeff seemed to carry on as normal.

After Sue had come out of hospital, I thought that was it and everything would get back to normal. However, she still had to have another dose of chemotherapy as an outpatient on 14 July.

When I looked out of the front window on 15 July, I noticed that the red fibreglass elephant had returned to Jumbo Self Storage across the road. I didn't like it any more than I had when it had first been displayed, but it's still there now.

I became more and more reluctant to do things because I found it increasingly hard work. On 23 July, I went for a walk along the road with Jeff, but my knees and back were playing up and I only made it to two houses from home. I didn't go for a walk from home after that, but I didn't stop doing so deliberately.

Jeff and Sue took me for a run to Wettonmill on 31 July and we had an ice lolly at a table outside the café. I decided to go to the toilet, but I couldn't get in with my wheeled walker because there was a bin in the way. Jeff had to move it and then put it back after I'd come out. It happened a second time just before we left and so Jeff decided to complain to the manager. She didn't want to know and said it was somebody else's responsibility. Jeff then complained to the National Trust, who owned the property, and they said they'd investigate, but he never had an answer from them, which was a poor show.

I'd been waiting to hear what had happened to Bridget Purcell and I read in *The Sentinel* on 13 August that, the day before, she'd been found guilty of murder and sentenced to at least 16½ years in gaol. The other woman, Stephanie Stubbs, who'd actually done the stabbing, had been given not less than fifteen years' imprisonment. I think the sentence was about right, but it seemed strange that the person who'd done the killing had had a lesser sentence than Purcell.

On 28 August, I was going down the stairs on the stair lift when it stopped working. I fiddled with the controls, but it still wouldn't go, so I was stuck about halfway down. I had to do something, so I carefully worked my way out of the seat, which was a struggle because I was afraid of falling down the stairs. I decided to walk backwards down the stairs and held the handrail on the way. I eventually got down and was thankful I was steady enough on my feet to have done so. I then tried the control on the wall and got the lift to work, so I was later able to get up to bed. The next day, I rang Stannah, the repair company, and the engineer who came replaced a broken spring on the lift. I had no further problem.

A fellow named John Pye had got in touch with Jeff after reading my story about his father, the singer, Ron Pye, in *The Way We Were*. John wanted to meet me and buy a copy of my book, so Jeff gave him my address and he called down on 1 September. We had a chat, I signed one of my books for him and he gave me a copy of a book he'd written, *The Force Was With Me*, which was about when he'd been a policeman. He seemed pleased with my book and I was very happy that he was interested in it.

My old hut, which Dad had erected before the war, was still standing and I was hoping to beat the record for having the oldest one in the world! It needed a new protective plastic sheet fixing on top of it because the old one was falling to pieces. So I rang the council and they put me in touch with a handyman, Matt Mace, who did the job for me on 5 September for £9.50, which was the cost of the materials! We got talking and he'd been reading my stories in *The Way We Were*, so he wanted a one of my books. Jeff delivered a signed copy to him and told me that Matt was so over the moon with it that he'd paid £20 for it. So I got my hut fixed at a profit!

Jeff rang me on 20 September and told me that he'd been walking down his road and seen the council's mobile library parked, so he'd popped into it. To his surprise, he'd spotted a copy of my book on its shelves and noticed that it had been taken out twice already. I thought it was incredible that a book of a poor, lowly author like me was on travelling show and it was a thrill to have heard about it.

There'd been quite a bit of banging at Nancy's old house next door and I found a note on my doormat on 22 September, apologizing for the noise. Eventually, it stopped and I was told by a neighbour that the house had been done up for a student from Staffordshire University to live there, but I've still not met her!

In late September, Jeff and Sue were on holiday in Pembrokeshire and, on the 29th, went on a boat trip from Tenby to Caldey Island. There were big waves on the way back and the boat couldn't land on the beach as it should have done. Instead it put in at the bottom of the lifeboat launching ramp, with the lifeboat close by in the sea, I suppose in case there was an accident. The passengers were unloaded onto the ramp, which had no handrail, and had to walk up it to safety. Jeff and Sue could easily have fallen into the sea and been drowned, but Jeff didn't seem to have been very frightened by the experience.

Jeff's treatment had succeeded in getting his blood disorder under control and his doctor at the hospital (Dr Hameed) was pleased with his progress. Jeff's itching had improved and, after 6 October, he only had to have one more venesection until 26 January 2012. I was very pleased that he was doing so well.

Jeff and Sue took me to the Roaches Tea Rooms on 15 October and we each had an ice cream in a dish, but they were mean with the scoops. There wasn't even a full scoop each, so Sue complained to the waitress, who took them away, but pulled her face. A waiter then brought us our replacements, which amazingly had three scoops each!

On 25 October, a nurse came to get a sample of my blood to check if my warfarin dose was still right. It's changed from time to time, but it's mostly been pretty steady. She couldn't get the needle in a vein in either arm because I haven't got enough flesh to hold the veins in place while the procedure is being done, so they wobble about. Another nurse came the following week and this time she was successful.

Sue had had a plastic tube put in her chest when she was in hospital, so that the nurses could put her medicines in through it and take blood samples from it. Because it had taken her blood levels a long time to go up, the doctors had decided to leave the tube in, but by November the levels were getting back towards normal. So, on the 2nd, the tube was taken out, which meant that her hospital treatment had finally ended. She went back to work on the 17th, but only for one day that week, in a new job she'd got with Walsall Council as a public safety enforcement officer. It seemed a bit soon for her to be returning to work after she'd been ill all those months, but the idea was for her to start off gradually and then build up to working full time again. So she was still progressing, which was the main thing.

Jeff had been writing a new book about how things might have turned out differently in Vale's history. It was called *What If There Had Been No Port In The Vale?* and was published on 25 November. He launched it at the club shop that night and had Harry, Colin Askey and Peter Ford along, as ex-players, to sign copies of the book with him. I was confident that Jeff knew what he was doing because he does his publishing in a really professional way.

On 4 December, Jeff took part in a humorous play at Castle Bromwich Hall Gardens, near Birmingham. He dressed up as a Wild West gunfighter and played the part of Wild Bill Hitchcock, deliberately misspelling the real character's surname for effect! I wasn't surprised at him doing it because he did different things and it was good that he'd had the courage to do it.

Jeff and I did our weekly food shopping at Sainsbury's on 13 December and he had a chat with the checkout assistant about me and my book. Hey presto and she ordered a copy, so that was another book sold! It was a real surprise, but I hadn't put it past Jeff to chat people up to sell books to them.

I was 96 on 14 December and wished my age was going backwards, to about twenty. Jeff and Sue took me to Amerton Farm & Craft Centre, near Stowe by Chartley, near Stafford, for the afternoon. We had a nice lunch and then Jeff pushed me round the place in a wheelchair because it was too far for me to walk. They had a huge pig and a tiny cow and there was a potter, with whom we had quite a chat.

We then went back to Jeff's, where I opened my cards and presents before he and Sue took me to Miso, a Japanese restaurant, at 161-163 London Road, in Stoke, for the evening. I'd got used to foreigners running things, so I didn't think much about it being Japanese. I thought the starter was the main course, but I liked the sushi that was served up, although their green tea was too weak. It was an experience anyhow and when I was young, I'd have thought it romancing if somebody had told me that one day there'd be a Japanese restaurant in London Road!

By Christmas, Jeff had sold 388 copies of his new Vale book, but he was very disappointed about that because the number of sales was a long way down from those he'd achieved with his earlier books on the club. However, because he'd only had 500 printed, he didn't have a lot of copies left on his hands.

As usual, I went to Jeff's for Christmas and stayed for three days from Christmas Eve. Sue was with us, of course. It was very quiet, which is how I like it, and it was very enjoyable. Obviously, I liked opening my presents on Christmas Day and we had a trip to The Junction Inn, in Norbury Junction, on Boxing Day.

We all had a half of their own bitter, but it wasn't very nice, which made me think I'd lost the taste for beer, perhaps because I hadn't drunk much alcohol after Helen and I had stopped going to the Gas Club.

After I'd gone to bed that night, I seemed to be banging my head on something and it was a queer sensation. I appeared to be in a strange position in the bed and couldn't get comfortable. I must have been making a noise because I woke Sue up and she came in to see what was going on. She found me at right angles to the top of the bed and I'd been banging my head on the wall because there wasn't enough room for me to lie sideways! Anyway, she sorted me out and helped me to get the right way up.

Jeff had bought me four John Wayne DVDs for Christmas and, on the 27th, we had one of them on – *Stagecoach*, from 1939, which was supposed to be a classic, but it was a poor thing, with not much action. After that, we watched a heat of *The World's Strongest Man* on television and it was better than the film.

On New Year's Eve, I went to bed about eleven o'clock or half past eleven, as usual. In the old days, I had to go to work on New Year's Day, so I never bothered much with the celebrations and they've never appealed to me. 2012 was to be the 98th year which I'd lived in, but it didn't sound a big number to me, just an ordinary year, and I intended to carry on just as usual.

10 Then And Now

There are a lot of advantages living now compared with when I was young. Most people in Britain can afford to buy a car, but many of them have it on the never-never. Most people seem to be living comfortably, but they're always on about poverty on the television and I heard about a child starving to death. There are a lot of things that are swept under the carpet, so that you don't hear about them.

There are also a lot of things against the way people live in the modern age. Jobs aren't safe and redundancies are coming up all the time. Unemployment – it's the modern scourge, but it was there in the 1930s when there was the "Means Test", which meant humiliation.

Working conditions used to be bad, but now there are those many people policing the way firms are run that companies have to keep more or less within the rules. When I was young, we stuck together when we went on strike, but there wasn't a lot of comradeship in the factories where I worked or on the Post Office.

There is much more help now. You used to have to pay to see a doctor if you wanted more advice or better medicine than the basics. Today, most of it's free, except for prescriptions for working people to get medicines.

Everything is so fast in modern times. Everybody's rushing around and nobody's got a minute. It only used to be like that if you were on piecework.

There was less entertainment in the old days and a lot of people couldn't afford holidays before the Second World War. Now they go flying to the other side of the world on foreign holidays. It didn't used to cost much to entertain people, but now it costs a fortune to go out anywhere.

The films don't seem to be very good nowadays, but then people's tastes are different than they used to be. When I was young, we used to like slapstick comedy and cowboy and gangster films. I liked to see a bit of gun work, but I wouldn't have liked to have been a gunfighter because I might have got shot! Now movies are full of technical stuff and computer animation. In the old days, films were all about the goodies and baddies, but today you can't work out who's what!

Jazz was just coming in when I was young and it was a young person's entertainment, but now there seems to be a lot of rubbish about. You can't properly remember what the tunes of the songs are. Working men's clubs used to be all the rage and an advantage of that was that you could take children with you to them, whereas they were banned from the pubs. Those clubs have dropped out of fashion now and people seem to wander round the towns binge drinking.

It's hard to choose whether life was better when I was young. There's more money about today and better health, but jobs are less safe. People cared more in the old days, but how bothered are they now whether you live or die? For a long time, I knew everybody nearby in Leek Road, but now I only know a few people because so many of them move in and out all the time. Overall, though, I can't make a decision either way about which time was the best.

Postscript

It was originally intended that this book would end with the passing of the year 2011 and that it would be published before Easter in 2012. Unfortunately, Cyril unexpectedly died on 6 February 2012 and, as his only son and his editor and publisher, it became my very sad task to update the readers on the short remaining period of his life, so that his story would be complete.

It might be considered rather complacent of Dad that on the cusp of 2012, at the age of 96, he had every intention that his life would carry on as before. He had already enjoyed over 32 years of retirement from work and had lived twenty years beyond male life expectancy in Stoke-on-Trent. Also, his health was not as robust as it had been and there were potential risks to his life, although they seemed to be under control through medication. There appeared to be no imminent danger, although his legs were gradually becoming weaker and I wondered if he'd remain fit enough still to be living relatively independently in his home by the end of the year.

On 1 January 2012, I rang Dad as soon as I got up in the morning, as I always did, to check that he was alright. He was fine. During the day, he had his usual four meals and was pleased that he'd been able to bend down to cut his toenails. At night, I called him before his bedtime, to confirm that he was still okay, which he was. The new year had begun much as he'd intended, with him carrying on just as usual in his inimitable calm and contented manner. That was what he'd intended to do for almost all of his life and it was probably one of the factors explaining his longevity.

On the 4th, I picked Dad up and took him to Sainsbury's, in Hanley, where we did our weekly food shopping as normal, and he went round the store without any problem. The following day, there was proof that his brain was still in excellent working order because a fireman went to Dad's house, at his instigation, and replaced his electric blanket for free!

The next nine days were uneventful as Dad continued with his usual routine, but on the 15th, Sue and I took him to Tittesworth Reservoir Visitor Centre, where he asked for a cappuccino coffee in the café straight away. Sue bought us a bag of Quavers, a cheese-flavoured potato snack, to share and Dad was so taken with them that he ordered a second bag! He was more talkative than normal and the only downside was that his walking was very slow, although it remained steady.

I was still using Dad's 1982 Volkswagen Polo for short journeys, to limit the wear and tear on my PT Cruiser. On the 18th, the Polo was given a new MOT and a service by Kennerley's at a total cost of £381.28, which was paid for by Dad, and so the old machine motored on to its thirtieth anniversary on the road. Although the car had practical value to me, for both of us the real driving force for our retention of it was nostalgia.

After I picked the car up, I drove us to do our food shopping. As Dad got to the checkout, he told me that his legs were giving way because he was so tired, but they didn't. After he'd had a short sit down, he was fine and we took our shopping back to the car.

Dad had been in touch with Revival Home Improvement Agency, of 308 London Road, in Stoke, to arrange for a handyman to fit a new weatherboard on his coal house to help protect the door. The non-profit-making agency was owned by Staffordshire Housing Association and provided property repairs for elderly and vulnerable people. The workman did the job on 20 January and, while he was there, Dad arranged for him to make a new door for the coal house as the old one was rotting. Therefore Dad was still planning effectively for the future.

The 21st was a Saturday and I went to Dad's to have lunch with him as usual. Normally, when I got there, he'd have already laid the table, put the dessert out and got our pizza ready for me to put in the oven. However, that day he hadn't completed his preparations because he hadn't felt like it. I noted in my diary that he was slowing up even more than he had been before and that his voice had gone rather deep, as a result of catarrh, so we thought. He had no trouble eating his food, though!

Two days later, Dad rang me as usual just before he went to bed, so that I'd know he was okay. He regularly called after 10.30, but that night the phone went at 9.50 and it wasn't the only time he checked in earlier than normal, which further seemed to indicate that he was slowing up.

On the 25th, I went to pick Dad up for us to do our food shopping, but he said he couldn't go because his legs were 'terrible' and he'd only been bothered to do half his shopping list, so I had to complete the rest for him. While I was with him, I noticed a large damp patch around the crotch area of his trousers, which smelled of urine, so I took them off, washed him and helped him to put a clean pair on. I formed the impression that he hadn't felt bothered to go to the toilet when the need had arisen, but he said that some urine must have dribbled out without him noticing. Any way round, it was a worrying development. When I got back from doing the shopping, though, he was finishing making his tea, so his legs had obviously held up for him to do that and at night he reported that they'd improved.

The following morning, Dad told me that, in the night, he hadn't been able to lift his legs up to get back into bed after having gone to the toilet. So he'd pressed his Lifeline alarm button and the centre had sent emergency help to put him back to bed. He also said he'd struggled to get downstairs in the morning and, soon after, Care Homes rang me, saying that Dad's morning carer was concerned about his mobility. I advised Dad to ring the Harley Street surgery as a priority, to get a doctor to pay him a home visit, and to call me when the doctor arrived.

I'd heard no more by lunch time, so I rang Dad, who told me that Dr Przyslo had just left! I asked Dad what the doctor had said about his mobility and involuntary urinating, but he replied that neither matter had been discussed, adding, 'He could see that I couldn't get about very well.' Unfortunately, Dad had long had the idea that doctors should know what the problem is with their patients without the latter having to comment on it. I'd told him more than once that doctors aren't mind readers and that it is imperative to draw medical problems to their attention, but I hadn't succeeded in changing his mind on the matter.

I therefore rang the surgery, but it was only possible to arrange a further home visit for the following day. As a result, I alerted Care Homes to the situation, but, as it turned out, Dad's legs rallied and he managed okay after that.

On the 27th, I went to his house to be present during the doctor's visit. Dad wanted me to do his lunch, but I needed to check his capabilities and so I had him do it for himself. He was very slow about it, but he seemed steady on his feet.

Then Dr Jayanti arrived and gave Dad a thorough examination. The doctor suspected that constipation was creating Dad's involuntary urinating and advised him to take Fybogel for a week to see if the problem would clear up. He also said that he thought that Dad might have anaemia, which would explain his overall weakness, and so a blood test would be arranged. Dad's voice remained deep, so Dr Jayanti examined his throat, but found nothing wrong with it.

On the 29th, Sue and I took Dad for a run out to Kingsley & Froghall Station. Although his walking was slow, he got from the car to the café okay. He ordered a cappuccino and when Sue asked if he'd like a packet of Quavers, his face lit up and he laughed with excitement. We had two bags between us and saw a steam train come in and go out before we left and Dad walked back to the car more quickly.

Two days later, Dad made one or two comments about the photo album of me as a child that he'd put together at the time and I wrote them down in his own words in his handwritten book. Little did we know that they'd be his final contribution to his life story.

On 1 February, I picked Dad up for our weekly visit to Sainsbury's, but he was very reluctant to walk down his front steps, fearing that he'd fall, although he was steady enough when he finally tackled them. Also, he went round the whole of the supermarket okay when we got there. However, when I pulled up outside his house, it took him five attempts to get out of my car and then he struggled to put one foot in front of the other. It was very cold and I became quite concerned about him, as it took him twenty minutes to walk across the pavement, climb his seven steps and get back into the house. Once inside, though, he was okay.

The following morning, he was still alright, but around 4.30 p.m. I came home to find two recent messages on my phone. The first one was from Dad and said that he'd got a pain in his chest. The second was from Lifeline, whom he'd rung because he hadn't been able to contact me, and it gave the same information, but also said Dad couldn't breathe properly and that an ambulance was on the way to his house. I rang him straightaway and spoke to a paramedic, who was at the scene. He said that Dad seemed okay in himself, but that his heart rate was 'all over the place'. I then spoke to Dad, who said he felt alright unless he got up from his chair when a sharp pain would shoot across his chest.

I then drove to A & E, where Dad had already arrived and was being attended to, by Dr Richard Evans in the Resuscitation Unit. Dad seemed alright and, after a number of tests had been done, Dr Evans said he thought Dad had anaemia, which was probably the cause of his chest pain. I noticed on the medical notes that his haemoglobin count was very low, at only 7.7, so it was no wonder that he was having problems. Nevertheless, he was deemed to be a non-urgent case and was moved to Room 3 in Ward 21 of the Infirmary. Nothing much happened while I was there, but I stayed with him, chatting, until 10.30. Dad was aware that I'd have to call at his house to do one or two things before finally making something to eat and he said, 'Now don't get rushing!'

The next morning, the anaemia diagnosis was confirmed to me and arrangements were made for the causes of it to be investigated, with internal bleeding being suspected. I then spoke to Dad on his mobile phone and he seemed okay, sitting in a chair, having had his breakfast. I went to see him at visiting time, but he was in transit to the short-stay Ward 18. There, he was given a blood transfusion and when I got to see him, he looked well and was altogether more alert than he'd been in the recent past. As a result, we had a good chat and it was clear that he was taking his latest stay in hospital in his stride, just as he had his previous confinements.

Unfortunately, several hours of sticking snow were predicted from lunch time the following day (the 4th), so I rang the ward in the hope of visiting Dad in the morning, but I was told that it wasn't possible until their usual time of 2 p.m. At about 12.30, snow began to fall and it quickly built up on the ground, so it would have been foolish to have driven to the hospital. As chance had it, I was unable to tell Dad because his mobile was dead and he was waiting for me to take his battery charger, to get it back into action again, so I asked a nurse to explain my absence to him.

That afternoon, he was then transferred to Ward 10, into the care of Dr Roffe. The evening visiting time started at 6.30, but it was still snowing then, there were about four inches of lying snow and I hadn't seen a car go past on the road for hours. So again I rang the hospital and asked for my apologies for not visiting to be passed on to him. Although I was unhappy at not being able to see him, my presence at his bedside didn't seem vital and I was reassured that he was okay and told that he'd just had a cheese sandwich and a pudding.

As soon as I woke the following morning, I rang the ward and was informed that Dad was 'up and walking'. Sue came with me to visit him in the afternoon and when we arrived, he was sitting in a chair next to his bed, D7. He looked up, we waved and he smiled a greeting to us. He seemed really pleased to see us and he and I briefly held hands. He was chatty and his voice was more or less back to normal. He said he hadn't expected me to come in the snow the previous day and he wanted to know how Stoke had got on in their match against Sunderland. He said he'd been eating his three meals each day and that he'd been walking with a frame with the physio that morning, although he was still experiencing chest pains when he got up.

Periodically, he coughed up a bit of catarrh and he said he'd got 'rubbish' on his chest. I thought it was the cause of his recent deep voice and that the catarrh was loosening and therefore clearing. Also, I noticed that his breathing was a little laboured and that he had to take a breath halfway through each sentence. I wasn't alarmed by it, but I was sufficiently unhappy about it to point it out to Staff Nurse Mini Biju, who was in the vicinity. She put him in bed and then took his blood pressure (which was 122/70), his pulse rate (69 beats per minute) and his oxygen saturation level, and was satisfied with the results. Nevertheless, she said she'd keep an eye on his breathing and so I was reassured by that. Dad then fell asleep and, ten minutes after visiting time ended at 4 p.m., Sue and I decided we'd better leave. I shook Dad slightly, to tell him we were going, but he barely stirred, so I left it at that because I thought it wouldn't be right to wake him.

It seemed to be unnecessary to drive back to the hospital for the 6 to 8 p.m. visiting slot, so, in the evening, I rang the ward and asked a nurse to tell Dad to switch on his mobile so that I could call him. I then tried him three times over a period of time, but there was no reply. I was disappointed, but assumed that the message hadn't got through or that he'd forgotten to put his mobile on. I then settled down to do some editing work on his forthcoming book and burned the midnight oil, satisfied that Dad was in safe hands.

As fate had it, while I was looking into his past, unknown to me Dad was fighting for his future existence as events wholly unexpected by anyone unfolded in Ward 10. About 10 p.m., soon after Staff Nurse Emily Waqanivere had come on duty, she noticed that Dad was a bit breathless, but felt he was okay. However, just before 11.45, another staff nurse, Jocelyn ("Josie") Cabie, saw that he looked pale and different, so she asked her more experienced colleague, Emily, to have a look at him. Emily found him cold, not breathing and without a detectable pulse. She shouted at him, but there was no response. She pressed the emergency button and gave him oxygen and cardiac massage. Within twenty seconds, three doctors were on the scene and by then Emily had succeeded in resuscitating Dad, so that he was breathing again. A tube was put down his throat and a lot of accumulated phlegm, which was obstructing his airways, was removed.

Dad regained consciousness and his breathing, with the aid of oxygen, went back to normal, but he was very restless and kept trying to take off the mask, presumably because he found it uncomfortable. In order to try to get it removed, several times he cried out: 'Let me go! I don't want this!' He was agitated and appeared to be confused, perhaps having suffered brain damage and not understanding the situation he was in. He also tried to climb out of his bed, quite possibly perceiving himself to be in a fight or flight situation, and it was decided that Josie would stay with him for the rest of the night to look after him and make sure that his oxygen mask stayed on.

At about 1.30 a.m. (on the 6th), Josie rang my mobile, to tell me the news, but, as I wasn't expecting any calls, it was switched off. I was still up at the time and had she also rung my landline, I'd have taken the call and immediately driven to the hospital. She tried my mobile at least another four times during the night and also rang my landline, but by then I was asleep upstairs and entirely unaware of the seriousness of Dad's situation.

Dad remained restless and agitated, but from time to time he settled down and slept. After 4 o'clock, his condition noticeably deteriorated, as his airways became increasingly blocked again, and so Josie rang for assistance. The night registrar, Dr Samubam, arrived soon after, examined Dad and decided that further intensive intervention was inappropriate, apparently because the chance of him surviving was slight and did not justify the extra distress that more emergency treatment would cause him. Therefore, in the absence of the hospital having obtained my consent for his proposal, Dr Samubam decided that no further attempts to resuscitate Dad would be made.

Some time after 5 a.m., Dad became calmer and gradually slipped into unconsciousness. From around six o'clock, his breathing became irregular and he was quiet and peaceful. His breaths became increasingly shallower and ceased altogether at 6.55 when he passed away, with Josie by his side. At 7.28, he was officially pronounced dead by Dr Mangat, a speciality registrar. Dad's extremely long journey in time since being born during the First World War was finally, but unexpectedly, over.

After Dad had died, Josie contacted West Mercia Police [sic], to ask them to inform me of his death. Unfortunately, the staff at the ward thought that I lived with him and, in any case, the police went to the wrong address – a house in Telford!

When I got up that morning, I was about to ring Dad, to see how he was and to tell him I'd be visiting him as usual, but I was alarmed to discover three messages from the hospital on my landline answering system. The first was from Josie, at 3.55 a.m., sounded urgent and said, 'Your father is really poorly. If you could give us a ring.' The second was also from her, at 6.50, just five minutes before Dad died, and said: 'Could you give us a ring as soon as possible? Cyril is really, really poorly now.'

The final message, at 9.23, was from Rebecca Wheatley, a nurse on the next shift, and was much more matter of fact: 'If you could ring the ward as soon as possible, please.' The implication of this final call was clearly that Dad had died and it wasn't lost on me.

I rang the ward straightaway, but the line was engaged, so, after the briefest of washes, I threw on some clothes and was about to rush through the door when Rebecca rang back and asked me, in a non-urgent way, to go to the hospital. I hit the road and arrived at the ward at 11 a.m. I was told to go into a side room, where a nurse would see me. I knew for sure then that it was all over and I tried to brace myself for the awful news.

Rebecca arrived and asked, 'Do you know what's happened?'

I said, 'He's died, hasn't he?'

She said, 'Yes, but it was peaceful.'

I wailed and walked rapidly round the room sobbing. After a few minutes, I calmed down somewhat and Rebecca asked if I'd like to see Dad. Of course, I said I would and was taken to his bed, around which the curtains were drawn. I went through them and found him lying on his back, wearing his green hospital pyjamas, looking peaceful, with his eyes almost closed and his mouth wide open. I asked to be left alone with him and cried profusely as I kissed his face and head. I'd dreaded the moment for years and it had finally come. I held one of his hands and said, 'Come on, Dad, we've got your book to finish off!'

I'd rung Sue and asked her to come and she joined me at about 12.45. We sat there, both very upset, for an hour until Rebecca told us they needed to wash Dad, ready for him to be taken to the mortuary. So, soon after, Sue and I left him. I took his watch and mobile and, on the way out, we bumped into Dr Roffe. She invited us into her office, where we were given details about Dad's death, and she said there'd probably be a postmortem examination of his body because it had been unexpected. I said I didn't want him to be tampered with because it would serve no useful purpose and she noted my wishes on the front page of her report.

Sue and I then went straight to Dad's house, which felt empty without him there, and I took out everything that I could find which was important or valuable. We then left for my house, where I began the unenviable task of informing relatives and friends of Dad's passing, but I had a little consolation from the many wonderful tributes to him that followed.

The next day, I rang Robert Williamson, of Williamson Brothers, to start making the funeral arrangements. They'd done a splendid job with Mum's funeral and I had every confidence in them to repeat the success. To ensure that I had the time to put together a personal hands-on event, as we'd had for Mum, the date was arranged for the 20th, at 1.30 p.m.

I then got a call from the hospital's Bereavement Support office, which informed me that Dad's death certificate was ready to pick up. That fortunately meant there wouldn't be a postmortem. Sue and I collected the certificate, which gave respiratory failure as the specific cause of death, as a result of bronchopneumonia, which had developed through atrial fibrillation and hypertension, though to me the background factors didn't seem to stack up.

Sue and I then went to the chapel of rest in the mortuary, where Dad was laid out on the same long table that Mum had been and, except for his head, he was covered by a cherry-coloured sheet, with gold strips. He didn't look much different than he had the previous day, but obviously he was cold. Sue stayed for fifteen minutes and I left after another ten because the attendant told me that visitors had arrived to see someone else who'd died. I returned there the following two days because I wanted to be with Dad while there was still time.

Dad had expressed the wish to be buried with his parents in Hanley Cemetery (in grave number 16364) and, of course, since then Mum had been interred there too. However, in 2008, when Dad and I had discussed what specific funeral arrangements he wanted, he hadn't seemed very bothered, had expressed no preference for a religious service and had said: 'Whatever. Go along with it.' So that left it mainly up to me and I thought that, as Mum's funeral service had gone so well at Zion Church, it would be most appropriate for Dad's to be held there too. So I rang Lily Birch and she put me on to the pastor, Paul Owen, who very kindly offered to hold the whole event at the church for free.

On the 8th, Sue and I went to an appointment I'd arranged with Dr Roffe, to discuss the causes of Dad's death because the rapidity of his demise remained a mystery to me. She said that he'd been improving and that, on the day before he died, nothing had suggested that he'd rapidly go downhill overnight. She also said that she'd done tests on him the same day and they'd shown no sign of any infection. Therefore, Dad hadn't been given antibiotics because he hadn't shown symptoms which required them. Dr Roffe said that the main problem had been that his heart was enlarged, which had put strain on his breathing. She added that although pneumonia usually takes a few days or a week to become critical, frail elderly patients are at particularly at risk of more rapid attacks. She also said that after I'd brought my worry about Dad's breathing to the attention of the staff nurse on the 5th, a doctor should have been informed, although there was no evidence in the medical notes to suggest that that had happened. Dr Roffe believed, though, that it would have made no difference to the outcome because of the shortage of time available to act. Because she hadn't been present at Dad's death and the full notes of the events hadn't been compiled, we agreed to have a follow-up meeting to try to tie up the loose ends.

Two days later, Dad was moved to the Williamson Brothers' premises in Birches Head, where he was embalmed. After the process had been completed, I went to be with him in their chapel of rest for a short while. He was lying on a trolley and was covered by a purple and lilac-coloured duvet. His eyes were closed and so was his mouth, and he was cold and stiff, but I found it therapeutic to be with him.

On the 12th, I selected Dad's "going-away" clothes, made up of colours which suited him and harmonized with his brown eyes: a green shirt, a dark brown jumper, a pair of light brown trousers and socks and his brown Filanto shoes. The following day, I took them to the undertaker's and called in to see Dad while I was there. When I left the chapel of rest, Robert gave me the lock of Dad's hair, which

I'd asked for.

I wanted to remove the many plants from the family grave before the necessary excavation began and had been told by the council's Bereavement Care Service department that I'd be able to do so until at least the 15th because digging wouldn't begin until the following day at the earliest. However, when I arrived at the undertaker's just after 2 p.m. on the 15th, Robert Williamson said he'd recently received a message that the excavation would begin after lunch! I rushed to the cemetery in less than fifteen minutes, but the mechanical digger was well into its stride. Although I halted the proceedings immediately and the gravediggers had removed the plants that they'd seen, numerous bulbs were buried in a great mound of earth next to the grave. As the work was half finished, I had no option but to allow it to resume and, when the gravediggers had completed their job, I sifted through the earth to rescue all the undamaged bulbs that I could find. By then, I was very upset, but I returned to the undertaker's to spend half an hour with Dad, who was fully dressed for his final big occasion and looked smart, but casual. He was lying in his coffin, which I'd chosen to be the same as Mum's – golden oak, with gold handles.

On the 17th, I visited Dad again and put a lock of my hair in his hands. The same day, *The Sentinel* published an extensive article about his death and it was accompanied by six photographs, which showed him at various stages of his life. I expect that Dad would have been pleased to have seen it, but wondered what he'd done to deserve such attention. The feature covered about two-thirds of a page, but, unfortunately, the funeral details were missing and needed to be printed in a follow-up piece.

The day of Dad's funeral was probably the biggest challenge of my life and it was suitably cold and grey. I went to see him in the chapel of rest for the final time and had trouble dragging myself away, but Sue and I had to do one or two things at the church and then had to go to his house to welcome the other main mourners. I noticed that there was a fine display of yellow crocuses in his front garden, which I'm sure he'd have enjoyed seeing. Harry, Gill, Helen Sargent, Lynn Halliburton, Dorothy Kent and Maureen Wallett arrived and then got in the funeral car. The small procession set off at about 1.20 for the short journey to the church. I walked slowly in front the front of the hearse to Egerton Street and then jumped into its passenger seat because of the dangerous roundabout ahead.

We followed the coffin into the church, which was nearly full. I'd selected Johann Pachelbel's *Canon in D Major* as being appropriate entrance music, but the organist played something different and unknown to me! Paul Owen then got the service under way, with its hymns and readings that I'd selected. After we'd sung *The Old Rugged Cross*, a favourite hymn of my parents, I walked to the head of Dad's coffin, put my right hand on it and bowed in silent tribute. I then read the eulogy that I'd written for him and it was by far the most difficult piece of public speaking I'd ever done, but my experience got me through as I'd thought it would. Several times, as I looked around, I noticed that Sue was crying. When I'd finished, I turned to the coffin and stood silent again. That signalled the start of two minutes of silent reflection by the mourners. Paul then continued the service and we sang the hymn, *Rock of Ages*, which I'd selected because it was featured in *Warlock*, a favourite Western film of Dad and me, but unfortunately the version played wasn't the one that was generally known.

At the end of the service, Dorothy went to the coffin and put a hand on it. The curtains were then drawn so that I could say my final goodbye to Dad. The coffin lid was removed and I read my farewell to him. At 2.35, I kissed him on the head and had a final look at him as the lid was screwed down. Everyone then slowly walked out behind the coffin.

The other main mourners got back in the funeral car while I rode in the hearse to the top of Egerton Street. There, I got out and walked in front of the procession again. At Dad's house, we stopped for one minute, as a mark of respect, and then continued along Leek Road, Cauldon Road and Avenue Road. The junction with Stoke Road was difficult for a slow-moving procession to negotiate, but we managed it without incident and arrived at the cemetery.

Dad's coffin was carried to the grave and Paul gave a reading. I then walked to the head of the grave, touched the coffin and read my farewell again. Dad was lowered into the grave and I sprinkled some soil on top of the coffin, as Sue then did too. She'd handed out red roses to the mourners and we all threw them on top of the coffin. All the mourners then departed except for Sue and me. I shovelled earth into the grave, determined to cover the coffin myself, but it was very hard work to fill in such a large area and eventually I asked one of the gravediggers for help. Being used to hard physical labour, he worked at twice my speed and the task was soon completed. I then left him and his colleagues to finish the job and Sue and I returned to the church, to join the reception.

By the time we got back, most of the mourners had left, but I wasn't worried about that because I felt I'd honoured my father. I really needed a rest, but there was socializing to be done and I thought it was appropriate to circulate. Ros had attended and was still there. She kindly told me that my delivery of the eulogy was 'professorial' and we chatted away until only she, Sue and I were left. Ros still made no move to go and the world seemed surreal – I'd just buried my dad, and my partner, my ex-wife and I were socializing together in a church. Finally, Sue said we'd have to go, which we did.

Sue and I went back to Dad's house and straightened the furniture up before we returned to the cemetery. By then, the gravediggers had gone, but it had started raining, so I spent five minutes standing under my umbrella, looking at the various bouquets of flowers on top of the freshly-laid soil.

I discovered that the names of 37 people had been entered into the book of remembrance, which had previously been used at Mum's funeral service, and, as before, most of them had put comments. There had been 54 mourners at the church, but a reminder about signing the book hadn't been given at the end of the service, so some people must have left without remembering that they could have left a written tribute. The word 'gentleman' appeared regularly in the comments and Ros had put, 'He was the one man I've known of whom no-one ever said a bad word.' It made me feel very proud of Dad and I realized then that he was a special person to others as well as me.

That night, Sue and I ate at the Pasta di Piazza restaurant, in High Street, Stone, because it would have been very depressing to have stayed in. I felt really strange, but also a sense of relief after the traumatic experiences of the day.

My immediate priority after Dad had died was, of course, to deal with his affairs. Fortunately, because he'd remained in fine mental shape and had continued to run the essentials of his life effectively, it was much easier to do than it would have been otherwise.

I paid the Williamson Brothers' bill of £2,247.08 and gave Zion a donation of £100. A sizable number of letters needed to be written and phone calls made to adjust Dad's affairs to the changed situation, so that most of them were resolved over the following few weeks.

With regard to Dad's grave, I decided to let the earth settle on it, perhaps for a year, before doing anything permanent. My general idea was to make it into a garden grave, as it had been after Mum had died, but I also intended to have a small headstone made, containing the names of the four occupants, which included Dad's parents.

On 2 March, Sue and I finally got to see Dr Roffe for our follow-up meeting. Not surprisingly, the events she described and assessments made weren't dramatically different from those outlined in our first meeting, but some pertinent new points came to light. She said that, although the rapid onset of pneumonia hadn't been expected, a C-reactive protein test on the afternoon before Dad died had showed the inflammatory indicator to be high, which normally suggests the presence of an infection. Nevertheless, he wasn't given any antibiotics and by the time the situation became serious, it was too late for them to be prescribed. Dr Roffe said he was also suffering from heart failure and there was fluid on his lungs, and so: 'All his reserves were being used up. When an infection came, he didn't have the strength to fight it, so it was overwhelming.' She said that, while he was conscious during the crisis, he'd have been aware that he was breathless and been pretty uncomfortable, but that he wouldn't have suffered any pain. She seemed to think that hypertension wasn't a cause of death, but suspected that Dad's anaemia was the result of a tumour or an ulcer, which might well have led to very difficult times ahead had he not contracted pneumonia.

On 5 March, I went to Ward 10, where I met Emily Waqanivere to hear her description of Dad's last hours, so that I'd understand what had happened to him. It was distressing to hear about the end of his life, but I had to know about it. Five days later, I met Josie Cabie in the ward and, like Emily, she'd kindly come in in her own time to see me. Josie also described the relevant events and I was grateful that, although I hadn't been with Dad when he died, at least I had some knowledge of what he'd gone through.

The funeral flowers on my parents' grave were going well off by the middle of March, so, on Mothering Sunday (the 18th), I removed them. Despite being interrupted by rain and hail showers, I then dug a plastic container into the earth at the head of the grave, filled it with water and placed in fifteen red roses. After that, I put in new flowers every so often when the old ones had died.

On 21 March, I picked up a message on Dad's phone from Revival Home Improvement Agency, telling him that his coal house door was ready to be fitted. When I returned the call, I explained that he'd had died, but was told that I could have the door free anyway. No doubt Dad would have smiled at the news! It was fitted on 18 April and seemed very solid. Peter Jones took the old door to use in a bonfire and I primed the new one before paining it, on 29 May, in the same Crown Forest Pine-coloured gloss as the original had been. When I'd finished, I looked at it and thought to myself that Dad would have been very pleased.

Jeff Kent, Cotes Heath, November 2012